Competing Germanies

D1028650

signale
modern german letters, cultures, and thought

Series editor: Peter Uwe Hohendahl, Cornell University

Signale: Modern German Letters, Cultures, and Thought publishes new English-language books in literary studies, criticism, cultural studies, and intellectual history pertaining to the German-speaking world, as well as translations of important German-language works. *Signale* construes "modern" in the broadest terms: the series covers topics ranging from the early modern period to the present. *Signale* books are published under a joint imprint of Cornell University Press and Cornell University Library in electronic and print formats. Please see http://signale.cornell.edu/.

COMPETING GERMANIES

Nazi, Antifascist, and Jewish Theater in German Argentina, 1933–1965

ROBERT KELZ

A Signale Book

CORNELL UNIVERSITY PRESS AND CORNELL UNIVERSITY LIBRARY
ITHACA AND LONDON

Cornell University Press and Cornell University Library gratefully acknowledge the College of Arts & Sciences, Cornell University, for support of the Signale series.

Copyright © 2019 by Cornell University

All rights reserved. Except for brief quotations in a review, this book, or parts thereof, must not be reproduced in any form without permission in writing from the publisher. For information, address Cornell University Press, Sage House, 512 East State Street, Ithaca, New York 14850.

First published 2019 by Cornell University Press and Cornell University Library

Library of Congress Cataloging-in-Publication Data
Names: Kelz, Robert Vincent, author.
Title: Competing Germanies : Nazi, antifascist, and Jewish theater in German Argentina, 1933–1965 / Robert Kelz.
Description: Ithaca, NY : Cornell University Press : Cornell University Library, 2020. | Series: Signale : modern German letters, cultures, and thought | Includes bibliographical references and index. | Summary: "Following World War II, German antifascists and nationalists in Buenos Aires believed theater was crucial to their highly politicized efforts at community-building, and each population devoted considerable resources to competing against its rival onstage. Competing Germanies tracks the paths of several stage actors from European theaters to Buenos Aires and explores how two of Argentina's most influential immigrant groups, German nationalists and antifascists (Jewish and non-Jewish), clashed on the city's stages. Covered widely in German- and Spanish-language media, theatrical performances articulated strident Nazi, antifascist, and Zionist platforms. Meanwhile, as their thespian representatives grappled onstage for political leverage among emigrants and Argentines, behind the curtain, conflicts simmered within partisan institutions and among theatergoers. Publicly they projected unity, but offstage nationalist, antifascist, and Zionist populations were rife with infighting on issues of political allegiance, cultural identity and, especially, integration with their Argentine hosts"—Publisher's Web site.
Identifiers: LCCN 2019042099 (print) | LCCN 2019042100 (ebook) | ISBN 9781501739859 (hardcover) | ISBN 9781501739866 (paperback) | ISBN 9781501739873 (adobe pdf) | ISBN 9781501739880 (epub)
Subjects: LCSH: Freie Deutsche Buehne in Buenos Aires—History. | Deutsches Theater (Buenos Aires, Argentina)—History. | Ethnic theater—Argentina—History—20th century | National socialism and theater—Argentina—History. | Jewish theater—Argentina—History—20th century. | Germans—Argentina—History—20th century. | German drama—20th century—History and criticism.
Classification: LCC PN2451 .K45 2020 (print) | LCC PN2451 (ebook) | DDC 792.098209/04—dc23
LC record available at https://lccn.loc.gov/2019042099
LC ebook record available at https://lccn.loc.gov/2019042100

To my family

Contents

ILLUSTRATIONS

ACKNOWLEDGMENTS

Many people and institutions have supported me throughout this project. This study would never have existed without the guidance and encouragement of my mentors at Vanderbilt University, including Meike Werner, Vera Kutzinski, John McCarthy, Christoph Zeller, Dieter Sevin, Barbara Hahn, and Edward Friedman. Grants from Vanderbilt's Center for the Americas and the College of Arts and Sciences funded multiple research trips to Argentina and Germany. Other companions from Vanderbilt who gave warm and valuable assistance include Kathrin Seidl, Gesa Fromming, Mark Looney, Brett Sterling, Elizabeth Weber, Ty West, Mayra Fortes, and Pablo Gomez-Zulaga. I thank my colleagues at The University of Memphis, including but not limited to Monika Nenon, Heike Polster, Fransisco Vivar, Pilar Alcalde, Will Thompson, Sharon Stanley, Carolina Quintana, Inma Gomez-Soler, Ralph Albanese, and Jennifer Lastra for their comradery and insights. Patricia Simpson, H. Glenn Penny, Glen Goodman,

Andrea Orzoff, and Birger Vanwesenbeeck also have facilitated my research in many ways.

In Argentina I am deeply obliged to the National Library Mariano Moreno, particularly to the staff of its newspaper archive and, especially, my dear friend and coauthor, Silvia Glocer. Regula Rohland de Langbehn has been extremely supportive, and I am grateful for the impulses of participants at her colloquiums including Hans Knoll, Ben Bryce, Ana Weinstein, René Krüger, Alfredo Bauer, Reinhard Andress, Alicia Bernasconi, Ximena Alvarez, Alfredo Schwarcz, Fedor Pellmann, Alfred Hübner, Arnold Spitta, Germán Friedmann, and Claudia Garnica de Bertona. The staff at the archives of the Fundación IWO, the Goethe School, and Pestalozzi School have aided me in searching for primary sources. Finally, Jacques Arndt, Cornelia Martini, Regine Lamm, Ursula Siegerist, Beatriz Pfeiler, and Hertha Scheuerle also shaped this study by taking time to talk with me about their experiences acting with the Free German Stage and Ludwig Ney.

In Germany, a research grant from the German Academic Exchange Service was fundamental to the realization of this project. Frithjof Trapp and Marin Jettinger at the Paul Walter Jacob Archive, the archivists at the Political Archive of the German Foreign Office, and the librarians at the Ibero-American Institute also contributed significantly to the research that went into this book. Ottmar Ette of the University of Potsdam, Hans-Jürgen Schings at the Free University of Berlin, and Ursula Seeber at the Literaturhaus Wien have offered valuable advice and support.

I also wish to thank Regine Lamm for permission to reproduce the images in figures 2 and 10, the Fundación IWO for permission to reproduce the images in figures 3 and 4, and the Argentine National Library Mariano Moreno for permission to reproduce the images in figures 5 and 6.

Marian Rogers has been very helpful in revising the manuscript. Finally, I am deeply indebted to Peter Hohendahl, Kizer Walker, and the Signale editorial board for their feedback and patience.

Abbreviations

Archives

BB	Bundesarchiv Berlin
CNC	Cornelia Ney Collection
ELW	Exilbibliothek im Literaturhaus Wien
GSA	Goethe School Archive
IWO	Fundación IWO
JAC	Jacques Arndt Collection
PAAA	Politisches Archiv des Auswärtigen Amts
PSA	Pestalozzi School Archive
PWJA	Paul Walter Jacob-Archiv
PWJAK	Paul Walter Jacob-Archiv Korrespondenz

Newspapers, Magazines, Yearbooks

AT	*Argentinisches Tageblatt*
BAH	*Buenos Aires Herald*
DAD	*Das Andere Deutschland*
DiA	*Der Deutsche in Argentinien*
DLPZ	*Deutsche La Plata Zeitung*
FP	*Freie Presse*
JdVA	*Jahrbuch des deutschen Volksbundes in Argentinien*
JW	*Jüdische Wochenschau*
LN	*La Nación*

Organizations

FFO	Federal Foreign Office (1945–1966)
FGS	Free German Stage
FO	Foreign Office (1934–1945)
JCS	Jewish Cultural Society
MP	Ministry of Propaganda
WGE	West German Embassy

COMPETING GERMANIES

Introduction

Argentina's Competing German Theaters

> There exists a single German people, which is not subject to borders, but instead can be found anywhere where German people live who speak German, think in German, and feel themselves to be Germans.
>
> —JOSEPH GOEBBELS, REICH THEATER WEEK,
> VIENNA, 1938

Reprinted in the widely read Argentine newspaper *La Razón*, Joseph Goebbels's speech at the 1938 Reich Theater Week pinpointed the root of the bitter conflict that had enveloped German Buenos Aires at least since 1933.[1] Celebrating the Nazification of Austrian theater, Goebbels asserted that, essentially, claims to German identity were not defined by political boundaries, but rather were contingent upon national affection and cultural representation. Not only did Goebbels underscore the importance of culture in National Socialist visions of Germanness, but he unwittingly bolstered the position of exiled German antifascists, who posited themselves as the true representatives of Germany by upholding German culture's accomplishments in painting, music, literature, and theater.

---

1. "Semana del Teatro en Viena," *La Razón*, June 14, 1938.

For this reason they named the first large antifascist conference in exile, held in Paris in 1935, "In Defense of Culture."[2] In Argentina, too, supporters and opponents of Nazism weaponized culture to define and claim a single legitimate German identity, as well as attack their adversaries and advance their own agenda among the nation's large German-speaking populations. Moreover, in nominally neutral Argentina these cultural battles were waged with an impassioned urgency. For nationalists, antifascists, and Zionists in Buenos Aires, the enemy was not only across the ocean—it was across town as well.

"The Argentines Came on Boats"

Contrasting the South American country with his native Mexico, Carlos Fuentes affirmed Argentina as a nation of immigrants when he commented: "The Mexicans come from Indians (indios), but the Argentines came on boats."[3] From 1881 to 1930, nearly six million immigrants entered Argentina. Across the Americas, only the United States received a greater number of immigrants in this period. Primarily as a result of these arrivals, Argentina's population increased more than fourfold, from 1.8 million in 1869 to 7.9 million in 1914, when foreign nationals comprised 30 percent of the population.[4] In Buenos Aires, the number of inhabitants skyrocketed from 177,787 in 1869 to 2.4 million in 1936, of which 870,000, or 36 percent, were foreign nationals.[5] Most immigrants hailed from Italy and Spain, accounting for 39.4 percent and 35.2 percent of foreign nationals in the country in 1914, respectively. By comparison, German, Austro-Hungarian, and Swiss citizens made up 3.4 percent of the total number of foreign nationals in Argentina, having dipped from 4.2 percent since 1895.[6] Between 1857 and 1914, there were

---

2. Hermand, *Culture in Dark Times*, xv.
3. Leiva, "La inmigración en la Argentina de posguerra," 8.
4. Bryce, *To Belong in Buenos Aires*, 14.
5. "Del Archivo: El Censo de 1936," 106.
6. *Tercer Censo Nacional*, vol. 1, *Antecedentes y comentarios* (Buenos Aires: Talleres Gráficos de L.J. Rosso y Cía, 1916), cited in Bryce, *To Belong in Buenos Aires*, 17.

62,006 German, 136,079 Austro-Hungarian, and 33,057 Swiss immigrants to Argentina.[7]

Numbers for German speakers are more elusive, because many Swiss and Austro-Hungarians did not speak German, but some arrivals from other countries did. German speakers entering Argentina from neighboring South American countries may have been registered as Paraguayans, Brazilians, Bolivians, and so on. There also was a steady flow of German-speaking immigrants from the Volga region of the Russian Empire to the Argentine provinces of Misiones, Santa Fe, Entre Ríos, and Buenos Aires from the 1870s to the 1920s. At a recent symposium in Buenos Aires, Horacio Walter of the National University of La Plata claimed that there may well have been more arrivals from the Volga region than from Germany itself.[8] If true, this would upend the math on German speakers, because according to government immigration data it would mean that the largest number of them were registered as Russians. Furthermore, the accuracy and comprehensiveness of government statistics must be taken with a dose of skepticism. In the last analysis, both historical and current calculations are imbued with conjecture.

Leo Mirau, a historical contemporary, calculated that in 1920 there were more than 100,000 Germans and over 200,000 speakers of German in Argentina.[9] Buoyed by Argentina's neutrality during World War I and spurred by economic and political crises in Europe, during the 1920s the number of German-speaking immigrants increased, by some estimates reaching 25,000 annually in the early interwar period.[10] From 1923 to 1930 Argentine authorities also noted immigrants' mother tongue and classified just shy of 94,000 entries as native speakers of German in this period. Ronald Newton calculates that this rate would mean that from 1918 to 1932 between 130,000 and 140,000 German speakers

---

7. Bryce, *To Belong in Buenos Aires*, 169.

8. Walter, "Los Alemanes de Rusia en la Argentina."

9. Mirau, *Argentinien von heute*, 119.

10. Anne Saint Sauveur-Henn, "Die deutsche Einwanderung in Argentinien," in Meding, *Nationalsozialismus und Argentinien*, 12.

entered Argentina, a figure corroborated by Heinrich Volberg.[11] By contrast, in his extensively researched book *To Belong in Buenos Aires*, Benjamin Bryce places the number of German-speaking immigrants from 1881 to 1930 at 100,000.[12]

Other forms of identification and affiliation, such as religion, social class, gender, and generation created contrasting communities of German speakers; however, most earlier immigrants favored the Wilhelmine monarchy over the Weimar Republic and, generally, welcomed National Socialism as a return to strong, conservative, patriotic government. Their presence was countered by the arrival of approximately 45,000 Jewish refugees and political dissidents during the Nazi regime. This influx meant that nearly 20 percent of German speakers in Argentina were victims of National Socialism, a figure that was much higher in the capital and, of course, had a transformative impact there.[13] Adding these exiles to the existing population, Georg Ismar estimates that the total number of German speakers in Argentina during World War II was roughly 250,000.[14] Argentina received just over 100,000 German- and Austrian-born emigrants in the decade following World War II, a significant percentage of whom were war criminals.[15] Throughout the time in focus, German Buenos Aires was charged with sharp and constantly evolving social and political tension.

Setting the Stage

While this book on emigrant theaters in Argentina is anchored in German exile studies, its import to our cultural knowledge stretches

11. Newton, *"Nazi Menace" in Argentina*, 81; Volberg, *Auslandsdeutschtum und Drittes Reich*, 6.

12. Bryce, *To Belong in Buenos Aires*, 14.

13. Saint Sauveur-Henn, *Un siècle d'emigration allemande vers l'Argentine 1853–1945*, 249; Schwarcz, "Die deutschsprachigen Juden in Argentinien," 204; Jackisch, *El nazismo*, 158.

14. Ismar, *Der Pressekrieg*, 12.

15. Gerald Steinacher, "Argentinien als NS-Fluchtziel: Die Emigration von Kriegsverbrechern und nazionalsozialisten durch Italien an den Río de la Plata 1946–1955," in Meding and Ismar, *Argentinien und das Dritte Reich Mediale und reale Präsenz, Ideologie Transfer, Folgewirkungen*, 243–244.

across historiography, dramatic theory, and literary criticism to link the disparate disciplines of German, Jewish, Latin American, and migration studies. Its tight *mise-en-scène* of smaller emigrant populations enables a sustained, nuanced look at the way more universal themes such as denominationalism, multilingualism, hybridity, and integration emerge and develop across decades. Meanwhile, the aesthetic tangibility and social dynamism of live theater map emigrants' contributions to the pluralism that is integral to all national identities, perhaps especially in the Americas. In this sense, multiple scholars agree that immigrants and ethnic minorities are in fact "normative Latin Americans" or, in my view, normative Americans writ large.[16] The challenges, clashes, and contradictions of forming a pluralistic society are the backbone of this book.

Dramatic literature and performances endure as occasions for memory and reinvention across both real and imagined borders of ethnicity, nation, and origin. The processes of remembering and reinventing inform cultural belonging and exclusion, especially when they are sculpted and reinforced by the volatile, in-the-moment interplay between actors and theatergoers. Thus, theatrical performances bring forth, manifest, and transmit senses of cultural identification and conflict within the intercultural matrix of the modern, cosmopolitan metropolis. The evolving laboratory of stage and city illuminates a key issue in the discipline of dramatic theory: the three-sided relationship of nation, history, and invention. The project of summoning a representative audience that will recognize itself onstage and abide by this depiction outside the theater depends on the ensemble and audience's mutual validation of certain works through their enshrinement in the repertoire.[17] Actors and spectators then assent to complex and imaginative schemes to imbue or refashion cultural identity through the dramatic presentation of these works. The degree of variation in the repertoire and the plays' depiction show us how theater reflects and propels the

---

16. Jeffrey Lesser and Ranaan Rein, "Motherlands of Choice: Ethnicity, Belonging, and Identities among Jewish-Latin Americans," in Foote and Goebel, *Immigration and National Identities in Latin America*, 156; Bryce, *To Belong in Buenos Aires*, 15.

17. Kruger, *National Stage*, 3.

evolution of spectators' views of their history, values, community, and sense of nationhood. In this way, Argentina's emigrant theaters render the mechanics of the epigram of Germany's national poet, Friedrich Schiller: the planks of the dramatic stage are boards that mean the world.

These emigrants' world was mid-twentieth-century Buenos Aires. The cultural landscape of the Argentine capital during this time was unique. No other major metropolitan city witnessed immediate, local, and fully open competition between Nazi, antifascist, and Zionist educational, media, and cultural institutions throughout the World War II period. Like Joseph Goebbels, who seized upon the Reich Theater Week to internationalize claims to Germanness, German-speaking nationalists, antifascists, and Zionists in Buenos Aires believed theater was crucial to their highly politicized efforts at identity formation and community building. Each group devoted considerable resources to competing against its rivals onstage. During the 1930s German emigrants in the Argentine capital founded the nationalist German Theater and its antifascist adversary, the Free German Stage. Created in 1938 by nationalist German emigrants, most of whom had arrived in Argentina in the early twentieth century, the German Theater performed to sold-out audiences at the National Theater, a cavernous venue with a seating capacity of 1,155. In a strategy of retaliation, the next year German-speaking Jewish refugees founded the Free German Stage, the only professional exilic theater worldwide to stage regular performances throughout World War II. Intense competition between these populations and their theaters continued for decades after 1945. Shaped by shifting cultural-political agendas in Europe, Argentina, and among their own ranks, both ensembles eventually recognized the imperative of integration with Argentine artists and audiences. By invoking their mutual cultural heritage and urging unity against communism, the West German embassy pushed the emigrant blocs toward reconciliation; however, its efforts were a charade contingent upon an unsustainable and indefensible amnesia of the past.

Although Buenos Aires is its epicenter, this book analyzes the competition for German cultural representation across much of

Argentina, from the Patagonian Andes to the rainforest corridor in Misiones province. The period in focus begins with a celebrity guest performance funded by the German government in 1934, the first major theatrical production overseas after Hitler came to power, and then covers the escalating competition between Argentina's German theaters through World War II, Peronism, and the first decades of the Cold War. The discussion concludes in 1965, when the West German Federal Foreign Office attempted to mollify enduring antagonism in German Buenos Aires by relocating Reinhard Olszewski's German Chamber Theater from Santiago, Chile, to the Argentine capital. In the process, it eliminated subventions to the Free German Stage, effectively terminating its ensemble.[18] Along the way, I address the following core questions: How did the German Theater and the Free German Stage contribute to transatlantic and transnational projects, such as delineating and consolidating German identity in South America, advancing political agendas, and integrating with the Argentine host society? Why, arguably more than any other form of art or cultural representation, did theater have such wide, enduring, and polarizing appeal in German Buenos Aires and beyond? Finally, how does putting theater at the center revise perceptions of German-speaking nationalist, antifascist, and Zionist populations in Argentina?

The conclusion revisits these questions, distilling the evidence presented and analyzed over the course of the book into a concise response to each. The dynamics of live dramatic events, which Freddie Rokem has referred to as "theatrical energies," are central to these discussions. The emotive spectacle of shared dramatic depictions can potentiate and elevate polemics from private to public discourse. In so doing their theaters defined, stabilized, coalesced, and then frequently redefined, disrupted, and cleaved nationalist, antifascist, Zionist, and apolitical blocs. Drawing from the broader context of German Buenos Aires as well as select theatrical presentations, this study highlights key themes, such as the influence

---

18. The Foreign Office relocated a new theater company to Buenos Aires, Reinhard Olszewski's German Chamber Theater, a postwar outfit formerly based in Santiago, Chile.

of theater on memory, community cohesion and polarization, national and political allegiance, and intercultural integration over the course of decades. To evaluate this impact, on- and offstage factors are considered, including repertory, cast, reception, funding, and, especially, performance theory. For example, even as many other factors shifted, Ludwig Ney's steadfast adherence to fascist drama theory and the positive reception of such presentations in the German and, later, the Argentine population demonstrates the constancy of National Socialist aesthetics among many nationalist Germans as well as their acceptability in Peronist Argentina. Concentrating on both fascist and antifascist theater reveals issues, interactions, and modes of analysis that have been underexplored in secondary literature on Germans in Latin America, and in migration studies in general. Thus, this work utilizes a fresh perspective to provide a more rounded portrait of diverse German trajectories from emigrants to immigrants in Argentina.

Extant Scholarship

According to the Society for Exile Studies, during the 1970s and 1980s scholars of German exilic literature created a framework that defined the field as research on "the circumstances of flight and . . . cultural, scientific, artistic, and political accomplishments of the German-speaking emigration from 1933 to 1945."[19] Although the term *emigrant* is politically neutral, the implication has always been that exile studies was concerned with refugees fleeing fascist persecution, and representative publications by leading scholars confirm this agenda.[20] A sampling of studies from the same time span with a narrower focus on specific locations, art forms,

---

19. *Exil*, Gesellschaft für Exilforschung, http://www.exilforschung.de/index. php?p=2.

20. Berendsohn, *Die humanistische Front*; Walter, *Deutsche Exilliteratur 1933–1950*; Durzak, *Die deutsche Exilliteratur 1933–1945*; Köpke and Winkler, *Exilliteratur 1933–1945*.

and artists also emphasizes antifascists and refugees.[21] It is impossible to catalog all publications in the field here; however, the yearbook of the Society for Exile Studies, *Exilforschung*, functions as a bellwether for the discipline. From its inception in 1983 to the present, *Exilforschung* has emphasized topics such as common destinations of exiles,[22] Jewish exile,[23] remigration,[24] inner emigration,[25] as well as politics,[26] music,[27] women,[28] science,[29] and journalism in exile.[30] By the 1990s there was concern about the continuing relevance of the field, exemplified by Bernard Spies's statement that many Germanists considered exile studies to be an "obsolete, closed chapter."[31] A few years later Claudia Albert claimed the discipline had grown stagnant, because for decades it had tended toward projects of meticulous data-collecting that often neglected issues of aesthetics, cultural theory, and migration. The foreboding title of Albert's article, "The End of Exile Studies?," underscored her uncertainty about the future.[32] Perhaps in consequence, research in German exile studies has since expanded far beyond its original scope. Gender transitions, cultural transfer, migration and diaspora studies, linguistics, networks and transnational

---

21. Emmerich, *Lyrik des Exils*; Lützeler, *Hermann Broch*; Pfanner, *Exile in New York*; Spalek and Strelka, *Deutsche Exilliteratur seit 1933*; Wächter, *Theater im Exil*.

22. Koebner, Köpke, and Radkau, *Stalin und die Intellektuellen und andere Themen*; Koebner et al., *Fluchtpunkte des Exils und andere Themen*; Krohn et al., *Metropolen des Exils*.

23. Koebner et al., *Das jüdische Exil und andere Themen*; Krohn et al., *Jüdische Emigration*; Bannasch, Schreckenberger, and Steinweis, *Exil und Shoah*.

24. Krohn et al., *Exil und Remigration*.

25. Krohn et al., *Aspekte der künstlerischen Inneren Emigration 1933–1945*.

26. Krohn et al., *Politische Aspekte des Exils*; Krohn et al., *Exil und Widerstand*.

27. Krohn et al., *Kulturelle Räume und ästhetische Universalität*.

28. Krohn et al., *Frauen und Exil*.

29. Koebner et al., *Vertreibung der Wissenschaften und andere Themen*.

30. Krohn et al., *Publizistik im Exil und andere Themen*.

31. Bernhard Spies, "Exilliteratur—ein abgeschlossenes Kapitel? Überlegungen zu Stand und Perspektiven der Literaturwissenschaftlichen Exilforschung," *Exilforschung* 14 (1996): 11–30, at 11.

32. Albert, "Ende der Exilforschung?," 182.

communities, multigenerational studies, and the possibilities of transfer and comparison across multiple historical situations are current themes.[33] Edited by Claus-Dieter Krohn, the massive, 1,356-page *Handbuch der deutschsprachigen Emigration 1933–1945* covers German emigrant scientists, historians, philosophers, and pedagogues, as well as architects, writers, actors, musicians, and painters, across five continents.[34] Beyond famous exiles, scholarship now also includes less-researched emigrants to Palestine, Bolivia, Uruguay, Argentina, China, India, and other nations.[35]

The late 1970s and early 1980s saw greater interest in antifascist art and literature in Latin America, including Arnold Spitta's *Paul Zech im südamerikanischen Exil* (1978) and Wolfgang Kießling's *Exil in Lateinamerika* (1980).[36] Numerous studies on exilic literature and theater in Latin America and, specifically, Argentina followed.[37] All emphasize victims of Nazism exclusively. Of course, ample research on pre- and postwar nationalist German emigration to Argentina also exists.[38] German scholars Holger Meding

33. For example, presentations at the 2018 symposium of the North American Society of Exile Studies at Loyola University Chicago included Pamela Caughie, "Between Nations, Between Genders: Transgender and the Experience of Exile"; Julia Elsky, *Heimatlose* and *en exil*: Adamov's French Translations of Rilke"; Sarah Voke, "Seher Çakir: Poetry Framed by Exile"; Wendy Pearlman, "Alienation in and from the Homeland: Narratives of the Lived Experience of Exile among Syrian Refugees in Germany and Beyond"; Shida Bazyar, *Nachts ist es leise in Teheran* (Cologne: Kiepenheuer & Witsch, 2016).

34. Krohn, *Handbuch der deutschsprachigen Emigration 1933–1945*.

35. Buxbuam, *Transit Shanghai*; Bannasch and Rochus, *Handbuch der deutschsprachigen Exilliteratur*; Maaß and Philipp, *Handbuch der deutschsprachigen Exiltheaters*; Franz, *Gateway India*.

36. Spitta, *Paul Zech im südamerikanischen Exil, 1933–1946*; Kießling, *Exil in Lateinamerika*.

37. Naumann, *Ein Theatermann im Exil, P. Walter Jacob*; Rojer, *Exile in Argentina, 1933–1945*; Douer and Seeber, *Wie weit ist Wien*; Rohland de Langbehn, *Paul Zech y las condiciones del exilio en la Argentina*; Roca, *Días de Teatro*; Silvia Glocer, *Melodias del destierro: Músicos judíos exiliados en la Argentina durante el nazismo* (Buenos Aires: Gourmet Musical Ediciones, 2016).

38. Newton, *"Nazi Menace"*; Meding, *Flucht vor Nürnberg?*; Jackisch, *El nazismo*; Pace, *La via del demoni*; Goñi, *La auténtica Odessa*; Ismar, *Der Pressekrieg*; Ben-Dror, *Catholic Church and the Jews*; Steinacher, *Nazis on the Run*; Argachá and Busiello, *Nazismo y otros extremismos en Entre Ríos*.

and Georg Ismar extensively analyze current events and politics in nationalist German media, such as *Der Weg* and the *Deutsche la Plata Zeitung*, respectively. Meding implicitly links the neofascist *Weg* to the study of German emigrant literature—if not precisely exile studies—by referring to it as an "emigrant magazine."[39] Yet, scholarship on German nationalists does not examine their artistic pursuits. Generally written by historians, research on nationalist emigration to Argentina appears to regard the cultural production of these emigrants as mostly outside its sphere of interest.

To sum up, despite the large-scale expansion of German exile studies and the plethora of historiography on Germans abroad, research on the artistic output of German nationalists abroad remains scarce. Additionally, while groups such as the Society for Exile Studies and the Austrian Society for Exile Research first defined themselves as dedicated to victims of Nazi persecution, both have long since exceeded their initial parameters. Nonetheless, they still exclude nationalist German emigrants, even though in the postwar period many of them were refugees.[40] To be sure, in German studies *emigration* is associated with victims of Nazism; however, reserving such a wide concept for this selective group is problematic. It is challenging to find a suitable term for the many nationalist German artists and journalists who resettled abroad if they cannot be referred to as emigrants. Furthermore, participation in cultural life forms an integral component of emigrant identity irrespective of political values.

While its focus on German drama abroad during the Nazi period continues the line of inquiry inherent in exile studies, this study encompasses not only Jewish and antifascist refugees, but also German nationalists. The first inclusive, book-length examination of German theater in Argentina, it argues that the cultural production of all Germans abroad merits study. Its emphasis on both victims and adherents of Hitlerism breaks sharply with the conventional purview of German exile studies. Furthermore, as reams

---

39. Meding, *"Der Weg."*
40. Holger Meding, "Der Nationalsozialismus und die deutsche Einwanderung an den Rio de la Plata," in Eick, *Nach Buenos Aires!*, 31–36.

of academic scholarship, popular history, and even pulp fiction attest, Argentina's fraught relationship with fascism extends beyond the World War II period. This book tracks Argentina's German-speaking refugees well into the postwar period; however, unlike previous models it also examines the cultural activities of German nationalists and postwar emigrants, some of whom collaborated on projects of fascist propaganda in Europe and later in Argentina. By including supporters, opponents, and victims of Nazism, I analyze the evolving relationships not only within, but also among antagonistic German-speaking populations. Despite their obvious differences, these factions and their theaters had much in common, including their countries and cultures of origin, language, and the mutual challenge of prospering as immigrants in Argentina. Furthermore, regardless of our perspectives today, emigrants during both Nazism and the postwar period saw themselves as refugees fleeing tumult, impoverishment, and persecution in their homeland. Thus, this study brings together groups and topics that scholars have tended to separate or bypass. In addition to investigating the conflicts that pervaded German Buenos Aires, I ask whether their common condition as emigrants in Argentina provoked nationalists, antifascists, and Zionists to take parallel tracks in community building, dramatic theory, integration, and transnational alliances, as well as fund-raising and commercial competition. Exploring these questions reveals elements of universality in the challenges intrinsic to immigration, and informs how to confront them.

Other than period newspaper and magazine reports and my own research there is nothing published on the German Theater.[41] Nonetheless, the success and influence of this stage and its founder, Ludwig Ney, are indisputable. Not only did the German Theater perform Goethe, Schiller, and Lessing to tens of thousands of spectators throughout World War II, but Ney continued directing German- and Spanish-language performances of canonical European authors in theaters across Argentina through the early 1970s. No figure from any stage in German Buenos Aires can claim such longevity, and Ney's artistic adaptability, professional opportunism, and

---

41. Kelz, "El teatro y la concepción de lo nacional."

ideological constancy constitute a novel blend of border skills that problematizes conventional views on nationalist emigrants. I also discuss several other, lesser-known nationalist theater companies in postwar Argentina. Although research on German culture abroad traditionally has emphasized antifascist artists, the music, theater, literature, and painting of nationalist German emigrants are vital to this topic. During the Nazi period and for decades beyond, Argentina's German-speaking populations supported antifascist *and* nationalist theaters. No investigation of German cultural production in this country can be complete without examining both.

Scholarship on the Free German Stage is more plentiful, but this book is a pioneering study in several ways.[42] Published research on the Free German Stage excludes Ludwig Ney's theater, even though Argentina's German ensembles competed in extraordinary proximity to each other. Performing at venues separated by just ten city blocks, the two troupes were inextricably linked. Not only did the German Theater spur antifascists and Zionists to establish their own competing theater, but each stage also influenced the repertoire, marketing, and the personnel of its rival for years thereafter. The contrasts, hostilities, and surprising approximations between these ensembles cannot be fully disclosed and analyzed unless both are in focus.

Extant scholarship on the Free German Stage also tends to focus on its founder, Paul Walter Jacob, marginalizing other members of the enterprise's twenty-plus-person cast, some of whom went on to

---

42. Wolfgang, "Paul Walter Jacob und die Freie Deutsche in Argentinien"; Naumann, *Ein Theatermann im Exil, P. Walter Jacob*; Pohle, "Paul Walter Jacob am Rio de la Plata: Rahmenbedingungen und Bestimmungsfaktoren eines exilpolitischen Engagements"; Pohle, "Paul Walter Jacob am Rio de la Plata: Der Kurs der FDB—eine exilpolitische Gratwanderung"; Pohle, "Paul Walter Jacob am Rio de la Plata: Exilprominenz und Zwang zur Politik"; Frithjof Trapp, "Zwischen Unterhaltungsfunktion und der Erwartung politischer Stellungnahme: Spielplan und künstlerische Konzeption der 'Freien Deutschen Bühne' Buenos Aires," in Koch, *Exiltheater und Exildramatik 1933–1945*, 118–137; Lemmer, *Die "Freie Deutsche Bühne" in Buenos Aires 1940–1965*; Rohland de Langbehn and Vedda, *Teatro y teoría teatral*; Germán Friedmann, "La cultura en el exilio alemán antinazi: El Freie Deutsche Bühne de Buenos Aires, 1940–1948," *Anuario del Instituto de Estudios Históricos Sociales* (2009): 69–87; Kalinna, "Exil und Identität"; Kelz, "Desde la emigración a la inmigración"; Kelz, "German Buenos Aires Asunder."

illustrious careers in Argentine theater and film. Many nationalist and antifascist artists were women, so this study also contributes to the history of female emigrants and their integration into the host society. Crucially, up to now scholars have not analyzed the dramatic presentations themselves, tending instead toward narrative history, biography, and, to a lesser degree, reception. While these approaches are informative, the Free German Stage was first and foremost a working theater company. Live performances were the bedrock of its existence. Fortunately, multiple sources inform investigations into the troupe's productions. In addition to reviews in local media, many of the original promptbooks—some of which diverge profoundly from published versions—are accessible at the Paul Walter Jacob Archive in Hamburg, and hundreds of photographs of performances exist in the Alexander Berger Collection at the Fundación IWO in Buenos Aires. I also have interviewed numerous thespians, whose memories help to illuminate productions at both stages. Drawing from theoretical scholarship, I pool primary sources to analyze several key productions at the Free German Stage and the German Theater, as well as their postwar incarnations.

This book on German theater in Argentina draws from primary sources in six languages from archives and personal collections in Argentina, Brazil, Germany, Austria, and the United States. Among these sources are oral testimonies, personal correspondence, and autobiographical writings. Memories can change and may reflect the interviewee's or author's aims of the moment, as well as their relationship to each other. Letters may also be shaped by the writer's personal objectives and his/her relationships to other correspondents. There are limits to the utility of oral history, personal letters, and autobiographical writings as a means of locating facts; however, these sources are indispensable for grasping people's interpersonal, emotional worlds and gaining a sense of the texture of daily life.[43] Impressions of one's cultural identity and national belonging, of a dramatic performance's personal and public

---

43. Farnsworth-Alvear, *Dulcinea in the Factory*, 204, in McGee Deutsch, 9.

resonance, and of discord or harmony in one's professional and social environments all fit into these categories. Therefore, such subjective perceptions add valuable emotional depth to this study. I have vetted interviewees' assertions of facts by comparing them with multiple primary and secondary sources. I have carefully evaluated every document, because all sources have biases, blind spots, agendas, and target audiences.

German Buenos Aires Onstage and Off

At the core of each colony's emphasis on the dramatic genre is the concept of theater as a community-building institution. In contrast to reading, generally an individual experience, the theatrical performance requires the bodily copresence and collaboration of actors and spectators, thus gaining a vital social dimension. Theater scholars have noted that the performance calls for a social community, since it is rooted in one and, on the other hand, since in its course it generates a community of thespians and theatergoers.[44] Furthermore, the collective sacrifices of time, effort, and money required to preserve the theater in times of crisis fortify the social union that the performance brings forth. Supporters of both the German Theater and the Free German Stage mobilized this social union to advance projects of theatrical nationhood, in which the emigrants' inchoate, tenuous sentiments of collective identity and national affection were articulated, developed, and reinforced through dramatic representation.[45] Collective identities, whether they are cultural, national, or even transnational, grow from a subjective understanding of history.[46] Both the German Theater and the Free German Stage vigorously participated in representations and debates about the past. Each produced dramatic depictions of recent and distant past events, in which thespians, theatergoers,

---

44. Max Herrmann, "Bühne und Drama, Antwort an Prof. Dr. Klaar," *Vössische Zeitung*, July 30, 1918, cited in Fischer-Lichte, *Theatre, Sacrifice, Ritual*, 19.
45. Kruger, *National Stage*, 3; Holdsworth, *Theatre and National Identity*, 2.
46. Rokem, *Performing History*, 3.

reviewers, and sponsors selectively contested or underscored hegemonic understandings of the historical heritage on the basis of which their collective identities were being formed. Whereas antifascists strove to forge intercultural alliances through inclusive theatrical performances, German nationalists and, to an extent, Zionists aimed to create a bond among theatergoers that represented a nationality in the modern sense—an insular ethnicity organized by historic fiction into an imagined community.[47] In the liminal stages of emigrant identity construction, the German Theater and the Free German Stage also functioned as laboratories for what Sandra McGee Deutsch calls border skills: flexibility, adaptation, and reinvention.[48] Through the shared spectacle of dramatic performance, audiences and ensembles alike negotiated lines that defined their identities, such as victims and oppressors, emigrants and immigrants, conformists and dissidents, as well as Jews, Germans, or Argentines. On- and offstage thespians and theatergoers reacted to these lines in different ways, disputing, crossing and crisscrossing, evading, hardening, and reproducing them. Identity formation also relies on differentiation, that is, defining identity by representing cultural and political difference. By means of encountering difference through theatrical excursions beyond their colony's fringes, nationalists, antifascists, and Zionists imagined communities of illusory fullness by performing and sometimes even becoming what they believed they were not. Together, these tactics of staging cultural representation were vital for the ways in which theatergoers and thespians tackled the project of concocting collective identity through conformism and transgression. The German Theater and the Free German Stage unleashed volatile theatrical energies that intervened directly, forcefully, and sometimes unforeseeably in the ideological debates that splintered and suffused German Buenos Aires.

One must place this study on emigrant theater within the context of German Buenos Aires and, more broadly, German emigration to Argentina. German-speaking emigrants to Argentina were

---

47. Roach, *Cities of the Dead*, 103.
48. McGee Deutsch, *Crossing Borders, Claiming a Nation*, 3.

not a monolithic group. Most scholars divide emigrants into two populations: a nationalistic "old colony," which arrived in Argentina between the late nineteenth century and the 1920s, and an anti-Nazi "new colony," composed mostly of Jewish refugees from Nazi Germany. This book largely abstains from the terms "old" and "new," because dates of emigration varied among members of each group. Many supporters of the Free German Stage belonged to earlier waves, and two leading actors at the nationalist German Theater arrived after 1933. The nationalistic and anti-Nazi colonies in Buenos Aires also fractured further into many distinct subgroups. While the repertoire and reviews of the German Theater dovetail with the National Socialist sociopolitical platform and conservative German drama theory, performances staged by other members of the nationalist population demonstrate salient divisions on several issues, most controversially Nazi racial ideology and integration with the Argentine host society. Later, tens of thousands of German emigrants to Argentina during the postwar period brought a new diversity to the nationalist faction. Having experienced National Socialism firsthand, many of them had a fundamentally different view of the Nazi period, World War II, and Argentina than less recent emigrants, the overwhelming majority of whom had not visited Europe from 1933 to 1945. Even though Ludwig Ney's renamed New Stage struggled to negotiate the divergent viewpoints of its postwar audiences, both nationalist media and the West German embassy insistently utilized the stage as means of trying to prevent a new rift from opening in German Buenos Aires.

The anti-Hitler population likewise was characterized by variance and even outright conflict. Some scholars have already established subgroups of German-speaking Zionists, antifascist activists, and other emigrants who were not politically engaged.[49]

---

49. Avni, *Argentina y la historia de la inmigración judía (1810–1950)*; Rojer, *Exile in Argentina, 1933–1945*; Schwarcz, *Trotz allem*; McGee Deutsch, *Crossing Borders, Claiming a Nation*; Schirp, *Die Wochenzeitung "Semanario Israelita"*; Schnorbach, *Por "la otra Alemania"*; Neumeyer, Schopflocher, and Traub, *"Wir wollen den Fluch in Segen verwandeln"*; Eick, *Nach Buenos Aires!*; Alfredo Bauer,

Since members of each group were present on both sides of the curtain at performances by the Free German Stage, this theater brings the full diversity of the anti-Hitler colony into focus. Onstage their thespian representatives projected unity, but offstage sectarian organizations incited conflicts over political allegiance, national affection, and intercultural integration. Influence over the stage's repertoire signified control of the messaging at the most popular entertainment venue for all German-speaking refugees from Nazism. Therefore, the private correspondence, promptbooks, ticket sales, and media reviews of its performances locate the Free German Stage at the center of an impassioned power struggle among antifascists, Zionists, and more moderate theatergoers. Many antifascists saw the theater as a vehicle to fuel anti-Nazi activism and uphold essential German cultural values in exile, thus preserving a moral foundation for a reformed postwar Germany. Zionists, on the hand, argued that Jews must reject Germany altogether and clashed with antifascists on the issue of collective German guilt for Nazi crimes. They regarded the Free German Stage as an exclusively Jewish theater, and insisted that its repertoire convey a Zionist worldview. Finally, most refugees were neither antifascist activists nor Zionists. Although their voices were underrepresented in local media outlets, these predominantly Jewish theatergoers exerted a decisive influence at the box office by rebelling against Zionist and agitprop theater (though not eschewing political and religious drama altogether). The Free German Stage is a revealing lens for exploring the political, religious, and cultural engagement of this large group, which tends to be less prominent in scholarship on Jewish and German Buenos Aires. During the postwar period, efforts to deploy the theater as a means of reconciliation exacerbated tensions within the anti-Hitler population. Guest performances by thespians who had been popular in Nazi Germany enraged Zionists and many antifascists. These events even drew some nationalist Germans to the Free German Stage, where they sat alongside victims of Nazi persecution and watched Theo

---

La Asociación Vorwärts y la lucha democrática en la Argentina; Friedmann, *Alemanes antinazis en la Argentina*; Schopflocher and Niefanger, *Buenos Aires*.

Lingen, Hans Moser, Viktor de Kowa, and others perform with a cast consisting almost entirely of Jewish refugees. Attempting to unify German Buenos Aires against the proliferation of communism, the West German embassy also feigned reconciliation by enforcing an untenable code of silence among actors, audiences, and reviewers.

Through their theaters, I show that Argentina's German-speaking colonies were subject to intensely antagonistic, transatlantic political pressures, and some individuals enthusiastically espoused and perpetuated this hostility. Despite their political and religious discord, however, these groups also had much in common. During World War II and beyond, the rival factions in German Buenos Aires shared positions constitutive of exile: all were caught between isolation from their homeland and adaptation to the Argentine host society. Qualities associated with cultures of diaspora—taboos and postponements of return to the native country, connections among multiple communities, and forms of longing, memory, and (dis)identification—apply to nationalist, antifascist, and Zionist emigrants alike and found expression in their dramatic performances.[50] As actors and audiences of both theaters morphed from emigrants to immigrants, many of them underwent similar processes of adaptation and reinvention, including the struggles to establish financial stability, learn a new language, construct social and professional networks, and contend with the societal norms of a foreign culture. Moreover, in their competition to define the boundaries and center of Germanness, nationalists, antifascists, and Zionists shaped each other's cultural production and political objectives. Reciprocal tactics of representation, differentiation, and retaliation via dramatic performances were inherent in the projects of identity formation and community building that were underway in each of these competing populations. German Buenos Aires can only be fully understood by exploring the interplay that existed among its constituent groups. Indeed, considering their geographical proximity, it is hard to imagine otherwise.

---

50. Clifford, *Routes*, 10.

I also argue that cultural life constitutes an essential part of emigrant identity construction, regardless of its political tilt. Specialists on Germany under National Socialism note that the word "culture" probably appears more often in Nazi propaganda than any other term, with the possible exceptions of "race" and "nation."[51] Although historians who work on the political and anthropological aspects of nationalist German emigrants do not emphasize their artistic output, during World War II[52] and the postwar period[53] German nationalist publications devoted a remarkable amount of space to poetry, short fiction, and serialized novels, as well as to reviews of concerts, theatrical performances, and cinema. Throughout the period in focus nationalist Germans stressed cultural activities to consolidate and project their sense of nationhood in Argentina. From 1934 to 1965, the German Theater and subsequent nationalist stages strengthened the cohesion of Argentina's nationalist German population, reinforced its members' ties to the fatherland, and

---

51. Hermand, *Culture in Dark Times*, 3.

52. The 1941 *Jahrbuch des deutschen Volksbundes in Argentinien*, for example, features ten poems, four short stories, a review of German cultural events in Buenos Aires, and an obituary of Josef Ponte, a German poet who had visited Argentina a few years earlier: Margit Hilleprandt, "September 1940," 43; Hermann Löns, "Wir fahren gegen England," 68; Heinrich Lersch, "Grabschrift," 70; Will Vesper, "Mahnung," 100; n.a., "Nun geht die deutsche Reise an," 101; n.a., "Wir kehren heim ins Vaterland," 101; n.a., "Aus Wolhynien sind gezogen," 102; Werner Hoffmann, "Der verlorene Sohn: Ein Legendenspiel," 132–134; Johannes Franze, "Das künstlerische Leben in Buenos Aires," 134–141; Wilhelm Lütge, "Zum Gedächtnis von Josef Ponte," 145–147; Wilhelm Rabe, "Ans Werk," 146; Fritz Berkhan, "Wir haben gesiegt," 158; Maria Kahle, "Das Gebet der Toten," 167; Margit Hilleprandt, "Tito, der Seehund," 175–177; Margit Hilleprandt, "Wolken, Wellen und Wind," 177; Karl Schade, "Para éste no hay perdón," 177–181; Karl Herrmann, "Erntendankfest," 180; Maria Brunswig, "Der Totenkranz: Eine Geschichte aus Patagonien," 197–201.

53. One example is the April 1948 issue of *Der Weg*, which included essays on Nordic music and a review of Wilhelm Furtwängler, as well as fictional works by German prisoners of war, Christian August Winnig, and a recent emigrant to Chile, Susanne Torwandt: Ernst Aufrecht, "Nordische Musik," 220–223; n.a., "Wilhelm Furtwängler: Zu seinen Konzerten im Teatro Colón," 260; n.a., "Zwei Gedichte eines deutschen Kriegsgefangenen," 248–249; Christian August Winnig, "Im Kreis verbunden," 228–233; Susanne Torwandt, "Menschen und Tiere am Rio Negro," 234–239.

inculcated them with propaganda from successive governments in Germany. During the Nazi period, this included the cult of the leader, virulent anti-Semitism, and militaristic expansionism. After the war, conservative actors and reviewers denounced the Allied occupation and the expulsion of German inhabitants from Eastern Europe before eventually siding with the West German embassy in its crusade against communism. An enduring conduit for government messaging, theatrical performances also revealed divergences between nationalist emigrants and their European countrymen, thus undermining officials' efforts to forge a transatlantic National Socialist community and, later, hindering Bonn's attempts to unite and mobilize German Buenos Aires against leftist activism. Furthermore, earlier nationalist German emigrants often portrayed Argentina as a second homeland, thereby illustrating a fundamental distinction between older and newer waves of migration, as well as between themselves and Germans across the Atlantic.

Chapter Overview

A cursory glance at the table of contents reveals the asymmetrical chapter lengths of this study. The first two compact chapters provide historical and biographical foregrounding for the main body of the book. The following three chapters are lengthier, because they examine the competing theaters at the heart of this project. While this entire book is based on extensive archival research, the third and longest chapter draws from the exhaustive archive of Paul Walter Jacob, founder, manager, director, and lead actor of the Free German Stage from 1939 to 1949. Jacob's collection of promptbooks, correspondence, and personal notes permits a penetrating restoration of the institutional alliances, personal relationships, and theatrical presentations of this period.

The first chapter contextualizes Argentina's thriving German-theater scene in (1) German emigration patterns to Argentina; (2) the interplay between German emigrants and their Argentine hosts; and (3) the tensions among local nationalist, antifascist, and Zionist German-language religious, educational, and media institutions.

Primarily constituted by emigrants who arrived in the late nineteenth century and in the 1920s, the nationalist colony was characterized by nostalgia for the Wilhelmine monarchy, aversion to the Weimar Republic and, eventually, support for Hitler. The antifascists consisted of a minority of earlier emigrants who supported the Weimar Republic and mostly Jewish German-speaking refugees who fled to Argentina during Nazism. Nominally neutral until late 1944, Argentina permitted pro- and anti-Hitler German media, schools, and cultural centers to flourish, thus whetting extant hostilities among emigrants. Conflict also pervaded the refugee population, which was divided on issues of cultural identity, Jewish integration into the Argentine host society, and collective German guilt for the Shoah.

Four case studies in circum-Atlantic migration mark the origins of Argentina's competing German theaters. Beginning with his success as director of a state-funded touring ensemble in Nazi Germany, the second chapter traces the journey of the German Theater's founder, Ludwig Ney, from Europe to Paraguay and, ultimately, Argentina. Shifting to Jewish actors, I reconstruct three Jewish thespian refugees' flights to South America and explore how their work onstage both exposed them to Nazi persecution and facilitated their escapes to an unlikely reunion in Argentina. This discussion emphasizes the interdependency between actors and audiences at theaters in times of crisis, casting dramatic performances as a laboratory for testing survival strategies amid the rise of European fascism. Another focus is the evolution of theater management during the 1930s. Bereft of state subventions, stages were compelled to upend the tradition of cultural theater, adopting instead a market-based approach to repertoire and advertising similar to popular entertainment venues, like the cinema. This controversial model became the blueprint for the Free German Stage in Buenos Aires.

Founded in 1939 and composed entirely of professional thespian refugees, the Free German Stage fomented anti-Nazism through an international blend of lighter comedies and serious dramas, nearly all of which were banned in Germany. A box-office stalwart and psychological urgency, the lighter muse conveyed a buoyant message of intercultural community to the theater's public. Yet, comedies also stirred tensions in the refugee population. Leftist antifascists and Zionists accused spectators of preferring escapist flights into a chimerical European past over engagement with current events. Against the resistance of most theatergoers, antifascist and Zionist activists demanded uncompromising agitprop and Jewish dramas. Based on private correspondence and ideological battles waged in local media, I examine the rancor that political and religious plays stoked among refugees. Finally, chapter 3 investigates backlash against the Free German Stage from Nazi Germany, nationalist German emigrants, and the Argentine government.

Founded in 1938 by the emigrant actor Ludwig Ney with funding from the German government, the German Theater staged dramas by propagandists, canonical authors, and members of the local community, instilling a sense of a common cultural heritage among its public. As chapter 4 shows, reviews in local media emphasized Nazi tropes, such as anti-urbanism, the leader cult, mania for Aryans and Teutons, the glorification of war, and racial anti-Semitism. Though they were Nazi loyalists who enthusiastically supported Ney's ensemble, local dramatists and theatergoers also emphasized their cultural hybridity and affinity for Argentina, which estranged them from the fatherland and undercut Nazi officials' efforts to construct a transatlantic National Socialist community. Later, when the war and the Argentine regime turned against Germany, comedies formed a larger proportion of the ensemble's repertoire. Spectators at both the Free German Stage and the German Theater embraced the comedic genre to cope with the overlapping psychological and emotional duress that they incurred as emigrant populations whose nations of origin were at war.

Spanning the period 1946 to 1965, the fifth chapter tracks the trajectory of Argentina's German theaters against a changing political landscape and new waves of European emigration. In the postwar period, director Paul Walter Jacob endeavored to attract all German speakers to the Free German Stage; however, his failed efforts at reconciliation underscored the polarized environment in the Argentine capital. Without ever renouncing fascism, Ludwig Ney adopted a strategy of interculturalism to succeed professionally in Peronist Argentina. German-speaking artists from across the political spectrum embarked on cross-cultural projects, and their transformative impact on theater in Argentina is still evident today. Meanwhile, in its crusade against communism, the West German embassy intervened at both stages. Carefully staged depictions of German heritage and reconciliation reflected a specious contrivance, contingent on edited memories of the recent past. The intractable animosity ultimately led to a move away from German dramatists in favor of canonical European playwrights, such as William Shakespeare.

1

German Buenos Aires Asunder

German emigration to Argentina has a history as old as the city of Buenos Aires itself. According to popular legend one of the original four founders of the city in 1536 was the German adventurer Ulrich Schmidl, who is celebrated for this feat in the drama *Utz Schmidl* (1940), penned by another German emigrant, Werner Hoffmann. Larger waves of German emigrants reached the River Plate in the latter third of the nineteenth century and peaked when hyperinflation ravaged Germany after World War I. Argentina had remained neutral in the conflict, which is attributable to the profitable business of exporting agricultural goods to both sides, resistance among the nation's huge Italian population against going to war with Italy, and ties between the Argentine and Prussian militaries. Argentina's neutrality was of great importance to German industrialists and policy planners, whose capital holdings in the country increased during the war years and were augmented again in the early 1920s by major investments in dependencies of German chemical, pharmaceutical, metallurgical, electrical, and heavy-construction combines. In part because of German, British, and US investment, in the 1920s Argentina emerged as a far more prosperous and developed country than its neighbors.[1]

The country was an appealing destination for tens of thousands of Germans seeking to escape hyperinflation as well as social and political turmoil in Germany in the 1920s. During the brunt of Germany's economic crisis in the early 1920s, over 25,000 Germans emigrated to Argentina annually, and from the end of World War I to the beginning of the global financial crisis approximately 135,000 German speakers entered the country.[2] While locally they split into many subgroups based on religion, social class, gender, age, and other factors, these emigrants were in general frustrated by financial and social instability in Germany and disseminated negative views on the Weimar Republic and nostalgia for the monarchy among Argentina's German population.

As noted in the introduction to this book, estimates of the number of German speakers in Argentina vary widely. The following statistics draw from previous scholarship to compile figures that are by no means intended to be authoritative. Immediately after World War I, roughly 30,000 German speakers resided in Buenos Aires alone, among them 11,000 who had been born in Germany.[3] By the 1930s, due in large part to arrivals of Jewish refugees and a smaller number of political dissidents, there were 60,000 people of German descent in the city, 20,000 of them German born.[4] As of 1937, approximately 47,000 German nationals lived in Argentina, and the total German-speaking population had reached 250,000,[5] although some scholars put the number as high as 400,000.[6]

---

1. Ronald Newton, "Das andere Deutschland," in Jackman and Borden, *Muses Flee Hitler*, 307.

2. Saint Sauveur-Henn, "Die deutsche Einwanderung," 12.

3. Ebel, *Das Dritte Reich und Argentinien*, 23.

4. Volberg, *Auslandsdeutschtum und Drittes Reich*, 16.

5. Volberg, *Auslandsdeutschtum*, 9.

6. As noted earlier, in the introduction, this vast discrepancy stems primarily from uncertainty regarding the number of Volga Germans and their offspring.

Between 1920 and 1945, the percentage of Germans among total emigrants to Argentina rose dramatically, beginning with 6 percent for the time span 1920 to 1930 and reaching 28 percent from 1933 to 1945.[7] Argentine emigration authorities estimated that 31,000 Jewish refugees fled to Argentina from Nazi Germany;[8] however, this figure fails to account for the many illegal and unrecorded emigrants, as well as refugees who entered legally from other countries.[9] The Jewish Philanthropic Society places the sum of Jewish refugees in Latin America at 101,500. The countries along Argentina's borders—Chile, Bolivia, Paraguay, Brazil, and Uruguay—received a total of 50,300 refugees (12,000; 5,000; 800; 25,500; and 7,000, respectively).[10] In particular, neighboring Paraguay, Uruguay, and Bolivia conducted a lucrative business selling visas to desperate Jews during the late 1930s. Borders were porous, and Argentina, with a GDP more than twice the average of the nations along its limits, offered refugees the brightest economic prospects in the region.[11] Argentina's large Jewish population of roughly 250,000 also attracted refugees from throughout South America.[12] These conditions, supplemented by ample anecdotal evidence, indicate that many Jews who initially disembarked elsewhere proceeded to take clandestine mountain, jungle, and river routes to settle in Buenos Aires. Most estimates place the total

---

7. Saint Sauveur-Henn, "Die deutsche Einwanderung," 11–13.

8. Jackisch, *El nazismo*, 158.

9. Ronald Newton estimates that the number of illegal Jewish emigrants exceeded the number of Jews who entered the country legally. Newton, "Das andere Deutschland," 304.

10. Hilfsverein deutschsprechender Juden/Asociación Filantrópica Israelita, *Zehn Jahre Aufbauarbeit in Südamerika/10 años de Obra Constructiva en América del Sud 1933–1943*, 9.

11. Alan Taylor, "Foreign Capital Flows," in *The Cambridge Economic History of Latin America*, ed. Victor Bulmer, John Coatsworth, and Robert Cortés Conde (Cambridge: Cambridge University Press, 2006), 76.

12. Newton, "Das andere Deutschland," 304.

number of German-speaking Jewish emigrants to Argentina from 1933 to 1945 at 45,000.[13] Per capita, worldwide only Palestine received more refugees.[14]

Such statistics reflect a sweeping cultural and religious shift in German and Jewish emigration to Argentina. Until 1933 most German emigrants to Argentina were Gentiles; afterward the overwhelming majority were Jews. Unlike previous waves of Jewish emigration to Argentina, during the Nazi period most Jews arrived from central Europe and had belonged to cosmopolitan, professional social classes. Most earlier Jewish emigrants, by contrast, hailed from the shtetls of eastern Europe. The religious, social, economic, and cultural gaps between these groups were profound.[15] Most German-speaking Jewish refugees were unwilling or unable to attend theatrical performances or read newspapers in Yiddish. Many earlier Jewish emigrants rejected the German language, which they associated with Nazism.[16] Such divergences impeded efforts to form a cohesive Jewish community in Argentina. Furthermore, during the 1930s German-speaking emigration to Argentina morphed from a rural to an urban phenomenon. Many earlier emigrants formed colonies in the arable regions of the interior, especially in the provinces of Misiones, Santa Fe, and Entre Ríos, but after 1933 most settled in Buenos Aires to practice urban trades.[17] This pattern of migration laid the foundation for an extensive network of antifascist and Zionist German-language educational, cultural, political, and media organizations in the Argentine capital.

To Govern Is to Populate? Argentina's Immigration Policy

After gaining independence from Spain in 1820, Argentina maintained a liberal immigration policy that favored Europeans in

---

13. Saint Sauveur-Henn, *Un siècle d'emigration allemande vers l'Argentine 1853–1945*, 249; Schwarcz, *Trotz allem*, 204; Jackisch, *El nazismo*, 158.

14. Rojer, *Exile in Argentina, 1933–1945*, 81.

15. Schwarcz, *Trotz allem*, 58.

16. Forum Sionista to Keren Kayameth Leisreal, November 18, 1942, Paul Walter Jacob-Archiv Korrespondenz (PWJAK).

17. McGee Deutsch, *Crossing Borders, Claiming a Nation*, 15–21.

general and northern Europeans in particular.[18] Even today, the constitution still obliges the Argentine government to encourage European immigration to the country.[19] The primary objective of this policy was to populate Argentina's rural interior; however, the nation also welcomed urban immigration until workers' protests caused restrictions in 1902 and again in 1910. Regulations were loosened during the prosperous 1920s, then tightened from 1930 to 1934 because of the global financial crisis. Although Argentina was reluctant to admit Jewish refugees, the total number of immigrants entering the country rose steadily from 21,000 in 1935, to 27,000 in 1936, then 44,000 in 1937, and finally 40,000 in 1938.[20] Immigration in 1938 would have surpassed the total for 1937 if not for tight restrictions passed in August of that year.

The growing number of refugees entering the country created concern among Argentine conservatives, who fretted about serving as a receptacle for Europe's unwanted.[21] In August 1938, President Roberto Ortiz's administration issued a decree limiting immigration to persons with immediate family in Argentina and those with start-up capital who had the explicit intention of pursuing agriculture in the interior.[22] Justified as necessary to prevent increased unemployment, the measures provoked a debate between the antitotalitarian newspaper, the *Argentinisches Tageblatt*, and nationalist media. The *Tageblatt* rejected the explanations of the Ortiz administration, claiming that recent emigrants had created jobs by launching small businesses.[23] Furthermore, the paper cited the Argentine constitution and claimed that the restrictive legislation opposed the will of the Argentine population as well as the nation's foundational legal document.[24]

---

18. Rodriguez, *Civilizing Argentina*, 33–34.
19. www.argentina.gov.ar/argentina/portal/documentos/constitucion_nacional. pdf, 4.
20. Spitta, *Paul Zech im südamerikanischen Exil, 1933–1946*, 39.
21. Ebel, *Drittes Reich und Argentinien*, 138.
22. Spitta, *Paul Zech*, 34.
23. "Argentinien sperrt die Grenzen," *Argentinisches Tageblatt* (*AT*), August 26, 1938.
24. "Argentinien braucht Einwanderer," *AT*, October 23, 1938.

The *Deutsche La Plata Zeitung*, mouthpiece of the nationalist German colony, entered the immigration debate as well. Initially it focused on Europe, lauding successful government policies that had pressured Jews to leave Germany.[25] With time, the *La Plata Zeitung* became more aggressive and localized its perspective on the River Plate. Without directly referencing Argentina, in its Spanish section the newspaper indicated its approval of the new legislation by citing reports that the political and economic stability of neighboring Uruguay, which had a more open immigration policy, was threatened by the infiltration of undesirable Jewish refugees. The *La Plata Zeitung* quoted complaints in the Uruguayan newspaper *La Tribuna Popular* about the nuisance of Jewish emigrant street peddlers. Concluding with a warning against the penetration of the River Plate region by Jewish emigrants, the *La Plata Zeitung* admonished Argentine authorities to enforce anti-immigration legislation rigorously.[26]

The debate on Argentina's immigration policy devolved into a bitter feud between antifascist and nationalist German media about integration and loyalty to the host country. Published by the homonymous political organization, the antifascist journal *Das Andere Deutschland* accused nationalist Germans of creating a fifth column to undermine Argentine sovereignty. The *Argentinisches Tageblatt* likewise expressed outrage at Nazi barbarism and exhorted the government to prevent toxic racism from poisoning the atmosphere in Buenos Aires. The paper made its position clear, declaring sympathy and solidarity with democratic Jews worldwide.[27] The nationalist *Jahrbuch des deutschen Volksbundes in Argentinien* countered by accusing antifascists of abusing the generosity and liberality of their Argentine hosts in order to extend their fight against Germany and everything German to Argentina.[28] Antifascist and nationalist media employed parallel methods, accusing the other German colony of disloyalty to their Argentine hosts, in an attempt to protect their own readership. Moreover,

25. "Zur Auswanderung der Juden aus dem Reich," *Deutsche La Plata Zeitung* (*DLPZ*), December 13, 1938.

26. "En el Uruguay comienzan a alarmarse de la silenciosa infiltración judía," *DLPZ*, February 8, 1941.

27. "Protest gegen Nazibarbarei in Argentinien," *AT*, November 15, 1938.

28. "Ein Nachwort zum Jahre 1938," *Jahrbuch des deutschen Volksbundes in Argentinien* (*JdVA*), 1939.

throughout the conflict neither side acknowledged the other as German, reserving this designation for itself.

The *Jahrbuch* defended nationalist emigrants by referencing Domingo Faustino Sarmiento, the seventh president of Argentina (1868–74), who had argued that German immigrants were "particularly desired by nations for their proverbial honesty, work ethic, and pacific, calm character."[29] The *Jahrbuch* quoted Sarmiento in his native Spanish, aiming to demonstrate the nationalist colony's history of integration and contributions to Argentine society. Mirroring the methods of German nationalists, yet supporting the opposite bloc, Free German Stage (FGS) founder Paul Walter Jacob argued in the yearbook of the Jewish Philanthropic Society that in addition to infusing Argentina with their industriousness and innovation, Jewish refugees were not merely transitory migrants, but immigrants who were in their new Argentine homeland to stay.[30]

Both nationalist and antifascist German populations adopted the tactic of accusing the other side of treason against Argentina while claiming to be the more loyal, contributing immigrant German culture. The evolving relationships between the various contingents of German immigrants and their Argentine hosts is a central theme throughout this book. With mixed results, nationalist, antifascist, and Zionist blocs, as well as both the Free German Stage and the German Theater, sought to build strength and exert influence internally through collaborative projects with local Argentines who, of course, also were a diverse population. Furthermore, the embattled factions of German speakers weaponized integration as a competitive menace against the rival ensemble and its public.

The Infamous Decade: Argentine Politics in 1930–1945

Following a trajectory of growth and development that began in the 1870s, by 1929 Argentina's liberal constitution and democratic government had enabled the construction of one of the

---

29. "Sarmiento," *JdVA* 1939.
30. Paul Walter Jacob, "Wissenschaft-Kunst-Theater," in Hilfsverein deutschsprechender Juden/Asociación Filantrópica Israelita, *Zehn Jahre Aufbauarbeit*, 140–142.

most ethnically diverse, politically open, and prosperous societies in the Americas. The nation's predominantly agricultural economy was a global breadbasket, and industrialization also was underway. In 1913 Argentina had the sixth highest per capita income in the world, and in 1929 it was among the world's ten wealthiest nations.[31]

Despite the apparent progress in Argentina from 1870 to 1930, some scholars argue that this period sowed the social decay and political authoritarianism that have troubled it ever since.[32] For all its economic growth and democratic reforms, Argentina did not achieve a more even distribution of wealth and power during this period. Its development was corralled by an oligarchy that aimed to maintain both the status quo of class hierarchy and its hold on the country's wealth. Freedom and equality were limited by the state as it suppressed political demonstrations and incarcerated dissenters. Many Argentine criminologists, psychopathologists, and government officials shared the pseudoscientific theories of Nordic and Anglo-Saxon superiority to other races, including Africans, indigenous peoples, and Jews.[33] Drawing from the work of European theorists, such as the Italian criminologist Cesare Lombroso and the French neurologist Jean-Marie Charcot, Argentine studies attempted to link race to criminality and psychological disorders.[34] State scientists strove to engineer a supposedly superior citizenry, and the government advanced repressive control through racially discriminatory practices, such as immigration policy and even state violence against racial groups that it regarded as inferior. This narrative suggests that Argentina's ambivalence toward fascism in later decades originated in its supposedly golden era.

This era ended with the world financial crisis in 1930, which marked a turning point in the nation's history. The tumult had

---

31. Della Paolera and Taylor, *New Economic History of Argentina*, 3.
32. Rodriguez, *Civilizing Argentina*, 1–40, 63–71, 84–94, 186–195. See also McGee Deutsch, *Las Derechas*, 26–31; Zimmermann, *Los liberals reformistas*; Botana, *El orden conservador*.
33. Rodriguez, *Civilizing Argentina*, 68–69.
34. Rodriguez, *Civilizing Argentina*, 68–69.

grave repercussions for Argentina's vulnerable export market as well as its young and fragile democratic institutions. The crisis plunged Argentina into social and political turmoil. In 1932 journalist Raúl Scalabrini Ortiz lamented that more than three million unemployed men suffered persecution by the police and stigmatization by the press and endured the most despicable misery.[35] This socioeconomic cataclysm rapidly worsened and provoked a political emergency that destabilized President Hipólito Yrigoyen's liberal Radical Party and opened the way for regime change at the hands of conservative elements in the military and agricultural sectors.

On September 6, 1930, a military coup deposed Yrigoyen and proclaimed the fascist sympathizer José Félix Uriburu as president. Uriburu abolished the nation's liberal constitution in favor of an authoritarian regime, an act that future president Juan Perón saw as a pivotal event in Argentine politics. According to Perón, Uriburu brusquely terminated the law of universal suffrage and voter participation, marking the beginning of a new epoch in which members of the conservative oligarchy controlled the government.[36] Fourteen months later Uriburu was ousted by Agustín P. Justo, who exploited earlier democratic reforms to organize a democratic façade legitimizing his government. Elections occurred and a parliament with majority and oppositional parties also existed; however, the Radical Party, reported to have the support of 70 percent of the population, was impeded from presenting candidates in national and provincial elections. Instead, votes were fixed by the government under the euphemism of patriotic fraud.[37] This political system of electoral fraud, intimidation, and cronyism held sway throughout the 1930s, known in Argentina as the infamous decade.

Justo looked to fascist movements in Italy and Germany for political models. Since many members of the military oligarchy had been trained in Germany, maintaining friendly relations with Hitler's regime was a natural foreign policy. Domestically, the

---

35. Ortiz, *Política británica en el Río de la Plata*, 167.
36. Perón, *Yo Perón*, 90.
37. Spitta, *Paul Zech*, 17.

government cultivated nationalism by demonizing communism. The newly created Special Section for the Repression of Communism banned the Communist Party of Argentina and incarcerated hundreds of activists under the anti-Communist Social Defense Law. The regime also supported the foundation of fascist groups and allowed National Socialist sympathizers to organize and operate freely. Grassroots organizations collaborated with the German consulate to work to coordinate German-language schools and media, as well as cultural and social organizations, with Nazism immediately after Hitler came to power. Antifascists, contrarily, were subject to continual harassment, even violence. The *Argentinisches Tageblatt* was temporarily banned twice in the 1930s, and its offices were firebombed in 1934. A meeting of the antifascist cultural group the Pestalozzi Society was disrupted by storm troopers in 1934. Attacks on leftist newspapers and synagogues followed later that year.

Particularly divisive among Argentines and German immigrants alike was the annexation of Austria in 1938. Nationalist Germans celebrated with a mass rally on April 10, 1938, at Luna Park, a large venue in central Buenos Aires. Attended by nearly 20,000 people, the event had many features of the stadium rallies in Germany, including mass chorus renditions of the "Song of Germany" and the "Horst Wessel Song" featuring Nazi organizations and their Argentine fascist counterparts. Dancers and musicians performed against the backdrop of an immense red curtain emblazoned with the words "One Nation, One Reich, One Führer" in towering black Gothic letters. Nearby, at Plaza San Martín, the Argentine University Federation and other activists protested the event. The counterdemonstration turned violent as protesters burned German flags and stoned German banks and other locales. Shortly after the rioting the Argentine interim chancellor of the Foreign Ministry, Manuel Alvarado, apologized publicly to the Nazi chargé d'affaires, Erich Otto Meynen, deploring members of the media and special interest groups who offended the German nation and harmed the "cordial relations between the two peoples."[38]

---

38. Newton, *"Nazi Menace,"* 187.

The ministry's thinly veiled reproach of the antifascist community and its sycophancy to NSDAP (National Socialist German Workers Party) officials exacerbated the tensions among native Argentine citizens and German emigrants alike.

In 1937 a civilian lawyer, Roberto Ortiz, became president of Argentina. Although he had gained office through the system of electoral fraud, Ortiz allied himself with the Radicals and worked to restore legitimate democratic elections to the country. Ortiz contributed to a shift in public opinion against fascism and passed an official ban on the National Socialist Party in Argentina on May 15, 1939. He declared his sympathy with the victims of Nazism in a message to Congress in May 1940, declaring that Argentine neutrality in World War II did not signify indifference and insensitivity.[39] Provoked by public outrage against the Nazification of German schools, Ortiz passed legislation forbidding the instruction of racial prejudice in private educational institutions. The first two years of Ortiz's presidency also coincided with the greatest waves of refugees to the River Plate. Nearly all the founding members of the Free German Stage arrived in Buenos Aires in 1938 and early 1939. In August and again in October 1939, however, Ortiz bowed to pressure within his government and passed prohibitive restrictions on immigration, practically eliminating legal admittance to Argentina.

Advancing blindness forced Ortiz to cede power to his vice president and archenemy, Ramón Castillo, in 1940. Oritz died in July 1942 without reassuming the presidency. Castillo was the political antithesis of Ortiz, and once in office he returned to the platform of Justo's regime. Though it remained nominally neutral in World War II, the new government was conservative, nationalistic, tolerant of fascist agitators, and unaccommodating to US calls for hemispheric solidarity. In a letter to the German embassy in 1942, chargé d'affaires Meynen reported that Castillo firmly believed in and desired an Axis victory in the war.[40] Further events confirm

---

39. Ismar, *Der Pressekrieg*, 31.
40. Meynen to Foreign Office (FO), July 20, 1942, Akten Büro Staatssekretär, Argentinien, Bd. 4, Politisches Archiv des Auswärtigen Amts (PAAA).

the tenor of Meynen's comments. When Ernesto Alemann, editor in chief of the *Argentinisches Tageblatt*, expressed his condolences after the bombing of Pearl Harbor in a telegram to the US ambassador, the Argentine postal service refused to deliver it, ostensibly out of concern for the preservation of the nation's neutrality. On the other hand, military airplanes delivered National Socialist newspapers to the rural Argentine interior for free.[41] The government intervened against the screening of antifascist films such as Charlie Chaplin's *The Great Dictator* (1940) and Emeric Pressburger's *49th Parallel* (1941), but the Nazi propaganda film *Victory in the West* (1940) was repeatedly shown to Argentine military officers.[42] On December 9, 1942, *The Voice of the Day*, an antifascist German-language radio broadcast from democratic, pro–Allied forces Uruguay, accused the Argentine regime of abetting Nazi espionage and propaganda as well as placing its own commercial interests above a commitment to human rights and international law.[43]

Conditions in Argentina worsened when a military conspiracy led by General Pedro Pablo Ramírez deposed Castillo in June 1943. Ramírez forbade political parties, dissolved student organizations, and restricted freedom of the press. In response to student protests, the government shut down all universities in October 1943.[44] For antifascists and Jews the situation became increasingly precarious. A temporary ban on Yiddish media in 1943 provoked a special report on anti-Semitism in Argentina in the New Yorker exile magazine *Aufbau*.[45] In June of the same year authorities shut down the *Volksblatt*, mouthpiece for exiled German Communists, and police briefly imprisoned one of its editors, Erich Sieloff. In consequence, the antifascist political organization and magazine *Das Andere Deutschland* temporarily relocated to Montevideo in 1944. Ramírez's policies also had repercussions for the Free German Stage, which was

41. Spitta, *Paul Zech*, 22

42. "Charlie Chaplin," *AT*, December 30, 1940; "Sieg im Westen," *DLPZ*, June 19, 1941.

43. Paul Walter Jacob-Archiv (PWJA) VII c) 408, Walter A. Berendsohn Forschungsstelle für deutsche Exilliteratur, Universität Hamburg.

44. Cane, *Fourth Enemy*, 156.

45. "Die antijüdische Front," *Aufbau* 43 (1943): 3.

nearly compelled to disband in 1944. During the same period the nationalist German Theater had its heyday. In 1943, its ensemble began playing at the National Theater, which had a seating capacity of 1,155 spectators and boasted a prime location in the heart of the Buenos Aires theater district, steps away from the iconic Obelisk, ground zero of the Republic of Argentina.

Despite the nucleus of Nazi sympathizers in his government, Ramírez was forced to break off diplomatic relations with Germany in January 1944. The Allies had intercepted Argentine plans to purchase arms from Germany, and US officials also threatened to publish documents allegedly proving Argentine participation in a coup that had overthrown the pro-Allies Bolivian government in 1943. Another supporter of the Allies, neighboring Uruguay, grew alarmed and allowed a fleet of US warships to anchor in the River Plate. Furthermore, the Allies threatened Ramírez that they would break off diplomatic relations with Argentina, a measure that held catastrophic consequences for the Argentine economy, if Argentina did not do so with Germany. When Ramírez complied, almost certainly against his will, he enraged Nazi sympathizers in the Argentine military. Three weeks later he was deposed, and on February 24, 1944, the Axis supporters General Edelmiro Farrell and Juan Domingo Perón assumed the offices of president and vice president, respectively. Perón, who had gained national prominence as secretary of labor under Ramírez, also held the office of war minister in the new administration. Some scholars have speculated that the Farrell-Perón regime initially planned to try Ramírez for treason and reopen diplomatic relations with Germany.[46]

Despite the political and economic disadvantages of its position, Argentina continued to support the Axis powers long after it was clear that fascism had lost the war. Even in May 1944 the *Neue Zürcher Zeitung* reported that the new government was inciting attacks against Jewish property in Argentina.[47] The military oligarchy and the conservative elite governed according to neither the will nor the welfare of the populace. Instead it perpetuated

---

46. Newton, *"Nazi Menace,"* 309.
47. Spitta, *Paul Zech*, 29.

the authoritarian system that ensured its monopoly on wealth and power. Rising nationalism and pretensions of hegemony in South America also motivated Argentina to oppose the United States and Great Britain, whom it saw as its principal competitors on the continent. The US government refused to recognize the Farrell-Perón regime and pressured others to follow suit. Facing Allied sanctions and mounting malcontent among its own population, on March 27, 1945, Argentina became the last country in the world to declare war on Germany. Argentina sent no troops to fight in the conflict; its declaration of war represented a purely cosmetic gesture of so-called hemispheric solidarity. In 1969 Juan Perón, who had become president of Argentina in 1946, reflected upon the measure: "Without question the war was decided by 1945. We would have remained neutral, but it was impossible to continue this policy. In agreement with the Germans in Argentina we declared war on Germany. Naturally, that was a mere formality."[48] Argentina resisted the Allied war effort throughout World War II. Even in the postwar period, Perón continued to sympathize with nationalist Germans. Nonetheless, throughout the period in question, Argentina's government permitted the expression of pro- and anti-Nazi positions with an openness that was singular worldwide in countries with a sizable German population.

Argentina's government and citizens are essential to this book's examination of German immigrant theaters. For all their success, both the Free German Stage and the German Theater always performed at the whim of Argentine authorities and were subject to a local environment beyond their control. Had the nation followed the repressive policies of neighboring Brazil toward its German population during World War II, neither stage could have survived. Thereafter, under Peronism, intercultural professional opportunities existed for nationalist and antifascist artists, facilitating both ongoing discord and integration into local society. In the Cold War, the West German embassy vigorously intervened at both theaters to advance its anti-Communist agenda. While Argentina's German

---

48. Meding, *Flucht vor Nürnberg?*, 50.

communities enjoyed unique liberties for much of the time covered in this book, their ability to exercise self-determination was always limited. This book therefore also evaluates how local external forces shaped the political and cultural altercations onstage in German Buenos Aires.

Trouble at the Theater: Ferdinand Bruckner's *Race* in Buenos Aires, 1934

Argentina's ambivalent political posturing permitted singularly open competition between its nationalist and antifascist German-speaking populations for nearly the full duration of Hitler's regime. The first high-profile clash occurred at the theater. Dramatic performances can bring forth a social community that unites actors and spectators; however, in the politically charged atmosphere of 1930s Buenos Aires, agitprop theater united certain groups by excluding and denouncing others. Productions of political theater thus exacerbated the animosity between antifascists and nationalists. Foreshadowing the competing German Theater and Free German Stage, the Spanish-language production of Ferdinand Bruckner's antifascist farce, *Race*, was a local harbinger of such antagonistic community building.

When *Race* premiered in December 1934 at the 500-seat Comic Theater, German Consul Edmund von Thermann immediately complained to the Argentine Foreign Ministry that its caricatures of Nazi leaders were injurious to Argentine-German relations. In turn, the ministry obsequiously appealed to the municipal censor to strike numerous offensive passages, the theater adhered to its demands, and performances commenced. To great acclaim, Bruckner's biting satire transcended nation and language. A derisory rendition of the "Horst Wessel Song," for example, was sung in both German and Spanish. Irate, the German consulate fretted to Berlin that the play could seriously damage the Reich's reputation in Argentina.[49] The *La Plata Zeitung* printed an indignant review, deploring scene after scene in which the German chancellor and the German people were reviled in the most hateful and egregious manner imaginable.[50] Nationalist Germans protested the performances, and on December 16, 1934, they organized a violent riot in the theater. Heinrich Volberg, a Nazi supporter who attended the presentation, reported the buildup to the event and the ensuing fracas. According to Volberg, a whispering campaign made sure that party members and supporters occupied about a dozen rows of the theater. In advance, they agreed to watch the piece in silence until a scene in which a drunken SA man played a record with the "Horst Wessel Song." At the first note pandemonium broke out. Whistles, noisemakers, loud boos, and jeers overwhelmed the thespians onstage. At the same time several men jumped onto the stage, smashed the record, tore down the swastika flag, and roughed up the actor portraying the SA man. The melee in the audience worsened when Argentine soldiers, who were among the spectators but allegedly had no idea what was happening, drew their bayonets and forced their way to the exits.[51] The Argentine police then appeared at the premises and arrested sixty-eight members of the audience, who spent the night in jail but were released the next day when the German consulate paid municipal fines in full.

The riot caused the *La Plata Zeitung* to appeal for clemency and a halt to performances of the piece based on the 100-year, untarnished friendship between Argentina and Germany.[52] The Comic Theater refused to yield, however, and presentations continued amid protests, disruptions, and threats of violence from German and Argentine Nazi sympathizers. On February 13, 1935, the police captured an Argentine with explosives in his possession, who confessed to plotting to firebomb the Comic Theater and named several accomplices. Many of the fourteen men implicated belonged to the Argentine fascist organization Civic Legion. The lone

---

49. Willi Köhn to Ministry of Propaganda (MP), December 18, 1934, Band R55, Akte 20553, Bundesarchiv Berlin (BB).

50. " 'Die Rassen' im Teatro Cómico," *DLPZ*, December 17, 1934.

51. Volberg, *Auslandsdeutschtum*, 124.

52. "Feindliche Hetzer," *DLPZ*, December 19, 1934.

German, Hans Hermann Wilke, an emigrant who worked at the German Bank of South America, was identified as the paymaster and sentenced to four years and six months in prison.[53]

In the aftermath, the *La Plata Zeitung* alleged that the true culprit in the incidents had been the antitotalitarian *Argentinisches Tageblatt*. The *La Plata Zeitung* exhorted local authorities to put a stop to the machinations of this newspaper, which had close ties to fearmongering rabble-rousers and cared nothing for honest journalism, but was interested only in cynical, self-serving muckraking.[54] For its part, the *Tageblatt* expressed sympathy for Bruckner's message and incomprehension regarding the municipal censorship and the riots at the Comic Theater. With an authoritarian, profascist government in power, a sharply polarized local population, large communities of German-speaking nationalists and antifascists, as well as increasing arrivals of Jewish refugees, already in 1934 Buenos Aires was fraught with violent and escalating political and cultural conflict.

Hitherto the hostilities had been confined to local German media outlets, but the spectacle of Bruckner's *Race* brought the simmering strife to an open uproar that incited emigrants and Argentines alike to action. Rehearsed, repeated nightly, and yet still spontaneous, live theatrical events consistently elevated to the public stage disputes that otherwise remained lurking behind the curtain. Live theater was not the origin—it was the detonator. In the coming years journalists, politicians, thespians, and spectators all mobilized the medium of theater to provoke and to polarize blocs of nationalists, antifascists, and Zionists, but also to attempt to reconcile them as well. This study explores the capacity of dramatic performances to potentiate, prolong, and surmount the polemics that suffused German Buenos Aires for decades.

A War of Words: German Media in Argentina

The most widely circulating German-language newspapers in South America during the World War II period, the *Deutsche La Plata*

---

53. Ismar, *Der Pressekrieg*, 101.
54. "Feindliche Hetzer," *DLPZ*, December 19, 1934.

Zeitung and *Argentinisches Tageblatt* are essential to any study of German emigration to Argentina.[55] Furthermore, the conflict-ridden history of these newspapers encapsulates the long-standing discord between Argentina's antifascist and nationalist German communities.

Founded by the German emigrant and entrepreneur Hermann Tjarks, the *Deutsche La Plata Zeitung* appeared without interruption from May 10, 1874, until October 18, 1944, when Argentina acquiesced to international pressure to ban pro-Nazi institutions. The *La Plata Zeitung* encouraged and actively recruited Germans to emigrate to Argentina, and by 1919 it was the most widely read German-language newspaper in the country. On March 2, 1878, the Swiss emigrant Johann Alemann, a journalist and expert on immigration policy, published the first edition of the *Argentinisches Wochenblatt*. The paper appeared daily as the *Argentinisches Tageblatt* beginning on April 29, 1889, and quickly became the *La Plata Zeitung*'s strongest competition for the German media market on the River Plate.

From the nineteenth century to the end of World War II, the two newspapers cultivated distinct readerships. The *Deutsche La Plata Zeitung* valued the preservation of German identity, whereas the *Argentinisches Tageblatt* advocated further integration with the host society. This divergence is reflected in their names: the "German newspaper on the River Plate" versus the "Argentine daily paper." Tensions between monarchist and republican German factions fueled feuding between the publications and their readers in the early twentieth century, and the animosity intensified upon the outbreak of World War I. Although economic interests caused Argentina to remain neutral during the war, anti-German sentiment was widespread and compelled the newspapers to take positions. Invoking its German heritage, the *La Plata Zeitung* unwaveringly

55. Beyond Ismar's *Pressekrieg*, scholarship on this rivalry is often tendentious, siding with the antifascists. See Gaudig and Veit, *Der Widerschein des Nazismus*; Schoepp, *Das Argentinische Tageblatt, 1933–45*; Manfred Pantförder, *"Das andere Deutschland"*; Arndt and Olson, *Die deutschsprachige Presse der Amerikas/ The German Language Press of the Americas, 1732–1968* ; Bussemeyer, *50 Jahre "Argentinisches Tageblatt."*

supported the German war effort. The *Tageblatt*, by contrast, viewed itself and its readership as Argentine and was a vocal critic of Germany's actions in Europe.

The rancor continued unabated after the war. The *La Plata Zeitung* had deep misgivings about the Weimar Republic, while the *Tageblatt* supported the new government. The tension stewed during the 1920s and accelerated into outright enmity with Hitler's rise. From January 1933 onward, the *Tageblatt* took a stridently antifascist position. The *Tageblatt* welcomed European refugees, nearly all of whom were Jewish, to Argentina and gained both readers and writers through this policy. Some of the better-known emigrants on its staff included Paul Walter Jacob, Balder Olden, Fred Heller, Carl Meffert, and Paul Zech. In the late 1930s, its circulation reached 28,000. The *La Plata Zeitung*, by contrast, was a staunch supporter of Nazism. As early as June 1931, the *Völkischer Beobachter* referred to the paper as "Hitler's banner" in Buenos Aires.[56] Likely motivated in part by large subventions from Berlin,[57] it denounced Jewish refugees as undesirables, and by 1935 had a circulation of 40,000 to 45,000.[58] The two papers' reactions to the Munich Agreement on September 29, 1938, which demanded that Czechoslovakia cede the Sudeten region to Germany, betrayed the irreconcilable dissension between the papers. Whereas the *Tageblatt* ran the headline "Agreement at Prague's Expense: A Nation Raped," the *La Plata Zeitung* celebrated the accord as a "Victory for Truth" under a giant headline "Peace!" flanked by portraits of Hitler and Mussolini.[59]

Not only readers of the *La Plata Zeitung* were offended by the *Tageblatt*'s reporting, which sometimes compromised journalistic integrity to defame German nationalists and galvanize the Argentine citizenry and government to punish pro-Nazi institutions.

---

56. Ismar, *Der Pressekreig*, 80.

57. The *La Plata Zeitung* received 25,000 reichsmarks in 1938 alone. Ismar, *Der Pressekreig*, 113.

58. Ismar, *Der Pressekreig*, 78.

59. "Einigung auf Kosten Prags: Eine Nation vergewaltigt," *AT*, September 25, 1938; "Frieden!," *DLPZ*, September 30, 1938.

The exposés it published about Nazi plots to annex Patagonia, as well as the provinces of Misiones and Corrientes, cited insidious sources and falsified documents with the express purpose of damaging relations between the nationalist colony and Argentines.[60] The *Tageblatt* relentlessly fought Nazism and supported refugees, often under very adverse circumstances, however its willingness to level wrongful accusations against the nationalist population exacerbated tensions among German immigrants and even alienated some opponents of National Socialism. A letter from a subscriber in Misiones exemplifies the reactions of many readers to its reporting: "Your newspaper has degenerated into a pack of lies. We are no friends of the Hitler regime, but we will not allow the entire nation to be dragged into the mud."[61] Some Germans chose the *La Plata Zeitung* not to support Nazism, but to protest the *Tageblatt*'s offensive tone.[62] Because of its tendentious standpoint the nationalist colony trusted nothing printed in the *Tageblatt*, including legitimate accounts of Nazi atrocities in Europe, which were absent from the *La Plata Zeitung*'s pages. The resultant animosity persisted long after the war's end, thwarting attempts at rapprochement by the West German embassy and the founder of the Free German Stage, Paul Walter Jacob.

The German writer Balder Olden, exiled in Buenos Aires and then in Montevideo, described the split between the nationalists and antifascists:

> There are two villages, one Republican and one nationalist, although the nationalist one is not half as Nazi as people say. . . . The two villages are utterly separate. A young woman, who is employed by a German firm, went to the theater with me one evening and was fired the next day—"untrustworthy in her private life." We have a theater and

---

60. "Naziotische Umtriebe in Misiones," *AT*, July 10, 1940; "Die Tätigkeiten der Nazioten in Misiones," *AT*, July 17, 1940; "Die Geschichte Nazi-Verschörung in Misiones," *AT*, July 21, 1940; "Bericht über Tätigkeit der Nazis in Misiones," *AT*, December 11, 1940; "Die Naziverschworungen in Sudamerika," *AT*, August 14, 1941.

61. Schoepp, "Das *Argentinische Tageblatt* als Forum der Emigration 1933–1945," 92.

62. "Leserbriefe," *AT*, April 29, 1939.

so do they. We each have a newspaper, a school, clubs, lectures—a German world and a German dystopia. . . . The separation is so absolute that you forget in one village that the other exists. I've been able do it so far, at least.[63]

While many scholars have taken this statement as evidence of a strict separation between two German-speaking populations, Olden's assessment represents a simplification.[64] First, Ben Bryce has argued convincingly that even far before World War I divisions existed among German immigrants along lines of education, religious denomination, gender, generation, and social class.[65] Furthermore, Germán Friedmann and I have pointed out that the quote itself is contradictory.[66] His friend's dismissal from her job after visiting the Free German Stage (FGS) proves contact between the two colonies. Attacks, reprisals, and other interactions between the two Germanies occurred regularly, making it hard for many people to be as successful as Olden in ignoring or even "forgetting" their adversaries.

Media coverage of the German theater scene was one area, however, in which the split was nearly absolute. The *La Plata Zeitung* covered Ludwig Ney's German Theater extensively from 1938 until 1944, providing publicity that was fundamental to the stage's success. The paper also reported frequently on drama in Germany and reviewed Argentine theatrical productions, but it never mentioned the FGS. For its part, the *Tageblatt* was one of the driving forces behind the establishment of the anti-Hitler FGS. The initial idea for the enterprise grew out of conversations between Paul Walter Jacob and Ernesto Alemann, owner, publisher, and editor in chief of the *Tageblatt*, who ran free advertising and reported on the troupe daily, while several members of the cast also wrote for the paper. Despite such close coverage, neither paper mentioned

---

63. Balder Olden, "Flucht und Hoffnung: Rückschau aus Buenos Aires," *Aufbau*, August 22, 1941.

64. Kießling, *Exil in Lateinamerika*, 73; Rojer, *Exile in Argentina*, 97; Lemmer, *Die "Freie Deutsche Bühne,"* 14; Ismar, *Der Pressekreig*, 29; Stuhlmann, *Vater Courage*, 146.

65. Bryce, *To Belong in Buenos Aires*, 163.

66. Friedmann, "Los alemanes antinazis de la Argentina y el mito de las dos aldeas."

the competing theater by name throughout World War II. After the war the *Freie Presse*, successor to the *La Plata Zeitung*, began reporting on the Free German Stage in December 1945,[67] but the *Tageblatt* did not print a single line about Ludwig Ney until 1956.[68] The war of words between the *Argentinisches Tageblatt* and the *Deutsche La Plata Zeitung* encompassed not only politics, but cultural life as well, including both theaters in German Buenos Aires.

German Schools

During his visit to Argentina as a delegate to the Congress of PEN Clubs in 1936, the exiled writer Stefan Zweig stated the tragedy of contemporary Europe lay in the inculcation of hatred in the minds of its children:

> Day after day, from sunrise to sunset, they taught hatred, and then at night, they dreamt of it. When the war ended, it was impossible to put an end to the hatred which coursed through everyone's veins. They could not turn it off . . . men, women, and children remained intoxicated.[69]

The author added that his most fervent hope was that the South American youth would never live under the hatred that agitated Europe in the 1930s.[70] But, as Zweig himself observed during his stay, the pedagogy of hate was already present in the Argentine capital.

In 1932, there were twenty German schools in Buenos Aires, with approximately 4,800 students, the largest concentration outside Europe. With few exceptions, by 1934 these institutions had been infiltrated by Nazi propaganda. The administration expelled all Jewish students, and other pupils subsequently remembered that the swastika and the "Horst Wessel Song" were ubiquitous in

---

67. "*Marilou,*" *Freie Presse (FP)*, December 3, 1945.
68. "*Zuviel für eine kleine Frau,*" *AT*, April 5, 1956.
69. "La propaganda del odio," *Crítica*, September 5, 1936.
70. "La juventud de Europa," *La Nación (LN)*, September 9, 1936.

the schools.[71] In its annual report for 1938, the Humboldt School, the largest German school in Argentina, thanked the German embassy and the Nazi Party for financial support.[72] Numerous schools received funds from the German embassy, and several teachers were dismissed for refusing to sufficiently support Nazism in the classroom.[73] Correspondence between administrators culminated in "Heil Hitler!"[74] and the Humboldt School calendar for 1938 celebrated the dictator's birthday as a school holiday.[75] One teacher at the Goethe School, Werner Hoffmann, read from Hans Grimm's *Volk ohne Raum* (1926) in class, and drew from the text to justify Germany's territorial and military expansionism.[76] The same calendar also highlights a theatrical presentation by the German Theater, and Ludwig Ney himself also taught in the Goethe School's drama program in 1938.[77] Ney worked in the arts curricula of the German school system through the early 1970s and was a key figure in connecting first-generation Argentines with their German cultural heritage.

In 1934, Ernesto Alemann spearheaded the creation of the Pestalozzi School to resist the spread of Nazism in local German schools. Stefan Zweig would later refer to the school and its pupils as "a little miracle."[78] The first rector of the Pestalozzi School, emigrant educator and journalist Alfred Dang, emphasized that the faculty's objective was to confront the demons of Nazi pedagogy with true humanity.[79] Furious, in a report to Berlin, Ambassador

---

71. Volberg, *Auslandsdeutschtum*, 187.

72. Annual report, Humbodlt-Schule (1939), Goethe School Archive (GSA), Vicente López, Argentina.

73. Claudia Garnica De Bertona, "Max Tepp, un intermediario entre dos mundos," *Anuario Argentino de Germanística* 5 (2009): 314.

74. Schroder to Preschel, November 13, 1940, GSA.

75. 1938 Calendar, Humboldt-Schule, GSA.

76. Mariana González Lutier, "La Comisión de Investigación de las Actividades Anti-argentinas: El caso de la Goethe Schule," *Cuadernos DIHA* 5–6 (2019).

77. Photographs of *Urfaust*, 1939, GSA.

78. "An die 'Pestalozzi'-Schüler," *Schülerzeitung der Pestalozzi-Schule*, September 1936.

79. "Die Humboldt-Schule eine naziotische Drillanstalt," *AT*, April 6, 1938.

Edmund von Thermann denounced the Pestalozzi School as adversarial to the new Germany.[80] In 1934, Dang became the first German in South America to be denaturalized by Hitler's regime.

From its inception, the Free German Stage collaborated with the Pestalozzi School and the Cangallo School, which also remained independent from the German embassy.[81] This effort was made at both pedagogical and economic levels. The FGS participated in fund-raisers for the schools and offered discounted ticket packages to pupils, parents, and teachers.[82] It initiated a close exchange between its ensemble and refugee children, mainly through dramatic representations of fairy tales. Conscious of the trauma that many pupils had experienced in real life, the cast edited the stories to shield Nazism's youngest victims from the violence, death, and fatalism in many tales.[83] In the spirit of both schools' pedagogical mission of intercultural harmony, the productions included songs in Spanish, new roles for immigrant children, and Argentine figures such as gauchos from the Pampas.[84] By infusing European fairy tales with local cultural markers, the presentations abetted the children's transition from emigrants to immigrants in Argentina. Furthermore, several pupils eventually acted with the adult ensemble of the Free German Stage.

Supporting Actors: Nationalist, Antifascist, and Jewish Auxiliaries

Whether motivated locally by self-interest, transnational agendas, or a combination of the two, the pre–World War I ties between local divisions of nationalist German groups in Argentina and their parent organizations in Germany facilitated rapid, transatlantic coordination upon the emergence of the National Socialist

---

80. Thermann to FO, May 10, 1934, Pestalozzi School Archive (PSA), Buenos Aires, Argentina.
81. PWJA VI h) 299.
82. PWJA VI c) 288.
83. *Schneewittchen*, PWJA VI j) 312.
84. *Die Prinzessin auf der Erbse*, PWJA VI j) 312.

state. The German Association of Employees was established in 1912 as a local division of the conservative German National Retail Clerks Association. When Hitler came to power, the Clerks Association coordinated itself voluntarily and changed its name to the German Labor Front. In April 1934, the Association of Employees in Argentina followed suit. Under the direction of Alfred Müller, who later took charge of the Nazi Party in Argentina, the Labor Front opened itself to professions beyond commerce, vastly increasing its representation in the German population. Following a decree passed on May 15, 1939, which obliged all Argentine organizations to cut their ties with foreign countries, the Labor Front changed the German version of its name to the League of Working Germans and feigned democratic reforms in conjunction with the new legislation. The Spanish version of its name was not altered, indicating the continuity of this organization after the 1939 decree.

As in Germany, local divisions of the German Labor Front and Strength through Joy in Argentina formed the labor and diversion wings of an organization devoted to building a close-knit community of working Germans in support of National Socialism. The group offered its members and their families vacation and recreational opportunities, including trips to Germany.[85] Until the decree of 1939, these programs were operated in conjunction with the Strength through Joy organization in Germany. The Labor Front also published a monthly magazine, *Der Deutsche in Argentinien*, which featured articles about current political and cultural events in Germany and Argentina. *Der Deutsche in Argentinien* reported a circulation of 10,000 for 1939 and was published until late 1944.[86] The magazine was clearly oriented to Germany, and it was committed to Nazism, including racial anti-Semitism. Contrary to antifascist claims, however, the magazine's contents do not demonstrate overt antagonism to Argentina.[87]

---

85. Newton, *"Nazi Menace,"* 71.
86. Volberg, *Auslandsdeutschtum*, 67. Figures for the circulation of *Der Deutsche in Argentinien* vary. In *Exil in Lateinamerika*, Wolfgang Kießling estimates a circulation of 700 in 1934. Volberg cites the publication's own statistics, while Kießling provides no source. Kießling, *Exil in Lateinamerika*, 64.
87. Dickmann, *La infiltración nazi-fascista en la Argentina*, 13–14.

Figure 1. Portrait of the German Theater's Irene Ney
in Manfred Hausmann's *Lilofee.*

Source: *Der Deutsche in Argentinien*, February 1941. Biblioteca Nacional
Doctor Mariano Moreno—Argentina.

The Labor Front exerted a profound influence on the German theater scene in Buenos Aires. Not only did *Der Deutsche in Argentinien* publish regular features on Ludwig Ney's German Theater, but the Labor Front also sponsored all the stage's performances during its inaugural year in 1938. The Labor Front and Strength through Joy were fundamental to Nazi propaganda and community-building efforts in Argentina, and they robustly deployed theater in this endeavor.

In 1937 the former member of the German parliament August Siemsen, a Social Democrat, led efforts to found *Das Andere Deutschland* (*DAD*), a multipurpose organization and political journal central to exiles in Argentina and the Southern Cone, until it folded in 1948.[88] Many antifascist activists in Argentina were members of *Das Andere Deutschland*'s executive committee, including Walter Damus, Heinrich Grönewald, Hans Lehmann, Rolf Ladendorff, Ernst Lakenbacher, and Rudolf Levy. Since local authorities refused to permit the establishment of an explicitly political organization, *DAD* consisted in effect of several thousand subscribers to a journal bearing its name. The founder of the Free German Stage, Paul Walter Jacob, was a frequent contributor to *DAD*.

DAD served as a liaison with Spanish and Italian antifascists and cultivated links to refugees in the far-flung corners of the Southern Cone. These exiles gathered political intelligence, which *DAD* passed along to Allied forces. The journal also distributed summaries of world events to provincial newspapers, whose limited resources rendered them vulnerable to Axis news agencies' offers to send them fascist propaganda for free. August Siemsen's activities for *Das Andere Deutschland* and the anti-Nazi Pestalozzi School drew the ire of Nazi authorities, who denaturalized him in 1938.[89] After the Argentine government passed a decree prohibiting the activities of various antifascist political parties and organizations

---

88. For thorough study of *DAD*, see Friedmann, *Alemanes antinazis en la Argentina*.

89. Geheimes Staatspolizeiamt Referat II B 3, September 7, 1938, PSA.

on January 17, 1944, *DAD* temporarily relocated its operations to Montevideo, Uruguay.[90]

Despite threats from abroad and within Argentina, *DAD* admonished German emigrants to participate in the fight against fascism. *DAD* indicted apolitical emigrants, accusing them of being no better than the Nazis themselves; however, the group never wavered from its faith in the integrity of German culture and the German people.[91] Even after the 1938 November pogroms, *DAD* repeatedly insisted that the German citizenry were not guilty of crimes against Jews. Instead, the organization asserted that socialists, democrats, and pious Christians suffered similar persecution. The German people, it sweepingly declared, were in fetters. They were victims, not perpetrators.[92] Throughout Nazism *DAD* championed the existence of another, better Germany which, it argued, was also the true Germany.[93] A nucleus for the most engaged antifascists in the region, *DAD*'s aggressive posture irritated some less zealous refugees as well as Zionist organizations, many of which indicted Germans collectively.

Numbering over 300,000, the pre-1933 Jewish population in Argentina was the largest in South America and had established Buenos Aires as an internationally prominent center for eastern Jewish cultural traditions. There existed numerous Yiddish newspapers, magazines, publishers, printers, and a widely acclaimed Yiddish-language theater, the Yiddish People's Theater or IFT.[94] In the 1930s Jewish refugees from Europe founded many new Jewish political, cultural, and social organizations. Some, such as the Jewish Philanthropic Society, were moderate in their religious and political positions. Founded in 1933, the Jewish Philanthropic Society assisted recent arrivals with social and economic integration. The group offered Spanish language courses, legal advice for illegal

90. Friedmann, *Alemanes antinazis en la Argentina*, 131–132.

91. "Ihr seid nicht besser," *AT*, August 28, 1938.

92. "Nacht über Deutschland," *AT*, November 20, 1938.

93. Heiden to Alemann, June 20, 1938, PSA.

94. Nouwen, *Oy, My Buenos Aires*, 140–141; Alejandro Dujovne, "Print Culture and Urban Geography: Jewish Bookstores, Libraries, and Printers in Buenos Aires, 1910–1960," in Brodsky and Rein, *New Jewish Argentina*, 98.

immigrants, and assistance in finding lodgings and employment. It also published a monthly magazine about events and services in the community. Within ten years its membership ballooned from 175 to over 2,000 heads of Jewish families. According to the Society, this number signified that 10,000 emigrants were linked to the organization, 20–25 percent of the total Jewish migration to Argentina during the Nazi period.[95]

Other Jewish institutions, such as the Jewish Cultural League, affirmed Zionist religious and political beliefs. The Cultural League issued a monthly news bulletin, organized a youth group, rented sporting facilities in the suburb of Olivos, and had garnered a membership of 1,500 by 1942.[96] According to League president Juan Zweig, by serving as a Jewish religious and cultural center the organization aimed to replace the milieu Jewish refugees had left behind in Europe, thereby rescuing them from spiritual isolation and psychological depression.[97] Considering that conservative estimates place Jewish emigration to Argentina at 40,000, the Cultural League had relatively low membership figures, indicating that most German-speaking Jewish emigrants to Argentina were moderate in their religious and political beliefs.

Two smaller Zionist organizations were the Group of German-Speaking Zionists, founded in 1936 or 1937, and renamed the Theodor Herzl Society in 1940; and the Zionist Forum, which was originally named the Zionist Forum Bar Kochba and was founded in 1937.[98] These institutions collaborated with the Free German Stage, which they pressured to perform Zionist dramas. When the ensemble staged Nathan Bistritzky's *That Night* in 1942, the Zionist Forum proclaimed its mission on the playbill for the event. The group promised to make every effort to deepen and disseminate Zionist values, as well as fulfill Zionist ambitions.[99] As news of the Shoah reached Argentina, Zionists voiced broad and bitter

---

95. Schwarcz, *Trotz allem*, 114.
96. Schwarcz, 145.
97. Schwarcz, 145.
98. Schwarcz, 154.
99. PWJA VI b) 281.

indictments of German culture and Germans, which put them at odds with antifascists, and to an extent, the FGS itself.

Local Jewish media also were involved in debates between Zionists and less religious organizations. In April of 1940 Rabbi Günter Friedländer and the lawyer Bernhardi Swarsensky, a Zionist activist who was also the president of the Theodor Herzl Society, founded the *Jüdische Wochenschau*. The *Wochenschau* was the only German-language Jewish newspaper in South America to gain a supraregional presence and withstand competition from the New York periodical *Aufbau*, which circulated throughout the Americas. A hard-line Zionist publication, the *Wochenschau* reviewed all productions by the FGS. It reported on cultural and political issues that were of interest to Jews and exhorted Jewish emigrants to return to their Jewish roots and rely on the principles of Judaism as a guide for life.[100]

The *Jüdische Wochenschau* and *DAD* clashed repeatedly. The *Wochenschau* rejected *DAD*'s appeals that all emigrants, whether Jews or Gentiles, should unite against Hitler. In an early, programmatic article Swarsensky clarified that unlike the members of *DAD*, Hitler had attacked him and his readership not as Germans, but as Jews. No Jew, Swarsensky continued, should ever forgive Germany for what it had done to the Jewish people. Only by returning to the Jewish spirit and way of life could they overcome the violent rupture that Nazism had inflicted on them.[101] In stark contrast to *DAD,* the *Wochenschau* severed all ties to Germany, advocating instead a Zionist interpretation of Jewish values and the return of all Jews to Eretz Israel. Acute discord between Zionists and political antifascists on issues of German identity and collective German guilt caused relations among refugees to steadily deteriorate throughout World War II and the postwar period.

The FGS, whose cast and public were composed of moderate Jews, Zionists, and antifascist Gentiles, was caught squarely in the crossfire of these hostilities. The troupe performed under the auspices of German antifascist and Zionist institutions. Both the

---

100. Kelz, "Los escritos de Hardi Swarsensky."
101. "Einig wie nie zuvor," *Jüdische Wochenschau* (*JW*), May 13, 1940.

Jüdische Wochenschau and *DAD* regularly reviewed the performances of the FGS and ran advertisements free of charge. This publicity was essential for the theater; however, offstage Zionist and antifascist institutions exerted considerable pressure on members of its cast to commit more resolutely to their respective political and religious positions. Furthermore, most German-speaking emigrants were politically and religiously moderate. These emigrants saw the FGS as neither an antifascist nor a Zionist institution, but rather an entertainment venue. As a professional enterprise without state funding—and one targeting a very limited and economically distressed public—the theater needed to attract all subgroups of the refugee population to its presentations, otherwise it would not remain solvent. The refugee colony and the ensemble were constituted by distinct groups with profoundly divergent perspectives. It was a daunting challenge for the Free German Stage to negotiate these internal and external fissures without alienating any specific group or betraying its own moral principles.

The preceding cross section of German Buenos Aires establishes its theaters as crucial community-building institutions at the center of the city's antagonistic nationalist, antifascist, and Zionist populations. The Free German Stage and the German Theater were a nexus for partisan immigrant media, educational, cultural, religious, and political organizations—all of which publicly celebrated the ensembles as standard-bearers while simultaneously vying to influence them from behind the curtain. Sharply divergent at first glance, their shared role as cultural bulwarks of immigrant populations raises the question of whether these stages and their constituencies deployed parallel approaches to community building, intercultural relationships, and dramatic theory. The lens of theater brings victims and adherents of Nazism into focus. Beyond defining difference, I draw from theatrical performances to search also for connections, overlaps, similarities, and even mimicry between these antithetical, fiercely conflictive groups.

2

THEATER ON THE MOVE

Routes to Buenos Aires

Ludwig Ney was born into a German military family in the village of Landau on May 29, 1901. The son of an officer, Ney was inspired to become as actor during his days as a cadet. Ney participated in a local theater project while stationed near the Baltic Sea and immediately realized that his future lay not in the army, but on the stage. Like his rival in Buenos Aires, Paul Walter Jacob, Ney faced vehement opposition from his family when he told them of his decision. He was forced to flee home, and at the age of twenty was living in an attic in Mannheim with no furniture, no money, and little food.[1] His dedication was rewarded when the City College of Music and Theater in Mannheim admitted him to its theater department. Shortly thereafter, in 1921, the Mannheim National Theater engaged him to perform bit pieces and minor roles. Though fortunate to have found work at this storied theater, Ney became

---

1. "Gespräch mit Ludwig Ney," *Teutonia*, September 1938.

frustrated by the limited roles available to a young, inexperienced actor such as himself.[2] He soon left Mannheim for a provincial stage in Sonneberg, Thuringia, where he could play leading roles. It was a humble start. Ney had to study his lines during intermissions because, with thrice weekly premieres, it was impossible to prepare well for each performance.[3] He even had to fashion his own costumes because of the theater's tight budget and the scarcity of supplies in rural Thuringia. Later, in Argentina, Ney claimed that these conditions were invaluable training for his work in South America, because they taught him optimism, resilience, and improvisation.[4] The formative days of Ludwig Ney's acting career reveal a buoyant appetite for adventure and passion for theater.

Like many actors of the antifascist Free German Stage, the early years of Ney's acting career mark a meandering course through the German provinces, passing through Konstanz, Detmold, and Bielefeld to his first major engagement as actor, director, and choreographer in Recklinghausen.[5] Thereafter, director Hanns Niedecken-Gebhard contracted Ney to collaborate on Handel's scenic oratorios with Kurt Jooss in Münster and later at the renowned cultural festivals held annually at the Heidelberg Castle. Esteemed by Joseph Goebbels, who entrusted him with artistic oversight for the opening ceremony of the 1936 Olympic Games in Berlin and performances honoring the German capital's 700th anniversary in 1937, Niedecken-Gebhard later reported to the Reich Theater Chamber that Ney's innovative vision would help to fill a palpable void in German theater. According to the *Deutsche La Plata Zeitung*, Ney's activities with these luminous figures earned him a position in the theater department at the Essen Folkwang School in 1931,[6] where Jooss directed the Department of Dance.[7]

---

2. "Ludwig Ney: 70. Geburtstag—50. Bühnenjubiläum," *AT*, June 3, 1971.

3. Ney, interview by author, February 3, 2009.

4. "Gespräch mit Ludwig Ney," *Teutonia*, September 1938.

5. "Ludwig Ney: 70. Geburtstag," *AT*, June 3, 1971.

6. The *La Plata Zeitung* has generally proven to be a reliable source on Ney's biography; however, I have been unable to confirm its report that he was employed by the Folkwang School.

7. "Zusammenarbeit mit einem Künstler," *DLPZ*, January 5, 1941.

While in Essen, Ney attended concerts and dramatic productions at the municipal theater, where a frequent conductor and director was none other than his future adversary in Argentina, Paul Walter Jacob. Within a year, just weeks after the establishment of the Propaganda Ministry on March 11, 1933, Essen's theater critics derided Jacob as a Jew and Social Democrat and forced him from the city's stages.[8] Whether or not Ludwig Ney read of Jacob's dismissal, the case clearly signaled that his own acting career was contingent on the goodwill of Nazi authorities. In 1934, together with his former student and future wife, Irene Winkler, Ludwig Ney left Essen to work full-time as an actor and director. In Berlin he founded a group called the Romantic Cabaret, which gained funding from the National Socialist Culture Community and Strength through Joy and toured throughout Germany from 1934 to 1936. Its life span thus coincided with National Socialists' efforts to consolidate their domination of German cultural life.

A branch of the German Labor Front, Strength through Joy had the self-declared goal of creating a National Socialist people's community while facilitating the perfection and refinement of the German populace.[9] Perhaps best known for its activities in the tourism sector, Strength through Joy also provided the German working class affordable access to cultural events, such as concerts and theater. The primary goal of such performances, as articulated in the theater journal *Die Bühne*, was to cultivate ethnic unity through shared experiences of German cultural heritage.[10] In addition to theater ensembles, critics were also conscripted into this endeavor. Pressured by the Reich Press Chamber and the 1933 Editors' Law, reviewers had the task of assisting—or impelling— theaters to inculcate citizens with Nazi values.[11] In the Romantic Cabaret's theater programs, Ney affirmed the National Socialist agenda of achieving a cohesive citizenry through cultural heritage by declaring his group's aspiration to reinforce the timeless virtues

---

8. "Randbemerkungen," *Essener National Zeitung*, March 26, 1933.
9. Baranowski, *Strength through Joy*, 40–42.
10. Strobl, *Swastika and the Stage*, 52.
11. Ruppelt, *Schiller im nationalsozialistischen Deutschland*, 116.

Figure 2. Ludwig Ney during a rehearsal.

Source: Regine Lamm Collection.

of the German race through art. As a "soldier of art" he exhorted his entire cast to devote themselves to this objective.[12]

On September 8, 1934, the Romantic Cabaret debuted at the well-known Tingel Tangel Theater, a political cabaret venue that had been founded in 1931 by the Jewish composer Friedrich Hollaender in the cellar of the Theater of the West in Berlin. Though Hollaender already had fled to Paris, in 1934 the Tingel Tangel had yet to be fully coordinated to Nazism. Remnants of its political program persevered until 1935, when the Gestapo arrested actors Walter Gross, Günther Lüders, and Walter Lieck for subversive remarks during performances. The venue's reputation notwithstanding, there appears to have been no subversion in Ney's debut, which garnered approving reviews from local media. The *Berliner Zeitung* praised Ney as the "father of the group," and

12. Romantische Kleinkunstbühne Program, July 1, 1935, Cornelia Ney Collection (CNC).

lauded the outstanding performances of his troupe.[13] The Romantic Cabaret's repertoire ranged from canonical figures such as Hans Sachs and Matthias Claudius to lesser-known regional folk songs from Mecklenburg and Franconia, many of which Ney had unearthed himself during his travels throughout Germany. Reviewers across Germany commended Ney for utilizing the cabaret genre to revitalize obscure works from the rich tradition of Germanic song, dance, theater, and poetry: "The director draws from the reservoir of history—German history."[14] Reporting on the ensemble's performance at the Residence Theater in Wiesbaden, the *Landeszeitung für Rhein-Main* argued that the Romantic Cabaret vitalized German cultural history to establish an emotional and intellectual rapport between spectators and performers.[15] Asserting that the presentation represented the soul of unadulterated German folklore, the *Würzburg General Anzeiger* reflected that Ney's greatest accomplishment was to have created cabaret-style ditties that cultivated and informed Germans' sense of national identity. Both papers glimpsed in the group's program a potential vehicle for fomenting German nationalism.[16]

Ney's focus on autochthonous German culture as an anchor for national affection neatly dovetailed with the Propaganda Ministry's vision for a new, ethnic German theater. However, Ney abstained from the bellicose depictions of German history that many dramatists were producing at the time.[17] Furthermore, reviewers sometimes wanted stronger affirmation of Nazi ideology in his productions. The *Berliner Zeitung* chastised the stage for its multicultural accents and was vexed when Ney introduced a Hans Sachs poem with—perhaps foreshadowing his emigration to

---

13. "Romantische Kleinkunstbühne," *Berliner Zeitung*, September 8, 1934.

14. "Romantische Kleinkunstbühne," *Berliner Zeitung*, September 8, 1934.

15. "Romantische Kleinkunstbühne," *Landeszeitung für Rhein-Main*, December 13, 1935.

16. "Ein heiter-besinnlicher Abend," *Würzburg General Anzeiger*, February 7, 1935.

17. Just a few examples include Hans Christian Kaergel's *Volk ohne Heimat* (1932), Kurt Eggers's *Annaberg* (1933), and Hans Kyser's *Lebenskampf der Ostmark* (1934).

Argentina—a tango.[18] Reviewers from Berlin to Nuremberg also asserted that the stage's historical focus rendered its performances insufficiently contemporary.[19] Perhaps the choice of the Tingel Tangel venue, his collaboration with future emigrant Kurt Jooss, and these instances of dissociation shed light on Ney's enigmatic decision in early 1937 to abandon Europe and start a new life in the South American republic of Paraguay.

The vast majority of emigrants from Nazi Germany were refugees. They were victims who fled Hitler's tyranny and sought safety abroad. In this context, Ludwig Ney's emigration is anomalous. Gentile Germans from military families, neither Ludwig Ney nor his partner, Irene Ney, had any apparent reason to fear Nazi oppression. It is possible that Ney had reservations about National Socialism, but his work with Strength through Joy demonstrates that he was not a dissident. Indeed, Ney had many reasons not to emigrate. Not only was his personal life anchored in Germany, but he stood to gain from Hitler's rise to power. The mass exodus of persecuted artists opened professional opportunities for racially and politically unobjectionable actors such as Ludwig Ney. Rainer Schlösser's Reich Theater Chamber recruited and funded artists for German stages, and, as an experienced thespian and pedagogue, Ney was in a fine position to profit from these programs. He had collaborated with major figures in the Nazi German theater milieu, such as Niedecken-Gebhard, and had directed his own modestly successful troupe for three years running. Additionally, he had secured funding from one of the nation's leading entertainment institutions, Strength through Joy. So why, with seemingly everything in his favor, did Ludwig Ney voluntarily emigrate and join the thousands of persecuted refugees fleeing Germany?

One theory is that the Nazi government contracted Ney to establish a German theater in South America. In fact, when Ney launched the German Theater in 1938, it was sponsored by the

---

18. "Romantische Kleinkunstbühne," *Berliner Zeitung*, September 8, 1934.
19. "Romantische Kleinkunstbühne," *Landeszeitung für Rhein-Main*, December 13, 1935; "Aus Kunst und Leben," *Wiesbadener Tageblatt*, December 19, 1936; "Das war Kleinkunst," *Fränkischer Kurier*, 1936.

Argentine branch of Strength through Joy. However, Ney's arrival and yearlong sojourn in Paraguay do not mesh with this scenario. Strength through Joy did not exist in Paraguay, and reports of Ney's theatrical activities in Paraguay do not mention any association with German institutions.[20] Ney's cooperation with Strength through Joy and the German embassy in Argentina appear to have occurred only after he had arrived in South America.

Cornelia Ney, Ludwig and Irene Ney's only child, claims that her father's adventurous spirit—specifically a friend's invitation to visit his farm in San Bernadino, Paraguay—inspired his journey.[21] As fanciful as this account seems, alternative narratives for Ney's emigration are scant. In interviews, former colleagues of Ney's spoke candidly about his collaboration with Nazi authorities in Argentina. Two of them, Ursula Siegerist and Regine Lamm, knew that he had spent time in Paraguay before arriving in Argentina. Yet nobody other than his daughter could explain why Ludwig Ney had left Europe in the first place. Various newspapers and magazines mention Ney's work in Germany, but only the *Deutsche Zeitung für Paraguay* and the *Deutsche La Plata Zeitung* note the year he spent in San Bernadino, and neither discusses his motivations for traveling to this far-flung, landlocked country.[22] Despite interviews with Ney's former colleagues and his family, as well very extensive archival research, I cannot explain why he left Europe in the first place.[23] Another theory is that his partner, Irene, had Jewish ancestry. Her maiden name, Winkler, could indicate Jewish genealogy. Such lineage might have motivated her and Ludwig Ney

---

20. "Die Pfingstkutsche," *Deutsche Zeitung für Paraguay*, May 20, 1937; "Deutsche Review in San Bernardino, Paraguay," *DLPZ*, May 30, 1937.

21. Ney, interview.

22. "Ludwig Ney: 70. Geburtstag," *AT*, June 3, 1971; Juan Marian Dafcik, "Ludwig Ney und das deutschsprachige Theater in Argentinien," *Maske und Kothurn* 10 (1964): 640–643; "Cuando empiezan a ser argentinos," *LN*, April 2, 1961; "Ausländisches Theaterwesen," *FP*, January 12, 1953; "Aus dem deutschen Theaterleben in Buenos Aires," *Der Weg*, June 1949.

23. "Ludwig Ney: 70. Geburtstag," *AT*, June 3, 1971; Dafcik, "Ludwig Ney und das deutschsprachige Theater in Argentinien"; "Cuando empiezan a ser argentinos," *LN*, April 2, 1961; "Ausländisches Theaterwesen," *FP*, January 12, 1953; "Aus dem deutschen Theaterleben in Buenos Aires," *Weg*, June 1949.

to emigrate, a decision that otherwise resists explanation. However, there is no hard proof to support this hypothesis; in the last analysis it is limited to conjecture.

In a biographical article following the 1940 theater season in Buenos Aires, the *Deutsche La Plata Zeitung* speculated that his seemingly innate pioneering spirit had brought Ney to South America.[24] From the day he left his home to attend acting school in Mannheim until his arrival in the Argentine capital, Ney was on the move. As he traveled throughout Germany and assumed a wide range of professional responsibilities, the only constant in his life was theater. His abilities as a pedagogue and director were immensely valuable in Buenos Aires, where some members of his ensemble were not professional actors. Furthermore, as he reiterated in interviews in Germany and Argentina, during his travels with the Romantic Cabaret Ney learned to achieve a maximum artistic effect with minimal resources.[25] As in provincial Germany, Ney's enthusiasm for his career eclipsed the challenges of acting in South America: "It is the greatest happiness to have a fulfilling profession, one that is a source of happiness in itself. In this situation, difficulties do not really matter."[26] Ney's upbeat outlook and professional experience were key attributes of his success as a pioneer of German theater in Argentina. Politically antithetical, Ludwig Ney, Paul Walter Jacob, and many of their colleagues were linked by a mutual, unrelenting passion for the dramatic stage.

Ludwig Ney began performing extraordinarily soon after his arrival to South America. Less than five months after his final engagement in Wiesbaden, the first reports of Ney's theatrical activities in Paraguay surface. Photographs from his first project in Paraguay, "The Pentecostal Carriage," performed on May 15, 1937, reveal very primitive conditions. Since rural San Bernardino lacked a proper facility, performances were held outdoors on a raised patch of grass. The costumes were simple, homemade improvisations.

---

24. "Zusammenarbeit mit einem Künstler," *DLPZ*, January 5, 1941.
25. "Ein heiter-besinnlicher Abend," *Würzburg General Anzeiger*, February 7, 1935; "Gespräch mit Ludwig Ney," *Teutonia*, September 1938.
26. "Gespräch mit Ludwig Ney," *Teutonia*, September 1938.

To compensate for these shortcomings, Ney took advantage of the open-air performance space and added a working carriage with live horses as a physical inspiration for the narrative frame of his drama. He also incorporated local Paraguayan and German musicians into the production, thus lending a new intercultural dimension to pieces he had performed in Europe. Entertainment was rare in the Paraguayan countryside, and many spectators traveled a full day by horse to the well-attended event. In militaristic jargon, the *Deutsche Zeitung für Paraguay* lavished praised on Ney's "Carriage." The Franconian folk song "It," now accompanied by live musicians instead of a phonograph, delighted the numerous spectators: "salvos of guffaws" roared through the audience. Reviewers were likewise impressed by Ludwig and Irene Ney's performance, referring to their acting as a "huge success."[27]

The "Carriage" may well have carried Ney all the way to Buenos Aires. Ten days after the piece in the *Deutsche Zeitung für Paraguay*, a full-page article about the performance appeared in the *Deutsche la Plata Zeitung* in Buenos Aires. The report almost surely caught the attention of Nazi officials in the Argentine capital. Galvanized by the success of sporadic guest performances in recent years, German consul Edmund von Thermann and Richard Schröder, regional leader of the German Labor Front, probably realized that a regularly performing local ensemble would be more effective in consolidating supporters of National Socialism in Argentina.[28] After reading about Ludwig and Irene Ney's activities in Paraguay, and especially upon learning that they had worked with Strength through Joy in Germany, Nazi officials in Buenos Aires likely glimpsed an opportunity to establish such an enterprise. For his part, Ney would have recognized that the size and resources of the German population in Argentina offered greater professional possibilities than in Paraguay.[29] Under the auspices of the German

---

27. "Die Pfingstkutsche," *Deutsche Zeitung für Paraguay*, May, 20, 1937.

28. "Deutsches Schauspiel 1934," *DLPZ*, May 29, 1934; "Kraft durch Freude Veranstaltung im Teatro Odeon," *Der Deutsche in Argentinien (DiA)*, July/August 1935; "2. Große 'Kraft durch Freude'-Veranstaltung: Besuch bei der Riesch-Bühne," *DiA*, October 1935.

29. Ney, interview.

embassy and Strength through Joy, Ludwig Ney's inaugural performance in Buenos Aires took place on May 19, 1938.[30] From his
debut, Ney would continue to be a prominent player on stages in
the Argentine capital for the next thirty-four years.

Even in 1937 Wilhelm Keiper, a prolific scholar and special ad-
viser on education to the German embassy from 1931 to 1938, had
deemed it impossible for German Buenos Aires to support a regularly performing theater.[31] Without funding from the Labor Front,
Strength through Joy, and the embassy, Keiper probably would
have been correct. Furthermore, the foundation of the antifascist
Free German Stage stemmed in large part from a will to compete
against the nationalist German Theater.[32] Nazi officialdom thus
had a germinal influence on both German theaters in Argentina.

Theater in Times of Crisis

Paul Walter Jacob was born to a middle-class Orthodox Jewish
family in Duisburg on January 26, 1905. In 1908 his family relocated to Mainz, where Jacob attended the Hessian Secondary
School and also studied music theory, history, and composition at
the Paul Schumacher Conservatory. When he completed his studies, Jacob decided to pursue a career as an actor or musician, which
enraged his family. His mother lashed him with a dog whip and insisted he become a merchant like his father.[33] This bitter conflict,
which Jacob described in letters to a childhood friend, discloses
a reserve of willpower essential to his perseverance in European
and South American exile. The letters also indicate that his parents
likely tried to prepare him for a career in business, which, ironically, later became fundamental to his artistic success. Both in Europe and South America, Jacob's achievements in theater can be
attributed in large part to his ability to marry creative talent with
business acumen.

30. "Deutsche Kleinkunstbühne Ludwig Ney," *DiA*, June 1938.
31. Keiper, *Der Deutsche in Argentinien*, 29.
32. Jacob to Felix Weil, January 29, 1941, PWJAK.
33. Naumann, *Ein Theatermann im Exil, P. Walter Jacob*, 23.

In 1923, Jacob left his family to study music and art history, philosophy, and journalism at the Frederick William University in Berlin. He also studied at Max Reinhardt's acting school at the German Theater, where he learned from the actor Ferdinand Gregori, a colleague of Otto Brahm. From 1926 to 1929 Jacob worked as assistant conductor at the Berlin State Opera. For the next three years, he found employment as a conductor, director, actor, and journalist in Koblenz (1929–30), Lübeck (1930–31), Wuppertal (1931–32), and Essen (1932–33). At these theaters he developed competencies as an artist, organizer, and businessman, which prepared him for the challenges he later faced in Argentina. Scholars have argued that Jacob learned these skills from others during his European exile; however, Jacob's memoirs from his years in Germany show that he began to hone his skills as a theater director and entrepreneur before 1933.[34] Moreover, Jacob cultivated his strategy on managing theaters in times of economic and political crisis largely on his own and often against the will of his superiors.

The comparison may seem unlikely; however, conditions at German provincial stages in the early 1930s were in many ways analogous to the environment in Buenos Aires a decade later. In both settings, Jacob was confronted with the challenge of managing theaters in a politically volatile environment with precarious, insufficient finances, incomplete and traumatized ensembles, and a small, beleaguered public. As a result of a budget shortfall in late 1931, Jacob's first season at the Wuppertal Municipal Theater, local authorities resolved to shut down the city's theater down the following July. Management was forced to rapidly refashion the stage into a solvent business enterprise while maintaining its cultural value. As the representative for the Guild of the German Stage in Wuppertal, Jacob played a leading role in this effort.

At the Wuppertal Municipal Theater and numerous venues throughout Germany, the core of the predicament was dwindling audiences. According to Jacob, Wuppertal's theater was failing because it had neglected its obligations as a community institution.

---

34. Lemmer, *Die "Freie Deutsche Bühne" in Buenos Aires 1940–1965*, 18; Naumann, *Ein Theatermann im Exil*, 61.

Consequently, it had grown estranged from spectators, a potentially fatal development. Jacob believed the theater could reconnect with theatergoers and boost attendance, but only after comprehensive reform. It had to recover its historical, emotional, and moral appeal. Furthermore, it needed to implement pragmatic business tactics to persevere in the harsh economic climate of 1932. Jacob believed three crucial steps were required to accomplish these goals: (1) establish a close and direct rapport between the theater and the residents of Wuppertal; (2) increase the theater's pull and profile as a popular entertainment option through an aggressive, modernized advertising campaign; and (3) reform its repertoire to better suit the tastes of theatergoers in the turbulent early 1930s. To its details, Jacob's successful strategy for rescuing the Wuppertal theater laid the groundwork for the program he followed to found and sustain the Free German Stage in Buenos Aires. Furthermore, and perhaps unexpectedly, Jacob's plan overlaps significantly with the tactics for publicity and community outreach that Ludwig Ney implemented at the nationalist German Theater.

Jacob believed the crises of 1932 could strengthen the bond between the stage and its local community. He hoped to initiate a sense of interconnectedness between Wuppertal's residents and their theater by publishing open letters to readers of the local newspaper, *Bergische Heimat*. For stage and populace alike 1932 represented, as Jacob presciently described, a grave hour on the threshold of a dark, menacing future.[35] Against this backdrop of shared struggle, he outlined his vision of a close, interdependent relationship between Wuppertal and its theater. Depicting their theater as a cultural edifice, constructed with sacrifice by generations of Wuppertal's citizens, Jacob conveyed the ruinous fate of its cast should the stage close its doors. He then exhorted his readers: "Rescue art and artists! Save culture from its downfall!"[36] In his appeal, Jacob evoked his readers' sense of empathy for local artists while simultaneously empowering them to protect and preserve their cultural traditions.

---

35. Jacob, "An die Bevölkerung Wuppertals," *Bergische Heimat*, January 1932.
36. Jacob, "An die Bevölkerung Wuppertals," *Bergische Heimat*, January 1932.

The relationship between theater and city, Jacob stressed in *Bergische Heimat*, was interdependent. Amid deep economic and social tumult, just months before the National Socialists' resounding victories in the Reichstag elections of 1932, Jacob claimed that theater would strengthen and unite Wuppertal as it confronted the looming peril: "*In times of distress, German theater has always given you solidarity and edification!*"[37] Jacob reminded citizens that literature, in this case performed on stage, was always an essential source of guidance in times of crisis. A dynamic and highly regenerative repository of knowledge for living, literature provided audiences a vast store of accumulated wisdom, moral support, and guidance.[38] Dramatic performances then tested these ideas in a fictional laboratory, enabling theatergoers to hone survival strategies for precarious external environments. Crucially, Jacob noted, theater was a shared experience. An interactive event among thespians onstage and spectators offstage, as well between these two groups, the dramatic performance requires the bodily copresence of the ensemble and the audience.[39] While reading is an experience generally limited to individuals or small groups, in live theater literature gains a vitalizing social dimension. Dramatic presentations are rooted in social community. As they unfold they also nurture community between actors and spectators. Moreover, the communal commitment to the labor, time, and funding required to sustain the theater fortify the social union that each performance engenders.

Jacob's article in *Bergische Heimat* closed with a message that both he and German nationalists would reiterate and reinforce years later in Argentina. The Free German Stage and Ludwig Ney's German Theater each echoed Jacob's urgent conclusion: "Become the standard-bearers of a great German future! Preserve the German stage!"[40] For all their differences, the immigrant blocs agreed that German theater had a pivotal role to play in the tenuous transition

---

37. Jacob, "An die Bevölkerung Wuppertals," *Bergische Heimat*, January 1932 (emphasis in original).
38. Ette, "Literaturwissenschaft als Lebenswissenschaft," 5.
39. Fischer-Lichte, *Theatre, Sacrifice, Ritual*, 19.
40. Jacob, "An die Bevölkerung Wuppertals."

from despair to prosperity. In Buenos Aires, victims and supporters of Nazism advocated that the theatrical experience would consolidate the local community as well as inform and inspire its efforts to withstand times of crisis such as the Nazi and postwar periods.

In tandem with these goals, Jacob elaborated a pragmatic business model that he followed closely in Wuppertal and later in Buenos Aires. Without public funding, in a free-market economy the theater can only survive as a solvent business enterprise. Rather than cutting costs and thereby reducing the quality of presentations, Jacob focused on maximizing income by increasing attendance. An aggressive, modernized advertising campaign was fundamental to this strategy, thus challenging contemporary notions that the highbrow cultural theater was above competing with popular entertainment, such as cinema. Regardless of its status as a sacrosanct German cultural institution, Jacob asserted that the theater was subject to the same competition as any other business enterprise and had to formulate corresponding marketing tactics.[41] Failure to promote its accomplishments amounted to suicidal snobbery.[42] Essentially, each theater should mirror not only the artistic but also the commercial and administrative spirit of its city. Thus, by adopting a modern business model Jacob also saw an opportunity for the theater to approximate its community.

To firmly anchor the Wuppertal theater in the local population, flyers, posters, programs, and actors promoted upcoming productions throughout the city. Presaging the Free German Stage's engagement with antifascist schools in Argentina, as well as Ludwig Ney's projects with the Goethe, Humboldt, and North Schools, Jacob implemented a publicity campaign in Wuppertal under the maxim "The theater has no future unless it wins over the youth." The cast put on dramas and workshops targeting younger audiences, and made attendance affordable through special ticket packages with discounts for group purchases by educational institutions.

Beyond direct advertising, theaters had to make far better use of local news outlets, a key means of integrating with the community.

---

41. Jacob, "Bemerkungen zu Theateretat," PWJA IV c) 253.
42. Jacob, "Denkschrift zur Frage Theaterbewerbung," PWJA IV c) 253.

Anticipating cooperation between the Free German Stage and the German Theater with the *Argentinisches Tageblatt* and the *Deutsche La Plata Zeitung*, respectively, Jacob envisioned thorough previews, personalized anecdotes from backstage, reports on social and economic issues facing the theater, updates on the national theater scene, essays about works being prepared for performance, and written contributions by members of the cast. By deploying newspapers as the primary form of offstage communication between the audience and ensemble, both Paul Walter Jacob and Ludwig Ney aimed to forge a community identity centered around theater.

The third and most polemical tenet of Jacob's program for a modernized theater was to reform the repertoire. A quicker rotation of dramas would best exploit the theater's promotional activities, because the previews and reviews are forgotten if a play remains in the repertoire for months. Furthermore, reducing the number of performances of each drama would diversify the productions and attract larger audiences, thereby enabling management to lower prices.[43] While a faster rotation limits rehearsals, Jacob reasoned that this could also be energizing for thespians, whose portrayals could become stale after an excessive number of presentations. Moreover, Jacob insisted that his suggestions must not have a detrimental effect on quality, because the foundation of any marketing is the performance itself.[44] For this reason, his plans were contingent on a seasoned ensemble working under a director who knew each individual well and understood how to distribute roles for each piece. Finally, an increase in premieres would encourage habitual theatergoers to visit the theater more frequently, generating greater ticket sales and cultivating a closer relationship between audiences and actors.

Most polemically, Jacob argued that highbrow theaters had to attract a broader public by balancing the German classics and literary dramas with a greater number of contemporary selections, including simple, lighthearted comedies. The Guild of the German

---

43. Jacob, "Bemerkungen zu Theateretat."
44. Jacob, "Denkschrift zur Frage Theaterbewerbung."

Stage was firmly opposed to this measure; however, Jacob was convinced that a rigid position on the issue was untenable. The core of the repertoire had to be literary dramas but, especially in turbulent times, these would be carried by popular, profitable lighter genres, such as the operetta or the farce.[45] A firm policy at the Free German Stage, this approach has been vigorously debated ever since the group's inaugural performance in 1940.[46] Jacob formulated his plan in 1932, theorizing that in a period of emotional and economic depression theatergoers would favor the lighter muse.[47] The theater could assuage audiences' hardships by offering respite from a troubled reality.

Jacob's strategy helped to save the Wuppertal Municipal Theater and was a cornerstone to his success with the Free German Stage in Argentina. Furthermore, in Buenos Aires, Ludwig Ney incorporated many of these ideas at his rival German Theater. Each enterprise took a remarkably similar approach to community building, advertising, and creating repertoires. Though harshly criticized by friends and foes alike, the survival of all three stages under immensely challenging circumstances lends credence to Jacob's tactics.

"Jewish mimes unwanted": Paul Walter Jacob

At the outset of the 1932–33 theater season, Paul Walter Jacob appeared to have a promising future on German stages. His accomplishments as a director in Wuppertal earned him strong praise from the theater's general intendant, Manfred Maurenbrecher: "Your excellent work . . . has found my fullest recognition. You represent a new, young and progressive generation, which will exert

---

45. Jacob, "Denkschrift zur Frage Theaterbewerbung."

46. Julius Bab, "Deutsches Theater in Argentinien," *Sonntagsblatt: Staats-Zeitung und Herold*, May 16, 1948; Pohle, "Paul Walter Jacob am Rio de la Plata: Der Kurs der FDB—eine exilpolitische Gratwanderung"; Trapp, "Zwischen Unterhaltungsfunktion und der Erwartung politischer Stellungnahme."

47. Jacob, "Bemerkungen zu Theateretat."

a formative influence on our stages."[48] That year Jacob also began a more prestigious position as director and conductor for theater, opera, and operetta in Essen. Yet, the Nazis' ascension to power abruptly halted his professional development. On March 26, 1933, the *Essener National Zeitung* printed a sinister preview of Wagner's *The Flying Dutchman*:

> The conductor, of all people, is the Jew and Social Democrat Walter Jacob.
>
> One question [to the opera administration]: Are you so secure that you can dare to insult the German people with a Jewish conductor now that the Jewish spirit has finally been eliminated from German stages, thank God?[49]

Jacob was dismissed from the Essen Municipal Opera and Theater immediately. On March 30, 1933, the *Essener National Zeitung* rejoiced that he would no longer continue to defile German art, and threatened Jewish thespians with further attacks.[50] The next day Paul Walter Jacob purchased a one-way ticket on a night train to Amsterdam.

Theater was a precarious, liminal space for Jewish actors in Europe during the 1930s. The public nature of their work on the stage exposed them to anti-Semitism very quickly, often forcing them into an early exile. For Jacob, theater was a source of both survival and peril in exile. It created opportunities and earned him a living, but it was a visible profession that made him vulnerable.

Jacob's European exile corresponds to Bertolt Brecht's poetic portrait of exiled artists, who changed countries more often than their shoes.[51] After working as a journalist in Amsterdam and Paris, Jacob was engaged as an actor and director in late 1935 by a newly founded Luxemburg touring theater, The Comedy, under Walter Eberhard. Although Eberhard promised good pay and an

---

48. Maurenbrecher to Jacob, Wuppertal, May 19, 1932, PWJA II b) 203.
49. "Randbemerkungen," *Essener National Zeitung*, March 26, 1933.
50. "Jüdische Mimen nicht mehr gefragt," *Essener National Zeitung*, March 30, 1933.
51. Bertolt Brecht, "An die Nachgeborenen," in Grimm, *Bertolt Brecht*, 72.

ambitious repertoire, his enterprise went bankrupt in less than two years. Rather than having learned from Eberhard, as some scholars have claimed, in fact Jacob attempted to advise his older colleague on personnel and budgeting.[52] One example is the two men's conflicting views on contracting personnel. In Jacob's view, The Comedy's precarious finances required it to maintain a small ensemble. Despite his repeated warnings, Eberhard contracted several new thespians following the 1935 season.[53] Then, a few months later, the director realized he could not afford such a large cast and terminated their contracts. By contrast, Jacob insisted that for an exilic theater sustainable budgeting is a moral obligation, because its refugee ensemble will be in dire circumstances if the stage fails. When The Comedy went bankrupt in 1936, its cast was left penniless and unemployed. The actors even had to sue Eberhard for unpaid wages.[54] In Buenos Aires Jacob took every precaution, even against the will of his colleagues, to ensure that the Free German Stage did not repeat the fiasco of Luxemburg.

After The Comedy collapsed, Jacob arrived at the final station of his European exile: Teplitz-Schönau, Czechoslovakia. This resort town of approximately 50,000 inhabitants had a very limited public, similar to the refugee population in Buenos Aires. Jacob implemented a repertory featuring a wide variety of plays with an extremely fast rotation, just six presentations per drama. Thanks to this policy, the Teplitz-Schönau City Theater enjoyed successful seasons in 1936 and 1937. However, this respite could only be temporary.[55] Jacob's work exposed him to Nazi authorities as an antifascist Jewish actor and journalist, and in March 1938 he was stripped of German citizenship.[56] The German annexation of Austria followed later that month. In July, he wrote to a former colleague that the "living space for myself and my peers has become

---

52. Lemmer, *Die "Freie Deutsche Bühne,"* 18; Naumann, *Ein Theatermann*, 61.

53. Jacob to Eberhard, December 17, 1935, PWJAK.

54. Jacob to Eberhard, January 26, 1936, PWJAK.

55. Paul Walter Jacob, "In Prag vor fünf Jahren," *AT*, September 14, 1942.

56. *Deutscher Reichsanzeiger und Preußischer Staatsanzeiger*, April 20, 1938.

hopelessly small."[57] Frantic, by August 1938 Jacob had written to contacts of the vaguest kind in England, Sweden, Switzerland, Greece, Palestine, the United States, South Africa, and Australia—all to no avail. His acquaintances warned him either that conditions were intolerable or that acquiring an entrance visa was impossible.

Jacob's chance to flee Europe arrived through his work in Teplitz-Schönau, where he met Liselott Reger, a Jewish actress and Argentine citizen. As the situation in Europe worsened, they became romantically involved and decided to escape together to Argentina. Jacob had renewed his German passport in May 1937, and in Prague he was able to purchase a visa to Paraguay. With this document he procured a transit visa for Argentina, which he converted to a residence permit when he became engaged to Reger in Buenos Aires. Shortly thereafter Reger, Jacob, and a small auxiliary cast performed scenes from Curt Goetz's comedy *Menagerie* (1919) for an audience of potential donors. Six months later, with Reger and Jacob as founding members and business partners, the Free German Stage put on its inaugural performance.

In addition to Reger, several actors who played with Jacob at The Comedy and in Teplitz-Schönau also performed at the Free German Stage. In Luxemburg Jacob acted together with Georg Braun[58] and Jacques Arndt,[59] and in Czechoslovakia he shared the stage with Ernst Wurmser[60] and Liselott Reger.[61] As they were all Jewish antifascist thespians, their shared experiences in exile contributed to cohesion in the Free German Stage ensemble. Moreover, as he had noted in Wuppertal, Jacob's familiarity with his cast facilitated his plans for a diverse repertoire and quick rotation of dramas.[62] Separated for years and oceans at a time when hundreds of thousands of refugees were fleeing Europe, they were reunited, often through sheer coincidence, in South America's Southern Cone.

57. Jacob to Carl Ebert, June 7, 1938, PWJAK.

58. "*Der Mann, den sein Gewissen trieb,*" *Luxemburger Zeitung,* October 7, 1935.

59. "*Kabale und Liebe,*" *Luxemburger Volksblatt,* December 27, 1935.

60. "*Es ist serviert!,*" *Wegweiser,* June 21, 1937.

61. "*Kabale und Liebe,*" *Der Abend,* March 4, 1937.

62. Jacob, "Bemerkungen zu Theateretat."

The Makings of a Hitler Youth: Jacques Arndt

Having married an Argentine citizen, Paul Walter Jacob's path from his last performance in Europe to his debut in South America was relatively smooth. For Jacques Arndt, whose career on Argentine stages spanned six decades, the journey was more adventurous. This section discusses Arndt's winding route from Vienna's Court Theater to the Free German Stage in Buenos Aires.[63]

Although he was born in Sarajevo, Arndt's family moved to Vienna when he was still an infant, and from his earliest childhood Arndt's parents took him to the theater. As a young boy he began acting at the prestigious Court Theater, where he played smaller supporting roles for children.[64] After he finished middle school, Arndt enrolled in the Viennese State Academy of Music and the Performing Arts, where many of his instructors were actors in the Court Theater's first ensemble. Simultaneously, Arndt acted in the Youth Theater at the Vienna People's Opera.[65] Targeting a youthful audience, this theater gave less experienced actors opportunities to play leading roles in canonical dramas.

In July 1938, shortly after the German annexation of Austria, the Youth Theater staged Schiller's *Wallenstein*.[66] Enthusiasm for the Nazi regime was at a high pitch, and even before the presentation had begun, an official gave a speech that culminated: "Hail the new day! Hail the new *Führer*!"[67] Backstage the Jewish Arndt was

---

63. The interviews I conducted with Arndt represent the most thorough account of his emigration that I have encountered; however, I consulted multiple sources for verification: Guy Stern, "Die Odyssee Jacques Arndts: Vom Theater der Jugend in Wien zum argentinischen Musical-Star," *Aufbau*, November 22, 1985; Naumann, *Ein Theatermann*, 116; Douer and Seeber, *Wie weit ist Wien*; Lemmer, *Die "Freie Deutsche Bühne,"* 104–105; "Vom Burgtheater ins Exil," *Die Furche*, August 11, 2005; "Evocaciones," *LN*, July 9, 2006; "Der verhinderte Burgschauspieler," Radio Österreich 1, August 14, 2006.

64. Posters, *Der Kaiser von Amerika*; *Die Majorische*, December 30, 1933; Jacques Arndt Collection (JAC)/Exilbibliothek im Literaturhaus Wien (ELW).

65. Poster, *Des Meeres und der Liebe Wellen*, April 10, 1935, JAC/ELW.

66. "*Wallenstein* im Theater der Jugend," *Neues Wiener Tagblatt*, March 11, 1938.

67. Arndt, interview by author, August 2, 2006.

appalled, but onstage his role of hunter-cum-soldier harmonized with the new order. The contradiction proved untenable. In one scene the hunter, flush with admiration for the great general, rallies a skeptical cuirassier to join his troops. The fateful moment occurred when Arndt uttered the lines: "Only with strength is freedom mine, I'll live and die with Wallenstein!"[68] Arndt spoke his character's lines with conviction, but the audience's reaction horrified him. His lines incited the young audience, which understood "strength" as the annexation and Wallenstein as Hitler. A pro-Hitler demonstration erupted, and "Heil Hitler" chants disrupted the performance. Aghast, in the emotion of the moment Arndt committed an actor's worst sin—he fell out of character and openly rebuked the audience from onstage.[69] His performative identity gave way to his phenomenal one, and he was held accountable for expressing his true opinions. When a spectator threatened to report him, Arndt exited his role again, this time retorting with a quote from Goethe's *Götz of Berlichingen*—"Lick my arse."[70]

Arndt's inability to adhere to his fictional role held potentially fatal consequences. A few days later two policemen entered his apartment, where he lived with his mother. Born into a patriotic family, Arndt's deceased father had been an army officer, his mother a nurse in World War I. To his death, Arndt remained uncertain who these men were, but he imagined they must have come to his home because of his father's role in the military. The strangers admonished his mother that her son had to flee immediately, because his name was on an arrest list. Decades later Arndt concluded that they, too, were actors: double agents. Jeopardized by his error onstage, from this moment forward his survival depended on his acting ability. The two men described an intricate route out of Nazi territory, but he was not permitted to write any of it down. Instead, he had to memorize all the information, which was, as

---

68. Friedrich Schiller, *Wallenstein* and *Mary Stuart*, ed. Walter Hinderer, trans. Jeanne Wilson (New York: Continuum, 1991), 42.

69. Arndt, interview, 2006.

70. Goethe, *Johann Wolfgang von Goethe: Werke, Kommentare und Register*, 4:143.

Arndt later reflected, no problem for a young actor.[71] The problem was the route itself, which was even more terrifying than remaining in Vienna.

The men instructed Arndt to escape the Gestapo by heading straight to Germany. There was logic to the idea, bizarre and fearsome though it seemed. The men explained to him that the only Austrian border where guards would not be looking for him and other fugitives was the frontier with Germany. Most people fleeing the Nazis would try to cross into Switzerland, Italy, or Hungary, and that is exactly where the authorities would be waiting for them. Arndt's escape route followed a zigzag course on commuter trains and local buses across Germany, from the border near Salzburg north almost until Berlin and then southwest to Trier. Despite the rationale behind the plan, Arndt still shook his head seventy-five years later as he recalled the men's advice: "utter insanity, going to hell to flee the devil."[72] He had to remember the proper trains, imitate local customs, and speak with regional accents to avoid arousing suspicion, all the while behaving as if each situation was nothing out of the ordinary. The French actor and director Jean-Louis Barrault described the skills of an accomplished thespian as an exceptionally strong will and well-trained pliability of body posture, as well as a high degree of flexibility in breathing and range of voice.[73] These were all skills Arndt had been honing since his childhood. Convincing the people around him that he was an ordinary German was a matter of performance, and he had already rehearsed for the role. In 1935, reviewing his portrayal of Eital in Maurice Rostand's pacifist drama, *The Man I Killed* (1930), the *Luxemburger Volksblatt* noted: "Jacques Arndt has the makings of a Hitler youth."[74] Arndt's work as an actor had cultivated the talents he now needed to escape Nazi persecution.

---

71. Arndt, interview, 2006.

72. Jacques Arndt, interview by author, December 25, 2008.

73. Barrault, *Ich bin Theatermensch*, 177.

74. "Theater im Volkshaus," *Luxemburger Volksblatt*, October 7, 1935. See also "Vorschau auf Winterspielzeit," *Luxemburger Zeitung*, September 27, 1935; "Bunbury," *Luxemburger Wort*, November 11, 1935; "Prinz Übermuts Fahrt ins Märchenland," *Der Landwirt*, December 7, 1935.

Later, when people asked him if he had been frightened during his journey, Arndt offered the simplistic, almost childish response that his actor's imagination had enabled him to remain calm and confident. As he crossed Germany, acting skills became survival skills: "I imagined it like a play in the theater. Ten meters ahead of me, the SS troops marched and I watched them as if I were onstage. I was young, blond, and completely convinced of my role in this crazy drama."[75] The philosopher and sociologist Georg Simmel has claimed that a compelling actor gives the impression that he is presenting himself; his actions and sufferings should seem to unfold in real life. In other words, the actor's phenomenal body—his bodily being in the world—should be indistinguishable from his performative body in his fictional role onstage.[76] Arndt believed strongly enough in his self-created drama that he achieved this effect: "I just followed the script, and nobody paid me any heed. They never asked: 'Hey, who are you anyway?'"[77] Nobody saw the fleeing Jew behind the ordinary German.

When he arrived in Trier, Arndt's instructions were to act as though he were a tourist and stroll among the Roman ruins, slowly making his way down to the Mosel River. After crossing the Mosel and following the left bank past its intersection with the Sauer River, he would reach the least guarded way out of Germany. Here he would verify that there was no major patrol in the area, then dive into the Sauer and swim across to Luxemburg. If all went well, he quickly would be in safety. If border guards saw him, however, they would shoot. Everything went according to plan until he reached the middle of the Sauer, at which point he heard gunshots. Diving underwater he swam hard, holding his breath until he reached the far bank. He was hardly a great athlete, Arndt explained, but "in this situation, everyone is Diego Maradona. It is a matter of life or death."[78] In this moment, Arndt indicated, his

---

75. Arndt, interview, 2006.

76. Georg Simmel, "Zur Philosophie des Schauspielers," *Internationale Zeitung für die Philosophie der Kultur* 9 (1920–21): 339–340.

77. Arndt, interview, 2006.

78. Arndt, interview, 2006.

phenomenal body merged with his performative body, which on-stage is capable of acts it could never accomplish in reality.

Arndt's next destination was a charity organization in Luxem-burg City, which doubled as an underground refugee assistance network. Wary of infiltration, they made him repeat his story doz-ens of times to see if he might eventually reveal inconsistencies.[79] Finally convinced, the group found him shelter in an attic and told him to keep a low profile, although they occasionally sent him out on small errands so neighbors would grow accustomed to seeing him about, and he would feel more comfortable in his environ-ment. On one of these errands Arndt brought a letter to an of-fice. When he delivered it, the recipients told him to go straight to the train station. Several other refugees already were waiting there, all strangers to him. A member of the relief organization ordered them to board the next train to Marseille, where another agent would greet them by reciting the first line of a French poem to which Arndt, the lone French speaker, would respond with the second line. Each refugee was told to sit in an exact seat in sepa-rate compartments. They had neither tickets nor passports. When they reached France, border guards entered Arndt's compartment and checked all the passengers' documents, except for his: "It was the same for everyone else. I don't know how they did it, but the escape was masterfully organized."[80]

When they reached the station in Marseille a man came up to the group and mumbled a few words as he walked past. Unsure, Arndt remained silent, and the man disappeared. The group then stood on the platform for several hours, with no documents, no money, and no contacts in a foreign city. Finally, the man returned and said something. Arndt, still unsure—and terrified—responded with the corresponding line. "Hurry, come with me," the man an-swered. Arndt and his companions then rushed through the streets of Marseille, following a complete stranger. Abruptly, the man shoved them inside a small door that opened to a flight of stairs leading under an adjacent building: "It was the cellar of the beggar

79. Jacques Arndt, telephone conversation with author, April 2007.
80. Arndt, interview, 2006.

king Jeremiah Peachum from the *Threepenny Opera*. There were beggars, fake beggars, false blind men, and us suddenly in the middle of it all!"[81] Aided by his actor's imagination, Arndt compared the scene to Brecht's play, which concludes with an unlikely happy ending, and was able to create an uplifting sense of familiarity.

Before sunrise, another man brought Arndt and his companions to the port and instructed them to wait for a signal. Given up to the hands of others, he had no choice but to continue following the script. Suddenly a sailor whistled, shoved a board through an opening in a freighter and motioned for him and a few others to climb in. The same sailor returned later with blankets and appeared once daily with food. For weeks Arndt and several other refugees huddled among cargo crates in the middle deck. They were cold, hungry, and with absolutely no idea of what awaited them, as Arndt put it, "in the next act."[82] Gradually, the weather grew warmer and the days longer. The ship docked at various harbors. After one stop, the sailor informed them that they had just departed from Santos, Brazil. The next stop was Montevideo, in democratic Uruguay. Here, the stowaways would disembark. The sailor gave them fake passports with their real names, plus forged vaccination records. There was a ten-dollar bill in each passport. At the last minute they scurried out of the ship on a wooden plank, just as they had boarded in Marseilles. The sailor called out "Good luck!" as the freighter left port.[83]

And there he stood. The twenty-four-year-old Jacques Arndt spoke no Spanish, could not place Uruguay on a map, and with ten dollars and fake papers had to begin his life anew. Unsuccessfully, he tried to speak with passersby in German, French, and bits of English. He attempted time and again until finally a person stopped and responded in a foreign language he somehow understood, Yiddish. Arndt claimed to have had no contact with Yiddish in Vienna, but he could understand the man well enough to follow his directions to a pension.[84]

---

81. Arndt, interview, 2006.
82. Arndt, telephone conversation, 2007.
83. Arndt, interview, 2006.
84. Arndt, interview, 2006.

Next, he began to look for work. His acting ability had rescued him from the Nazis, but guests told him it would not get him employment in Uruguay: "Someone asked me, 'What are you?' And I said proudly, 'I'm an actor.' 'Ah, very interesting. What language?' 'German.' 'Mmm, no good. Not useful here.'" But scores of German-speaking emigrants were arriving in Uruguay every week. Businesses run by refugees for refugees were springing up all over Montevideo. One such enterprise was Hermann Gebhardt's antifascist radio program, *The Voice of the Day*. The talented lawyer from Berlin designed content, found advertisers, did the accounting, even wrote copy—but he stuttered: "For him it was a godsend to find a professionally-trained speaker. And for me it was a miracle to find work on a German radio show in Uruguay. My salary was very small, but it was a start."[85]

Arndt quickly learned customs, mannerisms, and some Spanish by observing and mimicking his environs. As a young, blonde, Viennese actor, he was something of a curiosity. The Uruguayan owners of the radio station enjoyed chatting with Arndt, who held their attention with his scanty repertoire of words, plus hands, feet, and gestures. One day they approached him with a record. To his astonishment, the men requested that he announce the song, a Viennese waltz, on the airwaves. When he had finished, they asked him to do this daily with a few waltzes, narrating an anecdote before playing the record. It was, Arndt recalled, an effective if intimidating form of language instruction: "They forced me to learn Spanish by speaking it live on the radio."[86] As an actor Arndt had developed skills in language acquisition and communication, abilities that now gained him employment and facilitated his integration into Uruguayan society.

Arndt's knack for entertainment and his comical efforts at Spanish pleased listeners. The gimmick received positive reviews and became a full-scale program, *Viennese Stamps*, which aired twice weekly on the station, The World. One radio magazine urged readers not to miss the "young European actor of elegant bearing and refined culture, who tells the most charming and diverse tales from

---

85. Arndt, interview, 2006.
86. Arndt, interview, 2006.

Austria's great city."[87] A few weeks later he was surprised by two men waiting for him when he arrived at the station. When Arndt confirmed that he was the actor named in the article, the men told him to expect them at the studio later that evening. Flattered by his success, Arndt had forgotten that he was in Uruguay illegally. Now, he was afraid that he would be deported. He was thus perplexed when, as they drove off, one of the men called out to him that he should put on a tie.

When the men returned, they wordlessly whisked Arndt into the car. Upon reaching their destination, they escorted him up a wide flight of marble stairs and through the grand entrance of a government building. Bewildered, Arndt was brought to a table where several well-dressed civilians, military officers, and a bishop were seated. Clearly, Arndt remembers thinking at the time, "this here is no prison."[88] Strangely, everybody knew him. Eventually, one person asked who wrote the texts he read on the airwaves. Arndt explained that he wrote them himself; most he had experienced personally. This led to more questions, and Arndt told them about his childhood in Vienna, the German annexation, and his expectations for the future. As he struggled to grasp who these people were, Arndt wondered why he was at this banquet, where he was so utterly out of place: "Actors can speak about one topic while thinking about something entirely different. As I spoke, I sensed that this situation was an opportunity." He confessed to his companions that he had no right to be dining with them. They were dignitaries; however, he had no idea who they were. Surprised, the others at the table introduced themselves as the chief of the Montevidean police, the minister of the interior, an army general, and so on. Arndt responded that in this case he had even less of a right, because he was in Uruguay illegally as a refugee: "They answered that if it this was only the problem, they could help me. Forty-eight hours later I had a Uruguayan visa, residence permit, everything. Suddenly, I was a free man!"[89]

---

87. "Jacques Arndt evoca en 'Estampas Vienesas' el romanticismo de la bella ciudad austriaca," *Mundo Uruguayo*, December 6, 1940.
88. Arndt, interview, 2006.
89. Arndt, interview, 2006.

Shortly after Arndt had acquired his papers, he received a letter from Paul Walter Jacob, who had read about the radio show and needed a younger male actor for the Free German Stage.[90] A few weeks earlier the trip to Argentina would have been impossible, but now it was no problem. Seduced by the opportunity to play regularly in a professional theater, he traveled to Buenos Aires: "Then I got my first role, my wages, and was an actor again. Actually I had been acting the entire time since leaving Vienna, but now I was back onstage."[91] Jacob engaged Jacques Arndt as stage designer and young male actor for the 1941 season. Affiliated with the Free German Stage until 1962, he performed in Argentine and international theater, radio, and film for the next sixty-eight years.

Jacques Arndt's story typifies an interpersonal acumen inherent in numerous cases of successful immigration. He and other members of both the Free German Stage and the German Theater demonstrated what the literary scholar Ottmar Ette has identified as a critical tenet of survival skills: knowledge for living together.[92] Their faculty for deftly navigating an array of human relationships enabled many immigrant actors to integrate into Argentine society. As Arndt stressed repeatedly, of all the talents he needed to reach the triumphant conclusion of his extraordinary journey and continue on to a flourishing acting career in Argentina, much of his fortune came down to an ability to get along with others.[93] Irrespective of their politics, ethnicity, and religion, thespian emigrants thrived only if they understood how to improvise and adapt amid a foreign constellation of individuals and institutions. In German Buenos Aires such "border skills" were transcendent; they were a prerequisite for victims and supporters of Nazism to attain professional and personal prosperity in Buenos Aires.[94] Arndt and his fellow immigrants acquired this knowledge for living together through intense engagement with literature in a capacity, as thespians, that

90. Jacob to Arndt, January 23, 1941, PWJAK.
91. Arndt, interview, 2008.
92. Ette, "Literature as Knowledge for Living, Literary Studies as Science for Living," 989.
93. Arndt, interview, 2008.
94. McGee Deutsch, *Crossing Borders*, 3.

created a very close link between reading and living. Exemplified by Arndt's tale, their biographies are testimony to the Lebanese writer Elias Khoury's thesis that literature and life should not diverge, but rather should inform and enrich one another.[95] Drawing from the myriad of relationships and situations they encountered in literature and onstage, antifascist and nationalist actors accumulated the reservoir of knowledge for surviving and living together that facilitated their adept transition from emigrants to immigrants in South America.

Theater to the Rescue: Ernst Wurmser

Liselott Reger and Paul Walter Jacob had the fortune to begin a new, fully legal existence in Buenos Aires, the wealthiest and most cosmopolitan city in South America at the time. Despite his dangerous escape from Europe, Jacques Arndt was also lucky to quickly become a legal, employed immigrant in democratic Uruguay. The experiences of Viennese comic Ernst Wurmser followed a contrasting trajectory, one shared by many blue-collar refugees.

Born in Vienna on March 20, 1882, Ernst Wurmser was a comic actor on stages in Prague, Vienna, and Berlin, where Wurmser also launched a promising career in film. Between 1931 and 1933 he played minor roles in ten feature productions, including *The Captain from Köpenick* (1931) and *Poor as a Church Mouse* (1931). After the NSDAP seized power in 1933, the Jewish Wurmser fled to Czechoslovakia, where he coincided with Paul Walter Jacob and Liselott Reger in Teplitz-Schönau.[96]

Like many last-minute refugees, including several of his colleagues, Wurmser purchased visas for himself and his wife to Bolivia, one of very few countries that accepted emigrants after 1938.[97] Often corrupt, Bolivian officials in Paris and Prague issued

---

95. Mejcher, *Geschichten über Geschichten*, 131.
96. Te-The-Re Cabaret Program, February 28, 1938, PWJA V c) 262.
97. The actors Georg und Lotte Braun, Olga Keller, Erna Terrell, and Ernst Wurmser all received visas for Bolivia through the country's embassy in Prague.

visas at exorbitant prices.[98] Though fortunate to escape Europe, emigrants found scant opportunity to begin new lives in Bolivia, which was the poorest and least developed nation in South America. Indigenous Aymares and Quechuas, most of whom were illiterate and spoke little or no Spanish, made up 95 percent of its population. Furthermore, in 1939 Bolivia was in political turmoil, its economy obliterated after the nation's loss in the 1935 Chaco War. Most refugees in Bolivia were bitterly poor, and professional life was often reduced to a daily regimen of manual labor for meager pay.[99] Georg Braun, who had acted with Jacob and Arndt in Luxemburg, even wrote that he was near starvation.[100] As a friend of Jacob's wrote from Oruro, a mining town, those who did eke out a living still suffered, because they were deprived of intellectual stimulation.[101] The dearth of cultural life made it nearly impossible for actors to earn a living in the theater, especially in German. Ernst Wurmser, too, lived in material and cultural poverty in Bolivia. When he learned in October 1940 that his former colleague had founded a German theater in Argentina, he wrote him asking for work immediately.[102] The Free German Stage played a vital role for refugees because, as the only regularly performing exilic theater worldwide, it represented a unique opportunity for thespian refugees to earn a living in their chosen vocation.

The psychological importance of this prospect can hardly be overstated. Many persecuted thespians felt a deep inner drive to act and were devastated when they were unable to practice their profession in exile. As Wurmser wrote to Jacob from Cochabamba, for him theater was a vital necessity. He left the terms of his employment entirely up to Jacob, because he was lost without collaborating in a dramatic ensemble and performing for an audience.

Approximately 7,000 German-speaking refugees emigrated to Bolivia, nearly all of them after October 1938.

98. Douer and Seeber, *Wie weit ist Wien*, 38.

99. Schwarz, *Keine Zeit für Eichendorff*, 64–90.

100. Braun was engaged by the FGS in 1946. Braun to Arndt, February 13, 1946, JAC.

101. Olga Keller to Jacob, October 9, 1941, PWJAK.

102. Wurmser to Jacob, October 21, 1940, PWJAK.

In Bolivia he saw no hope in working toward a more prosperous future, the raison d'être of immigration. He pleaded with Jacob: "We've always gotten along well . . . it would be very kind if you could answer me *immediately* . . . I'm desperate for your reply."[103] Despite Wurmser's entreaties, Jacob was in the midst of the Free German Stage's inaugural season when the letters arrived. He was, he later explained, too busy for correspondence of any sort.[104] Three weeks later Wurmser wrote again. His second entreaty was that of a frantic man, verging on suicidal: "I urge you to send me a contract (even a fake contract) with the FGS, so I can get the visa. . . . Life here is unbearable and probably in a short time utterly impossible! I beg you to help me find my way to back to the theater, otherwise I will perish completely. Please answer me!!"[105] Ernst Wurmser saw the Free German Stage as his only chance to escape Bolivia and withstand the trauma of exile.

Jacob's measured response to Wurmser in January 1941 gives detailed information about the FGS's procedures for engaging refugee actors. Pleased to contract an experienced and familiar actor, he offered Wurmser roles for serious older characters as well as slapstick comedy. Nonetheless, Jacob warned, everybody had to play even the smallest bit parts. Since the stage produced weekly premieres, there were no days off. The cast had two full rehearsals even on days without performances. Although he promised to help by organizing benefit events, he could not guarantee wages for the six-month offseason. The salary, 120 Argentine pesos monthly, sufficed to provide an austere livelihood.[106]

When communicating with prospective actors Jacob always took care, consistently using the same phrase verbatim, "to describe things exactly as they are."[107] Unlike Wurmser, Jacques Arndt pondered joining the Free German Stage from a relatively

---

103. Wurmser to Jacob, October 21, 1940, PWJAK.

104. Jacob to Wurmser, January 1941, PWJAK.

105. Wurmser to Jacob, November 11, 1940, PWJAK.

106. Jacob to Wurmser, January 1941, PWJAK.

107. Jacob to Wurmser, January 1941, PWJAK; Jacob to Marc Lerner, February 8, 1941, PWJAK.

comfortable situation in Uruguay. Initially, he was unsatisfied with Jacob's offer and requested higher wages. Jacob flatly refused, explaining that he was determined not repeat the fiasco they both endured at The Comedy back in Luxemburg. Two principles, he continued, guided his management of the FGS. First, he assured Arndt that he was a reliable, honest director. The pay was low, but Arndt would receive his full, promised salary punctually (unlike at The Comedy).[108] Secondly, he maintained a very tight, disciplined budget to ensure the theater's financial viability. Jacob stressed to colleagues and donors alike: "Because of the twenty people who would lose their job and basis of existence anew [if it failed], maintaining the stage is a moral duty to me."[109] Cognizant that the Free German Stage was exiled thespians' only chance to continue acting in South America or probably anywhere at all, Jacob took utmost caution to ensure its solvency.

Ernst Wurmser was one of these twenty people. Effusively grateful for the prospect of performing theater again, Wurmser accepted all of Jacob's conditions, declaring himself ready to play any role necessary. The next concern was to procure travel and legal documents, which he worried would be extremely difficult from Bolivia.[110] This was another crucial function that the FGS fulfilled; every actor gained an entry visa and residence permit for Argentina. Jacob even intervened personally at the Ministry of Immigration for difficult cases, such as Wurmser's.[111]

Ernst Wurmser debuted at the Free German Stage on April 27, 1941, and remained in its ensemble until his death in 1949.[112] The *Jüdische Wochenschau* newspaper described his debut, a bit part in Ferenc Molnár's *Delila* (1937), as "infinitely accomplished, infinitely touching."[113] For Wurmser and many others, a contract with

---

108. Jacob to Arndt, January 23, 1941, PWJAK.

109. Jacob to Felix Weil, January 29, 1941, PWJAK.

110. Wurmser to Jacob, January 23, 1941, PWJAK.

111. Jacob to Maspero Castro (General Director of Immigration), February 20, 1941, PWJAK.

112. "Ernst Wurmser gestorben," *AT*, December 13, 1949.

113. "*Delila*," *JW*, May 2, 1941.

the FGS signified a truly decisive turn of fate.[114] There was tension in the cast, but, as Jacob attested after the debut season, its members found strength and solidarity in their collective fortune to play in the only regularly performing exilic theater worldwide.[115] It was vital for the morale of thespian refugees to recover the creativity, comradeship, and material subsistence that they derived from their work in theater. By providing them with residence and labor permits for Argentina, as well as modest but reliable incomes in their chosen vocation, the Free German Stage enabled victims of Nazism to rebuild their self-worth and establish new lives with prospects for the future.

Despite their obvious differences, Ludwig Ney, Paul Walter Jacob, Jacques Arndt, and Ernst Wurmser had overlapping backgrounds, including their central European origins, language, vocation, professional experiences, and the mutual challenge of prospering as immigrants. In Argentina, they underwent similar processes of adaptation and reinvention, including the struggles to establish financial stability, learn a new language, construct social and professional networks, and contend with the societal norms of a foreign culture. Particularly in the cases of Paul Walter Jacob and Ludwig Ney, their experiences in Germany taught them essential survival skills for professional success and personal perseverance as emigrant thespians. Their story reveals overlapping tactics to surmount the universal challenges inherent in migration.

114. Wurmser to Jacob, January 23, 1941, PWJAK.
115. Jacob to Felix Weil, January 29, 1941, PWJAK.

3

STAGING DISSIDENCE

The Free German Stage

When planning his escape from Europe, Paul Walter Jacob had
every intention of continuing his career in theater.[1] Upon arrival
in Argentina he made contacts with numerous antifascists in the
country, most importantly Ernesto Alemann, owner and editor
of the antitotalitarian *Argentinisches Tageblatt*. On January 19,
1939, the *Tageblatt* printed an article celebrating the composer
Felix Mendelssohn Bartholdy. Written by "Paul Walter," the piece
initiated a close professional and personal relationship between
Jacob and Alemann. When Jacob suggested forming a German-
language stage, the *Tageblatt* owner glimpsed a possibility to deploy theater as a cohesive force among antifascists and refugees on
the River Plate. Alemann's connections to local antifascists were an
invaluable source of networking for Jacob as he worked to gather

---

1. Jacob to Enrique Susini, December 5, 1936, PWJAK.

enthusiasm and start-up capital for the enterprise. Additionally, the *Tageblatt* ran nearly daily coverage on the troupe and printed advertisements for free. By far the most widely circulating newspaper in the anti-Hitler colony, the *Tageblatt*'s support for the Free German Stage was decisive.

Paul Walter Jacob and Liselott Reger began to raise start-up capital to rent a theater, engage an ensemble, and establish reserve funds to protect the stage from premature failure. For months Jacob and Reger met with bankers, industrialists, merchants, and wealthy individuals. Potential donors were skeptical, citing the small size of the antifascist population, which, moreover, was split into several distinct groups. According to Jacob, the turning point was a presentation of Curt Goetz's *Menagerie* during a charity benefit on June 17, 1939. It was a simple production, but, having seen an actual performance, donors saw the theater's potential both as an entertainment outlet and as a community-building institution. Jacob's plan to load its repertoire with popular dramas and comedies convinced them that the troupe could attract a broad public. The fund-raising gained momentum, and by August Jacob and Reger had achieved the target sum of 5,000 pesos, equivalent to one season's wages for the entire ensemble. Most contributions came from the German-speaking Jewish bourgeoisie. The textile industrialist Heinrich Fränkel and the banking firm Shaw, Strupp, and Co. were particularly generous supporters. They received regular financial reports from Jacob, and wielded ample influence over the frequency of premieres, length of the season, and composition of the repertoire.[2] While Jacob and Reger oversaw administrative and artistic matters, donors shaped the original concept for the theater.

Felix J. Weil, professor of sociology at Columbia University and cofounder of the Institute for Social Research in Frankfurt, Germany, made the final donation to reach 5,000 pesos. Jacob's correspondence with Weil, whose family ran a large grain export firm out of Buenos Aires, conveys detailed information on the theater's finances.[3] In 1940 the Free German Stage employed a staff

---

2. Jacob to Leopold Lewin, March 1943, PWJAK.
3. Jacob to Weil, January 29, 1941, PWJAK.

and ensemble of fifteen people. The average monthly wages were 120 pesos, except for the leading man and lady, who received an extra 30 pesos. Jacob and Reger earned three average wages, or 360 pesos monthly, based on their extra workload, which included playing major roles and directing twenty premieres, as well as managing the theater's accounting, correspondence, marketing, and legal affairs.[4]

Monthly expenses, covering four premieres and twelve to fifteen performances in total, varied from 5,500 to 6,000 pesos. This paid for wages, rent for the 350-seat House of Theater, performance rights from authors, acquisition of scripts, advertising and printing, stage props, costumes, and cosmetic styling.[5] Despite the tight budget, lists of stage props for each act of each production are quite detailed,[6] and records of stage props and designs for each production show close attention to authenticity, placement, and proportion.[7] With very limited capital, the FGS faced the task of putting on quality productions for audiences accustomed to theater in major European cities. It was a tall order, and the theater posted a 1,500-peso deficit for the 1940 season. This shortfall was reduced by half through a fund-raising dance, and donors covered the difference.[8]

Throughout the World War II period Jacob successfully urged backers to continue their support by connecting charity to politics, repeatedly stressing that the troupe was composed entirely of refugees whose livelihood depended on the theater.[9] Though publicly promoted as an inclusive social space for antifascists, Zionists, and apolitical refugees, in private correspondence Jacob initially hoped the stage would become a center for anti-Hitler activists. Soliciting funds, he cited the imperative of competing against Ludwig Ney's German Theater, because the nationalist colony in Buenos

---

4. Jacob to Weil, January 29, 1941, PWJAK.

5. Jacob to Weil, January 29, 1941, PWJAK.

6. Stage Props, *Jean, Hokuspokus, Menschen auf der Eisscholle*, PWJA IV a) 280.

7. Photos of Gorki's *Nachtasyl*, Bayard Veiller's *Der Prozess Mary Dugan*, Fundación IWO.

8. Jacob to Weil, November 22, 1940, PWJAK.

9. Jacob to Lewin, March 1943, PWJAK.

Aires would declare a great victory should the FGS fail against their "Nazi stage."[10] This argument resonated with sponsors, who believed the FGS also proved to the Argentine population the existence of a free, humane, and civilized Germany.[11] The enterprise was guided by politically inspired principles of antifascist community building and competitive cultural representation vis-à-vis the Argentine host society and, especially, against the nationalist bloc. From the outset, their conflictive relationship was immanent to the identities of the Free German Stage and the German Theater, as well as many of their supporters.

The FGS's efforts at inclusiveness also revealed tensions among anti-Nazi groups. Zionist institutions supported the stage, but its public was dominated by apolitical Jews, some of whom even resisted their Jewish identity. During the search for qualified thespians Hermann Geiger-Torel, an early and influential member of the ensemble, wrote to Kurt Hellmer, a journalist for *Aufbau* in New York. Geiger-Torel, himself a Jew, sought a leading man. To placate Zionists the actor had to be Jewish but because of pervasive anti-Semitism among other, *Jewish* theatergoers, he had to look as non-Jewish as possible, which Geiger-Torel referred to as a self-mutilation complex.[12] The letter provides an early glimpse into the challenges facing the FGS. The small size of the antifascist colony obliged it to accommodate everybody while offending nobody, an impossible task, given the the diversity of its target audience. Furthermore, this disunity existed internally among its personnel, which included Zionists, Communists, Social Democrats, Germans, Austrians, Gentiles, and refugees who were neither politically nor religiously engaged. The cast was a microcosm for the fragmented anti-Nazi colony.

Paul Walter Jacob was not the only exile with plans to establish a German theater in Argentina. Both the Troupe 38, an amateur group that put on political cabaret in the leftist Forward Club,

---

10. Jacob to Weil, January 29, 1941, PWJAK.
11. Alemann to Jacob, May 8, 1943, PWJAK.
12. Geiger-Torel to Hellmer, December 25, 1940, PWJAK.

and Josef Szekely's Comics' Cabaret, an artist's collective that played only sporadically, could coexist with the FGS. However, Max Wächter's German-language Stage of Argentina targeted the same public and had a similar repertoire. The population could not support two theaters, yet neither Jacob nor Wächter, who had performed with the Jewish Cultural League in Hamburg, was willing to compromise. When each declined offers to join the other, the two theaters were at an impasse.[13]

Jacob did not believe that Wächter could establish a regularly performing, professional exilic theater as he conceived the FGS. Wächter's group performed only fourteen times in ten months, which was insufficient to generate a living wage for its cast. This caused excessive turnover, which lowered the quality of its performances. The *Argentinisches Tageblatt* expressed similar misgivings in its review of Franz Arnold and Ernst Bach's farce, *The Real Jacob* (1924), asserting that Wächter's direction was inadequate and the ensemble featured too many amateurs.[14] Wächter appears to have selected dramas without ensuring he had the proper personnel, which is substantiated by last-minute advertisements scrambling to fill parts by engaging "talented" amateurs.[15] Jacob, who had been a representative for the Guild of the German Stage, viewed this practice as a crime against unemployed professional thespians. He argued that the purpose of an exilic theater was to

---

13. Wächter to Jacob, February 28, 1940, PWJAK. The FGS planned twelve presentations monthly.

14. According to Anne Lemmer, Wächter's refusal to cooperate with Jacob provoked a press campaign against the former's theater; however, her claim is questionable. Jacob first offered Wächter a place in the FGS on January 2, 1940, but as of February 23, Wächter had not replied. The *Tageblatt*'s review of *The Real Jacob*, printed on January 3, could not have been motivated by Wächter's refusal, because according to Jacob himself, Wächter had not yet refused. Moreover, the paper published positive reviews of Wächter's group on February 15 and March 11. This second piece appeared well after Wächter had declined to join the FGS. There is no evidence that the *AT* systematically defamed Wächter. Compare Lemmer, *Die "Freie Deutsche Bühne*,*"* 24.

15. *AT*, February 24, 1940; flyer, *Liebelei*, Max Wächter Collection, Institut für Theaterwissenschaft, Universität Hamburg.

help refugees work in their chosen vocation, not to exacerbate their struggles by doling out roles to amateurs.[16] Wächter also had not matched Jacob's fund-raising and could not offer the same job security. Consequently, all the professional actors in Wächter's group transferred to the FGS.[17] When Jacob also wrested the House of Theater venue away from the German-language Stage, Wächter was compelled to join his competition.

The *Tageblatt* depicted this arrangement as an amicable accord,[18] but in truth Wächter had yielded only under heavy pressure from the Zionist community, specifically Bernhardi Swarsensky, editor of the *Jüdische Wochenschau*.[19] Wächter eventually lamented his decision and often complained about the bit parts he received. In response, Jacob questioned Wächter's claims about his acting experience and asserted there were many plays that he would not have produced if he had had no better actors than Wächter to fill the main roles.[20] The polemic sowed partisan strife within the ensemble. Zionists consistently sided with Wächter, while most others aligned themselves with Jacob. The chronic agitation among thespians left an indelible mark on participants. Sixty-five years later, Jacques Arndt still referred to Wächter as a "poor sap."[21]

In addition to actors from Wächter's stage, several joined the FGS from other stations in exile, some responded to advertisements, and Ernesto Alemann recruited a few more, including Hermann Geiger-Torel and Hedwig Schlichter-Crilla. A graduate of the Hoch Conservatory in Frankfurt, Geiger-Torel had conducted in Buenos Aires under Erich Kleiber at the Colón Theater in 1934, 1938, and 1939. He directed over thirty productions at the FGS before becoming director of at the Uruguayan national opera in 1942.[22] Another key addition was Hedwig Schlichter-Crilla, who

---

16. Jacob to Geiger-Torel, March 27, 1940, PWJAK.

17. "Deutschsprachige Bühne in Argentinien," *AT*, January 1, 1940; "Deutschsprachige Bühne in Argentinien," *AT*, March 5, 1940.

18. "Deutschsprachige Bühne in Argentinien," *AT*, April 2, 1940

19. Wächter to Jacob, October 11, 1942, PWJAK.

20. Jacob to Wächter, October 14, 1942, PWJAK.

21. Arndt, interview, August 2, 2006.

22. Geiger-Torel conducted in Montevideo (1943–44) and Rio de Janeiro (1945–48) and was lead conductor of the Canadian Opera Festival Association (1959–76).

had collaborated with Leopold Jessner and Julius Bab in Berlin and starred in the feature film *Girls in Uniform* (1931). An acclaimed actress, Schlichter-Crilla also acted with French companies under Louis Jouvet, Rachel Berendt, and Madeleine Ozeray in Argentina.[23] The arduous task of composing an ensemble sowed enduring conflicts. Nonetheless, when the Free German Stage held its inaugural performance it featured a full cast of experienced, professional actors.

The curtain rose at FGS on April 20, 1940, Adolf Hitler's birthday, a conscious act of reclaiming German culture from the Nazi regime.[24] The date was a forceful political statement but the play, Ladislaus Bus-Fekete's *Jean* (1937), was not. A simple comedy, *Jean* offered theatergoers an escape from the psychological and economic hardships of exile. Reviewers, all favorably disposed toward the new enterprise, concurred that *Jean* was something less than an antifascist manifesto. The *Tageblatt* merely described it as harmless,[25] but *La Nación*, a prominent Argentine paper with a discerning arts section, criticized the play as "predictable," "coarse," and "improbable."[26] In a subtle way, *Jean* actually did correspond to the theater's internationalist and antifascist platform. Its author, Ladislaus Bus-Fekete, was a Hungarian Jew whose works were banned in Nazi Germany. Like much of the repertoire, *Jean* evinced a calculated effort at compromise. Bus-Fekete's background satisfied antifascists and Zionists, while the work itself appealed to apolitical theatergoers, most of whom favored entertainment over politics.

The setting of the performance was also significant. The House of Theater, where the FGS played for its first four seasons, was modern and comfortable, with seating for 350 people. Available for the desirable Saturday night and Sunday matinee time slots, it was located on Santa Fe Avenue, a central thoroughfare, easily accessible from the entire city. Importantly, the building also

---

23. Julius Bab, "Zehn Jahre deutsches Theater in Argentiniens Hauptstadt," *Staatszeitung New York*, September 10, 1950.

24. Arndt, interview, December 25, 2008.

25. "*Jean* von Bus-Fekete," *AT*, April 21, 1940.

26. "Teatro alemán en la Casa del Teatro," *LN*, April 21, 1940.

Figure 3. Ensemble of the Free German Stage following
its debut season in 1940.

Source: Fundación IWO, Alexander Berg Collection.

housed a residence for retired Argentine thespians. Current and
future presidents of Argentina, Agustín Justo and Roberto Ortiz,
attended the inauguration ceremony in 1938, at which the minister
of public education, Jorge de la Torre, described the institution as a
"fraternal embrace of the entire Argentine theater family."[27] In this
spirit, the FGS cultivated contacts in the Argentine theater world,
including Pedro Pico, president of both the House of Theater and
the Argentine General Society of Authors. An invaluable resource,
Pico facilitated bureaucratic procedures for the procurement of
visas, licensing for performances, and other municipal permits. The
House of Theater suited the FGS's public and facilitated actors'
integration into Argentine society.

27. "Inaugurado ayer el edificio de la Casa del Teatro," *La Prensa*, January 5,
1938.

Behind the Curtain: Working at the Free German Stage

Two interlinked features dominated the Free German Stage's repertoire and schedule during the World War II period. The first was
the number of productions, a dizzying 150 premieres and 500 total
performances from 1940 through early 1946.[28] In part this explains the second notable detail: a clear majority of the plays were
comedies. The FGS premiered twenty-five works yearly, one per
week during a six-month theater season from April to October. It
averaged eighty-five productions per season, but performed each
piece only three to four times. By comparison the Players from
Abroad, a German-language theater company founded in New
York City in 1942, produced three to four premieres per year for
a total of fifteen to twenty presentations. The rotation of pieces
at the FGS was extremely fast, and the number of overall performances was extraordinarily high.

The stage established a ticket subscription system that ran in
six-week cycles, and promised its audience a new premiere weekly.
In time a regular work schedule emerged. Sunday mornings were
free, and on Sunday afternoons the previous premiere had its third
performance. Monday afternoons and evenings were devoted to
initial preparations for the next piece; directors assigned roles and
composed lists for props, while Jacques Arndt and Hans Schön,
previously the stage manager for the German Theater in Prague,
collaborated on set designs. Tuesday and Thursday mornings and
evenings were devoted to stage rehearsals. On Wednesday mornings rehearsals were held again and, depending on demand, that
evening the fourth and final performance of Saturday's premiere occurred. Late Thursday night and early Friday morning, Arndt and
Schön assembled the props and scenery for the upcoming premiere.
Fridays were devoted to two dress rehearsals, one at midday and
the other in the evening, often continuing past midnight. On Saturday evenings, the group staged the premiere and first repetition

---

28. "Wasser für Canitoga," *FP*, May 26, 1946.

of the week's new play at 6:30 and 9:30 p.m., respectively. This schedule represents an ideal scenario—rehearsals often occurred closer together because of difficulties in acquiring materials for the stage design and preparing scripts, which actors often had to translate themselves into German. Jacques Arndt subsequently recalled Hedwig Schlichter-Crilla's frustrations:

> The room where we worked was, as she said with French influences, a "room *de merde*," . . . the theater was "a theater *de merde*." We had to translate works on airmail paper, so we could make copies with carbon paper. Obviously, the last copies were very weak. She said: "these shitty papers *de merde*." We all wanted to do it differently.[29]

Everyone at the FGS was accustomed to conditions in Europe. The duress of working longer hours under worse conditions at far less pay, and playing for an exigent and divisive audience—all amid the trauma of living as refugees—provoked acute stress and tension.

Issues of authority aggravated the strained relations in the troupe. Jacob regarded the Free German Stage as his theater and reserved the final say on all artistic and administrative matters for himself, yet others saw the stage as a collective. Finances were at the core of this disagreement. As Jacob wrote to prospective ensemble members, he could guarantee their modest wages only during the theater season. The actors, thus, were not only overworked but also had to worry about how they would survive the summer months. Together, Jacob and Liselott Reger earned three salaries, plus royalties from Jacob's journalism, so they had significantly more income than their colleagues. However, the theater's deficit also was their legal responsibility. The ensuing anxiety and misunderstandings often led to feuding between Jacob and Reger and the rest of the cast.

Over time, this discord escalated. One example is the homage that Jacob and Reger organized for the famous director, Max Reinhardt, upon his death in 1943. On November 17, 1943, over 1,000

---

29. Cora Roca and Jacques Arndt, "Recordando a Hedy Crilla," in Rohland de Langbehn and Vedda, *Teatro y teoría teatral*, 19–20.

people filled the sold-out Grand Splendid Theater.[30] An artistic and financial success, the festivities featured a lecture by Jacob, recitations by Reger, and a screening of Reinhardt and William Dieterle's *A Midsummer Night's Dream* (1935). Jacob and Reger held the event in the name of the FGS and disposed of the revenue as they saw fit, which technically they were entitled to do. Many of their colleagues disagreed, however, arguing that Jacob and Reger could not use the FGS name without including them in the presentation and decisions about the allocation of proceeds.[31] They expressed their disapproval to donors and even purchased tickets for the tribute independently.[32] Enraged, Jacob accused Alexander Berger, the ensemble's representative, of infringing upon his authority. Jacob claimed that he and Reger had the right to act in the name of the FGS unilaterally, since they had founded the stage, and they alone were legally responsible for its financial commitments, including paying the deficit, renting venues, and disbursing wages.[33] Furthermore, he had not claimed any of the profits personally, but had used the income to finance the deficit and refurbish funds set aside to support the cast during the off-season.[34]

The FGS accounts show that Jacob's actions benefited the entire cast, yet everyone was exhausted from the theater season, as well as the burden of world events and exile. The affair degenerated into a three-month, vitriolic letter exchange among Jacob, Berger, Reger, and another actor, Wolfgang Vacano. A competent but headstrong manager, Jacob repeatedly reproached Berger for utter cluelessness and directed numerous sardonic insults at Berger in their correspondence. Moreover, Jacob refused to apologize, insisting that all offenses came from the other side.[35] The belligerence eventually gave way to an uneasy peace, because nobody truly wanted the theater to fail. Nonetheless, Vacano and Reger both left the stage

---

30. "En memoria de Max Reinhardt," *Noticias Gráficas*, November 19, 1943.
31. FGS Ensemble to Jacob, November 19, 1943, PWJAK.
32. Vacano to Berger, December 12, 1943, IWO.
33. Jacob to Berger, November 22, 1943, PWJAK.
34. Jacob to Vacano, November 23, 1943, PWJAK.
35. Jacob to Berger, January 12, 1944, PWJAK.

after the 1943 season. Since Reger handled much of the business administration, she was unwillingly caught up in the altercation. Disillusioned, Reger relocated to Montevideo, where she worked on the *Voice of the Day* and at the theater The Comedy.[36] In 1946 she and Jacob were divorced. As she was a cofounder of the Free German Stage and director of over forty plays, the group lost one of its most energetic and influential members with her departure.

The Reinhardt fracas reached an exceptional degree of imbroglio, but the friction itself was not anomalous. The FGS's cast and public, as well as its donors and supporters in the media, were all rife with infighting. These groups' contrasting religious, political, and commercial agendas conflicted from the outset, and eventually spawned acerbic rivalries, which at times were eclipsed only by the mutual opprobrium of all parties toward Nazism. The fractious relations within the antifascist colony resulted in patterns of attrition, dysfunction, and disenfranchisement that markedly weakened the Free German Stage's efficacy to forge and sustain a united cultural front against German nationalism in Argentina. Cognizant of this dilemma, Paul Walter Jacob repeatedly invoked the comic genre as theatrical therapy to lower levels of stress and enmity. The next section evaluates the mixed results of his strategy.

Comedies: "Laughter, Ladies and Gentlemen, Is Stronger Than Tears"

As stated above, the Free German Stage performed far more comedies than any other dramatic genre. This did not escape the attention of critics near and far, including Julius Bab, who noted the prevalence of comedies, some of them quite lowbrow, with mild censure.[37] Yet, the theater did not neglect serious drama. In its first five years, it staged Ibsen, Schiller, Gorki, Maugham, Sudermann, Katajew, Zweig, Herzl, Ardrey, Holz and Jerschke, Hellman,

---

36. Reger to Berger, January 7, 1944, IWO.
37. "Deutsches Theater in Argentinien," *Staatszeitung und Herold*, May 16, 1948.

Capek, Rolland, Pirandello, Kaiser, and Schnitzler, as well as several religious dramas. This equals the totality of plays performed at the New Yorker Players from Abroad over the same time span. The FGS played far more serious dramas than exilic theaters in New York, Shanghai, Mexico City,[38] or Montevideo.[39]

Nonetheless, from motivations ranging from pragmatism to psychology, the troupe presented overwhelmingly more comedies than serious dramas. The rapid rotation of pieces left scant time for elaborate planning. For example, the cast began preparations for Lillian Hellman's *Watch on the Rhine* (1941) eight months before the premiere.[40] It was impossible to do this for more than a few dramas per season. The FGS lacked adequate time and personnel to present complex dramas for a public accustomed to seeing polished productions in European cultural centers.

Considering that theatergoers and cast alike were grappling with a horrific past, troubled present, and uncertain future, the physiology of humor also informs the prevalence of comedies at the FGS. Aristotle's *Poetics* posits laughter as a benign, cathartic form of discharging excess emotion or tension, and scientific research links his theory to concrete physiological phenomena. According to William Fry of Stanford University Medical School, laughter involves a rapid, prolonged acceleration of the heartbeat, which is invigorating during laughter and facilitates relaxation afterward. Laughing benefits the respiratory system as well. Guffaws catalyze heavy breathing, evacuating residual, carbon dioxide–laden air in exchange for new, oxygen-rich air. The improved air exchange replaces sluggishness with renewed mental verve. Laughter also produces catecholamines, chemicals that stimulate the nervous system. Together with improved air exchange, catecholamines trigger alertness and enhance cerebral functioning. Finally, laughing stimulates the secretion of endorphins, the body's natural anesthetics. If

---

38. Maaß, *Repertoire der deutschsprachigen Exilbühnen, 1933–1945*, 114–155, 69–73, 40–41.

39. Fritz Pohle, *Emigrationstheater in Südamerika abseits der "Freien Deutschen Bühne," Buenos Aires*, 28–29.

40. Jacob to Hellman, December 26, 1941, PWJAK.

external problems—of which refugees in Argentina had many—are provoking internal effects, such as a headache, a funny comedy is an effective remedy.[41]

In addition to its physical benefits, humor is a boon to the psychological health of oppressed individuals and communities. Holocaust survivor, neurologist, and clinical psychiatrist Viktor Frankl has argued that humor is essential to maintaining a healthy outlook on life, especially for individuals suffering from depression, self-doubt, and fear.[42] The person with a sense of humor can never be fully dominated, even by a government that imprisons him, for his ability to laugh at the situation will enable him to preserve a measure of personal freedom, at least in thought and spirit. Frankl, who survived Dachau and Auschwitz, said of the camps: "In the fight for self-preservation, humor more than anything else in the human make-up can afford an ability to rise above any situation."[43] Humor has been considered a fundamentally social phenomenon for centuries. Its communal character can be witnessed in cinemas and theaters everywhere—the fuller the house, the easier spectators are brought to laughter. Spreading from person to person, laughter also has a cohesive effect. Smiling and chuckling together, even if only at a piece of absurdity, brings people together and unites them at least temporarily.[44] A vitalizing force at the Free German Stage, humor was conducive to community building. Even the silliest plays played a serious role in helping refugees withstand the anguish of exile.

Brandon Thomas's *Charley's Aunt*

A rollicking, wildly successful farce, *Charley's Aunt* first premiered in London on February 29, 1892, and compiled a record-breaking original run of 1,466 performances. At the time of the FGS's premiere on October 11, 1941, Thomas's play had established itself as

---

41. Fry and Salameh, *Humor and Wellness in Clinical Intervention*, 125–133.
42. Frankl, *Doctor and the Soul*, 204.
43. Frankl, *Viktor Frankl Recollections*, 97.
44. Morreall, *Taking Laughter Seriously*, 115.

in the fourth line, the Aunt's identity blurred. With a darkening tone and faint cognizance of the present, Vacano's song gradually moved away from the fictional farce and approximated the actors and audience at the House of Theater. The lyrics were ambiguous, but many spectators also had been on the run, some had witnessed death personally, and nearly all of them had seen their past lives vanish like a whiff of smoke. The merry piano imposed a jovial mood, but serious undertones mounted:

I frolicked and felt content
on every continent,
learning languages on a spree
ja ja, yes yes, sí sí, oui oui.
But now travel is travailing!
Where can you get a visa?
And no ship sets sailing!
With no money to spend,
the world's a dead end.
But I know a trick for that
Just say you're luggage or freight
belonging to a diplomat—
you'll get into every state!

Jacob moved steadily closer to the spectators' own biographies, straddling the line between his performative and phenomenal identities. Hurriedly, Jacob's version of Charley's Aunt had learned the languages most commonly spoken by the emigrant audience. Her song—the difficulties of finding safe passage, the frustrated attempts to acquire a visa, and the exorbitant prices of procuring entry to foreign countries—told of a desperation that everyone in the auditorium had experienced firsthand. Finally, the Aunt cynically joked about a global hypocrisy in which freedom and safety are determined by connections, rather than justice. Paul Walter Jacob sang a story not about his character but about himself, his cast, and his audience. On the other hand, still cross-dressed, he invoked humor as a distancing mechanism. The incongruity between his performative and phenomenological selves provoked his audience to see humor in his narrative, enabling these refugees, at least

the second most-performed English drama in the world, surpassed only by *Hamlet*.[45] The well-timed event was staged shortly after the 1941 release of a Hollywood cinematic adaptation, starring Jack Benny. A surefire selection to generate robust ticket sales with an eye toward the lean summer months ahead, the play could be easily dismissed as a simple maneuver to fill seats; however, the presentation merits a closer look. It demonstrated the importance of humor for the morale of the refugee population, while also proving that even an irrelevant farce could be modified to include political elements.

Between scenes *Charley's Aunt* features musical interludes, and, without changing the plot, it was in these spaces that the FGS grafted its own perspective onto the script. Wolfgang Vacano replaced the original score with musical sketches, which altered the tenor of the play by adding a personalized undercurrent of nostalgia and political commentary. The published edition of *Charley's Aunt* opens with the "Eton Boating Song."[46] At the House of Theater, however, a portly Jewish man dressed in a pleated woolen skirt and frumpy blouse rushed in front of the curtain and, accompanied by a merry piano, addressed the audience directly:[47]

Yes! Smoke, ladies and gentlemen, smoke!
Smoking makes us feel so swell,
everyone likes to have a drag
regardless of where we dwell.
People, they run and they die,
they lie and might even love,
it all happens by the by,
and the only thing left is smoke.[48]

Lord Francourt Babberly, already disguised as Charley's Aunt and played by Paul Walter Jacob, began on a light note, flaunting his celebrity and building a rapport with the audience. Then,

45. "*Charleys Tante* in der FDB," *AT*, October 9, 1941.
46. Brandon Thomas, *Charley's Aunt* (London: Samuel French, 1935), 9.
47. Photographs, *Charley's Aunt*, IWO.
48. PWJA VI a) 280.

in the fourth line, the Aunt's identity blurred. With a darkening tone and faint cognizance of the present, Vacano's song gradually moved away from the fictional farce and approximated the actors and audience at the House of Theater. The lyrics were ambiguous, but many spectators also had been on the run, some had witnessed death personally, and nearly all of them had seen their past lives vanish like a whiff of smoke. The merry piano imposed a jovial mood, but serious undertones mounted:

> I frolicked and felt content
> on every continent,
> learning languages on a spree
> ja ja, yes yes, sí sí, oui oui.
> But now travel is travailing!
> Where can you get a visa?
> And no ship sets sailing!
> With no money to spend,
> the world's a dead end.
> But I know a trick for that
> Just say you're luggage or freight
> belonging to a diplomat—
> you'll get into every state!

Jacob moved steadily closer to the spectators' own biographies, straddling the line between his performative and phenomenal identities. Hurriedly, Jacob's version of Charley's Aunt had learned the languages most commonly spoken by the emigrant audience. Her song—the difficulties of finding safe passage, the frustrated attempts to acquire a visa, and the exorbitant prices of procuring entry to foreign countries—told of a desperation that everyone in the auditorium had experienced firsthand. Finally, the Aunt cynically joked about a global hypocrisy in which freedom and safety are determined by connections, rather than justice. Paul Walter Jacob sang a story not about his character but about himself, his cast, and his audience. On the other hand, still cross-dressed, he invoked humor as a distancing mechanism. The incongruity between his performative and phenomenological selves provoked his audience to see humor in his narrative, enabling these refugees, at least

the second most-performed English drama in the world, surpassed only by *Hamlet*.[45] The well-timed event was staged shortly after the 1941 release of a Hollywood cinematic adaptation, starring Jack Benny. A surefire selection to generate robust ticket sales with an eye toward the lean summer months ahead, the play could be easily dismissed as a simple maneuver to fill seats; however, the presentation merits a closer look. It demonstrated the importance of humor for the morale of the refugee population, while also proving that even an irrelevant farce could be modified to include political elements.

Between scenes *Charley's Aunt* features musical interludes, and, without changing the plot, it was in these spaces that the FGS grafted its own perspective onto the script. Wolfgang Vacano replaced the original score with musical sketches, which altered the tenor of the play by adding a personalized undercurrent of nostalgia and political commentary. The published edition of *Charley's Aunt* opens with the "Eton Boating Song."[46] At the House of Theater, however, a portly Jewish man dressed in a pleated woolen skirt and frumpy blouse rushed in front of the curtain and, accompanied by a merry piano, addressed the audience directly:[47]

Yes! Smoke, ladies and gentlemen, smoke!
Smoking makes us feel so swell,
everyone likes to have a drag
regardless of where we dwell.
People, they run and they die,
they lie and might even love,
it all happens by the by,
and the only thing left is smoke.[48]

Lord Francourt Babberly, already disguised as Charley's Aunt and played by Paul Walter Jacob, began on a light note, flaunting his celebrity and building a rapport with the audience. Then,

---

45. "*Charleys Tante* in der FDB," *AT*, October 9, 1941.
46. Brandon Thomas, *Charley's Aunt* (London: Samuel French, 1935), 9.
47. Photographs, *Charley's Aunt*, IWO.
48. PWJA VI a) 280.

to some extent, to put themselves above the tribulations of exile. Through humor Jacob initiated a confrontation with the past, a first step toward building the psychological fortitude necessary to surmount the challenges of the present.

The ditty concluded with the illustrious, irrevocable past of Charley's Aunt:

> Charley's Aunt is my name,
> across the globe spans my fame.
> For half a century
> I have performed on stages
> in every country,
> earning extravagant wages!
> By thousands I reeled them in
> with Guido Thielscher in Berlin.
> Ladies and gentlemen, you know it well,
> back then I always felt so swell.
> Everybody loved me
> from sea to shining sea,
> But things have changed since then,
> and all that's left is smoke.

Maintaining the tension between his role and his true self, Jacob narrated the play's trajectory, particularly its run in Berlin with the popular actor Guido Thielscher. In so doing, he tantalized emigrants with an idealized version of their own European lives. In Europe they, too, had been wealthier, enjoyed more prosperous careers, and often led fulfilling social lives. In exile most were poor, lonely, and worked outside their former professions. The Aunt did not shy away from the facts—nothing remained of their European pasts, only smoke. Nobody in the audience knew how close she was to the terrible truth.

In print, these final verses are strikingly somber for a song that introduces a riotous comedy. The context, however, belies the text. The ditty was sung by a heavyset, balding, well-respected artist and intellectual, but now he wore a pleated skirt, ruffled blouse, pink tights, and curly wig. Moreover, Jacob was not giving a scholarly lecture, but was singing along to a jolly piano. The humor followed

Schopenhauer's theory of incongruity, according to which laughter is caused by a mismatch between conceptual understanding and perception of the same object.[49] Through this incongruity Jacob taught his audience, at least occasionally, to view their struggles through the lens of humor. Moreover, he revealed that their sadness and sufferings need not be solitary. Their experiences as refugees were common to the actors, audience, and even the famed Doña Lucia d'Alvadorez, Charley's Aunt. For all their individual sorrows, the crowd could laugh together and gain solidarity through humor.

The FGS altered neither the original plot nor dialogue of Thomas's benign situational comedy, in which the problems created in the first two acts are resolved in the third as multiple pairs of lovers come together, concluding with a carefree, happy ending.[50] Before the third act, the published text calls again for the "Eton Boating Song," but at the House of Theater Jacob sang another ditty instead:

> An emigrant recently arrived by sea,
> he was unfamiliar with this country.
> But the others, who have been here quite a while,
> they welcomed and cared for him like a child.
> They helped with words and with deeds.
> A car, a house—he's got all he needs!
> The Charity also gives him money every day.
> I don't know if it's true, but that's what they say.[51]

Far more direct, this song was a quixotic vision of how refugees' lives might be, were their dilemmas so easily resolved as in a play like *Charley's Aunt*. Ideally, the refugees on- and offstage at the House of Theater also would have been greeted and supported by "the others"—that is, earlier waves of German emigrants, the nationalist, so-called old colony. Instead of helping, however, nationalist Germans shunned, reviled, and menaced refugees. The

---

49. Schopenhauer, *World as Will and Idea*, 1:76.

50. "*Charleys Tante*," *JW*, October 17, 1941.

51. PWJA VI a) 280.

"Charity," or the Jewish Philanthropic Society, did assist new arrivals, but it was overwhelmed by their numbers and provided only minimal financial aid. The arrival in Uruguay of Jacques Arndt, outfitted with nothing but ten dollars and illegal documents, more closely resembled the struggle of most emigrants, who had to restart life from scratch. Jacob's ironic parody contrasted the adversity of life outside the theater with the carefree fictional narrative within it, again winning humor by its incongruity. The tune concluded with self-reflexive cognizance of this disaccord, a lyrical wink betraying awareness of emigrants' struggles while refusing to relinquish hope and, especially, humor.

As the *Argentinisches Tageblatt* remarked, the unconventional roles in Thomas's drama created a space for younger actors such as Jacques Arndt und Walter Lenk to enjoy the blithe days of student life, which they had been denied as Jewish teenagers imperiled by Nazism.[52] Relations in the ensemble were often strained, so the cast was amused at the sight of their headstrong boss playing the cross-dressing Lord Francourt Babberly, often sniggering visibly onstage.[53] The laughter was contagious, spreading throughout the audience and into the newspapers. One reviewer took up the narrative of Vacano's introductory ditty, favorably comparing the guffaws to previous versions he had seen in Europe.[54] The Zionist *Jüdische Wochenschau*, too, joined in the fun, joking that "Doña Lucia de Alfajores, pardon, Alvadores" had lost none of her youthful charm.[55] Only emigrants to Buenos Aires would understand the play on words, which conflated the protagonist's surname, Alvadores, with an Argentine delicacy, pastries of cookie and caramel called *alfajores*. Such localized humor was a cohesive force among emigrants; it demonstrated that they were a community bound by experiences, customs, and cultural markers unique to themselves.

The FGS received many grateful letters for *Charley's Aunt*. One, addressed to the cast and the audience, noted that Thomas's droll,

---

52. "*Charleys Tante*," *AT*, October 10, 1941.
53. "Montevideo Gastspiel," *AT*, March 19, 1942.
54. "*Charleys Tante*," *AT*, October 10, 1941.
55. "*Charleys Tante*," *JW*, October 17, 1941.

fun-loving Aunt was, in a sense, a relic of spectators' former, happier lives in Europe. Written by Peter Bussemeyer, a journalist for the *Tageblatt*, the private letter wistfully recalled better and safer days, lamenting that if anything remained of the past it was bitter memories of an easier time, when one could cross borders with neither passports nor mortal fear. In Buenos Aires, the writer continues, Charley's Aunt would never be more than an "ersatz-Aunt." She could not restore the winsome days of Guido Thielscher in Berlin. For many emigrants, remembering the past underscored the misery of today. Yet the letter only feinted nostalgia to confront the present. Insisting that emigrants must not succumb to grief and loss, Bussemeyer argues that their current situation, represented by Jacob's ersatz-Aunt, is not futile. After all she still brought four couples together and caused the entire theater to erupt in guffaws; she continued to be a very comforting ersatz-Aunt. Seeing the farcical figure onstage, this theatergoer attributed an earnest function to Charley's Aunt offstage. By means of comedies, theatergoers and ensemble—"we"—had recovered the most buoyant and enduring of human sentiments—joyous, unrestrained, infectious laughter. The Aunt's most valuable accomplishment, the letter concluded, was to have conveyed one decisive, edifying truth to the refugee population: "Laughter, ladies and gentlemen, is stronger than death and tears."[56] All dramas are pliant when subjected to the dynamics of theatrical performance. Even the most unlikely of genres, the farce, can become relevant, resolute, and political.

In its presentation of *Charley's Aunt*, the FGS purposefully and effectively utilized comic theater as a restorative memory machine. Mutual participants in the presentation, refugee theatergoers and thespians were compelled to confront their traumatic past, learn to view it from a sounder perspective, and rekindle a sense of humor and hope that fortified them for the future. In the instance of Thomas's farce, the FGS harnessed the energy of live theater to build emotional grit and togetherness by depicting a shared past in a dramatically familiar, if still physically foreign, context. Yet,

---

56. Peter Bussemeyer to Jacob, October 18, 1941, PWJA VI f) 293.

performing history unleashes theatrical energies that are volatile and varied.[57] Neither the Free German Stage nor the rival German Theater proved capable of consistently channeling their force.

Carl Rössler's *The Five Frankfurters*

The greatest box-office smash at the FGS was Carl Rössler's idyll of the Rothschild family, *The Five Frankfurters* (1911), which was presented ten times in Buenos Aires and Montevideo from 1941 to 1944. Between laughs, Rössler's drama addressed issues of Jewish identity and integration that were the object of vigorous debate among Argentina's German-speaking refugees. Rössler's portrait of Frankfurt's famous Jews' Alley endowed the sold-out premiere with poignant kinship. Describing the atmosphere before the first curtain as akin to a family reunion, the *Jüdische Wochenschau* invoked images of tightly knit Jewish communities in Europe and Argentina.[58] In neither place were Jews as close as the paper suggested, yet this incarnation of Jewish traditions onstage, carefully reconstructed amid exilic disruption, enabled the invention of such intimacy.

To a degree, the destruction of European Jewish culture inspired its cultivation in exile and catalyzed a dynamic, if divisive, campaign for religious and cultural preservation among Jews in Buenos Aires. The Free German Stage supported this effort by reenacting European Jewish memory and community through theatrical performances, such as *The Five Frankfurters*. Its depiction of Jewish religious and cultural continuity was spatially anchored in Frankfurt's Jews' Alley, ever present through the windows of the Rothschild family residence. Jacques Arndt's mise-en-scène, in which individual space was made impossible through overlapping stacks of porous dwellings, bolstered this tightly bound religious family architecturally.[59] The image of kin was reinforced by the trajectory of Rössler's drama, whose main characters are Gudula Rothschild,

---

57. Rokem, *Performing History*, 25.
58. "*Die fünf Frankfurter*," *JW*, June 27, 1941.
59. Sketch, *The Five Frankfurters*, JAC.

and her five sons. Their travels from abroad to a reunion in the alley evoke a suspended diaspora. Portrayed as precious, precarious, and corruptible, throughout much of the play Jewish identity and community are jeopardized by the widening cultural and religious gaps of different generations.

Spatially, the plot moves along two axes: the (imagined) autochthonous, which is personified by the aging Gudula and depicted physically by Jews' Alley, and the diasporic, represented by the migration and integration of the five brothers into external Christian society, which threatens to efface their Jewishness. The play begins in the Rothschild home, where the youngest brother, Jacob, who lives in Paris, meets Gudula. His refined, cosmopolitan bearing contrasts markedly with his mother, who enters with prayer book in hand and dressed in an orthodox Jewess's ankle-length, long-sleeved, black dress. She has come from the temple, where she was commemorating the death of her father. In this place of worship and memory, the family's genealogy is palpable across generations.[60] Gudula's worship represents a performative practice that maintains religious and familial continuity. Living memory, conveyed by mnemonic materials, such as speech, image, and gesture, transmits culture from one generation to the next by means of restored behavior. Mnemonic materials principally give expression to (1) genealogies, particularly of leading families, and; (2) practical formulas of daily living and special observances, particularly those deeply imbued with "religious magic."[61] Gudula's ritualized commemoration of her father's death, visions of her own Kaddish, and the Frankfurter dialect evince and vitalize her social and religious heritage.[62] By contrast, Gudula senses that her worldly sons' links to Jewish mnemonic materials are in peril.[63]

The ensuing scenes, in which the Rothschild brothers display alienation from the living memory embodied by their mother,

---

60. Promptbook, *The Five Frankfurters*, 3, PWJA VI j) 350.

61. Le Goff, *History and Memory*, 58.

62. The Jewish Rössler wrote in German, and many spectators in the House of Theater spoke no Yiddish.

63. Promptbook, *The Five Frankfurters*, 3.

confirm her fears. When Salomon arrives from Vienna, he heads straight to the stock exchange in Frankfurt's center, circumventing Jews' Alley outside the city walls. He and his brothers then pressure their mother to relocate outside the alley; however, Gudula adamantly recounts an entire life cycle of the family—her marriage, the birth of her children, and her husband's death—as bonds of identity that hold her fast to the Rothschild family home. Her sons, contrarily, prioritize acculturation in Christian society. When Salomon tells his family that the Austrian Kaiser has bestowed the title of baron on the Rothschilds, only Gudula and Jacob demur. Gudula references institutionalized anti-Semitism, specifically recent urban laws in Frankfurt prohibiting Jews from public sidewalks, when she recalls that the same royal family forced her father to jump into a ditch as their coach drove past.[64] Jacob cites the rally cry of widespread pogroms just three years before the play's setting in 1819: "Hepp! Hepp! Death and ruin to all Jews!"[65] While audiences at the House of Theater shuddered at this clairvoyant vision of European Jewry's catastrophic future, onstage Jacob's brother Nathan retorted that the aristocratic title would protect the family.[66] Committed to joining the German nobility, Salomon divulges his plan to exploit the Duke of Taunus's need for a loan to pressure him into marrying his daughter, Löttchen, arguing that marriage will consolidate the Rothschilds' ascension into the aristocracy. When Jacob raises concerns, Salomon's response encapsulates his willful alienation from his Jewish roots: "You're *meschugge*!!"[67] Whereas his mother uses mnemonic tools, such as language, to effect cultural preservation and social continuity, Salomon inverts this usage and deploys the etymologically Yiddish term *meschugge* to sever the Rothschilds from their Jewish lineage.

The brothers' visit to the Duke of Taunus, however, confirms that dissonance between Jews and Gentiles persists. Before the Rothschilds arrive, the nobles express varying degrees of anti-Semitism,

---

64. Fuchs, "Concerning the Jews of Frankfort," 20.
65. Rohrbacher and Schmidt, *Judenbilder*, 263.
66. Promptbook, *The Five Frankfurters*, 10.
67. Promptbook, *The Five Frankfurters*, 12.

exposing their hopes for fuller integration and acceptance as illusory. The Duke's majordomo, Fehrenberg, charges that the inhabitants of Jews' Alley are a competing, parasitic society.[68] In a
dialogue struck from the promptbook, the Duke's uncle, Count
Moritz, evokes contemporary Nazi propaganda by insinuating that
Jews are sexual predators, and then barricades his daughter from
the brothers as if they were a virus. In retaliation, the Duke sternly
reproaches the Count for his anti-Semitism. He also remarks to
Eveline, a minor, Gentile character, that his uncle belongs in the
eighteenth century, whereas he himself should have been born
100 years later. In the published edition of the play these are crucial
scenes, because the distinction they illustrate conveys the drama's
clearest hope for future tolerance. Though childish and egotistical,
the Duke is open-minded, and he accepts Salomon's proposition.
He would never marry Löttchen were it not for her fortune, but
the compliments he pays to her even before Salomon's proposition
also give the impression that he is not motivated by money alone.
Furthermore, his acceptance is contingent on the condition that
his daughter consents of her own free will. The Duke's willingness
to marry Löttchen reflects self-interest *and* a progressive attitude
toward Jewish-Gentile relations.

Salomon's ambitions cause distress in the Rothschild household.
The marriage would require Löttchen to convert to Christianity
and discontinue the family's generational presence at the temple,
thus breaking irrevocably with the mnemonic materials and living
memory that Gudula preserves. Salomon dismisses her conversion
as a formality, and his brother, Karl, views baptism as a superficial
maneuver whose social gains justify any religious concessions.[69]
The family's debate depicts the vulnerability of Jewish identity
within a larger constellation of intercultural relations, social ambitions, and commercial interests. The transmission of Jewish religion and culture across generations is enshrined in traditional,
ritualistic events, such as marriages. In Löttchen's marriage the
synagogue, a mnemonic space intrinsic to Judaism, will be replaced

---

68. Promptbook, *The Five Frankfurters*, 15.
69. Promptbook, *The Five Frankfurters*, 16.

by the church. Christian traditions will supplant sacred Jewish rituals. Gudula describes her grandchild's wedding, a Christian ceremony in a Christian mnemonic space, as an act of abandonment. According to Gudula, the introduction of a Gentile would disrupt the family's genealogy, corrupt its identity, and cost the Rothschilds their blessing. Metonymically representative of the greater Jewish community, the Rothschilds' faith is inextricably linked to their family—both would be endangered by fully intercultural, familial relations with Gentiles.

Despite its divisive impact, Salomon is determined to push the marriage through. This sets up the drama's decisive final scenes, which were unedited in the FGS's promptbook. The Duke arrives in the alley, proposes to Löttchen, and, although the marriage would force her to renounce her religion, rejoices over the fusion of the two faiths as a sign of progress. The timing of his remarks, just before receiving a loan of one million florins, casts doubt on his sincerity. Gudula rejects his views along with her new title of baroness, saying she is an elderly Jewess, not nobility. Gudula's unwavering sense of Jewish identity convinces Löttchen to reject the Duke, explaining that he has come a century too soon. Instead, she marries her young uncle, Jacob. Rejecting the notion that Jews are eternal wanderers, she argues that her "home" is in Jewish faith and culture.[70] She neither confirms nor dismisses the possibility of integration in the long term, but by marrying Jacob, Löttchen commits to preserving her family's Jewish heritage. Gudula praises the choice as a return to community, tradition, and thus, happiness. Finally, Salomon capitulates and affirms his mother's triumph as proper and just.

The published edition of Rössler's *The Five Frankfurters* can be interpreted as a patient appeal for full integration. The Kaiser's decree and the Rothschilds' business relationships demonstrate functional interaction between Jews and Gentiles in legal and professional spheres. The divergent perspectives of several older characters (Gudula, the Count) and their younger counterparts (Salomon, the Duke) indicate momentum toward more complete

---

70. Promptbook, *The Five Frankfurters*, 34.

integration. Even as Löttchen refuses the Duke's hand, she admits the possibility of mixed betrothals in the future. Rössler warns that such intimate integration risks cultural and religious alienation, but he never categorically denounces bonds between Jews and Gentiles in the familial sphere.

The Free German Stage's revisions to *The Five Frankfurters* accentuated the warnings. Although he was an important supporting character in the published version, Liselott Reger's adaptation omitted the Count. In an attempt to shield theatergoers from his insults, she also deleted passages that distinguish between the Count's virulent anti-Semitism and the Duke's more moderate attitude. Without these scenes, the Duke's other progressive comments, all made in the Rothschilds' company, can be discounted as self-interested and disingenuous. Furthermore, if the spectator is unaware of the Duke's remarks in act 2, Löttchen's explanation for refusing the Duke's proposal, "You're too early, wait another century," loses its purport. In an unabridged presentation her words would reference the Duke's own ideas, independently corroborate them, and—poignantly positioned in the drama's final scene—indicate an affirmation of fuller future integration. Reger's deletions render Löttchen's words incongruent, even brusque and sarcastic. The outcome of a Jewish marriage inside Jews' Alley validates Gudula's vehement opposition to all forms of acculturation. Salomon, an enthusiastic supporter of assimilation, accedes to his mother's conservative convictions. Unlike the published play, the FGS's presentation of *The Five Frankfurters* decisively rejected closer relations between Jews and Gentiles.

Current world events influenced the reception of *The Five Frankfurters* in Buenos Aires. Emigrants at the House of Theater, most of whom were Jewish refugees, had seen efforts at integration fail disastrously. European Jews' hopes for admission into Gentile society had indeed, as Gudula prophesied, led many of them to stray from their cultural heritage and religion, a sacrifice that had met with calamitous results. Zionists argued that Nazism was cogent evidence against assimilation and in favor of a return to Jewish values. Reactions in local media advocated a corresponding interpretation of the play. The *Jüdische Wochenschau* posited the Jewish community anchored in Jews' Alley, and isolated from Christian society, as a model for future generations of Jews. Its reviewer also lauded Gudula's resolute adherence to tradition as an inspiration for a new, devout, exilic community.[71] Writing for the *Argentinisches Tageblatt*, the exiled Jewish author Balder Olden interpreted Rössler's drama as the beginning of Jewish emancipation. Praising Rössler's "entirely" Jewish philosophy, Olden criticized Salomon as a naive assimilationist, and, like the *Wochenschau*, he upheld the figure of Gudula as a model for contemporary Jewish audiences.[72] In its review, the *Diario Israelita* referred to the Free German Stage as a German-language Jewish theater, both misinterpreting its title and neglecting the Gentiles in the troupe.[73] Reception of *The Five Frankfurters* in 1941 stridently affirmed Jewish identity, and buttressed efforts to build a faith-centered community that excluded other emigrant groups.

Performed ten times from 1941 to 1944, Rössler's drama, and its reception, permit the tracking of developments within the refugee population against the backdrop of a single play. Upon its first presentation, Zionists viewed the play as an appeal to traditional Jewish values and an unmitigated indictment of integration, positions that did not correspond to the cultural affinities and religious practices of antifascist Gentile and moderate Jewish theatergoers. By 1944, this divergence had degenerated into unconcealed conflict. Amid reports of genocide in Europe, a position of uncompromising animosity toward all Gentile Germans gained currency among Zionists in Argentina. Most actors at the FGS, by contrast, believed in the possibility of a reformed, multicultural postwar Germany, putting them at odds with some spectators, especially Zionists. When the troupe produced *The Five Frankfurters* in 1944 to celebrate Rössler's eightieth birthday and its own 100th premiere, the cast seized the occasion to disseminate a message of tolerance and inclusion. On bilingual programs, they wrote a letter to "Papa Rössler" on behalf of the entire FGS community,

---

71. "*Die fünf Frankfurter,*" *JW*, June 27, 1941.
72. "Brief an Carl Rössler," *AT*, June 21, 1941.
73. "*Die fünf Frankfurter,*" *El Diario Israelita*, June 27, 1941.

"public, thespians, and director." Contradicting Olden's analysis of Rössler's "entirely" Jewish philosophy, the letter hoped for a new Germany guided by the dramatist's liberal, tolerant, and cosmopolitan attitude.[74] During the festivities Paul Walter Jacob thanked numerous supporters, but, conspicuously, not the Zionist *Jüdische Wochenschau*. The letter and speech reflected fallout between moderate Jewish and Gentile antifascists on the one hand, and Zionists on the other.

The final performance of *The Five Frankfurters* engendered stark dissension among Jewish refugees.[75] One theatergoer took offense that the company had written its letter to Rössler on behalf of the entire audience and underlined what he considered to be the most offensive passages, including the hope for a "happy future."[76] Rabbi Günter Friedländer, cofounder of the *Jüdische Wochenschau*, complained that Jacob publicly allied himself with the religiously neutral press organs to the detriment of the Zionist *Wochenschau*. It was hard to believe, he continued, that this behavior was not politically motivated. After specifically citing the production of *The Five Frankfurters* as the immediate impetus for his reproaches, Friedländer demanded that the "Jewish" Free German Stage alter its posture.[77] From 1941 to 1944, the reception of Rössler's *The Five Frankfurters* reveals marked deterioration in relations between Zionists, who renounced Europe altogether, and antifascists, who were convinced that a reformed postwar Germany was possible. Divergences are traceable to the drama's premiere, yet by its final presentation interactions among public pillars of the refugee population, including the FGS, the *Argentinisches Tageblatt*, and the *Jüdische Wochenschau*, were increasingly characterized by open animus.

Rössler's *The Five Frankfurters* and Brandon Thomas's *Charley's Aunt* underscore the capacity of dramatic performances to vitalize the past and bring individual experience to bear on collective

---

74. Program, *The Five Frankfurters*, May 24, 1944, PWJA VI b) 281.
75. Spectator (signature illegible) to Jacob, May 26, 1944, PWJAK.
76. Rodolfo Rauscher to Jacob, May 26, 1944, PWJAK.
77. Friedländer to Jacob, June 2, 1944, PWJAK.

projects of identity formation and community building. Depictions of distant and recent history at the FGS deviated from published editions of the works. The ensemble deliberately put the personal, polemical, and often private topics of memory, solidarity, integration, and future prospects onstage, sharing them with its audience and catapulting them into public discourse. The ensuing conversations were charged with mercurial theatrical energies that could both cohere and cleave the nascent communities under construction. Recognized by all as a puissant player among the emigrant population's grappling factions, the FGS struggled to steer its sway. Some presentations potentiated polemics in ways that were unintended and even antithetical to the theater's own objectives.

Pedro Pico and Samuel Eichelbaum's *The Nutshell*

The Free German Stage was founded with the explicit aim of fostering intercultural inclusion and integration through theater. The ensemble advocated internationalism through its repertoire: within its first four months of performances, it presented dramatists of six different nationalities, almost all of whom were banned in Nazi Germany, and was reviewed in the German, Spanish, English, Yiddish, Hungarian, and Czech press.[78] Many luminaries of the Argentine theater world also attended productions at the FGS. Playwright/director Chas de Cruz spoke for many: "As an Argentine, I am proud that it is in my country that this enterprise undertakes its magnificent labor."[79] At the same time as they enable intercultural communication, dramatic performances also make visible the play of difference and identity between immigrant and host cultures. Presentations often blended Argentine and German cultural markers. Before the performance of Carl Rössler's

---

78. "Jean, Lustspiel von Ladislaus Bus-Fekete," *JW*, April 26, 1940; "Dos Funciones de Teatro Alemán Ofrecerán Hoy," *Notícias Gráficas*, April 27, 1940; "Free German Stage," *Buenos Aires Herald (BAH)* April 9, 1940; *Di Presse*, August 13, 1940; "Független Német Szinház," *Délamerikai Magyarság*, July 20, 1940; "Lidé Na Kre," *Czecoslovakia Libre*, July 22, 1940.

79. Cruz to Jacob, August 16, 1948, PWJA VI h) 299.

The Five Frankfurters on July 9, 1941, Argentina's independence day, the theater played the Argentine national anthem. Midway through the hymn the curtain rose to reveal the set for the first scene of the drama—the Rothschild family home in Frankfurt's Jews' Alley.[80] Such occasions were interactive sites of willingness for and resistance to integration. The FGS showcased successful interculturalism, but it also exposed disharmony between the refugee population and their Argentine hosts.

A landmark in the integration of German and Argentine cultures onstage was the FGS's production of *The Nutshell* (1922) by Pedro E. Pico and Samuel Eichelbaum on June 28, 1941, the first performance ever of an Argentine drama in German. Both dramatists were widely respected figures in the local theater world. A prolific playwright whose oeuvre is dominated by comedies with a leftist political tilt, Pico also served as president of the House of Theater and the Argentine Authors' Association. The son of Jewish immigrants from Russia, Samuel Eichelbaum was a dramatist, journalist, and critic for many influential publications in Argentina, including *Caras y Caretas*, *La Nación*, and the *Jüdische Wochenschau*. Eichelbaum was one of the most renowned writers of his generation and won Argentina's exalted National Drama Prize in 1957.

The Nutshell is not a famous play, so some foregrounding is useful. In the early twentieth century, it was common for Argentine men to be married to women of high social standing and simultaneously carry on affairs with women of a lower class. Eichelbaum and Pico imagined that such an affair could hold a moral dilemma whose outcome is tragic and comic at once. The drama's protagonist, Ricardo, marries Maria Victoria, a wealthy heiress, without ending an ongoing romantic relationship with a poor schoolteacher, Alicia. Comfortably married, Ricardo is ready to terminate the affair when Alicia becomes pregnant. When the child is born, and his marriage with Maria Victoria remains infertile, Ricardo realizes that the pull of Alicia's squalid shack, the "nutshell," is stronger

---

80. "Die zweite Spielzeit der Freien Deutschen Bühne," *AT*, July 9, 1941.

than his legitimate, luxurious, but childless home. Maria Victoria fights for Ricardo, but without malice toward her rival. Ricardo hesitates, but then his son falls gravely ill. As the child lies sick in bed, Ricardo realizes that his paternal instincts surpass all other affections. For her part, Maria Victoria knows the child's death would signify her triumph, but she never utters such a malevolent wish. The baby's rescue is her perdition, and when she learns her husband's son will survive, an afflicted Maria Victoria exits the scene with tragic grace.

The production of *The Nutshell* brought Argentine customs and moral values closer to a public still adapting to its new environs. *La Nación* described the choice as daring. It considered that in a subtle but profound way, the play's plot and especially its conclusion presented to recent immigrants a world that was particularly Argentine.[81] *La Nación* believed that Ricardo's abandonment of his wife, although she does him no wrong, rendered the play foreign to European spectators. Moreover, this action goes unpunished. The *Jüdische Wochenschau*, too, viewed *The Nutshell* as a fundamental departure from European values. As the play was set in Argentina, its reviewer asserted, neither the drama's outcome nor Ricardo's actions needed to adhere to European morality or social norms. Instead the plot turns on one man's search for happiness, which he finds in fatherhood. Law and order are subordinate to parenthood, and the Argentine spirit holds sway.[82] Writing for the *Argentinisches Tageblatt*, Balder Olden argued that in the context of modern European literature Ricardo's actions are nonconformist precisely because he finds happiness by founding a family. Olden accounted for this divergence by contrasting American and European visions of nationhood. Citing the nineteenth-century Argentine political theorist Juan Bautista Alberdi, he argued that a new nation's path to growth and greatness passes through the health and proliferation of its families. Olden found this principle reaffirmed in *The Nutshell*, in which the good of the nuclear

---

81. "Teatro Alemán Independiente," *LN*, June 19, 1941.
82. "*Die Nussschale*," *JW*, July 4, 1941.

family trumps all other concerns.[83] This transitional drama conveyed crucial contrasts between Europe and Argentina to emigrant theatergoers, with the intention of facilitating their adaptation to the latter.

Both Pico and Eichelbaum attended the performance in person and received ovations after the second and third acts. Pico wrote an open letter to theatergoers, which was printed in programs for the event. Expressing his wish that the production would trigger a vibrant exchange between "German and Argentine brothers in art," Pico posited live theater as a form of communication powerful enough, in his opinion, to overcome the barrier of language.[84] Addressing the audience directly, Eichelbaum saw in theater a conduit to intercultural understanding among artists and spectators.[85] A bilingual production, the program featured Pico's note in Spanish and summarized the play and its reception in both languages. In the Argentine daily *Crítica*, Liselott Reger promoted the upcoming performance as proof that the true spiritual and cultural Germany, that of Heine and Goethe, was united with other nations by humanist values that could never be extinguished.[86] At the event itself, Paul Walter Jacob emphasized the troupe's goal that art would bring all nations together in a new egalitarian spirit of the future.[87] Confronting the German embassy in Buenos Aires, polyglot antifascist artists from host and immigrant cultures envisioned and strove to create an intercultural society characterized by tolerance, awareness, and cooperation.

Many emigrants resisted their efforts. They sought in theater a retreat from the challenges of integration, preferring escapism and nostalgia to engagement. The *Jüdische Wochenschau* took its readership to task for lackluster attendance of *The Nutshell*, arguing that the future consisted either in integration with Jewish Argentine society or, hopefully, aliyah to Eretz Israel. It was

---

83. "*Die Nussschale*," *AT*, June 30, 1941.
84. Program, *Die Nussschale*, June 28, 1941, PWJA VI b) 281.
85. "*Die Nussschale*," *AT*, June 30, 1941.
86. "Teatro Alemán Independiente," *Crítica*, April 13, 1941.
87. "*Die Nussschale*," *AT*, June 30, 1941.

Figure 4. Scene from the 1943 production of *Abie's Irish Rose* by
Anne Nichols at the Free German Stage.

Source: Fundación IWO, Alexander Berg Collection.

convinced that Jews had nothing to gain from longing for their past
lives in Europe, and scorned any possibility of rapprochement with
European nations. Therefore, *The Nutshell* should have resonated
with Jewish refugees: "One might have expected" that this presentation "would meet with broad understanding, enthusiasm, and
approval." The editor Bernhardi Swarsensky reprimanded theatergoers for their inexplicable reluctance to exit well-trodden paths,
choosing to support sanguine portrayals of an illusory, idealized
past instead of welcoming attempts to move in a new direction.[88]
Audience polls corroborate the *Wochenschau*'s criticism; for the
1941 season *The Nutshell* received only 3.2 percent of the vote for
favorite production.[89]

88. "*Die Nussschale*," *JW*, July 4, 1941.
89. Audience poll 1941, PWJA VI f) 293.

Resisting the Lighter Muse

To the chagrin of Zionists, politically engaged antifascists, and the FGS cast, theatergoers consistently chose light European comedies over political and religious dramas. Comedies played buoyant psychological and social roles among refugees, and some of them, like *The Five Frankfurters* and *The Nutshell* or even Anne Nichols's *Abie's Irish Rose* (1922), also explored more complex sociopolitical and religious themes, yet the Free German Stage was obliged to favor this genre to such an extent that political and religious activists grew disgruntled. On May 4, 1940, two weeks after the stage's inauguration, Liselott Reger affirmed in an interview to the *Tageblatt* that the cast wanted to perform the German classics and political dramas. However, Reger continued, the FGS was an independent professional theater beholden to the mandates of the ticket office. If certain groups wished to see a specific genre, she advised, they had to ensure that such dramas were well attended.[90]

The theater's attempt to include the German classics in its repertoire represents an early example of this conundrum. Considering its humanist agenda and the large number of plays it produced, it is surprising that the FGS did not put on Lessing once during World War II. An early draft of the schedule for its inaugural season in 1940 included *Minna of Barnhelm*; however, Jacob ultimately opted to replace *Minna* with Schiller's *Mary Stuart*.[91] Jacob probably made Lessing's drama his first choice because he suspected the classics would be a tough sell to his audience. He reasoned that, because it was a comedy, there would be less aversion to *Minna* than to tragedies. However, memories of a government-funded guest performance of *Minna* by the celebrity ensemble German Drama in Buenos Aires in 1934,[92] and the popularity of *Minna* in Nazi Germany—Hans Schweikart's film *The Girl from Barnhelm* (1940) was released that same year—appear to have led to the replacement of Lessing's drama with *Mary Stuart*.

---

90. "Kulturträgerinnen unter uns: Die Frau mit den drei Berufen," *AT*, May 4, 1940.

91. "Spielplan 1940," PWJA VI, f) 293.

92. See chapter 4 for the ensemble German Drama.

As the *Tageblatt* noted in previews, *Mary Stuart* was an artistic and commercial "experiment."[93] The presentation was a test to gauge whether further productions of the classics were commercially viable. By staging the classics, the FGS endeavored to build an audience beyond the antifascist population. It hoped that not only recent emigrants but also "native-born and longtime residents"—an unequivocal reference to the nationalist population, often called "the old colony" because most of its members had arrived before 1933—would attend dramas such as *Mary Stuart*.[94] By all accounts, the event was an artistic success. The *Jüdische Wochenschau* reported that long, demonstrative applause emphasized the deep impression that Schiller's tragedy made on "everyone who saw it."[95] This concluding qualification shows that despite numerous appeals, attendance of the production was disappointing. Nationalists saw the Free German Stage as ideological anathema. Meanwhile, refugees appear to have rejected Schiller as a propagandized dramatist whose works emblematized the literary traditions of a nation that had ostracized and assailed them. Furthermore, theatergoers consistently shunned the tragic genre. Always just a few box-office failures from bankruptcy, the theater did not stage the German classics again until the postwar period.

Emigrant media organizations recognized the difficulty of the FGS's position, but they refused to absolve it from all responsibility. Two vigorous critics were the political group and journal *Das Andere Deutschland* and the Zionist *Jüdische Wochenschau*. Despite broad support for the FGS in the refugee population, already in August 1940 *Das Andere Deutschland* began expressing reservations about the amount of light entertainment in its repertoire. Aware that the theater would not survive if it prioritized politics over ticket sales, the journal indirectly reprimanded theatergoers for favoring comedies.[96] As time passed, its patience waned. Following the 1941 season *DAD* stated outright that it was displeased by the lack of agitprop

---

93. "Maria Stuart," *AT*, July 14, 1940.
94. "Maria Stuart," *AT*, July 11, 1940.
95. "Maria Stuart," *JW*, July 19, 1940.
96. "Ein Sieg auf der Kulturfront," *DAD*, August 1940.

theater in the FGS's program, insisting that any "free German stage" had certain inexorable obligations as an anti-Nazi institution. The antifascist mouthpiece also chastised the so-called comedy public, which it accused of striking against political presentations.[97] Finally, *DAD* advised that in 1942 it expected more political dramas.

The *Jüdische Wochenschau* initially refrained from criticizing the Free German Stage, believing it morally imperative to support Jewish artists. It also recognized and valued the psychological uplift and community-building function the theater provided to all Jewish refugees. Eventually, however, it too grew exasperated. When, in 1943, the stage put on A. A. Milne's comedy *Mr. Pim Passes By* (1919) to celebrate ensemble member Josef Halpern's forty-fifth career anniversary, the *Wochenschau* questioned why a worthier work had not been chosen for the occasion.[98] Reviews disclosed widening divergences between the uncompromising *Wochenschau* and the more indulgent *Argentinisches Tageblatt*. Earlier, both publications had accepted laughter as an end unto itself. In two years' time, the *Tageblatt*'s posture had changed only slightly. When the FGS played Ludwig Hirschfeld's comedy *The Swedish Match* (1933) on June 11, 1943, the *Tageblatt* praised the performance and made no reproach to an audience looking for nothing but laughs.[99] The *Wochenschau* demurred. It castigated the troupe for stagnating in plays that were neither innovative nor inspirational, but squarely pinned the blame on a public that chose shallow comedies over serious dramas. Caustically invoking refugees' struggles, it wondered "if this crowd's nerves are so shot that it's happy for any joke that lets it laugh."[100] The *Wochenschau* was no longer willing to accept the past as a reason to evade the present.

Two weeks later, after the premiere of Elmer Rice's *Flight to the West* (1940), the paper approved the selection while advising that this presentation should initiate a run of provocative period plays, lest the Free German Stage should fail to live up to its name,

97. "Freie Deutsche Bühne," *DAD*, December 1941.

98. "*Mr. Pimm kommt vorbei*," *JW*, May 7, 1943.

99. "*Das schwedische Zündholz*," *AT*, June 6, 1943.

100. "*Das schwedische Zündholz*," *JW*, June 11, 1943.

especially in such a year as 1943.[101] The *Tageblatt*, on the other hand, reiterated that both contemporary political dramas and simple comedies had a place in the repertoire. Both papers had critical words for the audience, however, betraying varying degrees of impatience. The *Tageblatt*, which hitherto had abstained from criticizing theatergoers, gave them a gentle slap on the wrist for their distaste for anything that was not a comedy from yesteryear. Its critic patiently speculated that in time the FGS would inspire its audience to antifascist activism, citing Rice's North American compatriots as an example of isolationists who had been convinced to combat Nazism.[102] The *Jüdische Wochenschau* did not mince words. Accusing Jewish emigrants of egoism and apathy, the paper denounced spectators for closing their eyes to the sufferings of others, "satisfied enough to have saved their own precious lives." Dismissing apolitical, less religious Jews as worthless for the construction of a better future—let alone for influencing a theater's program—the *Wochenschau* warned that their posture risked exclusion from the refugee community.[103]

Nonetheless, most theatergoers continued to favor benign comedies, and their predilections did indeed shape the repertoire. After *Flight to the West*, which was more successful in the media than at the ticket office, the FGS presented Ladislaus Fodor's comedy *Dr. Juci Szabo* (1926). Whereas the *Tageblatt* emphasized the cast's acting and the audience's enthusiasm,[104] the *Wochenschau* decried the choice as a regression and disparaged Fodor's piece as superfluous and outmoded. It saved its most scathing criticism for theatergoers:

> This review should be entitled: "Criticism of the Audience." This is the formula for many reviews lately. . . . The FGS serves theatergoers, who desire nothing but comedies. They enjoy themselves more easily than at the cinema, where one at least must read the subtitles or understand the language.[105]

---

101. "*Flug nach dem Westen*," *JW*, June 25, 1943.
102. "*Flug nach dem Westen*," *AT*, June 20, 1943.
103. "*Flug nach dem Westen*," *JW*, June 25, 1943.
104. "*Dr. Juci Szabo*," *AT*, June 26, 1943.
105. "*Dr. Juci Szabo*," *JW*, July 2, 1943.

The *Wochenschau* suggested the theater conduct an audience survey, claiming that the comedy public endangered the whole enterprise, but comedies consistently outdid most serious dramas in audience polls.[106] The ultimate barometer was the box office, and here comedy was king.

Numerous political and religious groups argued that the disproportionate number of simple, profitable comedies in the FGS's repertoire compromised its objectives of community building, integration with Argentine society, and competition against the nationalist German presence in Argentina. Though correct to a degree, this evaluation is myopic. First, serious dramas and even some comedies stoked tensions within the anti-Hitler population. Second, quite a few comedies were about more than ticket sales and escapism. Light humor provided an imperative psychological uplift for audience and ensemble alike. It contributed to community building, at least among the so-called comedy public, which comprised most theatergoers. Comedies such as *Charley's Aunt*, *The Five Frankfurters*, and *The Nutshell* blended laughter with serious psychological, social, and political issues. The latter play in particular helped the stage to construct crucial networks with influential figures in the local Argentine entertainment industry. In the first two, performing history in the theatrical present provoked emotive discussions about coping with the trauma of racial persecution and the travails of the refugee experience, as well as debates on the interlinked themes of identity, religion, and integration.

Finally, in the last analysis, the FGS simply would not have survived without popular, profitable comedies. Without them, the enterprise almost certainly would have gone the way of other emigrant ensembles in the United States, Mexico, Palestine, and China—all of which either quickly failed or performed very irregularly.[107] For its refugee ensemble, this would have been a disastrous, perhaps even mortal setback. The great risk, of course, was that the theater would succeed as a business but fail elsewhere. Aware

---

106. Audience polls 1940–1942, PWJA VI f) 293.

107. Maaß, *Repertoire der deutschsprachigen Exilbühnen, 1933–1945*, 40, 60–64, 69–73, 95–116.

of this dilemma, the company tried to strike a balance. Paul Walter Jacob's polemical strategy from Wuppertal, to fund serious drama through profitable comedies, was the modus operandi in Buenos Aires. Though they were a comparatively small proportion of its repertoire, the FGS staged far more literary, political, and religious dramas than any other exilic theater. Moreover, without its anti-fascist opponent, the Nazified German Theater would have stood alone. Decades later, Jacques Arndt subordinated all the compromises and shortcomings to a single, transcendent accomplishment: throughout World War II, the only professional, anti-Nazi, exilic theater worldwide was the Free German Stage in Buenos Aires, Argentina.[108]

Confrontation and Conflict: Political and Religious Dramas, 1940–1945

An outspoken Social Democrat, Paul Walter Jacob vigorously defended his political convictions in the progressive Forward Club and the antifascist radio program *The Voice of the Day*, as well as in the political journal *Das Andere Deutschland* and the *Argentinisches Tageblatt*. As manager of the Free German Stage, however, Jacob's approach to politics was extremely cautious. The stage had to navigate the interests of distinct, often conflicting groups, including financial backers, antifascist activists, and Zionists. Plus, its cast was composed of actors with divergent political and religious views. In addition to tensions within the refugee population, the enterprise was subject to the politics, laws, and whims of Argentine authorities, which generally were unfavorable to antifascist organizations. Furthermore, the larger, wealthier, nationalist colony and official representatives of the Nazi government in Buenos Aires were antagonistic to the stage. The German embassy could harm the troupe in Argentina and also caused its members to fear retaliation against their families in Europe.[109]

---

108. Arndt, interview, 2008.
109. Jacob to Pauly, August 27, 1942, PWJAK.

Caution dictated Jacob's approach even before the FGS's debut, initially scheduled for August 1939. As he recalled, all preparations had been made when the outbreak of war in Europe provoked the postponement of the inauguration until the following April. During this crisis, donors, ensemble, and administration alike were concerned about potential repercussions from Argentine authorities. Of the four Argentine presidents during World War II, Roberto Ortiz (1938–42) was the only pro-Allies head of state. Scholars have argued that should have caused Jacob to feel a measure of security, yet the volatility of Argentine politics meant a profascist regime could come to power at any time.[110] Already in 1939 Ortiz suffered from severe diabetes, which eventually blinded him and forced him to cede the daily execution of his office to the vice president, Ramón Castillo, in July 1940. A fascist sympathizer, Castillo officially assumed the presidency in 1942, and under his authority Argentine politics shifted drastically to the right. Jacob and his sponsors also feared disruption by the nationalist German population, such as the riots that the German consulate had organized to sabotage productions of Ferdinand Bruckner's *Race* at the Comic Theater in 1934.[111] A similar affair at the House of Theater would have had cataclysmal consequences for the nascent FGS.

When the FGS opened in 1940, its guarded approach to tendentious drama continued even as it simultaneously attempted to placate political organizations, such as *Das Andere Deutschland*. Although *DAD* showed comprehension of the financial complexities facing the stage, it expected political agitprop theater. *DAD* enthusiastically promoted Maurice Rostand's pacifist drama *The Man I Killed* (1930), scheduled for April 1940, as an appeal for German-French fraternity and reconciliation, "a goal that we all desperately desire."[112] Bitterly disappointed when Jacob abruptly

---

110. Pohle, ""Paul Walter Jacob am Rio de la Plata: Der Kurs der FDB—eine exilpolitische Gratwanderung," 40; Trapp, "Zwischen Unterhaltungsfunktion und der Erwartung politischer Stellungnahme." Both Pohle and Trapp note infighting among refugees, but do not consider other threats to the stage.

111. Willi Köhn to MP, December 18, 1934, Band R55, Akte 20553, BB.

112. "Freie Deutsche Bühne," *DAD*, March 15, 1940.

replaced Rostand's play with Ibsen's *Master Builder* (1892), *DAD* speculated that a section of the FGS public had threatened to boycott *The Man I Killed* because they opposed its pacifist message.[113] In this context, the wording "we all" from its preview can be read as a preemptive effort to counteract protests against the play.[114] The conflict surrounding Rostand's drama pitted believers in the fundamental moral integrity of Europe, such as *DAD*, against others who had permanently renounced Europe and especially Germany—namely, Zionists. Sensing this as a warning of future confrontations, *DAD* urged immediate dialogue, identifying the debate as a decisive, fundamental question.[115] As early as 1940, conflicting views on issues of collective German guilt portended the polarization of the refugee population. Jacob later remembered the affair as a major altercation with his cast, public, and political associates.[116] Divisions among refugees, though yet to fully erupt, were already widespread on both sides of the curtain. Furthermore, promotions of Ibsen's drama as a timeless work relevant to all spectators in all countries also reflect efforts to mollify hostilities.[117] The replacement of *The Man I Killed* with *Master Builder* represented a calculated move away from divisive contemporary politics toward universal, enduring moral questions.

Contemporary political dramas also risked inciting Argentine authorities and nationalist Germans, obliging the FGS to line edit its promptbooks and omit any potentially polemical material. When the stage produced Bruno Frank's comedy *Storm in a Teacup* (1930) in 1940, Jacob deleted several passages, including probably the best-known line of the play, in which an older lady, speaking to a judge about her mixed-breed dog, blurts: "Well, it's nothing for Hitler anyway." Jacob explained: "Neither our political friends nor our Jewish friends understood, but I knew that if Hitler were named on a foreign-language stage in Buenos Aires, the

---

113. "Abgesetzt!" *DAD*, May 15, 1940.
114. "Freie Deutsche Bühne," *DAD*, March 15, 1940.
115. "Abgesetzt!" *DAD*, May 15, 1940.
116. PWJA VIII c) 454.
117. Jacob, *Sieben Jahre Freie Deutsche Bühne in Buenos Aires*, 29.

police would ban the Free German Stage the next day."[118] Already splitting his public into distinct groups, Jacob unequivocally stated that concerns about running afoul of the Argentine government motivated this self-censorship. The FGS took care to avoid political controversy during its infancy, because this was the surest strategy of preventing trouble with local authorities *and* of circumventing quarrels among refugees. Passages naming Hitler directly, even in a comedy like *Storm in a Teacup*, were deemed too hazardous for the new enterprise. With the lone exception of Vilém Werner's *Men on Ice* (1936), which is more concerned with generational conflict and moral decay than current politics, during the entire 1940 season the FGS did not produce a single play written after 1933.

Nonetheless, it was impossible for the theater to elude all controversy. Even before the debut of the FGS, *La Nación* introduced the troupe as artists who were forced to suspend their work on stages in Germany.[119] With an ensemble composed entirely of European refugees, most of whom were Jewish, it was a fait accompli that the group would be viewed as an antifascist entity. Moreover, as *La Nación* noted, the actors had claimed a political platform by naming themselves the Free German Stage. Local press outlets compelled them to choose sides. Before the theater's inauguration, the British *Buenos Aires Herald* sent a journalist to verify that the FGS was an anti-Nazi stage. During an interview with the *Herald*, Liselott Reger and Hermann Geiger-Torel took unequivocally antifascist positions on international events. Geiger-Torel declared that the cast stood with the British against Nazi Germany. Reger, who had acted in Czechoslovakia from 1928 to 1938, debunked the German propaganda effort leading to the 1938 Munich Agreement: "There was no repression. . . . Masaryk and Benes allowed all German expression there. To say the Czechoslovakia ill-treated its German minority was a lie."[120] In these declarations, the FGS affirmed its antifascist principles and indicted Nazi German diplomacy to a publication outside the refugee colony and in a language

---

118. PWJA VIII c) 454.

119. "Ofrecerá su primera función hoy el Teatro Alemán Independiente," *LN*, April 20, 1940.

120. "Free German Stage," *BAH*, April 9, 1940.

spoken far more widely in Argentina than German. Word spread quickly.

German ambassador Edmund von Thermann included a clipping of the article in a report to Berlin, describing Geiger-Torel's and Reger's comments as poisonous to the new Germany. The embassy's report included analysis of banned authors in the FGS's repertoire, as well as of the theater's advertising, ticket sales, and its potential to impact the greater Argentine public and theater scene. From Thermann's perspective, the greatest danger the group posed to Nazi interests was as a facilitator of integration between refugees and their Argentine hosts. Thermann evaluated the ability of the FGS to influence Argentine theater and mainstream opinion as low, claiming Argentines knew it represented an insidious anti-German propaganda campaign by Jewish emigrants, yet the ambassador's own report undercut his conclusion.[121] Although he argued that the FGS would be ineffective because few Argentines spoke German, Thermann noted that FGS productions were often reviewed in *La Prensa* and *La Nación*, two of the nation's most widely read newspapers, with a combined daily circulation of 450,000.[122] Including the *Herald* interview, Thermann's dispatch proved that the Spanish- and English-language press already covered the theater. The ambassador also mentioned that one actor, Walter Szurovy, was married to an opera singer at the Colón Theater. Though it was not included in Thermann's commentary, through cursory research Nazi officials could learn that Geiger-Torel and the actress Hedwig Schlichter-Crilla's brother, Viktor Schlichter, were well-known figures in the Argentine music scene. Finally, as a public institution and residence for local actors, the House of Theater was conducive to interaction with Argentine theater personalities. Thermann was dismissive, but his report might have raised concerns among his superiors in Germany.

Six weeks later, the Propaganda Ministry wrote to the Reich Theater Chamber blacklisting the FGS as a "Jewish enterprise"

---

121. Thermann to FO, October 4, 1940, Band R55, Akte 20553, BB.

122. In 1936 *La Prensa*'s circulation was 230,000; *La Nación*'s was 220,000 weekdays and 340,000 weekends.

and forbidding German publishers to send it any materials.[123] Then, in early 1941, an anonymous source accused Reger and Jacob of tax evasion. Only after Argentine financial regulators had scrutinized FGS accounting books, receipts, and contracts was the cast granted permission to perform the next season.[124] No direct proof exists that Nazi supporters or officials made the denouncement, but circumstances suggest suspicion of these groups. There were altercations among refugees, but an indictment of the entire theater for tax evasion would have served nobody and risked collateral damage. By contrast, the German embassy had connections to the Argentine police and fiscal authorities. During fund-raising activities, antifascist organizations repeatedly warned Jacob to be wary of Nazi chicanery.[125] Local adversaries reported on the FGS to Berlin and may have intervened against it on several occasions. Ambassador Thermann's dispatches also indicate that as the FGS gained recognition in local media and built relationships with Argentine artists, the embassy might have been provoked to intensify its campaign against the theater.

Nazi officials in Argentina and Europe took the FGS seriously, and especially worried that the antifascist troupe could weaponize integration against their interests in the region. For his part, Paul Walter Jacob feared that the nationalist population would mobilize its partnerships with Argentine institutions to attack his enterprise. As antifascists and nationalists antagonized each other, the FGS worked to cultivate intercultural networks as leverage against opposition. An example was the grand tribute for the legendary director Max Reinhardt upon his death in 1943. Although its aftermath was marred by infighting among cast members, the event was a resounding intercultural artistic and financial success.[126] Held on November 17, 1943, this spectacle of solidarity with refugee artists was attended by many celebrities of Argentine stage and screen,

---

123. MP to President of Reich Theater Chamber, November 21, 1940, Band R55, Akte 20553, BB.

124. Jacob to Berger, November 22, 1943, PWJAK.

125. PWJA VIII c) 454.

126. See above, pages 100–102.

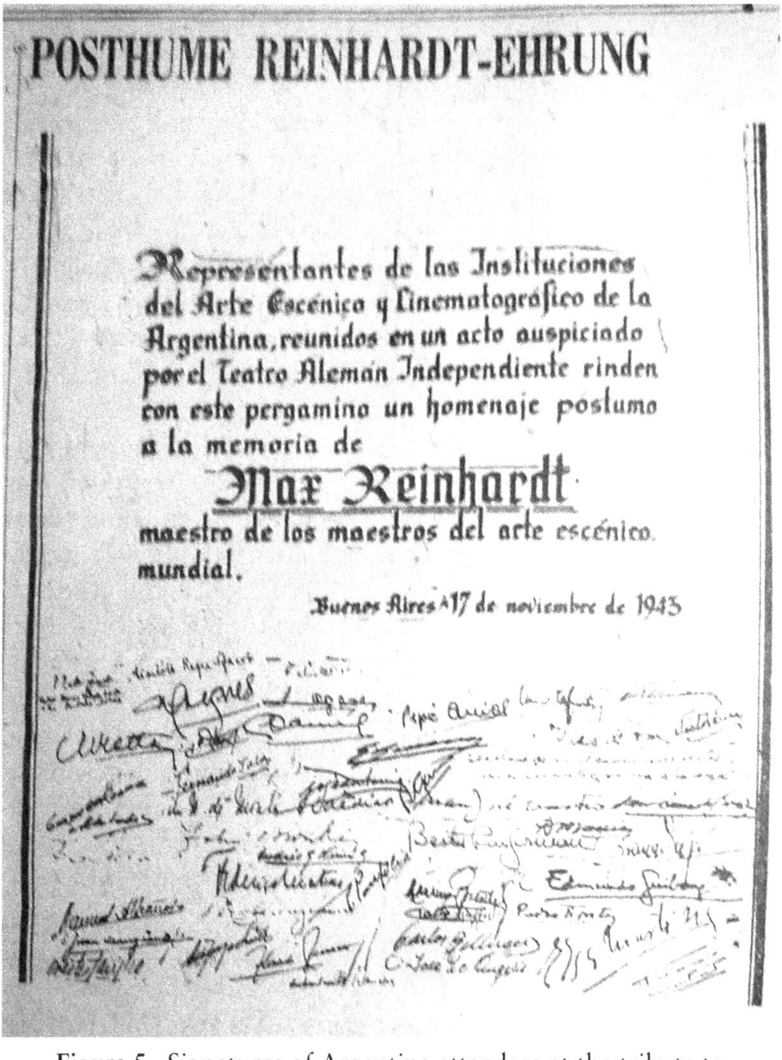

POSTHUME REINHARDT-EHRUNG

Representantes de las Instituciones del Arte Escénico y Cinematográfico de la Argentina, reunidos en un acto auspiciado por el Teatro Alemán Independiente rinden con este pergamino un homenaje postumo a la memoria de

Max Reinhardt

maestro de los maestros del arte escénico mundial.

Buenos Aires 17 de noviembre de 1943

Figure 5. Signatures of Argentine attendees at the tribute to Max Reinhardt on November 17, 1943.

Source: *Argentinisches Tageblatt*, November 17, 1943. Biblioteca Nacional Doctor Mariano Moreno—Argentina.

such as actresses Delia Garcés and Juanita Sujo, critic Chas de Cruz, actor and director Enrique de Rosas, producer Manuel Peña Rodriguez, as well as screenplay-writer, director, and producer Alberto Zavalía.[127] The event garnered the FGS notoriety in the Argentine entertainment industry, which was critical to creating the intercultural alliances the stage needed to survive. Despite their political differences, all blocs in German Buenos Aires recognized the power of integration and eventually utilized theater as a tool to achieve it.

The specter of attacks by German officials was not the only motivation to diminish conflicts with Nazi sympathizers. Like emigrant literati Balder Olden and Paul Zech, Paul Walter Jacob distinguished between local German nationalists and the German embassy, regarding many of the former as victims of propaganda and intimidation.[128] Personally convinced that theater would play a major role in reeducating Nazi supporters, as an entrepreneur he also realized that the enterprise's profits would increase significantly if it could draw audiences from throughout German Buenos Aires. As early as 1943, he began planning for this opportunity.[129] Jacob wanted to avoid an overly confrontational course with nationalist Germans because he believed the political and financial future of the FGS was hitched to both German colonies in Argentina. During World War II, the troupe could not stay afloat without backing from antifascists and Zionists, as well as from less politically and religiously engaged emigrants, so it worked to reduce infighting among these groups. Furthermore, it had to withstand aggression from the German embassy and local profascist groups. With an eye toward the postwar period, however, it also strove to achieve tenable relationships, or at least avoid open conflict, with the Argentine authorities and nationalist Germans. This daunting balancing act caused the theater's approach to political drama to be characterized by utmost caution.

It was not until 1942, when much of the Americas became directly involved in World War II, that the FGS began to put on

---

127. "En memoria de Max Reinhardt," *Noticias Graficas*, November 19, 1943.
128. "Deutsches Schauspiel 1934," *Argentinisches Wochenblatt*, June 9, 1934.
129. Jacob to Berger, November 22, 1943, PWJAK.

contemporary tendentious plays. It opened the 1942 season with Robert Ardrey's *Thunder Rock* (1939), its first presentation of a US-American playwright as well as its first serious contemporary drama. Antifascist and Zionist media organizations greeted this development enthusiastically. The Communist *Volksblatt* approved the choice and pressed for more agitprop theater. The paper asserted that it was incumbent upon Paul Walter Jacob to bring the wishes of his public in line with the moral obligations of performing exilic theater.[130] By meeting this challenge, the *Volksblatt* concluded, he could achieve greater loyalty among theatergoers, thereby improving ticket sales. Upon closer scrutiny, this strategy reflected an overly sanguine outlook. The *Jüdische Wochenschau*'s reviewer focused exclusively on the moral relevance of *Thunder Rock*, explaining that Ardrey depicted current dilemmas, which should not be withheld from those who did not attend the production.[131] This hinted at poor ticket sales, and even the *Volksblatt* acknowledged unsatisfactory attendance. Its arts section featured an exuberant review, but its youth page bemoaned empty seats and a dearth of younger spectators.[132] Despite mobilizing readers to vote for political dramas,[133] the *Volksblatt* was disappointed that *Thunder Rock* received just 6.6 percent of the vote in audience polls for the 1942 season.[134] The media did not convey the preferences of theatergoers, who still avoided tendentious plays.

Now in its third season, the Free German Stage had established itself as a popular cultural institution and entertainment venue by catering to a public that clearly preferred the lighter muse. As American nations became militarily involved in the war, however, its cast felt increasing pressure to put on more political plays.[135] In September 1942 *Das Andere Deutschland* served as a forum for Paul Walter Jacob and Hans Jahn, editor of *DAD*'s arts section, to

---

130. "*Leuchtfeuer* von Robert Ardrey," *Volksblatt*, May 7, 1942.

131. "*Leuchtfeuer*," *JW*, April 24, 1942.

132. "Jugendseite," *Volksblatt*, May 7, 1942.

133. "Fragebogen der F.D.B.," *Volksblatt*, November 1, 1942.

134. "Publikumsabstimmungen über den FDB Spielplan 1942," *AT*, November 22, 1942.

135. PWJA VIII c) 455.

exchange opinions about exilic theater. Though neither named the FGS directly, the title of Jacob's response, "Free German Theater—Today," left little doubt as to the subject of their discussion. Writing first, Jahn acknowledged that a refugee ensemble faced intimidating challenges, but he also insisted that such a theater had the ability to advance ideas that could not be expressed elsewhere and in a way that no other medium could. It must not shirk this duty. Displeased with the ratio of comedies to political dramas, Jahn addressed theatergoers. Showing sympathy for thespians whose livelihood depended on ticket sales, he scolded audiences for boycotting political dramas, forecasting the harsh judgment history would pass on "emigrant spectators."[136] In response, Jacob reiterated the case for lighter fare, emphasizing that comedies have an uplifting psychological influence on refugees. Next, departing from earlier, somewhat equivocal statements, Jacob argued that an exilic theater also must stage authors "who courageously confront our times and our world. As reflections, appeals, and accusations these plays speak to thespians and theatergoers directly."[137] Unlike in 1940, Jacob now recognized a duty to put on political plays, provoke audiences to grapple with current events, and catalyze them to action.

Jacob's deeds supported his words. In addition to *Thunder Rock*, the FGS staged *The Lamb of the Poor* (1929) by Stefan Zweig, who had twice visited Argentina before committing suicide in Brazil. In Argentina, under General Ramón Castillo's fascist military regime, Lieutenant Fauré's cry "Down with the dictatorship! Long live the republic!" represented a bold provocation.[138] The FGS had deceived the censor by deleting Fauré's lines from the summary of the play it submitted to the Argentine police.[139] Unlike its diluted rendition of *Storm in a Teacup* two years earlier, this production kept Zweig's play intact, including its most controversial passages.

In *DAD* Jacob also set forth the political convictions underpinning his evolving position on tendentious drama. Even in 1942, he

---

136. "Das Emigrantentheater und sein Publikum," *DAD*, September 1942.
137. "Freies Deutsches Theater—heute," *DAD*, September 1942.
138. PWJA VI j) 36.
139. PWJA VIII c) 455.

wrote, it still had not penetrated the collective consciousness that the truly revolutionary forces of the day were also the real conservatives. Hitler's enemies were striving for the preservation, rescue, and continued development of cultural, scientific, and artistic values. Contextualized in the pages of *DAD*, an antifascist publication, Jacob's words were unambiguous. By defining antifascists as conservatives, he rejected the Zionist position that German culture was inherently flawed. Fascism represented a recent corruption of the values of a nation that, in his view, was historically and fundamentally good. Nazism represented aberration, not essence. More explicitly, performing German-language theater in exile manifested faith in a restored and renewed postwar Germany.[140] As manager of the FGS, Jacob accommodated divergent viewpoints, but his declarations in *DAD* flatly contradicted the Zionist platform. Instead of evading religious and political themes, by 1942 Jacob was willing to engage with current political events and confront his public.

This new course was fraught with peril. In taking on Nazism and factions within the refugee colony, Jacob jeopardized the Free German Stage as a community-building institution. His new strategy found favor with international groups of antifascists in Buenos Aires, but it was sure to exacerbate the strife simmering in the emigrant population, as well provoke the ire of Nazis and German nationalists. In publicly standing with antifascists, Jacob no longer prioritized inclusion and restraint above all else. The deployment of dramatic presentations as divisive, politically charged events escalated partisanship among Argentina's German speakers. Bitter and hardened, the resultant polarization would prove very resistant to reconciliation.

Lillian Hellman's *Watch on the Rhine*

A clarion call for US-American intervention against Nazism, Lillian Hellman's *Watch on the Rhine* (1941) won the New York Drama Critics' Circle Award for best play of the 1941 season and was selected by President Roosevelt for a command performance

---

140. "Freies Deutsches Theater—heute," *DAD*, September 1942.

at the National Theater in Washington, D.C., in January 1942. In 1943, Warner Brothers produced *Watch on the Rhine* as a feature film starring Bette Davis and Paul Lukas, who won an Academy Award for best actor. Paul Walter Jacob referred to the Free German Stage's rendition of Hellman's drama as a watershed event, which made the Argentine theater world view the FGS cast as equals. Simultaneously, he remembered it as probably the most polemical presentation of the entire exile period.[141]

In December 1941, Jacob wrote to Lillian Hellman requesting her permission to put on *Watch on the Rhine* in German. He was searching, he explained, for a programmatic drama to "proclaim the antifascist position of our group."[142] Events between Jacob's letter to Hellman and the premiere rendered the selection more daring. During this period several countries bordering Argentina, including Brazil, Uruguay, and Paraguay, officially entered World War II. The United States exerted heavy pressure on Argentina to follow suit. Hellman's purpose in *Watch on the Rhine*, as the family matriarch, Fanny, says in the final scene, was to shake naïve, noninterventionist US-Americans "out of the magnolias" and make them aware of the threats fascism posed for their country and the world.[143] This message dovetailed with the aims of antifascists and Zionists, who were frustrated by emigrants' passivity. On the other hand, in a country under a profascist authoritarian regime with a large population of German nationalists, as well as official representation from Germany, Hellman's directive courted retribution. Having read and edited the script, Jacob decided that preparations had to be secretive.

To reduce the risk of preemptive actions on the part of nationalist Germans and Argentine authorities, Liselott Reger obscured the drama by translating its title to *The Unvanquished*. All advertisements referred to the play as either *The Unvanquished* or Spanish translation, *Los Invictos*, and most also omitted Hellman's name.[144] Next, Jacob wrote to the *Argentinisches Tageblatt*'s theater critic. After divulging that the piece was indeed *Watch on the*

---

141. PWJA VIII c) 455.
142. Jacob to Hellman, December 26, 1941, PWJAK.
143. Hellman, *Four Plays*, 330.
144. PWJA VI c) 289.

Rhine, Jacob explained that the volatile situation in Buenos Aires had provoked him to camouflage the play. He requested that the preview consist only of an announcement of the upcoming premiere, specifically warning against mentioning its plot and political tilt: "If the other side finds out, we can expect disturbances."[145] The *Tageblatt* obliged, and the premiere occurred as scheduled.[146]

Hellman's play unfolds in the Farrelly family home near Washington, D.C., in 1940. The matriarch, Fanny Farrelly, presides over a household whose inhabitants include her adult son, David, and a couple formed by an American friend of the family, Marthe, and her husband, Teck de Brancovis, an opportunist Romanian count, who collaborates with the German embassy. Forced into a loveless marriage with Teck, Marthe is engaged in a budding romance with David that brightens the drama with a campy subplot. The action begins when Fanny's daughter, Sara, returns home with her three children and husband, Kurt Müller, a German engineer, with whom she has been living in Europe. Suspicious, Teck searches the Müllers' room and finds money intended to finance underground antifascist operations in Germany. Shortly thereafter, Kurt learns that a fellow resistance fighter has been arrested in Berlin, and he resolves to return to Germany to assist him. Aware that Kurt will be in peril if the Nazis discover him, Teck demands $10,000 to keep silent, so Kurt kills him. Throughout the drama Fanny and David are reluctant to recognize the menace of Nazism, but now, finally convinced, they agree to hide the body and help Kurt escape.

The Unvanquished was eminently suitable for the environment of Buenos Aires in 1942. The Farrelly household is a diasporic space in which natives share ground with foreigners, who comprise supporters and victims of Nazism. Like the Argentine capital, the Farrelly home is territory in play, wedged among opposing groups who vie for influence. The FGS believed Hellman's drama would resonate among its public and bolster antifascist movements in Argentina; however, it also realized the play could stir controversy among refugees. While the translated title served to hide the

145. Jacob to Reinhard Pauly, August 27, 1942, PWJAK.

146. "Südamerikanische und deutschsprachige Erstaufführung von *Die Unbesiegten*," *AT*, August 28, 1942.

drama from nationalist Germans and the Argentine censors, Liselott Reger's translation of the original script incorporated numerous changes targeting the local audience. Notably, her translation was void of religious references. For example, she changed the name of Kurt's wife from Sara to Judith. Since a 1938 Nazi decree required all Jewish females to carry the name of Sara, theatergoers might have believed Kurt's wife was Jewish, which was not Hellman's intent.[147] Kurt's story about how he became an antifascist was edited, too. In Hellman's script, Kurt brings this monologue to its climax by quoting Martin Luther: "I say with Luther, 'Here I stand. God help me. Amen.' "[148] Reger included these lines, but Jacob, who directed the production, subsequently cut off the monologue directly before the reference to Luther.[149] The FGS closely edited its depiction of Kurt and his family to emphasize the potential in each person, regardless of religion, nationality, or political affiliation, to respond to the call of conscience and fight Nazism.

German antifascists in Argentina were convinced that despite Nazi crimes, German culture and character were not inherently bellicose or racist. Organizations such as *Das Andere Deutschland* avowed time and again that an extensive underground anti-Hitler resistance network existed in Germany. The anti-Nazi resistance fighter Kurt Müller, a Gentile, lent credence to this thesis.[150] Moreover, Kurt retains a sense of patriotism where, as he says, it is appropriate.[151] Hellman's contention that true German patriots rejected National Socialism dovetailed with Jacob's own views, but the two versions of the play diverged profoundly on Nazi culpability. Reger's translation of one conversation is so irreconcilable with the English original that it is expedient to cite both, beginning with Hellman's text:

Kurt: We may well some day have pity. They are lost men, their spoils are small, their day is gone. (*To Teck*) Yes?

---

147. Second Ordinance on the Implementation of the Law on the Change of Family Names and First Names, August 17, 1938.

148. Hellman, *Four Plays*, 277.

149. *Die Unbesiegten*, PWJA VI j) 329, 14.

150. *Die Unbesiegten*, PWJA VI j) 329, 32–33.

151. *Die Unbesiegten*, PWJA VI j) 329, 34.

Teck: (*slowly*) You have an understanding heart. It will get in your way
       some day.
Kurt: (*smiles*) I will watch it.[152]

Reger's German text, translated into English, reads:

Kurt: They are lost men, their spoils are small, their day is gone. (*To Teck*)
       Yes?
Teck: (*slowly*) You have an understanding heart, Mr. Müller. Things will
       turn out the way you expect.
Kurt: We'll make sure of it.[153]

Some of the slippage could be mistranslation rather than willful
deviation but, in either case, theatergoers in Buenos Aires saw a
profoundly different version of this scene than that witnessed by
North American audiences. First, Reger deleted Kurt's line about
"pity" for National Socialists. As refugees performing for spectators who had suffered persecution under Hitler in Europe, the Free
German Stage was unyielding on questions of Nazi culpability. Second, Teck's and Kurt's comments on the latter's "understanding
heart" are conflictive. In Hellman's dialogue Kurt's sense of empathy is a potential vulnerability, but the translation shows only a
keen and confident perception of the struggle between Nazis and
antifascists. Further, in the original play Teck doubts an antifascist
victory. In the German production, by contrast, both men agree
that antifascism will triumph. A warning to Nazi officials and collaborators, these lines likely intended to boost the morale of antifascists, whose situation in Argentina was precarious.

Although Hellman's depiction of Germans and Nazi collabo-
rators is nuanced, she does not downplay the danger that Nazi
officials represent. The true menace in the play is the German
embassy in Washington, D.C. Viewers never see the agents—they
remain ominous figures lurking offstage, much as most refugees
experienced Nazi officials in Buenos Aires.[154] All real peril in the

---

152. Hellman, *Four Plays*, 316.
153. *Die Unbesiegten*, PWJA VI j) 329, 33.
154. "Nazidiplomaten in Südamerika," *AT*, July 23, 1941; "Naziverschwörun-
gen," *AT*, August 12, 1941; "Nazitätigkeiten in Argentinien," *AT*, August 28, 1941.

drama emanates from the embassy. German diplomats enable
Teck to discover Kurt's identity, and their presence provides the
count with leverage to blackmail him. The embassy's illicit business with a contraband munitions dealer conveys its involvement
in larger-scale machinations. Hellman's portrayal of the German
government's parasitic arm in the United States bears uncanny
parallels to Nazi diplomats in Argentina. In October 1943 Oscar
Alberto Hellmuth, a German-Argentine carrying an Argentine
diplomatic passport, was intercepted at Trinidad by British forces
while on a secret mission to Germany. In collusion with German
officials in Buenos Aires, the fascist president of Argentina, Pedro
Pablo Ramirez, had sent Hellmuth to Berlin to purchase German
weapons and smuggle them to Argentina. The event, which rendered Argentina a pariah in the Americas, manifested the insidious
influence that Hellman claimed Nazi diplomats exerted on host
countries.[155]

An influential political drama, Hellman's play is also accessible
family entertainment. The Müller's children synthesize moments of
comic relief with a compelling motive for antifascist activism—the
future of the world's youth. Nine-year-old Bodo communicates his
father's weltanschauung with a simple vocabulary and an endearing
delivery. The drama's romantic relationships also contributed to its
appeal. Kurt's passionate farewell kiss to Judith resembles a Hollywood love story, and the final scene in which Marthe and David
affirm their love is more dime-novel romance than political theater.
Reviewers from the *New Republic* to the *Argentinisches Tageblatt*
lamented this subplot as a dispensable concession to mainstream
audiences, yet Hellman's self-proclaimed goal was to galvanize ordinary citizens to fight Nazism, and these scenes served that end.[156]
Other dramas with similar intent, such as Ardrey's *Thunder
Rock*, made fewer concessions but had limited reach. The FGS
put on *Thunder Rock* for 550–600 people; attendance of *The*

---

155. "Erklärungen des nordamerikanischen Staatsdepartementes," *AT*,
July 28, 1944; "Pressestimmen über Argentiniens Politik," *AT*, August 10, 1944;
"Wirtschaftskrieg gegen Argentinien," *AT*, August 19, 1944.
156. "*Die Unbesiegten* von Lillian Hellman," *AT*, August 31, 1942.

Unvanquished numbered in the thousands.[157] *The Unvanquished* won polls for favorite drama of 1942 with 23 percent of the vote, a huge proportion given that twenty-five dramas were in the running.[158]

The biographical overlaps among Hellman's characters, the cast, and theatergoers added poignancy. On November 14, 1942, the FGS presented *The Unvanquished* to a sold-out audience at Uruguay's national opera house with the young actor Frank Nelson playing the role of Bodo for the first time. Although he was instructed to wear a brave face as Kurt leaves in the final scene, the departure evoked such overwhelming memories of Nelson's own flight from Europe that he began to sob onstage.[159] In this scene Nelson's semiotic body, rooted in dramatic text and representing Bodo Müller, disappeared amid the true tears of his phenomenal person, his bodily being-in-the-world, thus violating the boundary differentiating the character being played and the actor's own body.[160] Transgression against the phenomenal/semiotic boundary can cause concern for the physical or emotional integrity of the actor, thus violating the rules of theatrical performance. The audience should feel compassion for the character within the framework of the fictional work, but not for the actor himself. In case of the contrary, the relationship between the spectators and the actor changes profoundly, becoming less professional and more personal.

Nelson was so appalled by his outburst that he was ashamed to face the crowd after the final curtain, but the audience empathized with him.[161] They reacted to Nelson as refugees who had suffered firsthand the anguish of departing from loved ones without knowing if a reunion would ever take place. When the director dragged Nelson back onstage, he was greeted with an ovation. His mistake as an actor added solidarity to the theatrical spectacle.

---

157. "Theater und Literatur," *DAD*, October 1942.
158. "Die Publikums-Abstimmung über den FDB-Spielplan 1942," *AT*, November 22, 1942.
159. Roca, *Días del Teatro*, 189.
160. Fischer-Lichte, *Theatre, Sacrifice, Ritual*, 4–5.
161. Roca, *Días del Teatro*, 189.

The *Tageblatt* noted the strong resonance among the public,[162] and Paul Walter Jacob later remembered the evening as the most emotional of his career.[163] Unlike Jacques Arndt's miscue a few years earlier, Nelson's error launched decades of success as an actor in South America. In Vienna a racially exclusive community rejected Arndt's phenomenal identity as a Jew; however, the spectators-cum-community in Uruguay empathized with Nelson as fellow refugees.

The Müller family's life as impoverished refugees on the run overlapped with that of thespians and theatergoers alike. In one scene Kurt Müller merged his biography with the many anonymous emigrants on the River Plate, referring to himself as a *"not* famous exile."[164] By adding italics absent from the original script, the FGS willfully emphasized these parallels. Most spectators, including many Jews, identified with the Gentile Müllers, whose travails recalled their own. Referencing Kurt's background as an exiled antifascist activist, Paul Walter Jacob claimed that the play was the FGS ensemble's "self-portrayal."[165] Not everybody agreed with him.

Zionists and antifascists clashed over Hellman's drama, and especially over the character of Kurt Müller. In a programmatically worded review, the *Tageblatt* declared that all emigrants thanked Hellman for clarifying that the fronts of World War II also ran through Germany.[166] The implication that Zionists were among those who should be thankful met with a vehement retort from the *Jüdische Wochenschau*. Whereas Jacob, Nelson, and others felt that the drama verged on biography, the *Wochenschau* argued that it rarely bridged the gap between truth and fiction. Describing Müller as pure fantasy, the reviewer caustically dismissed the notion a large antifascist movement in Germany: "In reality a duplicitous Romanian count is not necessary to betray the few righteous fighters of a truly different Germany. There are millions of

---

162. "*Die Unbesiegten*," AT, November 21, 1942.
163. Jacob, *Sieben Jahre Freie Deutsche Bühne*, 48.
164. *Die Unbesiegten*, PWJA VI j) 329, 15.
165. PWJA VIII c) 455.
166. "*Die Unbesiegten*," AT, August 31, 1942.

Germans who do the same work, but cheaper." Accusing Hellman of naivete, the paper asserted that it was no coincidence that a US-American had written the play—German authors knew there was no antifascist underground. In conclusion, the reviewer indicted the "overwhelming majority" of the German nation for supporting atrocities against Jews.[167] The *Wochenschau* contradicted antifascists, who insisted that ordinary Germans were victims, not perpetrators, of Nazi crimes.

The review did not go unanswered. The *Tageblatt* validated the play, claiming that Hellman's thousands of pages of notes attested to the thoroughness of her research.[168] *Das Andere Deutschland*, incensed by what it felt to be a direct attack on its legitimacy, was more confrontational. It flatly rejected the *Wochenschau*, asserting that its reviewer knew nothing of the thousands of imprisoned and tortured dissidents in Germany. The only explanation for such ignorance was that he had not fought Nazism himself, and was guilty of exactly the posture Hellman rebuked in her drama. If the reviewer had not actively resisted Nazism, he shared the blame for its rise.[169] Rather than ceasing to put on the drama, the FGS deployed Hellman's play to honor antifascist activism and encourage dialogue. Further presentations commemorated the German actor Albert Bassermann's birthday, the fifth anniversary of the death of Thomas Masaryk, and raised funds for prisoners at the Gurs concentration camp in France.

Paul Walter Jacob celebrated Bassermann as the thespian representative of Hellman's "unvanquished" antifascist Germans.[170] A colleague of Otto Brahm, Leopold Jessner, and Max Reinhardt, the German Bassermann protested the spread of militant nationalism before emigrating to Switzerland and then the United States with his Jewish wife, Else Schiff. Speaking at the performance, Jacob reiterated his belief in a reformed postwar Germany by wishing that soon a new world would greet the famous actor. Next, the

---

167. "*Die Unbesiegten,*" *JW*, September 4, 1942.
168. "Lillian Hellman," *AT*, September 16, 1942.
169. "Ein Unglücklicher," *DAD*, October 1942.
170. "Bassermann zum 75. Geburtstag," *AT*, September 6, 1942.

cast came before the curtain, read a birthday card to Bassermann, and then passed the letter around the theater so spectators could sign it, congratulate Bassermann, and, in so doing, imply their own approval of Jacob's antifascist platform.[171] Weeks later the actor responded gratefully, closing with "Pereat Hitler."[172] Bassermann ratified an intercontinental solidarity based on opposition to Hitler, sentiments the *Tageblatt* reinforced by publishing both letters in its Sunday edition.[173]

The Free German Stage next put on *The Unvanquished* to honor Thomas Masaryk, founder and first president of Czechoslovakia. The audience included well-known members of the local Czechoslovakian, Hungarian, Austrian, German, Dutch, French, English, and US-American populations. In its review, the *Buenos Aires Herald* noted that many members of the ensemble had emotional bonds to Czechoslovakia, "the last European country where they could play theatre freely."[174] Writing for the *Tageblatt*, Paul Walter Jacob extolled Masaryk as a universal model for leadership, guided by truth, tolerance, and courageous dignity. Jacob expressed solidarity with Czechs in Buenos Aires by hoping that a liberated Czechoslovakia would effect the broader European renaissance, "in which we will never cease to believe."[175] The presentation acclaimed Masaryk, another "unvanquished," and exhorted the diverse emigrant population in the Argentine capital to reaffirm antifascism in his memory. Staged just three months after Czech freedom fighters had assassinated Reinhard Heydrich, the acting governor of Bohemia and Moravia and head of the Reich Main Security Office, the Masaryk commemoration was poignantly timed. Proceeds went to the local Czech envoy for the reconstruction of the town of Lidice, destroyed by the Nazis in retaliation for Heydrich's assassination.[176] Propelled by the shared spectacle of live theater, an international

---

171. "Bassermann-Ehrung der F.D.B.," *AT*, September 7, 1942.
172. Bassermann to Jacob, September 30, 1942, PWJAK.
173. "Bassermann dankt der F.D.B.," *AT*, October 18, 1942.
174. "Tribute to Late Czech President," *BAH*, September 18, 1942.
175. "In Prag vor fünf Jahren," *AT*, September 14, 1942.
176. František Kadeřábek (Czech envoy to Argentina) to Jacob, September 18, 1942, PWJAK.

antifascist community confirmed its commitment to a resurgent postwar Europe.

On October 17, 1942, the FGS staged *The Unvanquished* for an unprecedented fifth performance in as many weeks. Displaying solidarity with victims of Nazi persecution, ticket sales went to aid internees in the Gurs concentration camp in Vichy France. The secretary for the Gurs charity, Carlos Hirsch, sent the cast a letter of gratitude, signed by all members of the organization's advisory board, including Bernhardi Swarsensky, editor of the *Jüdische Wochenschau*.[177] Hirsch expressed reservations about Hellman's drama, but his approach was measured. Performing *The Unvanquished* to support causes that resonated among all members of the refugee population, the FGS at least temporarily persuaded antifascists and Zionists to moderate their tone.

In November the troupe traveled to Montevideo, Uruguay, for its annual guest performance, featuring a final production of *The Unvanquished*. Though it did not endorse Hellman's directive, the *Wochenschau*'s preview praised the fund-raising performances and encouraged its Montevidean public to attend the drama.[178] Instead of stoking tensions with antifascists, the paper called for candid dialogue about *The Unvanquished*, which was less risky in democratic Uruguay than in authoritarian Argentina.[179] The FGS invited theatergoers to remain after the final curtain for an open exchange of opinions about the play.[180] By providing a space and impetus for its public to meet, converse, and engage in debate in person, the cast aimed to foster constructive dialogue and initiate reconciliation among emigrant blocs. Nonetheless, despite such efforts, ultimately the fallout from such tendentious dramas deepened divisions in German Buenos Aires.

Hellman's blend of political messaging, simple comedy, and romantic melodrama garnered the Free German Stage unprecedented attendance and fame. Perhaps more than any other play,

---

177. Hirsch to Jacob, October 17, 1942, PWJAK.
178. "Theater in Montevideo," *JW*, November 1942.
179. PWJA VIII c) 455.
180. "*Die Unbesiegten*," *AT*, November 21, 1942.

The Unvanquished bore witness to the capacity of theatrical energies to potentiate polemics, activate audiences, and construct
and cleave community. Charity presentations united emigrants of
multiple nationalities and faiths in spiritual and material support
of antifascism. Individually and collectively, the FGS cast drew
from these intercultural alliances to surmount political and professional challenges in the years to come. Yet, these were costly
achievements. By elevating disputes about German identity, antifascist activism, collective guilt, and the possibility of a reformed
postwar Germany to the theatrical stage, the FGS publicized
and hardened hostilities among refugees. The act of fomenting
solidarity among certain groups was contingent on the exclusion of others. While uncompromising Zionists were implicitly
pushed to the fringes of the community being built, supporters
of Nazism were explicitly ostracized and attacked. The dramatic
depiction of the fight against Hitler mobilized antifascists and
nationalists alike.

Retribution

While the Free German Stage worked with mixed success to transform the infighting about *The Unvanquished* into a constructive
debate among refugees, the reactions of nationalist Germans were
beyond its control. In an earlier report to the Foreign Office, Ambassador Thermann had indicated that his greatest concern was
the troupe's ability to reach beyond German-speaking refugees.[181]
The ambassador had deemed this to be unlikely, but after three
seasons of steady coverage in diverse media the stage had successfully disseminated its anti-Nazi message to a broader audience. In
consequence, German and Argentine authorities appear to have
retaliated. The Nazi government had already denaturalized Paul
Walter Jacob for his journalistic activities in 1938.[182] On October 3, 1942, Jacob learned in a communiqué from the Dutch Red

---

181. Thermann to FO, October 4, 1940, PWJAK.
182. "Bekanntmachung," *Deutscher Reichsanzeiger und Preußischer Staatsanzeiger*, April 20, 1938.

Cross that he had suffered another, more painful injustice. On September 18, 1942, just three weeks after the debut of *The Un-vanquished,* his parents committed suicide while facing imminent arrest and deportation by the Gestapo. Perhaps worse, the documentation from the Red Cross included a wire stating that his parents had waited for news from Argentina to no avail.[183] Jacob had sent letters, but evidently they had never arrived. He never knew how they might have influenced his parents. There is no direct evidence that Jacob's work with the FGS was connected to the accusations against his parents; however, the timing and circumstances of their deaths are suspicious.[184] Neither Jacob nor the ensemble ever discovered whether the events were related, but the tragedy intensified the psychological weight on the actors, many of whom had family in Nazi-controlled territory. According to Jacques Arndt, who lost contact with his mother in 1941 and later learned that she had been murdered in the Shoah, the cast seriously considered dissolving the stage when they received word of Jacob's loss.[185]

As the FGS raised its profile outside German Buenos Aires, Nazi officials correspondingly increased support for Ludwig Ney's German Theater. On December 4, 1942, the embassy wrote to Berlin requesting subventions of 4,000 reichsmarks for Ney's stage. The request, which the Ministry of Propaganda quickly approved, contrasted the German Theater with the FGS's repertoire featuring many playwrights prohibited in Germany. Thermann falsely argued that Ney warranted funding because large numbers of Argentines attended the German Theater's presentations of genuine German culture.[186] Emphasizing the German Theater's cultural legitimacy and propagandistic potential, the embassy reinforced it as a foil against the FGS. The proximity of a competing theater whetted the political edge of antifascist and nationalist groups.

---

183. Dutch Red Cross to Jacob, October 3, 1942, PWJAK.
184. Fanny Jacob to siblings, PWJAK. The undated letter is placed between correspondence from September 30 and October 3, 1942.
185. Arndt, interview, 2008.
186. Thermann to FO, December 4, 1942, Band R55, Akte 20553, BB.

The FGS incurred further adversity in January 1944, when it was evicted from the House of Theater.[187] Ostensibly, the motive was a reform in municipal regulations for theaters, which, following a spate of fires, now enforced a stricter safety code. Although the FGS had played there for four full seasons, the auditorium was not officially licensed as a theater, and the necessary reforms were prohibitively expensive. Turnover in the institution's administration also worked against the troupe. Pedro E. Pico, coauthor of *The Nutshell*, had resigned from his position as president of the House of Theater in 1943. Moreover, Arturo Mario, a renowned actor and manager of the House of Theater, died that August. Mario had secured the venue for the FGS in 1940 and was an invaluable contact for the stage as it navigated a foreign theater world. For months after Mario's death, theater programs for the FGS featured a bilingual notice mourning his passing.[188] These were its last productions at the House of Theater.

In addition to the regulations and the new administration, several actors wondered if other, unknown reasons motivated the expulsion of the company. As fascism gained currency among Argentina's military regimes, Jacob worried about the passage of decrees that could render further performances impossible.[189] There is no incontrovertible evidence that Argentine authorities or the German embassy intervened against the FGS, but there are reasons for suspicion. Jacob received hate mail throughout his time in Argentina; however, during 1943 and 1944 there was a spike in intimidation by nationalist Germans.[190] These letters came on the heels of a tense encounter between Jacques Arndt and the vice president of the House of Theater, Pascual Carcavallo.[191] The FGS urgently desired to continue using the auditorium, because the chances of finding a suitable substitute were slim. In January 1944

---

187. Jacob to Ensemble, January 15, 1944, PWJAK.

188. "Programmheft zu *Der Mann, der zum Essen kam*," PWJA VI b) 281.

189. Jacob to Ensemble, February 19, 1944, PWJAK; Jacob to Ensemble, March 17, 1944, PWJAK.

190. Anonymous to Jacob, May 26, 1944, PWJAK.

191. Jacob to Arndt, January 22, 1944, PWJAK.

Jacob offered to pay the rent for the coming season in advance, thus providing capital for the necessary renovations. Jacob entrusted Arndt, who spoke better Spanish, with presenting the proposal to the House of Theater administration. When Arndt met Carcavallo, the latter preempted Arndt and said all attempts were futile. The House of Theater had had problems with government agencies because of the FGS, and it would not allow the company to play there again. When Arndt explained that the advance rent would solve such problems, Carcavallo intimated that renovations were not the issue: "We no longer will allow . . . any foreign groups in this building. We are a public institution, we receive state subsidies, and it is, under the prevailing circumstances, impossible to maintain the status quo."[192] He insisted that Arndt remove all stage props from the premises immediately, lest he have more trouble with the authorities.[193] Instead of the municipal regulations, Carcavallo disclosed that the motive for evicting the FGS was government pressure against foreign-language theaters at the venue. Since the House of Theater was partly a state-sponsored institution, the government's intervention was decisive. This is striking because during the 1943 and 1944 seasons Ludwig Ney's group played at the National Theater, which also received public funding. The FGS may or may not have been specifically targeted, but these cases indicate that the rules against foreign-language theaters were not applied consistently. The Free German Stage would perform occasionally in unlicensed, privately funded auditoriums, but for the duration of World War II it never again played at any other state-sponsored locale.

This was a major blow, because replacing the House of Theater was impossible. Its size, central location, availability for weekend presentations and midweek rehearsals, and inexpensive daily rent were a singular combination. The FGS could not afford to rent any theater for the full season, and weekend prices for licensed auditoriums were prohibitive.[194] It finally arranged eight weeks of

---

192. Arndt to Jacob, January 20, 1944, PWJAK.
193. Arndt, interview, 2006.
194. Jacob, *Sieben Jahre Freie Deutsche Bühne*, 65.

performances at a ballroom in the north of the city. This was a solution beset with problems, including fewer presentations per piece, less desirable time slots, scant storage space, no on-site rehearsals, higher rent, and an inconvenient location.[195] Jacob was so desperate for an alternative that he offered a 100-peso reward for anyone who could find another locale—to no avail.[196]

Meanwhile, despite the growing likelihood of a German defeat in the war, the FGS faced strong headwinds under the overtly fascist regime of General Edelmiro Farrell, who took power in February 1944. Not only were Farrell's politics antithetical to the ensemble, but under Allied pressure Argentina had broken off diplomatic relations with Germany that January, causing increased restrictions on all German-language media and entertainment. The stage now required a police permit for each production, which further problematized securing a venue.[197] The volatile environment impacted its repertoire, too. After the 1943 season the FGS ceased performing political dramas. Amid such adversity Jacob openly doubted the enterprise's viability. The troupe could only begin its fifth season with an initial eight-week cycle of performances, beyond which there were no guarantees.[198]

Days before the 1944 season premiere, Jacob issued an unprecedented public appeal to theatergoers. Proud to announce that the FGS would launch its fifth year with its hundreth premiere, an astounding number, Jacob also posited the coming season as a proving ground for the FGS's value to the refugee community. He warned that its days were numbered if attendance for its first ticket cycle declined.[199] In desperate straits, the ensemble barely managed to play regular functions for the full 1944 season. It eventually relocated from the ballroom to the House of Catalonia, which was at least a true theater, though situated in the San Telmo neighborhood,

---

195. Jacob to Ensemble, March 17, 1944, PWJA 1944.

196. "Hundert Pesos-Prämie der F.D.B.," *AT*, March 26, 1944.

197. Jacob to Ensemble, January 15, 1944, PWJAK. The authorities did not enforce these measures on Ludwig Ney's German Theater.

198. Jacob to Ensemble, February 19, 1944, PWJAK.

199. Appeal to the audience of the Free German Stage, PWJA VI b) 281.

far away from the Belgrano district, where most refugees lived. Furthermore, it was not licensed for regular theatrical productions, so the FGS could play there only twice weekly. The enterprise finished the season with a deficit, but attendance was sufficient to keep it afloat.[200] Importantly, Argentine theater organizations began to recognize the FGS's achievements and sought its participation in administrative and celebratory functions. The Argentine Actors Association expressed a "special interest" that the cast attend its annual award gala, and the Artistic Cultural Association invited the cast to its meetings with the explicit motive of integrating them in the local theater community.[201]

In November 1944 the Free German Stage honored the German actor Conrad Veidt, who had died in Hollywood on April 3, 1943. Best known for his portrayal of Cesare in Robert Wiene's *The Cabinet of Dr. Caligari* (1920), Veidt was a vocal antifascist who emigrated in 1933 to protect his Jewish wife, Ilona Preger. The commemoration, held in the cavernous Grand Cinema Splendid, was crucial for the FGS, which needed a strong showing at the box office to salvage its balance sheets.[202] Thanks to collective efforts by the local theater and film industry, the event was a resounding success. The intercultural production featured the French opera star Jane Bathori; Ulises Petit de Murat, a poet, screenwriter, and Veidt's colleague; influential film and theater critic Chas de Cruz; and the famous singer and actress Berta Singerman. Many other Argentine celebrities attended the commemoration, which also included a speech by Paul Walter Jacob and a screening of Lothar Mendes's film *Jew Süss* (1934), starring Veidt in the title role.[203] The event found a strong media echo.[204] The film magazine *Cine*

200. Jacob to Albert Maurer, November 10, 1944, PWJAK.

201. Argentine Actors Association to Jacob, October 14, 1944, PWJAK; Artistic Cultural Association to Jacob, August 1, 1944, PWJAK.

202. Jacob to Maurer, November 30, 1944, PWJAK.

203. Unlike Veit Harlan's film of the same title, Mendes's *Jud Süss* is true to Lion Feuchtwanger's 1925 novel.

204. "Homenaje se tributó a Conrad Veidt," *Antena*, November 30, 1944; "Homenaje a Conrad Veidt," *El Plata*, May 14, 1944; "En memoria de Conrad Veidt," *Revista Familiar Israelita del Uruguay*, May 15, 1944.

reprinted Jacob's entire speech, which concluded: "Everything that he did during the final decade of his life was done to demonstrate to the world his convictions against racial persecution."[205] Veidt reflected the FGS's antifascist platform, and the illustrious guests at the event represented the international public's ringing approval.

In crisis, the FGS's many accomplishments came to the fore. Its integration into the local theater scene enabled the ensemble to win pivotal local and international support. Despite tensions among Zionists and political antifascists, audiences visited less comfortable, distant venues in sufficient numbers to sustain the enterprise during the tenuous 1944 season. Furthermore, after it finished the year with a large deficit, the emigrants and Argentine celebrities raised funds to save the theater. Despite worsening altercations with Zionists and German nationalists, its perseverance demonstrated that the Free German Stage had become an intercultural institution that was fundamental to the refugee community and increasingly interwoven with the national theater scene.

The Free German Stage: An Anti-Jewish Theater?

In a 1943 letter to the Jewish Cultural Society, Paul Walter Jacob asserted that the Free German Stage was indisputably a Jewish theater. Its public was overwhelmingly Jewish, its cast was 90 percent Jewish, and 80 percent of the authors in its repertoire were Jewish. Nonetheless, profound divergences existed on questions of Jewish identity among refugees.[206] The FGS struggled and ultimately failed to reconcile the postures of antifascist groups and moderate Jewish theatergoers with those of Zionist institutions, including the Zionist Forum, the Jewish Cultural Society, and the *Jüdische Wochenschau*.

At the close of the 1941 season, the *Wochenschau* congratulated the FGS on two years of performances, but then contended that its success was not attributable to broad support from German Buenos Aires. The paper put Gentile Germans, regardless of

---

205. "Conrad Veidt," *Cine*, December 14 and 29, 1944.
206. FGS Ensemble to JCS [Jewish Cultural Society], August 12, 1943, PWJAK.

political affiliation, in a separate colony, which was reluctant to visit the exilic theater. The *Wochenschau* designated the entire anti-Nazi population as Jewish and claimed that without its support the FGS would fail. Praising Jacob for employing Jewish refugees, the paper argued that Jewish organizations were obliged to aid these artists in the off-season, but not Gentile thespians. It then warned: "We expect adherence to Judaism and a Jewish way of life from all Jews, but especially from those who are themselves dependent on Jewish solidarity."[207] Having defined Jewish identity according to a Zionist view, which, for example, excluded Arthur Schnitzler from the ranks of Jewish playwrights, the *Wochenschau* asserted that FGS's repertoire must represent these values. It was incumbent on the company to present dramas that rejected European culture and advocated a return to the principles of Judaism as a guide for life. Otherwise, Zionists threatened to withdraw their support. During the 1942 and 1943 seasons, the FGS paid Zionists heed. It put on several plays with Jewish themes, including Nathan Bistritzky's *That Night* (1938), Hans Rehfisch and Wilhelm Herzog's *The Dreyfuss Affair* (1929), and J. Aialti's *Father and Son* (1943), and took part in events sponsored by the Theodor Herzl Society, the Jewish Cultural Society, and the Zionist Forum. Some actors joined these organizations as a gesture of solidarity, yet onstage such efforts were divisive. Dramatic depictions of Zionist interpretations of Jewish identity sowed discord, not solidarity.

On November 9, 1942, the FGS presented the American premiere of *That Night* by Nathan Bistritzky, a Jewish author living in Palestine. Organized by the Zionist Forum and Karen Kayemeth Leisreal to raise funds for Kfar Argentina, a group working to establish an Argentine moshav in Palestine, the event also memorialized the 1938 November pogroms. The program featured an image of a sapling growing inside the skeleton of a razed synagogue, thus visually associating the November pogroms with the Zionist mission. Inside, spectators found essays by the movement's foremost figures admonishing Jews to make aliyah, that is, resettle in their

---

207. "Kleine Chronik," *JW*, November 1, 1941.

natural and spiritual home of Eretz Israel. Other contributors, such as Hugo Benedikt of the local Bar Kochba organization, chastised refugees for neglecting their spiritual roots, failing to learn from the past, and risking further persecution in the future. In "The Incorrigibles and Us," Hugo Lifezis buttressed Benedikt's argument with the case of Hermann Oppenheim and Josef Ticho, leaders of UNION, the assimilationist opposition to Zionists in Vienna, who had to be rescued and resettled in Palestine after the German annexation of Austria. In their example Lifezis saw a moral imperative for Zionists: if Jews had not learned from history's lessons that assimilation is annihilation, then Zionists were obliged to rescue the incorrigibles *"against their will."*[208] According to Lifezis, the Zionist mission need not match the disposition of emigrant Jews. As an independent theater, the Free German Stage had a contrasting perspective. It had to cater to the predilections of its public; otherwise insufficient attendance would cause the enterprise to become insolvent.

The selection of Bistritzky's *That Night* reflected Lifezis's position. Although theatergoers clearly preferred comedies, Bistritzky's drama follows the model of a Greek tragedy. *That Night* dramatizes the eve of the Roman conquest of Jerusalem, provoking the Jewish diaspora from Israel. Bistritzky blames this disaster on the Jews themselves. Infighting, egoism, and spiritual decay splintered the Jewish people and their leaders in an hour that demanded unity and sacrifice. Bistritzky eternalizes the rabbi of Israel, Jochanan ben Sakai, who prophetically sees that the Jewish future is galuth. Feigning death, the rabbi encloses himself in a coffin to elude the Romans' attack, preserving the proud, unyielding Jewish spirit needed for a second Jerusalem.[209] *That Night* culminates in a double tragedy—Sakai's daughter mourns her father's false death as the Romans make their final assault on Jerusalem.

The play was harsh medicine for an involuntary patient, and both Argentine Jews and refugees spurned *That Night*. The *Jüdische Wochenschau* lamented that Bistritzky's play proved how

---

208. Program, *That Night*, PWJA VI b) 28 (emphasis in original).
209. "*In jener Nacht*," *AT*, November 9, 1942.

far Zionists were from persuading most Jews in Argentina to espouse the Zionist agenda. Sadly, Jews had not advanced a single
step in the past millennium. The same selfishness, partisanship, and
decline in piety continued to fester, hindering the realization of a
second Jerusalem.[210] Private reactions betrayed similar disillusion-
ment. In a letter to Karen Kayemeth Leisreal, the Zionist Forum
bemoaned: "The balance is morally and financially shameful."[211]
The Forum had advertised in the *Wochenschau, Jiddische Zeitung,
Mundo Israelita,* and *Argentinisches Tageblatt,* and on radio. It distributed 10,000 flyers, sent 120 formal invitations to Jewish organizations, and peppered street corners with posters. The results were
abysmal—40 percent of the tickets went unsold, and the Forum
calculated that only seventy Argentine Jews in total attended *That
Night.* At a loss to explain this lack of support, the Forum reasoned
that many Argentine Jews spoke Yiddish and thus could have followed the dialogue. An aversion to German, the language of Herzl,
Max Nordau (cofounder of the World Zionist Organization), and
Einstein, was incomprehensible. Finally, Bistritzky's commitment
to Jewish faith and unity should have appealed to all Zionists in
Buenos Aires. Instead, the opposite had occurred: "This was an opportunity to show togetherness. What happened? NOTHING!!!"[212]
Although offstage the Forum had trusted in a multinational community of like-minded allies, onstage *That Night* exposed the factious relations between Argentine and German-speaking Zionists.

Attendance among Jewish refugees was hardly better. Only
580 of them bought tickets, numbers that, had they endured for
a full month, would have bankrupted the FGS. Bistritzky's drama
flopped so badly that plans for a guest performance in Montevideo
were scrapped.[213] While the Forum felt that painful memories of the
November pogroms accounted for refugees' absence, the organization itself also was to blame.[214] The fiasco of *That Night* indicated

210. "*In jener Nacht,*" *JW*, November 13, 1942.
211. Zionist Forum to Keren Kayameth Leisreal, November 18, 1942, PWJAK.
212. Zionist Forum to Keren Kayameth Leisreal, November 18, 1942, PWJAK.
213. Jacob to Friedländer, August 20, 1943, PWJAK.
214. Zionist Forum to Keren Kayameth Leisreal, November 18, 1942, PWJAK.

that Zionists' sharp tone alienated most Jewish refugees and that genre played a major role in bringing spectators to the theater.

The following year, mounting reports of the mass extermination of European Jews heightened awareness of the Shoah in South America. In this historical context, Zionists in Argentina redoubled their efforts to win over more Jewish refugees. In August 1943 the Jewish Cultural Society sponsored the FGS's production of the world premiere of J. Aialti's drama *Father and Son*, which had appeared a year earlier as a serialized novel in *Di Presse*, a local Yiddish newspaper. Set in occupied Paris, the play centers on a young resistance fighter, Sokolowski. After a bomb he detonates kills several Nazis, the Gestapo gives notice that fifty civilians will be executed unless the perpetrator is reported to the police. When Sokolowski's name is divulged, his father is arrested and sentenced to death if his son does not surrender by dawn. When the younger Sokolowski moves to turn himself in, his mother tells him that his father wishes to die so he can continue fighting. The play closes with the surety of the father's execution and his son's determination to avenge his death.

Across the media spectrum reviews of the cast in *Father and Son*, like those for *That Night*, were positive. The *Diario Israelita* noted the biographical parallels between the play and the actors, and *Di Presse* gushed over an unforgettable performance.[215] The *Jüdische Wochenschau* demurred, criticizing what it considered to be a superficial depiction of Judaism, but otherwise its review was affirmative.[216] The *Tageblatt* and the Communist *Volksblatt* joined in the accolades, wishing the FGS packed houses.[217] Spectators did not cooperate. The weak attendance came as no surprise to Paul Walter Jacob, who had put on Aialti's play only to placate Zionist organizations. Writing to Rabbi Günter Friedländer, coeditor of the *Wochenschau*, Jacob reiterated that dramas favored by Zionists consistently repulsed audiences. It was no coincidence that

---

215. *"Vater und Sohn,"* *Di Presse*, August 24, 1943.

216. *"Vater und Sohn,"* *JW*, August 27, 1943.

217. "Ein Zeitstück von J. Aialti," *Volksblatt*, September 1943; *"Vater und Sohn,"* *AT*, August 22, 1943.

Father and Son had drawn the fewest spectators of any drama for the entire season, because promoting Jewish content always resulted in lackluster ticket sales. Jacob concluded that Zionists did not represent most refugees, and he retaliated against pressure to stage more specifically Jewish plays: "How should we show 'greater consideration' for Jewish audiences if they, as ticket receipts clearly show, want nothing to do with plays that speak to their Jewish interests?"[218] According to Jacob, *That Night* and *Father and Son* failed because of their Jewish content. Friedländer evidently lacked a counterargument, since he never answered Jacob's letter, yet an explanation existed. Aialti and Bistritzky flopped because of their somber tones and grim plots, not only their Jewish content.

Although theatergoers preferred entertainment over politics and religion, the most successful dramas, Carl Rössler's *The Five Frankfurters* and Lillian Hellman's *The Unvanquished*, combined elements of all three. Rössler and Hellman weaved humor and romance into plots that addressed serious issues of Jewish identity and antifascist activism, respectively. The FGS premiered over 100 dramas from 1940 to 1945, and ticket sales for these two plays far exceeded all others. Their unmatched success indicates that theatergoers favored dramas that addressed political and religious themes over benign, irrelevant farces.

As the *Argentinsches Tageblatt* observed, Bistritzky's *That Night* made no concessions to audiences, and Aialti's merciless, almost cruel mode of expression depicted a world of injustice, suffering, and death.[219] Carl Rössler, by contrast, lightened his treatment of Jewish integration with comedy and romance. Despite his sacrifices for the antifascist cause, Hellman's Kurt Müller plays the piano, enjoys a joke, and, above all, loves his family with warmth and tenderness. Bistritzky and Aialti's protagonists lacked this balance. Rabbi ben Sakai deliberately feigns death before his own daughter, and Sokolowski is a hardened combatant who expresses cold

---

218. Jacob to Friedländer, August 20, 1943, PWJAK.
219. "*In jener Nacht*," *AT*, November 9, 1942; "*Vater und Sohn*," *AT*, August 22, 1943.

insensitivity toward life.[220] He loves his father, but leaves him facing execution. As the *Diario Israelita* put it, when the curtain fell on Aialti's *Father and Son* the elder Sokolowski's Jewish piety earned him mortal punishment.[221] The dark review intimated that Sokolowski's murder was the collective fate of the Jewish people. A brooding drama that offers scant hope for resolution of the myriad of excruciating dilemmas it presents, *That Night* culminates in the certainty that God's chosen people will spend thousands of years in the anguish and dispersion of galuth. In the final lines of Rössler's *The Five Frankfurters*, by contrast, Salomon kneels at his mother's side and anticipates his daughter's Jewish marriage with tears of joy. Bistritzky's Rabbi Jochanan ben Sakai, scuttled away in a casket as Jerusalem burns, cuts a depressing figure in comparison.

One theatergoer's letter to Paul Walter Jacob contextualized audiences' aversion to tragedies in the psychology of living as a refugee. After Nazi persecution, flight from Europe, and struggle in exile, the writer, Mr. Talpa, wished only "to stop crying!"[222] For him and his peers visits to the theater were holidays, and on such occasions they preferred "cake" to "hard bread." Simple comedies and serious dramas alike could win over an audience; it just depended on fulfilling the public's emotional needs. Most important of all was the connection between the actors and their audience. Successful plays, Talpa explained, engendered intimacy, empathy, and affection between performers and spectators. Most refugees were tired of conflict, so they found the confrontational rhetoric of the Zionist Forum off-putting. They had little appetite for the elder Sokolowski's somber march to death and his son's aloofness. They did not empathize with such characters; thus the essential bond between thespians and theatergoers was absent. *Father and Son* and *That Night* were too harsh and despondent for a public whose prevailing wish was to cease crying. When offered "hard bread" instead of "cake," most refugees preferred to stay at home.

---

220. "*In jener Nacht*," AT, November 9, 1942; "*Vater und Sohn*," AT, August 22, 1943.

221. "*Vater und Sohn*," *El Diario Israelita*, August 22, 1943.

222. Talpa to Jacob, February 25, 1945, PWJAK.

The debacle of *Father and Son* culminated a full year of altercations among the FGS and Zionist organizations. Zionists were frustrated with the stage's reluctance to perform more religious dramas and resented Jacob's alignment with antifascists. The FGS actors countered that they had participated in events at Jewish organizations, volunteered in presentations for Jewish charities, and observed all Jewish holidays, even though this harmed their commercial interests.[223] The cast felt Zionists not only had failed to recognize their efforts at cooperation but were antagonistic toward the FGS. Jacob accused Bar Kochba and the Jewish Cultural Society of scheduling activities to compete with his enterprise, even claiming that they hired artists with links to fascist groups in lieu of supporting fellow refugees.[224] In August 1943, an administrator at the Jewish Cultural Society accused the FGS of being an anti-Jewish theater and objected to the presence of Gentiles in the troupe.[225] Although the board of directors later denounced the comments, Jacob and his cast maintained that this unforgivable "Jewish Nazism" was pervasive at the Society.[226] After years of failed productions and quarrels the Free German Stage, Jewish Cultural Society, and Zionist Forum decided that their differences were irreconcilable. Jacob canceled his membership in the Jewish Cultural Society, and the cast did not cooperate with Zionists for the remainder of the World War II period.

Performances about historical and current events directly disclose their ideological preferences within the specific social and the cultural context in which they have been created and presented.[227] The reception of this position gauges the tenability of the tenor and political perspective presented onstage. In the context of Buenos Aires during the Second World War, audiences supported depictions of Jewish identity and antifascist activism, themes that

223. FGS Ensemble to JCS, August 12, 1943, PWJAK.

224. Jacob to Curt Zacharias, September 14, 1943, PWJAK.

225. FGS Ensemble to JCS, August 12, 1943, PWJAK.

226. Arturo Nussbaum and Enrique Frohmann to Jacob, August 20, 1943; Jacob to JCS, September 14, 1943, PWJAK.

227. Rokem, *Performing History*, 24.

contributed to the formation of a resilient community of emigrant and native artists and theatergoers. The same spectators spurned Zionists' aggressive dogma and their choice of the tragic genre to advance it dramatically. Exposed and magnified by theatrical controversies, disputes among refugees became so intractable that the Free German Stage decided it could only prosper as an intercultural community-building institution by excluding Zionist organizations.

Franz Werfel's *Jacobowsky and the Colonel*

The FGS garnered glowing reviews and full houses for its production of the German-language premiere of Franz Werfel's *Jacobowsky and the Colonel* in the Americas.[228] In Werfel's self-described comedy of a tragedy, set during the Nazi invasion of France in June 1940, a German-speaking Jewish businessman, Polish Catholic colonel and his orderly, and a Frenchwoman—Jacobowsky, Stjerbinsky, Szabuniewicz, and Marianne, respectively—embark on a perilous and hilarious series of adventures in a race against time to escape their Nazi pursuers. Over and over, Jacobowsky's savvy survival skills save them from disaster. Jacobowsky leaves the group after an envious Stjerbinsky challenges him to a duel, but the four are reunited in the coastal town of St. Jean de Luz, where an undercover officer in the British navy is waiting to take Stjerbinsky to England. All appears for naught when he insists that only two places are free in the ship, but then Marianne decides to join the French resistance and Stjerbinsky refuses to abandon his antagonist-cum-comrade. The happy ending is complete when the officer finally agrees to take Jacobowsky along.

Jacobowsky's improbable escape, and the many individual miracles sitting in the theater that evening in Buenos Aires, reflected a special talent that Ottmar Ette terms "knowledge for surviving."[229] While fortunate, Jacobowsky's escape also is earned. A blend of wit, optimism, and affability is the basis of his survival skills. Some critics have accused Werfel of an excessively blithe approach to a

---

228. "Werfels *Jacobowsky und der Oberst*," *AT*, September 5, 1945.
229. Ette, *Zwischen Welten Schreiben*, 42.

dire moment in history, but his protagonist's wit has a serious role in this drama.[230] As previously noted, the Holocaust survivor, neurologist, and clinical psychiatrist Viktor Frankl has theorized that humor can afford the ability to overcome extreme psychological duress.[231] Jacobowsky deploys humor to reduce potentially overwhelming situations to more manageable proportions, comparing the bombardment of Paris to a toothache, for instance. A vitalizing force for himself and those around him, Jacobowsky's humor is inextricably linked to his resilient optimism. He sees two possible outcomes for every dilemma, one of them always good. Stranded on a pier as the Gestapo closes in from behind, Jacobowsky holds fast to his belief in free will. Cyanide capsules in one hand and pills against seasickness in the other, he has two final possibilities and opts against suicide. Only after this final act of optimism does British commander Wright, convinced of his courage, offer him a place on his ship.

Neither Jacobowsky nor audiences at the FGS were immune to the hardships of exile; however, evidence suggests that like Werfel's protagonist, theatergoers attempted to bear this trauma with a smile. Not only did they cultivate humor and optimism by attending comedies, but refugees also tried their hand at germinating cheer as well. At their 1943 theater ball, the troupe played a ditty written by a fellow refugee, entitled "Optimism." The merry tune describes an emigrant who, like Jacobowsky, does his best to buoy his spirits, "unflaggingly hoping that everything will get better soon."[232] "Optimism," and other similar skits and songs penned by refugees, indicate that survival strategies on- and offstage overlapped. Refugees in both contexts strove to stay upbeat, aware that if they succumbed to depression their chances of triumph were slim.

In Buenos Aires, too, Werfel's happy ending provoked criticism. The Socialist newspaper, *Freies Wort*, protested the drama's outcome: "Unfortunately the six million murdered Jacobowskies were

230. Wagener, *Understanding Franz Werfel*, 112.
231. Frankl, *Viktor Frankl Recollections*, 97.
232. PWJA VI a) 280.

not so clever."[233] Yet, the dramatist depicts the escape as narrow and unlikely. Upon reaching St. Jean de Luz, Jacobowsky's two possibilities comprise variations of his death; his optimism has vanished. The Nazis arrest far more characters than they overlook, such as the many guests at Marianne's hotel and dozens of people in the Café Mole. Furthermore, the seventeen suicides reported by the Gestapo represent the many victims who died in flight, compared to only two who can flee to safety. Historically and in Werfel's drama, many refugees did not make it out of France, but others did, including hundreds of spectators in the House of Catalonia.

The links between Werfel's exilic drama and German-speaking exiles in Buenos Aires were uncanny. Jacob, whose family name recalls Werfel's protagonist, played the leading role. As he narrated Jacobowsky's biography in the opening scene, Jacob essentially was telling his own life story. Acculturated Jews in pre-1933 Germany, Jacob and Jacobowsky grew up mistakenly convinced that they were Germans, and for both, their enthusiasm for German culture provoked the Nazis' ire.[234] At the time, Jacobowsky and Jacob each were on their fifth fatherland and shared several stations of exile, including Paris and Prague. Jacobowsky's purchase of two expensive visas to an exotic, landlocked country paralleled the exorbitant prices that Jacob and fellow actor Ernst Wurmser paid for passports to Paraguay and Bolivia, respectively. When an official burns Jacobowsky's papers, this was another bitter yet familiar situation for many thespians and theatergoers. Earlier that year Fred Heller, an exilic author and collaborator with the FGS, had published a collection of stories about emigrants who restarted life from scratch, *Life Begins Again*.[235] Perhaps nothing underscored the linkage among such disparate refugees more than the nullification of their former identities by Nazi persecutors.

Preparing to play the reactionary, bellicose Polish Catholic Colonel Stjerbinsky, the Jewish Jacques Arndt had the sensation

---

233. "Franz Werfels *Jacobowsky und der Oberst*," *Freies Wort*, November 1945.

234. "Jüdische Mimen nicht mehr gefragt," *Essener National Zeitung*, March 30, 1933.

235. Heller, *Das Leben beginnt noch einmal*.

of reading a dramatized version of his own flight from the Nazis.[236] Several reviewers referred to Arndt and Stjerbinsky as opposites; however, the *Jüdische Wochenschau* noted that both were refugees.[237] Under the pressures of exile, differences may give way to novel, often improvised similarities. On Nazi wanted lists, both Stjerbinsky and Arndt adopted analogous tactics to remain hidden in plain sight, such as engaging in role playing. Werfel introduces elements of metatheater at numerous junctures in *Jacobowsky*. When a German patrol confronts the four refugees, Stjerbinsky deceives them by playing a ward from an insane asylum, participating in a metatheatrical spectacle performed for German soldiers-cum-spectators onstage before an audience of refugees-cum-theatergoers. Throughout their escape, Stjerbinsky conceals his identity as a Polish colonel. These scenes evoked Arndt's path across Germany years earlier, when he played the part of a Hitler youth to hide his identity as an absconding Jew. Arndt and Stjerbinsky had distinct backgrounds and conflicting morals, yet when they were forced into the role of refugees their survival tactics matched to a remarkable degree.

In the immediate aftermath of the Shoah, not all media in Buenos Aires were receptive to the inclusive intent of Werfel's play. The *Jüdische Wochenschau* welcomed the play's focus on the victims of Nazism, but it saw this group exclusively as Jews and ignored the many Gentile refugees, including the Tragic Gentleman, the Intellectual, and the Monk, whose descriptive names signal their representation of a diverse civilian population.[238] As its title implies, both the Jewish Jacobowsky and the Catholic Stjerbinsky are essential to the drama. Their cooperation embodies Werfel's wish for interfaith harmony, also symbolized by the Wandering Jew and the Monk pedaling their tandem bicycle. Werfel's protagonists mirrored the cast of the FGS, an institution founded on intercultural

---

236. Arndt, interview, 2006.

237. "Franz Werfels *Jacobowsky und der Oberst*," *Freies Wort*, November 1945; "*Jacobowsky und der Oberst*," *AT*, September 21, 1945; "*Jacobowsky und der Oberst*," *JW*, October 2, 1945.

238. "*Jacobowsky und der Oberst*," *JW*, October 2, 1945.

antifascism and religious tolerance. In a letter to the Jewish Cultural Society, the ensemble declared: "Jewish and Gentile colleagues in our small company will stay loyal to the last. We are proud that 'racial' and religious prejudices play no role in our small enterprise. We all work together as like-minded artists."[239] In the spirit of the FGS's own political convictions, the *Tageblatt* posited *Jacobowsky* as an appeal for human rights and respect for diversity. Just six months after World War II, Werfel's drama provided moral guideposts to prevent such a catastrophe from recurring.[240] Despite the confident tone of their letter, however, the religious tolerance among the FGS's actors was always tenuous. Within and beyond the refugee colony, German Buenos Aires continued to be suffused by an intractable animosity that foretold the challenges of heeding Werfel's directive in the postwar period.

Some postliminary scholarship has perceived anti-Semitic "stereotypes" of the calculating, ingratiating Jewish businessman in Werfel's protagonist, yet no trace of such misgivings existed among thespians, theatergoers, and media in Argentina.[241] In 1995, the Viennese Court Theater invited Jacques Arndt to attend a commemorative presentation of *Jacobowsky*'s premiere in Buenos Aires. Decades after his expulsion from Austrian stages, Arndt returned as a guest of honor. When asked to compare the productions, he replied that the essential difference was one of community. At the Free German Stage actors and spectators had shared a theatrical event that evoked mutual, real-life experiences. In Buenos Aires, Arndt mused, Werfel's drama was performed by Jacobowskies for Jacobowskies.[242] The refugee population did not see stereotypes; they saw themselves.

The spiritual kinship between Paul Walter Jacob and S. L. Jacobowsky endured far beyond the 1945 production.[243] In 1947,

---

239. FGS Ensemble to JCS, August 12, 1943, PWJAK.

240. "Dichter sterben," *AT*, August 29, 1945.

241. Steiman, *Franz Werfel*, 174; Schwarz, "Franz Werfel und das Judentum." (lecture, Wiener Werfel-Symposium, Vienna, 1990)

242. Arndt, interview, 2006.

243. "*Jacobowsky und der Oberst*," *AT*, September 21, 1945.

the emigrant magazine *MMM* ran an article on Jacob entitled "Paul Walter Jacob-owsky."[244] Some of his closest friends henceforth began their letters "Dear Jacobowsky."[245] Others referenced Jacob's role in the drama when discussing their personal lives.[246] Perhaps because of this lasting, intimate association, Jacobowsky became Jacob's defining role. When Dortmund's city theater put on Werfel's drama in 1960, the West German Broadcasting service reviewed Jacob's portrayal in biographical terms: "There is a level of sorrow so high that afterward nothing worse can come. Jacob has reached this decisive point, and that is why he so endearing."[247] While this critic found Jacob's past disarming, other friends and colleagues believed that he was haunted by the insurmountable trauma of persecution, exile, and stymied reintegration.[248] Marvin Carlson's neologism, "ghosting," describes how actors can become trapped in certain roles by their audiences' memories.[249] Since his performative role as Jacobowsky so closely overlapped with his phenomenal person, Jacob was associated with this role on- and offstage. Historical plays, such as *Jacobowsky and the Colonel*, enable ghostly figures from the past to reappear onstage.[250] The actors depicting such figures are in a sense repeating history, prolonging and deepening its resonance in the present. Playing Jacobowsky time and again, Jacob repeated a fictionalized history that was his own biography. Onstage he performed the imagined historical event of a refugee's flight from France, yet, ghosted by his role inside and outside of theater, he also was continually reliving his real experiences as a refugee.

Jacob remigrated to Germany for good in 1951, becoming general director of the Dortmund theater system. He also founded a children's theater program in Dortmund, launched a prosperous

244. "Paul Walter Jacob-owsky," *MMM*, March 1947.

245. Fritz Busch to Jacobowsky, January 28, 1946; Maurer to Jacobowsky, December 24, 1946, PWJAK.

246. Jacob to Fränkel, December 28, 1945, PWJAK.

247. Naumann, *Ein Theatermann*, 197.

248. Naumann, 203–234.

249. Carlson, *Haunted Stage*, 7.

250. Rokem, *Performing History*, 6.

career on German television, and played on stages across the Continent, including Barcelona, Lisbon, Nice, Antwerp, and Vienna. In Europe he enjoyed more artistic freedom, disposed of greater resources, and commanded higher wages than in Buenos Aires. Still, he never felt at home in postwar Germany. His alienation reflects Max Horkheimer and Theodor Adorno's provocative statement: "Home is to have escaped."[251] According to the director Imo Wilimzig, even among close friends Jacob never overcame the psychological repercussions of this estrangement, which caused chronic loneliness.[252] Over and over Jacob requested the role of Jacobowsky for guest performances,[253] and attempted several times to return to the renamed German Stage in Buenos Aires.[254] He seems to have sought a way to recapture a sense of exilic solidarity that, like his native country, he had lost. Jacob later reflected that although he had not been aware of it at the time, his years in Argentina were also the peak of his career: "I never again felt the way I did with these people. We had a spiritual, indeed, I would almost say, existential bond. Our fates were all at each other's mercy."[255] Despite the abundant acting talent in Germany he claimed he could never cast *Jacobowsky* there, nor hope for the impact it had in Buenos Aires.[256] Jacob's comments are tinged by nostalgia. In addition to professional success, his years in exile were characterized by fear, feuding, and personal tragedy. Nonetheless, Jacob eventually grew certain that the Free German Stage represented an irretrievable sense of community and artistic achievement. In the alchemy of exile and return, Jacobowsky's ghost was relentless.

---

251. Horkheimer and Adorno, *Dialektik der Aufklärung*, 86.
252. Naumann, *Ein Theatermann*, 227.
253. Raoul Alster to Jacob, January 16, 1962, PWJAK.
254. Jacob to Willy Bodenstein, August 8, 1963, PWJAK.
255. PWJA VIII c) 455.
256. PWJA VIII c) 455.

4

HYPHENATED HITLERISM

Transatlantic Nazism Confronts Cultural Hybridity

Nazi officialdom wasted little time conscripting dramatic performances into their efforts to foment enthusiasm for Hitler's regime among Germans in Argentina. On April 5, 1934, the *Deutsche La Plata Zeitung* announced plans for a guest performance by the star-studded German Drama ensemble, featuring Gerda Müller, Eugen Klöpfer, and Käthe Dorsch, under the direction of Heinz Hilpert.[1] As it was a stridently nationalist paper, the *La Plata Zeitung*'s propagandistic intent was clear from the outset. Before the celebrity cast had even departed for South America, the paper reported that its rehearsals were preparations for an upcoming cultural "victory" of the new Germany, which would have a profound echo throughout South America.[2] When the North German Lloyd steamer *Sierra*

---

1. "Eugen Klopfer," *DLPZ*, April 5, 1934.
2. "Deutsches Schauspiel 1934," *DLPZ*, April 18, 1934. Although he featured prominently in advertisements for the group and oversaw its rehearsals in Berlin, Hilpert did not travel to Argentina.

Salvada docked in Buenos Aires on May 28, the *La Plata Zeitung* ran an article hailing its passengers as representatives of a new German theater liberated from the shackles of the egoism, sensationalism, capitalism, and intellectualism that had marred stages in the Weimar Republic. By contrast, this ensemble reflected theater in the new Germany, which the paper described as the essence and resurrection of the German soul.[3] Although preparations predated Hitler's rise, the German Drama performance in 1934 was a programmatic spectacle engineered to inculcate National Socialist visions of German identity in the Argentine capital.

The following day, the *La Plata Zeitung* reinforced this directive by publishing an open letter from Otto Laubinger, president of the Reich Theater Chamber, to his "countrymen" in South America. Noting that the upcoming event represented the first state-funded theater performance overseas under the Nazi regime, Laubinger goaded emigrants to prove their allegiance to Hitler by upholding the arts as the most exquisite blossom of national life.[4] He emphasized that the guest performance in Buenos Aires represented a rare opportunity to showcase the artistic accomplishments of Nazi Germany against a multinational backdrop. Metonymically representative of the Nazi regime and its cultural values, the celebrity thespians would assert the new Germany's rightful place among the national populations of the Argentine capital, including France, Italy, and Spain. In a separate article, the *La Plata Zeitung* revealed a more sinister side to the German Drama's cultural mission. Lambasting reports of censorship and repression in Nazi Germany as fatuous "horror stories," the newspaper marked its territory against the "enemies of our fatherland."[5] If the upcoming event demonstrated the nationalist population's unanimity with the new Germany, as Laubinger and the *La Plata Zeitung* touted, this expression was characterized by aggression and exclusion.

The troupe's performances of the German classics, which reviewers posited as symbolic of a newly awakened sense of national

---

3. "Deutsches Schauspiel 1934," *DLPZ*, May 29, 1934.
4. "Ankunft der Schauspieler," *DLPZ*, May 30, 1934.
5. "Deutsches Schauspiel 1934," *DLPZ*, May 29, 1934.

pride, were the cornerstone of the combative cultural politics.[6] The decision to put on the classics, and especially media reports on these productions, reveal that already in 1934 Nazi dramatic theory held sway among nationalists in Buenos Aires.[7] Echoing Julius Petersen, president of the Goethe Society (1926–38) and chair of the German Department at Frederick William University (1933–41); and Hanns Johst, dramatist, Nazi poet laureate, and president of the Reich Chamber of Literature (1935–45); the *La Plata Zeitung* emphasized the preeminence of the written text over improvisation in dramatic performance.[8] Both Petersen and Johst perceived actors' clear delivery of the text to be the gateway to establishing an ethnocentric theater in the service of "the national idea."[9] In an interview about the imminent production of Schiller's *Mary Stuart* (1800) and Lessing's *Minna of Barnhelm* (1767), actress Gerda Müller affirmed this theory, explaining that the classics had resurged in Nazi Germany as a result of the "awakening of a newfound nationalism and transformation of dramatic performances through a greater respect for the author's work."[10] Subsequent reviews confirmed her pronouncements.

The German Drama's performance of *Mary Stuart* emphasized Nazi aesthetics. The austere mise-en-scène broke with the elaborate stage designs of Expressionist theater, rejecting, as scholar Friedrich Rosenthal put it, the "flooding of the world with optical seductions."[11] Instead, the *La Plata Zeitung* argued, the stage design for *Mary Stuart* served to foreground the dramatic work and spectators' reflection on the presentation: "The setting is not a burden. Its thrift becomes the mind's wealth."[12] The 1934

---

6. "Gerda Müller," *DLPZ*, June 2, 1934.

7. In 1934–35, *Minna* received 280 performances in Germany. See Ann Schmiesing, "Lessing and the Third Reich," in Fischer and Fox, *Companion to the Works of Gotthold Ephraim Lessing*, 274; Drewniak, *Das Theater im NS-Staat*, 109.

8. Pfanner, *Hanns Johst*, 128.

9. Pfanner, *Hanns Johst*, 128.

10. "Gerda Müller," *DLPZ*, June 2, 1934.

11. Friedrich Rosenthal, "Verwüstung der künstlerischen Sprache," *Rufer und Hörer* 2 (1933): 487.

12. " 'Maria Stuart,' " *DLPZ*, June 2, 1934.

performance of *Mary Stuart* underscored the sanctity of the spoken word in Nazi dramatic theory.[13] Actors and directors alike adhered to the formula of minimizing the demands on theatergoers' eyes and reducing their lust for visual pageantry in favor of sharpening their focus on dialogue and carefully guided interpretations of thematic purport.[14] Correspondingly, in Heinz Hilpert's adaptation, Elisabeth's monologue replaced Mary's departure as the dramatic climax. Unlike its aesthetics, the thematic substance of Schiller's play resisted unambiguously pro-Nazi interpretations even in this propagandistic production. The *La Plata Zeitung*'s review described Hilpert's interpretation as relevant, contemporary, and nonpartisan, concluding that *Mary Stuart*'s many subplots and intrigues led spectators to the fundamental dilemma of the work: "The state ruthlessly exploits individuals to push its political and historical agenda."[15] In fact, this ambivalent conclusion could be interpreted to support both nationalist and antifascist platforms.

As if to compensate, coverage of *Minna of Barnhelm* was unabashedly sectarian. The *La Plata Zeitung* praised especially the actors' clear delivery of the dialogue, gushing that it was soothing to the ears "to hear the crisp ring of Lessing's crystalline German."[16] Furthermore, the purity of Lessing's prose temporarily held the "linguistic wilderness" in Argentina in check. The German Drama's rendition of Lessing's dialogue was exploited as a vehicle for aggressive nationalist posturing by an ethnic enclave that felt its identity was threatened by corrupting, foreign influences. Embellishing on these xenophobic overtones, the *La Plata Zeitung* synthesized Lessing's prose with a bellicose analysis of *Minna*. Brandishing the weaponry of literature, Lessing had carved out a place for himself in the ranks of those patriots who fought to liberate German culture from the shackles of foreign powers. Drawing parallels between the Seven Years' War

---

13. Hans Johst, "Die Helligkeit des Wortes," in Biccari, *"Zuflucht des Geistes"?*, 85.

14. Rosenthal, "Verwüstung der künstlerischen Sprache," 489.

15. " 'Maria Stuart,' " *DLPZ*, June 2, 1934.

16. "Lessings 'Minna von Barnhelm,' " *DLPZ*, June 7, 1934.

and the state of German theater in the eighteenth century, the paper perceived *Minna* to be a deliberate revolt against the "stifling French influence on German stages." Its theater critic depicted Lessing as a "rebel" and an early forerunner of current National Socialist revolutionaries, even wondering if the play had been written in 1763 or 1934. Criticism of the individual actors in the play also reinforced a nationalist identity based on exclusion. Actor Werner Pledath was censured for his portrayal of the Frenchman Riccaut de la Marlinière: "too moderate, too little sleazy pretension, too good-natured, instead of cold reasoning and Gallic greed."[17] Pledath's Riccaut failed to satisfy the *La Plata Zeitung* because he did not adequately fulfill the Francophobic expectations that state-sponsored nationalist German media held for Lessing's drama.

The antitotalitarian *Argentinisches Tageblatt*, by contrast, was livid about what it considered to be an insidious betrayal of German values and culture. *Tageblatt* contributor and emigrant Paul Zech, winner of the Kleist Prize in 1918, denounced the German Drama and its sponsors in a three-page harangue:

> They have the gumption to send out a troupe that brandishes Lessing, Schiller, and Goethe as the summit of German culture. The pawns of this new Germany force their interpretation on people who are decidedly less informed about the depths to which culture and artistic expression have fallen under Hitler.[18]

Zech trenchantly observed that the efficacy of Nazi cultural politics lay in the remoteness of populations such as Germans in Argentina, whose perceptions of their homeland were patriotically inclined to the positive and thus were vulnerable to the misinformation filtered to them by Goebbels's minions. The controversy surrounding the guest performance evinced this vulnerability, as well as the sharply discordant politics of cultural identity emerging in German Buenos Aires.

---

17. "Lessings 'Minna von Barnhelm,'" *DLPZ*, June 7, 1934.
18. "Deutsches Schauspiel 1934," *Argentinisches Wochenblatt*, June 9, 1934.

The German Drama was a seminal event for German theater in Argentina. As in Europe, the German Labor Front and Strength through Joy in Argentina formed the labor and recreation wings of an organization devoted to building a close-knit community of working Germans in support of National Socialism. Theater played an important role in this endeavor. Inspired by the 1934 guest performance, Consul Edmund von Thermann and Strength through Joy organized numerous theatrical productions. In June 1935 an ad-hoc ensemble of local actors sponsored by the Labor Front and the consulate staged Hans Lorenz and Alfred Möller's comedy *Christa, I'm Waiting for You* (1934).[19] Later that August the two organizations funded a guest performance of Ridi Walfried's *The Cobbler in Heaven* by the Riesch Stage, a touring company based in Santa Catarina, Brazil.[20] Held at the cavernous Odeon Theater in the heart of the Buenos Aires theater district, these events had the purpose of assembling, consolidating, and expanding a cohesive community under the swastika. Prices were kept low to foster sentiments of horizontal comradeship within the nationalist German colony. Regardless of the disparities of wealth and privilege that existed among its members, the monthly magazine *Der Deutsche in Argentinien* reminded its readership that in accordance with the National Socialist principle of equality, all tickets were general admission.[21] Within two days the thousand-seat venue was sold out.

The Labor Front exploited these occasions to advance allegiance to Nazi Germany and Adolf Hitler. In a speech preceding the performance by the Riesch Stage, Richard Schröder, regional leader of the Labor Front, urged the audience to form a transatlantic kinship with their compatriots in Europe and actively recruit other Germans to join the NSDAP community in Argentina. He longed to inform Hitler that a national community had united itself under the German Labor Front in Argentina.[22] Speakers at these events,

---

19. In 1936 Berlin upgraded the consulate to an embassy.

20. Walfried's play is better known as *Four Weeks in Heaven*.

21. "Kraft durch Freude Veranstaltung," *DiA*, July/August 1935.

22. "2. Große 'Kraft durch Freude'-Veranstaltung: Besuch bei der Riesch-Bühne," *DiA*, October 1935.

including Consul Thermann, directly elicited enthusiasm for Adolf Hitler: "In conclusion, the Consul found honorable words for the host country, Argentina, and ended his speech with a threefold *Sieg-heil* to the Führer and chancellor, which was echoed by hundreds of voices."[23] Although such assemblies were not antagonistic to the host country, Argentina stood in a subordinated role to Nazi Germany. Spectators were pushed to aver that their first allegiance was to Adolf Hitler and the Nazi government, metonymically represented by Consul Thermann onstage.

The potential they saw in these sporadic guest performances to build community and disseminate propaganda encouraged Thermann and Erwin Schriefer, who followed Schröder as chairman of the Labor Front in 1937, to establish a regularly performing local ensemble. When news of Ludwig and Irene Ney's activities in Paraguay reached Argentina, Nazi officials in Buenos Aires contracted them to launch such an enterprise. Ludwig Ney's German Theater, also called the Ney Stage, gave its first performance in Buenos Aires on May 19, 1938.[24] By June the small, unseasoned cast was staging variety shows in German neighborhoods throughout the Argentine capital.[25] Unlike Paul Walter Jacob, Ney entered an auspicious situation in Argentina. His troupe targeted a large, wealthy, and relatively unified population.[26] The Labor Front and Strength through Joy promoted his group in their media arm, the magazine

---

23. "Kraft durch Freude Veranstaltung," *DiA*, July/August 1935.

24. "Deutsche Kleinkunstbühne Ludwig Ney," *DiA*, June 1938.

25. "Gespräch mit Ludwig Ney," *Teutonia*, September 1938.

26. In *To Belong in Buenos Aires*, Benjamin Bryce makes a compelling case for the existence of distinct and at times conflicting communities among Argentina's German-speaking population between 1880 and 1930, especially according to denominational differences. These are the immigrants who would have become supporters of the German Theater, yet there is no trace of such tensions in sources on Ludwig Ney's theater. One can surmise that the absence is attributable to the diminishing importance of denominational difference among Gentile German speakers, exemplified by stagnate rates of baptism and congregational membership as well as frequent interdenominational marriages. The predominance of Lutherans in most nationalist Pan-German institutions was likely another factor. All sources on the German Theater indicate that its public was unburdened by the conflicts that splintered the antifascist population. Bryce, 147–149.

Der Deutsche in Argentinien. These organizations coordinated events in various districts and subsidized performances so that prices remained accessible to the entire nationalist colony. Strength through Joy sponsored guest performances in provincial cities like Rosario and contracted the Ney Stage to appear at well-attended community events, such as the Oktoberfest festival in Quilmes and the inauguration of the Strength through Joy park at Punta Chica in the capital.[27] Passages of the *Deutsche in Argentinien*'s preview for the park, a verdant ludic space for the nationalist population, resembled an advertisement for the German Theater. A section of the park was reserved exclusively for performances by the group, and, as the magazine assured its readers, all seats afforded an unobstructed view of the stage and background.[28]

Such publicity drew large numbers to the German Theater, enabling it to gain a foothold in the nationalist colony. Thanks to the support of Nazi officialdom, and in stark contrast to the Free German Stage, Ney was not constantly rushed to prepare productions. The German Theater produced an average of seven plays per season, usually with four productions in the capital plus additional performances in Buenos Aires province and beyond.[29] This allowed far more time for rehearsals, which was beneficial because some members of Ney's cast were not professional thespians. As a former performing arts instructor and ensemble leader in Germany, Ney was well trained to mentor younger actors. He also had the luxury of holding six rehearsals per week, normally beginning three to four weeks in advance of the premiere.[30] Presentations thus reached a high level, an accomplishment reflected in the central role the stage played in the solidarity of the nationalist German

---

27. "Heute in Rosario," *DLPZ*, October 22, 1938; "Münchner Oktoberfest," *DLPZ*, October 18, 1938; "Unser 'Kraft durch Freude' Park," *DiA*, December 1940.

28. "Unser 'Kraft durch Freude' Park," *DiA*, December 1940.

29. "Deutsches Theater," *DLPZ*, February 28, 1943.

30. "Große Vorbereitungen im Freilichttheater der Ney-Bühne," *DLPZ*, January 28, 1941; Egon Straube, "Ein Schauspieler spricht," in *Die Brücke* (Buenos Aires: Imprenta Mercur, 1942); "Schauspielproben," *DiA*, August 1943.

population.[31] In turn, the support of Nazi officialdom enabled Ludwig Ney to forge a loyal public as he molded his troupe into a polished theater company.

Closing Ranks: Comedies at the German Theater, 1938–1944

For German nationalists in Argentina, theater was inextricably linked to National Socialist visions of German identity, and comedies were no exception. The lighter muse provided cheerful entertainment, which grew increasingly urgent as the war turned against the Axis powers, and buttressed nationalist Germans' identification and enthusiasm for National Socialist doctrine. In its Spanish-language supplement, the *Deutsche La Plata Zeitung* claimed that for Germans artistic expression was intrinsic to nationhood.[32] Thousands of miles removed from its fatherland, the nationalist population's theater displayed unflinching loyalty to Nazi Germany. Ney's productions and writings advocated key tenets of Nazism, including the cult of the leader, military expansionism, and blood and soil ideology.[33] Though his anti-Semitism is less blatant, Ney's diatribes against intellectuals and theater entrepreneurs of the Weimer Republic do appear to target primarily Jews.

In a 1941 essay, Ney posited totalitarianism as an ideal form of government to cultivate the arts. He argued that grand artistic

31. Volberg, *Auslandsdeutschtum*, 65.

32. "Edición Castellano," *DLPZ*, July 28, 1940.

33. Based on new research, this view revises the position of my dissertation and contradicts Andreas Stuhlmann's statements about Ney in his book, *Vater Courage* (2016), on Reinhold Olszewski's German Chamber Theater in Latin America. My dissertation distanced Ney from Nazism to extent, and Stuhlmann also states that Ney was skeptical toward Nazism and did not disseminate Nazi ideology. This chapter and subsequent sections on Ludwig Ney demonstrate these theses to be false. In private, Ludwig Ney may have held reservations about National Socialism, but in public he actively promoted Hitlerism throughout the Nazi period and beyond. Even decades later, he never abjured these beliefs. Stuhlmann, *Vater Courage*, 151.

accomplishments of Nazi loyalists already should have debunked the view that Hitler's regime hindered artists' creativity, and also claimed that authoritarian governments are particularly adept at fostering the development of young artists. To prove his point, Ney narrated the story of a colleague who opened an acting school for aspiring young thespians in the back room of a friend's restaurant. The studio was humble, but "noble and pure," and eventually its students began to land roles at city stages and garner some repute in the Berlin theater world. Then, suddenly, the restaurant owner decided to move to the distant East Prussian town of Memel. The new owner was not interested in art, so the fledgling studio was left in the lurch. In the Weimar Republic the school would have been lost, Ney claimed, but in Nazi Germany it was saved because there existed a watchful and authoritative Reich Theater Chamber. Cognizant of its value, the Reich Theater Chamber granted the studio use of a small theater, where it staged modest productions of lesser-known authors. By 1941 several in its cast had landed roles in Vienna, Munich, and Königsberg. The moral of the story, Ney concluded, was that artistic will flourished in Nazi Germany because the state could rapidly and decisively deploy resources to identify and fund even the meekest enterprises.[34] Backed by the Labor Front and Strength through Joy organizations in both Germany and Argentina, Ney likely saw himself as such a beneficiary. His story may even have been loosely autobiographical. Convinced that National Socialism was a boon to artists at all levels, the German Theater unwaveringly supported the Nazi government's endeavor to create a loyal community of supporters in Argentina.

Ludwig Ney selected comedies exclusively by German playwrights, nearly all of which were frequently presented in Nazi Germany. A major objective during the troupe's first years was to renew among nationalist Germans a transatlantic sense of identity and belonging through dramatic performances. Ney believed that the impulse to participate, either as spectators or as actors, in theatrical productions was intrinsic to the German people, but was

---

34. "Geschichte einer jungen Schauspielschule," *DiA*, June 1941.

concerned that the many years his public had spent outside of Germany had alienated them from this urge.[35] Germans' risk of losing their cultural appetite in Buenos Aires was acute, Ney argued, because there had never been a German-language stage in Buenos Aires. Sporadic guest performances could not fill the void of a permanent local theater. Writing for the *Jahrbuch des deutschen Volksbundes in Argentinien* in 1943, Wilhelm Lütge, who had just a few years earlier argued that establishing a permanent theater was impossible,[36] reflected on Ney's accomplishment:

> The sense of togetherness with the local German stage can only develop gradually. When one considers this difficulty, it is astonishing how much Ney has achieved. Many of our countrymen feel the German Theater is "our" stage and visit its productions out of an inner drive to experience cultural solidarity.[37]

Ney believed that comedies, especially agrarian-themed pieces with strong links to the German homeland, could nurture the nationalist colony's innate enthusiasm for theater and reinforce its collective ethnic heritage. For nationalist media these plays about rural life in Germany were so evocative of their native landscapes and customs that they referred to them as homeland plays or, in German, *Heimatspiele*. Ney contextualized agrarian comedies in racial ideology, writing that the German farmer's blood of the dramatist August Hinrichs saturated his oeuvre with ethnic inspiration.[38] Recalling the National Socialist blood und soil mantra, the bond between German farmers and their land was fundamental to their cultural and racial identity.

Just beyond the city limits of Buenos Aires, the vast natural setting at the Strength through Joy park at Punta Chica enabled the German Theater to recreate the northern German pastoral environments of August Hinrichs's *All for Nothing* (1937) and *When the Rooster Crows* (1933). Reviewers identified Hinrichs's characters

---

35. "Das Programm unserer Ney-Bühne," *DiA*, January 1941.
36. Keiper, *Der Deutsche in Argentinien*, 29.
37. "Das deutsche Theater in der Spielzeit 1942," *JdVA* (1943).
38. "Die Ney-Bühne spielt 'Alles für Katz,'" *DiA*, April 1940.

as faithful representations of German nationhood, contrasting them with modern city dwellers, who had been alienated from their pure ethnic integrity. Shielded from the corrosive effects of modernity and multiculturalism, the farmers in this drama lived and acted like true Germans from millennia ago: "strong and vivacious, without a trace of decadent refinement."[39] Hinrichs's figures presented Germans in Buenos Aires with a mirror of cultural purity for them to emulate in their urban, foreign, and potentially contaminating environment. Open-air presentations in Argentina corresponded to popular outdoor theater performances in Nazi Germany, which also often emphasized the benefits of life in the countryside. These events at the Punta Chica park physically removed the audience from the crowded city, where they existed immersed among Argentines, and brought them to a racially insular enclave, sealed off from foreign influences. The *Deutsche in Argentinien* fantasized that the performance would enable spectators to "cross the ocean to our homeland with its vast pastures, where German people live a farmer's life."[40] Nationalist press organs claimed that the theatrical exposition of rural Germany enabled theatergoers to approximate their model countrymen by escaping both city and foreign country alike.

This agenda pertained to audience, performers, and even theater itself. The *Deutsche in Argentinien* posited the events at Punta Chica, which were attended by approximately 2,000 people, as a proving ground for Ney and his cast. Their success in this natural setting demonstrated that the German Theater was composed of true artists capable of creating theater self-sufficiently, not pseudothespian deceivers, who "can only dissemble a dramatic illusion in an artificial, stylized environment of theatrical contrivance."[41] Ney's open-air presentations broke with the elaborate theatrics of the Weimar Republic and kept the so-called old colony current with new developments in art across the Atlantic.[42]

Open-air theater was not only opportune because of the warm summer nights in Buenos Aires. Less than half of Argentina's

39. "'Wenn der Hahn kräht,'" *DLPZ*, November 8, 1940.

40. "'Wenn der Hahn kräht,'" *DiA*, September 1940.

41. "Unser 'Kraft durch Freude' Park," *DiA*, December 1940.

42. Ludwig Ney, "Wachsen und Werden des Deutschen Theaters," in *Die Brücke* (1942).

estimated 240,000 German speakers resided in the nation's capital. Many were farmers who cultivated land granted to them by the Argentine government in far-flung corners of the country, isolated from German culture. Berlin claimed to prioritize cohesion among geographically disparate German communities, so Strength through Joy funded expeditions by the Ney Stage to German agricultural colonies. Selecting dramas appropriate for such audiences was challenging. Nazi authorities emphasized the utility of theatrical productions to update Germans abroad on sociopolitical changes in the so-called new Germany, but producing contemporary dramas presented numerous obstacles in agricultural settlements. Popular contemporary playwrights like Curt Goetz relied on a familiarity with contemporary urban life that was utterly lacking in the rural interior. Many propagandistic works, such as Hanns Johst's *Schlageter* (1933), demanded infrastructure that made their production in agrarian Argentina impossible.

Hinrichs, on the other hand, was a perfect fit. The German Theater traveled to farming communities remarkably contiguous with the settings of Hinrichs's comedies. The characters, settings, and themes were drawn from much the same milieu as that of German immigrant farmers and required only modest props for performance. Ney and his cast brought essential props and then improvised according to whatever conditions awaited them. In 1940, the group traveled over sixty miles up the Rio Paraná to Brazo Largo, a German farming outpost. When the actors arrived, they found that recent flooding had washed away the facility where they had planned to perform. With no other suitable structure for miles around, the presentation had to be held outdoors. Together, residents and the actors erected a platform for the stage and built benches for the audience. The *Deutsche in Argentinien* reported: "Under the friendly light of petroleum lamps and a full moon an image of our Nordic home emerged on Ipicui Island. . . . This evening provided spectators and actors a wonderful experience of active national community."[43] The improvised production of *All for Nothing* in Brazo Largo illuminates how Nazi organizations pitched and concocted theatrical presentations as community-building

---

43. " 'Alles für die Katz' in Brazo Largo," *DiA*, April 1940.

events. The allure of German theater drew settlers from far and wide, and because so many individuals actively collaborated on the project, the endeavor to inculcate them with National Socialist propaganda and consolidate their allegiance to Hitler's nationalist community was likely quite effective. Collaborative, entertaining, and collective, live theater was as compelling a form of propaganda as speeches or party rallies. The German Theater manifested the Nazis' paradoxical fusion of an ethnocentric anti-urban message with a highly modern propaganda machine.

The open-air performances caught the attention of antifascists, who suspected Germany might establish a fifth column in rural Argentina, and perceived the large gatherings of nationalist Germans at Punta Chica as a menace.[44] Municipal authorities appeared during one production of *When the Rooster Crows*. They insisted on viewing the play, and then interrogated the organizers and the cast. A few days later, the municipality ordered Strength through Joy to close the Punta Chica park. Only after weeks of interviews with local police was the group allowed to reopen its facilities. In consequence, Strength through Joy resolutely declared that the Ney Stage would continue to play a key role in their competition against the antifascist colony in Argentina. Against antifascist pressure the nationalist population defiantly closed ranks around its theater, exacerbating tensions among German emigrant blocs.

Nationalist media discussed the incident at length, complaining bitterly about the cowardly hatred of their enemies, who set heaven and hell in motion to defame ethnic Germans. At the same time as it threatened that its adversaries' actions would not go unpunished, the *Deutsche in Argentinien* and the *La Plata Zeitung* exhorted their readers to show the local population and authorities "that we have nothing to hide, and that we will obey Argentine laws as disciplined and self-aware Germans." Ironically, the nationalist press pledged adherence to Argentine law in the act of declaring themselves to be, first and foremost, Germans. Furthermore, the

---

44. "Naziotische Umtreibe in Misiones," *AT*, July 7, 1940; "Nazis in Misiones," *AT*, December 12, 1940; "Nazioten Nester in Entre Rios," *AT*, August 4, 1941.

Deutsche in Argentinien concluded that the most imperative reason to comply with local authorities was because the "Führer" had issued this command.[45] Nationalist Germans submitted to Argentine governance, but the pro-Nazi media stated that devotion to Adolf Hitler—not loyalty to Argentina—compelled them to do so.

Agrarian comedies were popular entertainment, and their portrayals of cultural purity as well as blood and soil ideology also was effective propaganda. Nonetheless, plays about country life were somewhat at odds with the daily reality of many German nationalists in Argentina. The greatest concentration of theatergoers resided in Buenos Aires, a metropolis with roughly 2.5 million inhabitants. They lived in urban surroundings, had professions in an industrializing economy, and generally favored a modern lifestyle. During the first years of World War II, the German Theater attempted to satisfy this audience's desire for lighthearted, urban-themed fare without compromising its commitment to the National Socialist agenda.[46] As in Germany, the talk of indispensable cultural standards in the arts section of the *La Plata Zeitung* was ubiquitous and unrelenting. Whether in Europe or South America, these values were a direct extension of National Socialist ideology. The farce, for example, was anathema to Ludwig Ney, who derided the genre and its authors as capitalist speculators who cared nothing for artistic merit and were motivated by box-office profits alone.[47] His indictment, in this case directed against the popular Jewish playwrights Oscar Blumenthal and Gustav Kadelburg, carried anti-Semitic connotations. Ney and his supporters were uncompromising on this issue. From its inception until Ney's retirement in 1972, the German Theater and its successors never staged a Jewish dramatist.

The troupe did, however, produce contemporary propagandistic comedies, such as Maximilian Böttcher's *Trouble Backstairs* (1934), which also had been produced as a feature film under the direction of Veit Harlan in 1935. Set in the rear building of a Berlin tenement

---

45. "Gewollte oder ungewollte Missverständnisse," *DiA*, December 1940.
46. "An das Publikum," in *Die Brücke* (Buenos Aires: Imprenta Mercur, 1944).
47. "'Krach im Hinterhaus,'" *DiA*, August 1942.

house, Böttcher's play features a middle-aged widow whose own daughter unintentionally incriminates her in the theft of a cockle stove. Widow Bock then launches her own investigation and uncovers the true culprit of the crime. A light romantic comedy, *Trouble Backstairs* also upholds National Socialist institutions and policies. Böttcher's Nazi police, lawyers, and judges prove themselves capable and just by granting Bock probation while simultaneously laying a trap for the actual thief, the miserly caretaker. The play ends with a marriage between a mailman's daughter and a young attorney, which the *La Plata Zeitung* identified as representative of the social balance that National Socialism had achieved among different economic classes in the new Germany. Exalting the author as an advocate for the people, the reviewer authenticated the inhabitants of Böttcher's crowded Berlin tenement as emblematic of the German proletariat—rough and prickly outside, but inside honorable and determined.[48] The paper linked the resolve and vitality of Böttcher's figures with the nationalist colony, noting that the German Theater's Tilde Jahn played the leading role despite having broken her foot just days before the premiere. Except for the caretaker, the *Deutsche in Argentinien* observed, there were no villains in the piece; instead all conflict stemmed from cramped living conditions and insufficient "lebensraum."[49] The production of Böttcher's *Trouble Backstairs* by the Ney Stage reflected its strategic implementation of the comic genre. The humorous banter and cheerful plot amused audiences, while reviewers emphasized the egalitarian social and justice systems as achievements of Nazi social policy; reinforced Nazi visions of the innate virtues of the German people, exemplified both performatively and phenomenally by Tilde Jahn in the role of Widow Bock; and justified Germany's bellicose, expansionist foreign policy by identifying insufficient living space as the underlying cause of all strife in the play.[50]

In the first years of World War II both agrarian and urban comedies played a key role in establishing Ludwig Ney's German Theater as a conduit for Nazi propaganda and a nexus

---

48. "'Krach im Hinterhaus,'" *DLPZ*, August 13, 1942.
49. "'Krach im Hinterhaus,'" *DiA*, August 1942.
50. "'Krach im Hinterhaus,'" *DLPZ*, August 13, 1942.

for German nationalists throughout Argentina. Antifascists retaliated against its success, which provoked nationalists to rally around their theater and agitate against their perceived enemies. As its public grew, the German chargé d'affaires in Buenos Aires, Erich Otto Meynen, lauded the German Theater as the "cultural backbone of the German colony," which, he continued, "is of utmost importance for our community life and cohesion."[51] To an extent the success of the German Theater is measurable in ticket prices. Initially quite accessible or even free, by 1943 admission cost from 10 to 22.50 pesos. This was not cheap, considering that wages at the Free German Stage were 120 pesos monthly. Despite the rising cost, high demand for the 1943 winter season forced Ney to move from the 750-seat Politeama Theater into a much larger venue, the National Theater (Teatro El Nacional), which had capacity for 1,150 spectators and was located steps away from Buenos Aires's trademark Obelisk, ground zero of the republic of Argentina.[52]

Unlike the splintered factions of the refugee population, during World War II the nationalist population generally adhered to a single, coherent set of cultural values and political objectives. While it is possible that there was dissension behind the scenes, whatever tensions might have existed within the colony never degenerated into public altercations. Capitalizing on this accord, the German Theater augmented camaraderie among nationalists by performing dramas that upheld a unified, clearly defined cultural, artistic, and political platform. Its efficacy as a community-building institution during the first five years of its existence built a durable base of support for the tougher times that came when the war turned against Germany.

Laughter and Loyalty: Comedies from 1943 to 1944

In his introduction to the 1940 *Jahrbuch des deutschen Volksbundes in Argentinien*, Wilhelm Lütge worried about the potential

---

51. "Geleitwort," in *Die Brücke* (Buenos Aires: Imprenta Mercur, 1943).
52. "Deutsches Theater," *DLPZ*, March 4, 1943.

ramifications of a protracted conflict for Germans in Argentina.[53] His concerns were well founded, because as the war dragged on Argentine society grew increasingly inimical toward nationalist Germans. Although the national government continued to sympathize with fascism, the trajectory of the fighting emboldened antifascists. By 1943, anti-Nazi media organs in Buenos Aires were attacking local German institutions daily. Legislative action against fascist organizations gained traction in municipal and national governments,[54] and the likelihood that Argentina ultimately would yield to Allied demands for "hemispheric solidarity" increased.[55] Precedents in neighboring Brazil and Paraguay portended grave consequences for local Germans, and, indeed, when Argentina did break off diplomatic relations under immense pressure from Britain and the United States in October 1944, its government banned pro-Nazi media, seized properties, and closed German businesses, cultural centers, and schools. Many institutions did not reopen until years later, and some properties never were returned.

As the Allied offensive gained in lethality, Germans in Argentina feared for their livelihoods and for the lives of friends and family in Europe. A "Letter from Home," reprinted in the *Deutsche in Argentinien* in 1943, recounted the bombings of Hamburg:

> We were sitting in the air-raid shelter when the bombs hit. . . . Violent explosions, wood, glass, and stone shards flew around our ears, the air pressure compressed us and lime and mortar dust covered our faces. We hurried outside. Appalling images of destruction awaited us. . . . We unearthed a grandfather with his little granddaughter from the ruins, the grandmother was dead, the mother was badly wounded. . . . We found a second wounded mother nearby, her two little girls dead. . . . It was horrible.[56]

Under extreme duress, the nationalist German colony sought refuge in its theater. Although they were on opposite sides of the

---

53. "Zum Geleit," *JdVA* (1941).

54. The executive branch of the national government remained profascist; however, the lower congressional chamber's special Investigative Commission of Anti-Argentine Activities represented the momentum behind antifascism.

55. Newton, *"Nazi Menace,"* 217.

56. "Brief aus der Heimat," *DiA*, June 1943.

fighting, the Free German Stage and the German Theater adopted parallel approaches to attract and soothe audiences in times of crisis. As the news from Europe worsened, comedies came to comprise a large proportion of presentations at both stages. In 1944, reflecting upon the changing mood of the German Theater's public, Ludwig Ney explained that a "thoughtful tenderness" for theatergoers shaped the stage's repertoire.[57] As director, he had to intuit what genres and themes would satisfy his audience's psychological and emotional needs. Closely and inadvertently echoing Paul Walter Jacob's open letters to the citizenry of Wuppertal in 1932, Ney believed spectators visited the theater in search of reassurance and respite from an everyday suffused with fear, dismay, and doubt.[58] As he saw it, his challenge was to fulfill this role while affirming Hitlerism. During its final two years of performances, comedies at the German Theater served a three-pronged agenda: to fortify nationalist Germans with mirth and cheer during the grim final years of World War II; to reassure the theater's beleaguered public that its allegiance to National Socialist ideology was worthwhile; and to preserve nationalist German unity against escalating pressures that threatened dissension and atomization.

Plenty of dramas suitable for these goals existed in Germany, but as the war expanded it became nearly impossible in Argentina to obtain printed material from Germany, including current dramas.[59] The shortage complicated the German Theater's endeavor to satisfy demands for lighter fare without compromising Nazi cultural standards, so older works had to be refashioned to meet the exigencies of a time and public very different from those for which they originally had been intended. To render them fit for performance, Ludwig Ney and the nationalist press were compelled to transform such dramas altogether.

Presented in November 1943, Otto Ernst Schmidt's *Master Flachsmann* (1901) is an apt example. When it had premiered over forty years earlier, Schmidt's contemporaries understood the drama

---

57. "Was will das deutsche Publikum vom Deutschen Theater?," *JdVA* (1944).
58. "Was will das deutsche Publikum vom Deutschen Theater?," *JdVA* (1944).
59. "Zum Geleit," *JdVA* (1943).

as an indictment of the German education system. In *Flachsmann*, Schmidt criticizes the authoritarian atmosphere at a small, provincial school through his scathing portrayal of its despotic schoolmaster, Johann Flachsmann. He enforces absolute discipline at the institution, visually represented by an enormous poster of school rules that hangs above his desk. Given to dictatorial sayings, Flachsmann commands a militaristic conformity among students. As one faculty member remarks, the schoolmaster is determined to convert his school into a "military boot camp."[60] In 1943 in Buenos Aires allies and foes alike could easily construe such lines as critical of National Socialist educational institutions; indeed just a few years earlier the *Argentinisches Tageblatt* had used nearly identical language when it branded the coordinated Humboldt School a "Nazi boot camp."[61] The playwright's repeated acclamatory references to the Swiss pedagogue Johann Heinrich Pestalozzi were even more problematic. Schmidt's protagonist, Jan Flemming, acclaims Pestalozzi as an estimable, even saintly educator. Essentially, the plot is encapsulated in a pair of stage props: the clash between the schoolmaster's poster of rules and the portrait of Pestalozzi that hangs in Flemming's classroom. In Buenos Aires the Pestalozzi School, founded by a group of antifascists spearheaded by the owner of the *Argentinisches Tageblatt*, Ernesto Alemann, stood as a vehemently antifascist bulwark against dozens of Nazified German-language educational institutions.[62] Such glorification of the Swiss pedagogue was anathema to Nazi authorities. Indeed, Schmidt's play aligned with the political position of the anti-Nazi Free German Stage—*not* the nationalist German Theater.

Ney's troupe could not stage *Flachsmann* without major revisions. The drama was especially problematic on the eve of the 100th anniversary of German schools in Argentina, which antifascist media exploited to attack these institutions.[63] Before the

---

60. Otto Ernst Schmidt, *Flachsmann als Erzieher* (Leipzig: L. Staackmann, 1901).

61. "Die Humboldtschule eine naziotische Drillanstalt," *AT*, June 4, 1938.

62. Thermann to FO, April 18, 1934; Thermann to FO, May 10, 1934, PSA.

63. "Hundert Jahre deutsches Schulwesen," *DLPZ*, November 21, 1943.

premiere, the *La Plata Zeitung* preempted deviant interpretations by restricting the drama's call for reform to its turn-of-the-century setting. Its preview argued that today, in the new Germany, the school system was a model for education worldwide.[64] Instead, the paper amended *Flachsmann*, defining the play's central message as censure of an older generation that impeded the education system's progression to its current state under Nazism. Additionally, Schmidt's drama should propel further consolidation of National Socialist pedagogy in Argentina. The performance confirmed these revisions. The cast and community designed period costumes and stage props as visual markers that temporally compartmentalized the play to preclude unintended interpretations.[65] Ney removed Pestalozzi's portrait and erased the Swiss educator from the script, and also achieved welcome touches of heartwarming humor with his revisions.[66] The nationalist German press and the German Theater recast *Master Flachsmann* as a cheerful celebration of the Nazification of German schools in Argentina.

The case of *Flachsmann* was not singular. Emil Rosenow, a playwright, Social Democrat, and member of the German parliament, also was conscripted to further fascism on the River Plate. A satire about incompetent officialdom and the hardships of peasant life in rural Germany, Rosenow's naturalist milieu comedy, *Lampe, the Cat* (1902), seems a surprise selection for a theater funded by Goebbels's Ministry of Propaganda. Rosenow's play turns on the confiscation of a cat belonging to a poor wood-carving apprentice, Neumark, after it damages some furs belonging to a wealthy factory owner. Neumark eventually raises the money necessary to regain possession of his cat, but in the meantime Seifert, the impoverished village constable, has already slaughtered the animal and eaten it. Seifert is forced to confess when Neumark arrives with money, but he goes unpunished because his superior officer, who also had partaken in the meal, is assigned to lead the investigation. At times an endearing portrayal of village life in the Ore Mountains

---

64. "Deutsches Theater," *DLPZ*, November 11, 1943.
65. Albert Haigis, "Das Deutsche Theater—und wir," in *Die Brücke* (1944).
66. "Deutsches Theater," *DLPZ*, November 12, 1943.

and a comical satire of inept local officials, *Lampe* concludes with a laugh at the expense of the factory owner, who will not be compensated for damages to his property by the cat. Yet, drama cannot escape its somber undertones. The curtain falls without hope for change in the poverty-stricken village—corrupt politicians remain in power, civil servants continue to earn miserable wages, and the village laborers are doomed to further exploitation by the wealthy factory owner. The choice of *Lampe* is doubly perplexing because, like his compatriots in Germany, Ludwig Ney regarded naturalism as an abomination to National Socialist aesthetics. Writing for the German Theater's yearly almanac, *Die Brücke*, Ney disparaged naturalism as the attempt to reduce the stage to a "psychological bullring," a degrading experiment that had threatened to destroy theater altogether.[67]

The unsuitability of its naturalist aesthetics, grim outlook, and trenchant social criticism raise the question of why *Lampe, the Cat* was chosen for presentation at all. First, in 1936 Veit Harlan had reworked the play into a feature film, in which Aryan villagers rebel against the oppressive factory owner, who now is Jewish. Harlan also lightened the narrative by adding a romantic subplot. While Harlan's propagandistic vision stifled the play's Social Democratic message, in Argentina his film went unmentioned, probably because the German Theater desired a different effect. The chronological discrepancy between Rosenow's play, Harlan's film, and the German Theater's performances had created a double or even triple time register. Midway through 1943, both Rosenow's socialism and, to an extent, Harlan's anti-Semitic crusade were outdated for National Socialist propaganda, which by this time prioritized the war effort. Ney probably chose *Lampe* because the lack of current dramas from Nazi Germany in Argentina forced him to improvise. Instead of Harlan's defiance, Ney purveyed carefree humor and patriotic visions of the German homeland. His theater transformed Rosenow's work into a quaint homeland play. Although both the original drama and Harlan's film call for an austere setting of squalid huts, Ney created scenery designed to evoke idealized

---

67. Ludwig Ney, "Theater," in *Die Brücke* (1943).

memories of a German winter wonderland. The *La Plata Zeitung* instructed theatergoers to expect a fairytale landscape, replete with snow-covered houses, snowmen, and the holiday charm "that we all love at home." Ney even added a live brass band to the merry mise-en-scène. Rosenow's scenery might have reminded many emigrants why they had left Germany in the first place, but Ney's version, ironically, sought to transport them back to the Europe they had left behind: "The audience should forget that it is sitting in a theater in Buenos Aires. We should bridge the distance and feel as if we are far away at home."[68] Nationalist media praised the inventive stage design and the thorough revisions to the drama's text, which muted the exaggerated burden of social problems in favor of humorous, lighthearted dialogue.[69] This was logical, reviewers argued, because the National Socialist revolution had overcome the problems of Rosenow's time. Ney's group retouched the dreary German hinterland, its impoverished inhabitants, and the bleak outlook of Rosenow's *Lampe, the Cat* to metamorphose the tendentious drama into a "cozy homeland play," supplanting social criticism with a buoyant sense of nostalgia and patriotic cheer.[70]

Not all older comedies required such thorough revisions. In April 1944, the German Theater put on Leo Walther Stein and Rudolf Presber's *Liselotte of the Palatinate* (1921) to sold-out audiences at the grand National Theater.[71] Stein and Presber drew from Liselotte's correspondence to depict her life in France at the court of Louis XIV. As the Duke of Orleans's wife, she was for many decades second in rank only to the queen. Liselotte's political marriage obliged her to spend her adult life in France; however, she remained staunchly loyal to the traditions and values of her native Palatinate and expressed disdain for courtiers who treated her like a Frenchwoman.[72] Such sentiments resonated with nationalists, some of whom identified themselves as Germans and held

---

68. "Deutsches Theater," *DLPZ*, June 4, 1943.

69. " 'Kater Lampe,' " *DiA*, July 1943.

70. " 'Kater Lampe,' " *DiA*, July 1943.

71. Carl Froelich remade the drama into a feature film in 1935, but the media coverage did not discuss it.

72. Kroll, *Letters from Liselotte*, 243.

fast to German customs even after residing in Argentina for many years. Liselotte also persisted in writing in German, the language of over two-thirds of her correspondence.[73] The nationalist population likewise preserved their sacrosanct native tongue by establishing German-language media, schools, and cultural institutions.[74]

As exemplified by her own marriage, the French aristocracy functioned as a foil that accentuated Liselotte's Germanness. Whereas her husband, Phillip of Orleans, was a sickly spendthrift who loathed the outdoors, Liselotte was healthy, robust, and economical, and enjoyed nature. In her letters, health emerged as a strategy of not only resistance and survival, but also of identity formation: illness signified the decadent and corrupt French court, health the morally pure Germany. Depicting herself as a robust German, Liselotte maintained her national identity and individuality in an environment that was based on self-renunciation for the sake of the crown.[75] In this respect she matched the self-fashioned image of nationalist Germans in Argentina, whose institutions promoted outdoor activities to preserve the fundamentally German qualities of health and vivacity. The German Theater's agrarian comedies and guest performances in rural German settlements also represented the enthusiasm for nature and active, pioneering spirit that the German press traced to Liselotte of the Palatinate.[76]

Though centuries and oceans apart, Liselotte and nationalist Germans shared positions constitutive of exile—all were caught between isolation from their homeland and assimilation to the new, host society.[77] Cheerful in Germany, Liselotte believed that the homesickness she suffered in France was turning her into a melancholic. Her depression worsened when the king launched an invasion of her native Palatinate, in 1688, and led to her steady withdrawal from the French court to the private, intimate, and

---

73. Dirk Van der Cruysse, *"Madame seyn ist ein ellendes Handwerk,"* 15.

74. Irene Ney, "Sprachbildungsarbeit," in *Die Brücke* (1943).

75. Baumgartner, "Illness and Health as Strategies of Resistance and Identity Formation in the Letters of Liselotte von der Pfalz," 58.

76. " 'Liselotte von der Pfalz,' " *DLPZ*, April 13, 1944.

77. Strelka, *Exilliteratur*.

German world of her letters.[78] Nationalists in Argentina shared
this strategy—the epistolary form was often their closest, most
meaningful contact with their homeland. Local media also featured
letters from home that, as the war endured, echoed publicly the
desperate tone in Liselotte's letters about the devastation of the Palatinate. Reviews of the German Theater's performance reinforced
the deep historical roots of German nationalism in a hostile foreign
environment: "A clenched German rage emanated from the stage
and penetrated the auditorium. The audience felt as if they, too,
were defending this Germany that had always been threatened by
a thousand demons."[79] In *Liselotte of the Palatinate* theatergoers
embraced an emotive, transatlantic bond of mutual, unflinching
allegiance to their embattled German homeland.

Marginalized at the French royal court, in her nonfictional letters Liselotte was distraught about her inability to prevent a decade
of bloodshed in the Palatinate during the War of the Grand Alliance from 1688 to 1697.[80] In the German Theater's presentation,
however, she overcame the animosity of the French aristocracy and
ultimately gained great power and influence.[81] Although the *La
Plata Zeitung* credited her for arranging for her son's ascension
to power after Louis XIV's death, most studies cite the Parliament
of Paris as the determinant voice in the decision. Furthermore,
Liselotte's son, Philippe of Chartres, did not become regent until
1715, and even then Liselotte continued complaining to her correspondents about her life in France. Nonetheless, the *La Plata
Zeitung* explicitly declared that the drama seemed to reference the
immediate present and posited its heroine as a model German for
its readers to emulate.[82] The production of *Liselotte of the Palatinate* manifested the discursive and subjective power of performing
history. Instead of relying on historical documents, this live event
depended primarily on the director and his ensemble to convince

---

78. Baumgartner, "Illness and Health," 58.
79. "'Liselotte von der Pfalz,'" *DLPZ*, April 14, 1944.
80. Baumgartner, "Illness and Health," 71.
81. "'Liselotte von der Pfalz,'" *DLPZ*, April 14, 1944.
82. "'Liselotte von der Pfalz,'" *DLPZ*, April 14, 1944.

spectators that the actual historical past had been presented on the stage. Transformed into what Freddie Rokem has called "hyper-historians," the actors functioned as witnesses of the events vis-à-vis the audience, regardless of the historical veracity of the parts they played and the story they told.[83] This transformation enabled a reimagination of German memory concordant with the present-day exigencies of German supporters of Nazism in 1944 Buenos Aires. By inventing Liselotte's success and then attributing it to her perseverance, the German Theater and nationalist press legitimized theatergoers' loyalty to Nazi Germany and implied that they, like Liselotte, would prove triumphant.

From the inauguration of the German Theater in 1938 until Argentina broke off diplomatic relations with Germany in late 1944, comedies played an integral role in the stage's success as a National Socialist community-building institution. Performances of folkloric agrarian comedies in the early 1940s united emigrants throughout Argentina by evoking patriotic nostalgia for their German homeland. Later, in 1943 and 1944, as the war effort grew increasingly hopeless, Ludwig Ney's company approximated the antifascist Free German Stage through its preference for the lighter muse to attract, entertain, and fortify audiences undergoing existential crises in a time of war. The German Theater's productions of comedies harnessed the theatrical energies of performing history to sow mirth among audiences, encourage fealty to National Socialist dogma, and sustain unity within the nationalist German colony. Together, Ney's German Theater and the pro-Nazi press implemented propagandistic interpretive strategies, altered dramatic content, and depicted a revisionist account of historical events to achieve these goals.

Conscripting the Classics (Goethe, Schiller, Lessing)

From 1940 to 1943, the German classics comprised the core of the German Theater's repertoire. This program corresponded to the

---

83. Rokem, *Performing History*, 25.

agenda of Reich dramatist Rainer Schlösser, head of the Reich Theater Chamber and chief theater censor, who in 1935 announced
that the primary function of his office was to champion and elevate the German classics.[84] Ludwig Ney's troupe abided by this
policy, and, as the director noted in 1943, the works of Goethe,
Schiller, and Lessing consistently were its best attended and most
deeply resonating performances.[85] Unlike the Free German Stage,
Ney could count on patronage from government institutions and
did not need to issue an ultimatum about the consequences of poor
attendance. Instead he prepared theatergoers for upcoming presentations by endeavoring to make literary dramas accessible to them.
In an essay entitled "Fear of Art," Ney promised working-class
nationalists that nobody was ostracized from the "Reich" of art
and education.[86] Artists were fully integrated with other sectors of
the workforce; all labored together for National Socialist ideals.
The only group prohibited from Ney's collective were pompous
elites who did not share the work ethic incumbent on members of
this community, including artists. The classics were not an impen-
etrable morass of antiquated language and arcane allusions, but
conveyed timeless values of practical utility for all productive citizens. The German Theater emphasized inclusion. Goethe, Schiller,
and Lessing were agents of community building, and the entire nationalist population, regardless of social class and education, could
enjoy the German classics and benefit from them.

In previews of Goethe's *Faust I* (1808) in March 1942, Ney
conceded that this famously complex drama risked intimidating
theatergoers and sought to reassure them. Perversely, he contended
that *Faust* was an inclusive drama by excluding certain groups
from Goethe's purview. Writing in a populist tone, Ney invoked
Karl Moor from Schiller's *The Robbers* (1781)—"I am disgusted
with this age of puny scribblers"—to condemn intellectuals of the
Weimar Republic for sapping the work of its vivacity. Scholars during the so-called time of the system (*Systemzeit*) had seized *Faust*

---

84. Schlösser, *Das Volk und seine Bühne*, 27.
85. "Was will das deutsche Publikum vom Deutschen Theater," *JdVA* (1944).
86. Ludwig Ney, "Angst vor der Kunst," in *Die Brücke* (1944).

from its rightful audience by disseminating the falsehood that only an elitist intellectual cabal could understand it. In the weeks before the premiere, Ney asserted that in fact it was the Jewish intelligentsia who were incapable of grasping Goethe's "thoroughly German" masterpiece.[87]

The conservative actress Louise Dumont-Lindemann, for example, claimed in 1932 that because all art is an expression of its creator's ethnicity, only an artist's own people can arrive at a genuine understanding of his work.[88] Echoing Dumont-Lindemann, Ludwig Ney argued that access to the drama's true meaning is a matter of nationhood, not intellect, because Germans' bonds of Aryan blood with Goethe enabled them to understand the poet intuitively.[89] Ney's references to Nazi racial doctrine aligned with National Socialist interpretations of *Faust*. Franz Koch, author of the infamous *Goethe and the Jews* (1937), asserted that *Faust* and Faustian striving were symbolic of the Germanic race.[90] Hans Severus Ziegler, general director of the German National Theater in Weimar, theorized that Mephisto's comment "Blood is a very special juice" represented a basic truth undergirded by new scientific research in eugenics.[91] The Nazis mobilized well-known excerpts from *Faust* as ideological slogans and catchphrases. The *La Plata Zeitung* ratified the drama as a cultural birthright shared by all Germans, maintaining that such familiarity represented German ownership of the work.[92] Cultural fluency and inherent German traits, such as courage, sacrifice, and the primal German urge "to know what the world contains in its innermost heart," enabled

---

87. "Gedanken zur 'Faust'-Aufführung durch das Deutsche Theater, Buenos Aires," *DLPZ*, March 8, 1942.

88. Dumont-Lindemann, *Vermächtnisse*, 111.

89. "Gedanken zur 'Faust'-Aufführung," *DLPZ*, March 8, 1942.

90. Franz Koch, *Geschichte deutscher Dichtung*, cited in Thomas Zabka, "Vom 'deutschen Mythus' zum 'Kriegshilfsdienst': *Faust*-Aneignungen im nationalsozialistischen Deutschland," in Möbus, Schmidt-Möbus, and Unverfehrt, *Faust*, 315.

91. In Zabka, "Vom 'deutschen Mythus' zum 'Kriegshilfsdienst,'" 316.

92. "Warum spielt das Deutsche Theater Buenos Aires 'Faust'?," *DLPZ*, March 12, 1942.

them to comprehend Faust through "empathy" and "emulation."[93] Declaring that Goethe wanted to be understood in this spirit, Ludwig Ney cited the poet's instructions to Eckermann that his works should not only be studied intellectually, but also performed physically in a phenomenal sense.[94]

For Ney, the individualism of intellectual analysis was antithetical to spectators' emotional, even physical, participation in theatrical performances. Only this latter "theater community" could grasp key scenes in the drama, such as Gretchen's perdition.[95] The erudite but phlegmatic literati of the Weimar Republic made the futile attempt to understand the final scene of *Faust I* materialistically; however, in 1942 audiences sensed the drama's integral meaning viscerally via the conduit of their National Socialist worldview.[96] Like Georg Schott, who identified Hitler as the incarnation of the archetypal Faustian leader,[97] Ney exculpated Faust any misdeeds in his effort to fulfill his "transcendent idea."[98] Anticipating the perspective of Nazi literary scholars such as Paul Husfeldt, Ney wrote that Gretchen was a heroine compelled to sacrifice herself so Faust could achieve larger goals, including the creation of a new Reich.[99] Gretchen's perdition exposed the provocative connection between Nazi visions of community and their dependency on sacrifice.[100] Ney exploited this connection to elaborate a strategic interpretation of *Faust* that collectivized his constituency as racially privileged viewers entitled to the drama's fundamental truths. *Faust* was the exclusive domain of the nationalist German colony, favored by race, nationhood, and allegiance to Hitler.

---

93. "Gedanken zur 'Faust'-Aufführung," *DLPZ*, March 8, 1942.

94. "Warum spielt das Deutsche Theater Buenos Aires 'Faust'?," *DLPZ*, March 12, 1942.

95. "Publikum, aktiv!," *DiA*, August 1942.

96. "Gedanken zur 'Faust'-Aufführung," *DLPZ*, March 8, 1942.

97. Schott, *Goethes Faust in heutiger Schau*, 319.

98. "Gedanken zur 'Faust'-Aufführung," *DLPZ*, March 8, 1942.

99. "Gedanken zur 'Faust'-Aufführung," *DLPZ*, March 8, 1942; Paul Husfeldt, "Schuld und Tragik in Goethes *Faust*," *Dichtung und Volkstum* 44 (1944): 19–52.

100. Fischer-Lichte, *Theatre, Sacrifice, Ritual*, 121.

Paralleling reception of the work in Nazi Germany, the local press conscripted *Faust* into the war effort. As testimony to the drama's role as an inspirational linchpin in the unified German will to victory, Ludwig Ney cited the thousands of German soldiers who had attended presentations of *Faust* while on furlough.[101] In Buenos Aires, the German Theater depended on an enthusiastic, active audience to achieve the essence of the drama's Faustian, and thus German, spirit—the "Sieg."[102] Innate to all participants in the presentation, their transatlantic will to victory linked nationalist German theatergoers and thespians to their ancestral heritage as well as to fellow members of Hitler's national community in Europe. Reviews of the sold-out performances endorsed Ney's tactics.[103] According to the *La Plata Zeitung* the production riveted the entire audience, who all embodied this new "Reich" of the German spirit.[104]

The nationalist German media's treatment of *Faust* consistently affirmed propagandistic interpretations of the drama. This is noteworthy because reception of Goethe and *Faust* in Nazi Germany was diverse. Some scholars remained true to the humanism of Weimar classicism well after 1933.[105] Max Kommerell's remark that Goethe was infinitely interpretable indicated the myriad of approaches to *Faust* that existed in Nazi Germany.[106] Beholden to government funding, the German Theater, *Der Deutsche in Argentinien*, and the *Deutsche La Plata Zeitung* showed no nuance, not even in the instance of *Faust*. Instead they consistently sided with ideologues such as Franz Koch and Paul Husfeldt, who were zealous proponents of Nazi dogma.

The German Theater also undertook to substantiate the classics as common cultural currency by integrating them with daily life in the German colony. Although most would never become personally acquainted, the Ney Stage attempted to inculcate the image of a close-knit, cohesive national community into the mind of each

---

101. "Zur 'Faust'-Aufführung des Deutschen Theaters," *DLPZ*, March 17, 1942.
102. "Publikum, aktiv!," *DiA*, August 1942.
103. "Goethes 'Faust,' " *DLPZ*, March 29, 1942.
104. "Die zweite 'Faust'-Aufführung," *DLPZ*, March 24, 1942.
105. Mandelkov, *Goethe in Deutschland*, 2:88–89.
106. In Zabka, "Vom 'deutschen Mythus' zum 'Kriegshilfsdienst,' " 323.

individual theatergoer. In anticipation of Goethe's *Götz of Berlichingen* (1773), a reporter for the *Deutsche in Argentinien* followed Ney as he prepared for the upcoming premiere. Ney's errands to a German-owned café, bookseller, clothing shop, and beauty salon in the German barrio of Belgrano juxtaposed the medieval world of Goethe's Knight of the Iron Hand to everyday scenes from contemporary German Buenos Aires. The first stop was Pedro Wörns's general store, where the proprietor was rehearsing for a battle scene. Dressed in a full suit of armor and wielding a heavy sword, he challenged Ney to a duel in the back room of his shop. After numerous encounters in the same vein, the journalist joked that the actors seemed so utterly immersed in Götz's medieval world that he would not be surprised if one of them were to say in a café: " 'Upon my oath, waiter, an espresso.' Hopefully out of a sense of decorum he will refrain from adding the most famous quote from *Götz*."[107] Narrated in Belgrano German, a linguistic hybrid of High German and local Argentine Spanish, the joke embedded Goethe's eighteenth-century drama in a cultural context at once familiar and unique to Germans in Buenos Aires. Furthermore, Ney was on a first-name basis with everyone he met, and the involvement of so many local businesses in the preparations for *Götz* produced the sensation that the entire nationalist population had a hand in the upcoming production. Such previews bolstered efforts at community building, provided comic relief, and brought the disparate worlds of the German classics and 1940s Buenos Aires closer together. These tactics of constructing community through intercultural identity markers resembled reception of the Free German Stage's presentation of *Charley's Aunt*. Although the pro-Nazi *Deutsche in Argentinien* and the Zionist *Jüdische Wochenschau* occupied diametrically opposing ends of the political spectrum, each publication utilized a similar approach of cross-cultural humor to convince its emigrant readership that the German Theater or the Free German Stage, respectively, truly was *their* local stage. Viewed through the lens of emigration, even Nazis and Zionists approximated each other to an extent.

---

107. "Rund um das 'Götz'-Festspiel," *DiA*, June 1940.

Figure 6. Poster previewing the German Theater's performance of Goethe's *Götz of Berlichingen* on June 17, 1940.

Source: *Deutsche La Plata Zeitung*, June 16, 1940. Biblioteca Nacional Doctor Mariano Moreno—Argentina.

By positioning the classics as a German cultural cornerstone and emphasizing their value to all German nationalists in Argentina, Ney and the local press dovetailed with Julius Petersen, president of the German Goethe Society (1926–38) and chair of the German

Department at Frederick William University in Berlin (1933–41). One of the most influential Germanists of his generation, through his scholarship Petersen contributed significantly to the coordination of his discipline with Nazi ideology.[108] Petersen envisioned that a genuine national theater would arise from the consecration of the German classics as "sacred public property" of all Germans. Therefore, Petersen exhorted directors to overcome the opposition between the common people and academics as well as to fuse entertainment with education.[109] The *Deutsche in Argentinien*'s preview encouraged nationalist emigrants to regard *Götz of Berlichingen*

Figure 7. Audience at the German Theater's performance
of *Götz of Berlichingen*.

Source: *Deutsche La Plata Zeitung*, June 19, 1940. Biblioteca Nacional
Doctor Mariano Moreno—Argentina.

---

108. Petersen, *Die Sehnsucht nach dem Dritten Reich in deutscher Sage und Dichtung*.

109. Julius Petersen, *Das deutsche Nationaltheater: Fünf Vorträge, gehalten im Februar und März 1917 im Freien Deutschen Hochstift zu Frankfurt a.M.* (Leipzig: Teubner, 1917), cited in Biccari, *"Zuflucht des Geistes"?*, 87.

as familiar, approachable, and even funny. Postulating Goethe's drama as popular entertainment, the *Deutsche in Argentinien* and the *La Plata Zeitung* campaigned to draw a broad swath of their readership to the German Theater's performances.[110] The *La Plata Zeitung* voiced this goal in its review of *Götz*, reporting that Ney's cast had brought together German emigrants in a sublime hour: "This loyal commitment to Götz will long be an ideal sign of German unity in Buenos Aires."[111] The premiere, attended by 1,450 spectators, bore cogent witness to the German Theater's efficacy as a community-building institution not for all Germans as the *La Plata Zeitung* attested, but exclusively for the pro-Nazi German colony.

As the theater's popularity grew, the nationalist press familiarized its audience with its work as an ensemble.[112] These accounts stressed that the troupe's achievements were attributable to the actors' cohesion and work ethic. Drivers passing the Punta Chica park could see the intensity of rehearsals, the *La Plata Zeitung* observed, by the stage lighting, which still shined through the trees at 11 p.m.[113] Ney's blend of amateur and professional thespians concurred that the long hours were welcome, because they saw this work as the focal point of their personal and, often, professional interests. Actor Werner Loewer remembered how, in the first years of the enterprise's existence, its members had to create many of their own decorations, stage props, and costumes, and then travel with their bulky cargo to play at rudimentary facilities in rural villages.[114] While the public expressed gratitude and astonishment at such tenacity, Loewer felt that these challenges created a feeling of brotherhood in the enterprise. Deploying National Socialist rhetoric, Loewer described how during these journeys up rivers, across

---

110. "Klassiker als Unterhaltungsliteratur," *DLPZ*, January 14, 1941.

111. "Deutsches Theater," *DLPZ*, June 19, 1940.

112. "Aus der Welt des Schauspielers," *DiA*, November 1943; "Schauspielproben," *DiA*, August 1943; "Die Vision eines Schauspielers," *DiA*, October 1943.

113. "Große Vorbereitungen im Freilichttheater der Ney-Bühne," *DLPZ*, January 28, 1941.

114. Werner Loewer, "Das Deutsche Theater vom Schauspieler ausgesehen," in *Die Brücke* (1943).

the pampas, and through rain forest, the German Theater became their spiritual home. Individuals who did not embrace the imperative of collective sacrifice were quickly removed by Ney, "the führer of our fellowship." According to Loewer an egalitarian spirit reigned among the thespians, all of whom obeyed their director unquestioningly, confident that he would lead them to the fulfillment of the group's artistic mission.[115] Previewing the 1943 production of Schiller's *Robbers*, the *La Plata Zeitung* emphasized Ludwig Ney's role as an inspirational leader, who demanded dedication, humility, and selflessness from his cast. All actors were devoted to the realization of Hitler's cultural project, "to bring Germany's great minds closer to its people."[116] In a few years, the German Theater developed from a modest variety stage to a polished ensemble that staged Schiller, Goethe, Lessing, and Hebbel for thousands of spectators at the National Theater. Based on the fascist concept of the leader cult, the press showcased the troupe's commitment to discipline, sacrifice, and a rigid, hierarchical authority structure as a model for the nationalist German population.

Traditional approaches to onstage movement, speech, and gesture, such as Goethe's "Rules for Actors" (1803), stress repetition and consistency to set firm guidelines for each role.[117] As the actor Egon Straube explained, Ney's rehearsals established precepts for the minutiae of each scene to attain maximum coherency and prevent any awkward movement from distracting the audience's attention.[118] This conservative methodology spurned so-called transgressive forms of modern theater, in which actors' performances evaded conventional, standardized, and formalized movements, gestures, postures, or attitudes. In contrast to Max Reinhardt, Leopold Jessner, and other prominent directors of the Weimar Republic, improvisation was anathema to Ludwig Ney,

---

115. "Deutsches Theater," *DLPZ*, August 1, 1943.

116. Adolf Hitler, *Hitler: Reden, Schriften, Anordnungen: Februar 1925 bis Januar 1933*, cited in Biccari, *"Zuflucht des Geistes"?*, 110.

117. Goethe, "Regeln für Schauspieler," in Johann Wolfgang Goethe, *Johann Wolfgang von Goethe: Werke, Kommentare und Register*, 12:259.

118. Straube, "Ein Schauspieler," 10.

who believed that meticulous planning was the key to artistic accomplishment. The German Theater's rehearsals were in lockstep with National Socialist dramatic theory.

Theater scholar Gaetano Biccari has stated that the predominance of the written text over improvisational acting was a transitional marker that differentiated stages of the Nazi period from those of the Weimar Republic.[119] As I have noted above, both Julius Petersen and Hanns Johst perceived fidelity to the dramatist as a gateway toward fulfilling theatrical nationhood.[120] Petersen identified the link between textual primacy and nationalist theater to be the spoken word, claiming that each nation's identity coalesced around its language, which also was the most immediate expression of ethnic character.[121] Hanns Johst also glorified the sanctity of the word,[122] declaring "language conveys the mission of the theater and the life of the nation."[123] Language was a hallmark of conservative, nationalist approaches to German theater.

As an ethnic minority geographically isolated from its country of origin, nationalists saw their common native tongue as intrinsic to their endeavor to distinguish and insulate Germans from other nationalities in Buenos Aires, as well as to substantiate and deepen bonds between German emigrants and their European fatherland. Conservative theories of dramatic performance prevailed among nationalist theater critics in Argentina, who strongly emphasized language in reviews of the German Theater, especially its productions of the German classics. Evaluating Werner Loewer's depiction of Faust, the *La Plata Zeitung* applauded the actor's "linguistic perfection." The pivotal monologues of "Night" and "Forest and Cavern" achieved a spiritual resonance,[124] leaving the audience with indelible impressions of "the deepest image of the

---

119. Biccari, *"Zuflucht des Geistes"?*, 84.

120. Pfanner, *Hanns Johst*, 128.

121. Petersen, *Das deutsche Nationaltheater*, cited in Biccari, *"Zuflucht des Geistes"?*, 85.

122. Johst, *Standpunkt und Fortschritt*, cited in Pfanner, *Hanns Johst*, 259.

123. Johst, "Theater und Nation," 97, cited in Biccari, *"Zuflucht des Geistes"?*, 136.

124. "'Faust'-Aufführung des Deutschen Theaters," *DLPZ*, March 22, 1942.

German soul."[125] Language also dominated reviews of Lessing's *Minna of Barnhelm*, which were strikingly consistent with reactions to the same drama from the 1934 guest performance. The *La Plata Zeitung* declared the ensemble's greatest merit was its vibrant and rhythmic delivery of Lessing's dialogue. Irene Ney's portrayal of Minna was praised for being "a linguistic masterclass, utterly compelling in every accent and nuance."[126] Language conveyed the virtues of the German protagonists and exposed the depravity of the drama's single non-German figure—the Frenchman Riccaut de la Marlinière. On this point the *La Plata Zeitung* exceeded its coverage from 1934, in which the paper had criticized Werner Pledath for an insufficiently Francophobic performance of the droll Frenchman. Now, in 1943, Riccaut was vilified as a transgressor against German cultural values, especially language.[127] To make its point, the paper focused on Riccaut's dialogue with Minna, in which he tries to convince her to lend him money for his gambling habit. After a lengthy exchange in French, Minna explains to Riccaut that in her homeland she prefers to communicate in German. Riccaut then retorts scornfully: "German is such a poor language, such a graceless and inept language."[128] Assailing him as the antithesis of the other characters, reviewers distinguished the "dowdy" Frenchman from the honorable Germans by dint of his "putrid" speech.[129] For nationalist emigrants, Riccaut's greatest offense was his ridicule of their sacrosanct native tongue.

The German Theater's emphasis on language was well received. In January 1943, Irene Ney opened her own language and acting studio, specializing in elocution, recitation, and vocal formation. The school expanded several times until March 1945, when the Argentine government shut down most Nazified German institutions. Its self-avowed purpose was to enhance emigrants' appreciation for

---

125. "Zur 'Faust'-Aufführung des Deutschen Theaters," *DLPZ*, March 17, 1942.

126. "Lessings 'Minna von Barnhelm,'" *DLPZ*, April 7, 1943.

127. Schmiesing, "Lessing and the Third Reich," 274.

128. Gotthold Ephraim Lessing, *Minna von Barnhelm*, in Lessing, *Gotthold Ephraim Lessing: Werke*, 1:670.

129. "Lessings 'Minna von Barnhelm,'" *DLPZ*, April 7, 1943.

their "hallowed mother tongue."[130] The studio organized recitation evenings, in which the maxims of conservative theater scholars such as Louise Dumont-Lindemann's "power of the word," Friedrich Rosenthal's "theater of poetry," and Hanns Johst's "service to the word" found a strong echo.[131] Such precepts are tenets of a national aestheticism that emphasized the folkloric qualities of German drama, especially the classics.[132] The nationalist population warmly welcomed the preeminence of the word in national aestheticism, because language was a decisive element in the formation and preservation of its constituents' ethnic heritage and cultural identity as Germans abroad. A binding element among emigrants as well as between them and their countrymen in Europe, language linked the German Theater with Nazi dramatic theory across the Atlantic.

The embrace of national aestheticism carried clear political undertones. Reich dramatist Rainer Schlösser perceived the Nazi movement for literary theater to be a fusion of politics and art. By dint of the "force of their rhetoric, through the sculpting of the word," Schlösser regarded Goebbels and Hitler as both statesmen and artists. The fruit of intensive labor, their eloquence was inspiring for all Germans.[133] In defining the oratory of Goebbels and Hitler as performance art, Schlösser suggested that Nazi ideology and dramatic representation overlapped. The rigor of Ney's rehearsals typified Schlösser's theory and helps explain why Nazi supporters in Argentina believed theater to be vital for community building. Through intensive engagement with the written work, the actors sought to establish a profound bond with their public.[134] Their language and text-oriented preparation coincided with the Nazi front poet Otto Paust's formulation that the supremacy of the dramatic word manifested service to author and audience alike.[135] Beginning with an assiduous refinement of enunciation,

---

130. Irene Ney, "Sprachbildungsarbeit," in *Die Brücke* (1943).
131. "Sprechabend des Deutschen Theaters Rainer Maria Rilke gewidmet," *DLPZ*, June 20, 1943.
132. Biccari, *"Zuflucht des Geistes"?*, 101.
133. Schlösser, *Das Volk und seine Bühne*, 83.
134. Straube, "Ein Schauspieler," 8.
135. Biccari, *"Zuflucht des Geistes"?*, 122.

tone, and gesture, the group's highest objective was to attain an ecstatic sense of community, in which the ensemble and audience become one with the dramatic work.[136] The German Theater imagined theatergoers to be a "spiritual collective of individuals,"[137] which molded each presentation.[138] Together, spectators and thespians collaborated "in service of the people's sacred power."[139] The ensemble's ethnocentric charity performances for the benefit of the German Relief Organization reflected this principle. One event, entitled "The Little Theater of Daily Life," embedded the imagery of Goethe's works, such as Auerbach's cellar and Götz's castle, in contemporary German Buenos Aires. In support of their compatriots, the colony expressed a buoyant pledge through their shared reverence for German culture from the emotive perspective of South American dispersion.[140] Against the backdrop of emigration, sacrifice, and charity, the German Theater fulfilled ethnic Germans' patriotic duty to spiritual and material solidarity with their countrymen overseas.[141] Propagandists in Germany and Argentina portrayed the true bond between audience and ensemble as one of devotion to a transatlantic, racial ideal of nation.

At the core of emigrants' emphasis on the dramatic genre is a concept that Loren Kruger has termed "theatrical nationhood," a project in which inchoate, tenuous sentiments of national identity are articulated, developed, and reinforced through dramatic representation.[142] The German Club of Buenos Aires published an annual almanac for the Ney Stage, *Die Brücke*, which dovetailed with this agenda. Ney explained that the title *Die Brücke* (The Bridge) emphasized the troupe's three-pronged cultural mission: to create bridges between themselves and their public, between members of the emigrant population, and between Germans living abroad

---

136. "Vorwort," in *Die Brücke* (1944).
137. Carl Ludwig Schleich, "Psychologie des Publikums," in *Die Brücke* (1944).
138. "Publikum, aktiv!," *DiA*, August 1942.
139. "Zum Spielplan der Ney-Bühne," *DiA*, September 1940.
140. "Zum Fest des Deutschen Theaters am 5. September zu Gunsten des Deutschen Hilfswerks," *DLPZ*, August 23, 1942.
141. Haigis, "Das Deutsche Theater—und wir," in *Die Brücke* (1944).
142. Kruger, *National Stage*, 86.

and their cultural heritage in Europe.[143] Reprinted in the Argentine newspaper *La Razón*, a speech given by Joseph Goebbels at the 1938 Reich Theater Week in Vienna resonated with these objectives: "There exists a single German people, which is not subject to borders, but instead can be found anywhere where German people live who speak German, think in German, and feel themselves to be Germans."[144] During the Ney Stage's presentations, the Argentine National Theater became a surrogate for national theaters in distant Germany and Austria. In Buenos Aires, the provocative spectacle of theatrical performance summoned the idea of a transatlantic, National Socialist sense of German identity in the poignancy of the audience's absence from its fatherland.

The German classics were fundamental to this program. Nationalist media sought to validate Nazism as a nucleus for German cultural identity by claiming the movement had deep historical roots, thus touching on one of the problematic paradoxes of nationalism—a nation's objective modernity versus its subjective antiquity.[145] The press attempted to surmount this paradox by linking canonical dramas to the recent rise of Nazism. The 1943 edition of *Die Brücke* featured an article by the sociologist and historian Hans Freyer, head of the German Institute for Culture in Budapest from 1938 to 1944. In calling the nation to confront its future, Freyer asserted, statesmen also urge citizens to draw from the past, thereby uniting past and future in an eternal present. Hitler's regime had purposefully opened the inflow of history, shaping the new National Socialist Germany from the depths of millennia.[146] In tandem, the German Theater deployed performances of canonical dramas to claim and ratify the historical origins of Nazism.

Propagandists on both sides of the Atlantic grafted their own interpretations of national memory onto the German classics, which they believed directly addressed contemporary events. Literary

---

143. "Vorwort," in *Die Brücke* (1943).
144. "Semana del Teatro en Viena," *La Razón*, June 14, 1938.
145. Anderson, *Imagined Communities*, 5.
146. Hans Freyer, "Das neue Reich," in *Die Brücke* (1943).

works were not a product of their authors' intellect, but instead the author functioned as a conduit for the will of the people.[147] Nazi scholar Rudolf Ibel argued that the eternal German spirit inspired Goethe to articulate the still inchoate ethnic impulses toward National Socialism in *Götz of Berlichingen*, anticipating the "visible realization" of these values by future generations.[148] In a lecture to his cast, Ludwig Ney traced the Knight of the Iron Hand to National Socialist ideology—and not the other way around—when he described the drama as a literary expression of peasants' instinctive knowledge of their organic attachment to German blood und soil. Furthermore, Götz's scorn for the regional princes and reverence for the Kaiser reflected an intuitive, Teutonic longing for an authoritarian state.[149] The *La Plata Zeitung* theorized that Goethe's dramatization of the German Peasants' War (1525) was the first harbinger of the National Socialist revolution. Hitler's seizure of power proved how prophetically the poet had foreseen the coming changes.[150] Writing for the *Deutsche in Argentinien*, the cultural critic Johannes Franze, who in 1959 won the West German Federal Cross of Merit, listed several examples of how *Götz* accorded with contemporary world events.[151] Lerse and George, characterized by their tenacious loyalty to Götz, represented "precursors to the most recent German revolution, fighting only with different weapons and under different names." Franze also interpreted the timely intervention of Götz's ally, Franz von Sickingen, as anticipatory of Russia's military alliance with Germany in 1940. German nationalists excluded all other interpretations of the drama to secure its links to a National Socialist worldview; any reading not attuned to Nazism only masked *Götz* from true understanding.[152] Goethe's work represented a visionary expression of the eternal will of the German people, which reached its righteous zenith in Hitler's rise.

---

147. "Zur Aufführung des Schauspiels 'Die Räuber,'" *DiA*, August 1943.

148. "'Die Räuber,'" *DiA*, August 1943.

149. "'Götz von Berlichingen' und der Bauernkrieg," *DiA*, June 1940.

150. "Goethes 'Götz von Berlichingen,'" *DLPZ*, May 26, 1940.

151. Franze won the award with no resistance from the West German embassy. Bestand B8, Band 372, PAAA.

152. "'Götz von Berlichingen' und der Bauernkrieg," *DiA*, June 1940.

Reviews of productions of Schiller's *Robbers* and Lessing's *Minna of Barnhelm* in 1943 reiterated this message. Like *Götz, The Robbers* represented a visionary gaze into the future, a "certainty of what was coming, an early anticipation of our thinking."[153] Schiller's drama was set in the distant past, but it addressed political and intellectual problems that remained as current in 1943 as they had been in 1777. Karl Moor was an archetype of the great leader figure. Were it not for his brother, Franz, Karl could have inspired his nation to glorious conquests and victories. The *Deutsche in Argentinien* contrasted the Moors in terms evocative of anti-Semitism, labeling Karl "autochthonous" and "deeply rooted," whereas Franz was the "complete opposite of autochthonous." Karl naturally inspired comradeship, but Franz was incapable of amity or empathy. His purely calculating, materialistic nature ultimately drove him to suicide. The magazine concluded that this lesson was particularly relevant to the current global war of ideals. In the dizziness of technological advances entire cultures had been swayed by materialism, and they would end in the same self-destruction as Franz von Moor.[154] Schiller's *Robbers* proved that Nazi idealism would triumph over the philosophical poverty of its foes.[155]

Lessing's *Minna of Barnhelm*, set in Berlin shortly after the Seven Years' War (1754–63), was also celebrated for its contemporary relevance: "A great, soldierly epoch roars through the scenes of this drama. It seems to have been written in this war and not 170 years ago."[156] The *Deutsche in Argentinien* was convinced that all spectators discerned the closest similarity between these characters and their own lives in the mid-twentieth century.[157] Most importantly, as German chargé d'affaires Erich Otto Meynen put it, even in 1943 Lessing's drama continued to provide mirth and inspiration for all Germans.[158] Reviews of *Minna* undertook to

---

153. "Schillers 'Räuber,' " *DLPZ*, September 3, 1943.
154. "Zur Aufführung des Schauspiels 'Die Räuber,' " *DiA*, August 1943.
155. "Schillers 'Räuber,' " *DLPZ*, September 3, 1943.
156. " 'Minna von Barnhelm,' " *DLPZ*, April 5, 1943.
157. " 'Minna von Barnhelm,' " *DiA*, April 1943.
158. "Lessings 'Minna von Barnhelm,' " *DLPZ*, April 7, 1943.

establish historical links to Hitler's Germany and instill the nationalist colony with an uplifting confidence in National Socialism. The pro-Nazi media created a bond among its public that represented a nationality in the modern sense, an insular ethnicity organized by historic fiction into an imagined community.[159]

Drawing from historical precedents they traced to the German classics, theater critics in Europe and Argentina inculcated their readers with authoritarian hierarchical structures. The protagonist of *Götz of Berlichingen*, the Knight of the Iron Hand, prophesied the rise of a "powerful state" under the "führer figure" of Adolf Hitler.[160] Ernst Rudolf Huber, a leading architect of the Nuremberg Laws, praised *Götz* for its emphasis on state rule, hierarchy, and order.[161] In Buenos Aires, Ney averred that the tragic conclusion to *Götz* should cause Germans everywhere to be grateful for Hitler's clear leadership and creative energy.[162] The *La Plata Zeitung* attempted to legitimize absolute obedience to Hitler's regime on the basis of *The Robbers*. Referring to Kantianism, the paper argued that the actions of each individual must represent the laws of his nation.[163] This misinterpretation of Kant's *Critique of Pure Reason* (1781) revealed another paradox inherent in nationalism: political power versus philosophical poverty, even incoherence.[164] Hannah Arendt states in *The Origins of Totalitarianism* that compliance with the singular will of society becomes uniform in a perfect totalitarian government.[165] In Nazi Germany this meant obedience to Hitler, because the leader's words had the weight of law. Thus, the *La Plata Zeitung* contradicted Kant's rule that the principle of one's will must always be such that it can become the principle of general laws. Instead it demanded that, as loyal Germans, nationalist emigrants submit collectively to the absolute authority of Adolf Hitler. The hierarchical models of service and devotion in the works of

---

159. Roach, *Cities of the Dead*, 103.
160. "Goethes 'Götz von Berlichingen,'" *DLPZ*, June 16, 1940.
161. Mandelkov, *Goethe in Deutschland*, 2:100–101.
162. Notes, *Götz*, CNC.
163. "Schillers 'Räuber,'" *DLPZ*, September 8, 1943.
164. Anderson, *Imagined Communities*, 5.
165. Arendt, *Origins of Totalitarianism*, 136.

Lessing, Goethe, and Schiller—Just to Tellheim in *Minna*, Lerse and Georg to Götz, and the robber band to Karl in *The Robbers*—epitomized and buttressed loyalty to Adolf Hitler in German Buenos Aires.

As the war turned grim for the nationalist population, the German Theater conscripted the classics to encourage commitment to Nazism through both cheer and darker innuendo. For the German Theater's production of Schiller's *Wallenstein* (1798/1799) in March 1944, Ludwig Ney deliberately heightened the drama's relevance to World War II by striking all references to astrology and minimizing Max Piccolomini and Thekla's romance. Instead, Ney focused exclusively on the "fundamental moral" of *Wallenstein*—that is, treason and its consequences.[166] The *La Plata Zeitung* indicted the general as a war criminal and identified egoism as his downfall. Motivated more by his own lust for power than by patriotism, Wallenstein was doomed by his treasonous arrogance even before he acted against the emperor: "The mere thought of treason begets evil, even if it has not translated into action. Merciless vengeance ensues inevitably."[167] Given the tenuous state of Argentina's neutrality in the war, the review can be read as a veiled admonition to the nationalist population. Sanctified as the pure expression of an eternal German people, Schiller underscored the relations of power in the Nazi regime and issued grave warnings against even thinking about transgressing against this hierarchy. Hitler's chief diplomat in Argentina, Consul Edmund von Thermann, regularly attended the German Theater and metonymically reinforced Nazi authoritarianism at its events. Erika Fischer-Lichte has theorized that the bodily copresence and collaboration of thespians and theatergoers endow dramatic presentations with a vital social dimension; however, this theatrical energy is malleable and volatile.[168] The Free German Stage struggled to harness its capacities, unwillingly generating dissonance as well as harmony. Nazi propagandists, on the other hand, adroitly exploited theatrical intimacy as

---

166. "Schillers 'Wallenstein,' " *DLPZ*, March, 22, 1944.
167. "Schillers 'Wallenstein,' " *DLPZ*, March, 22, 1944.
168. Fischer-Lichte, *Theatre, Sacrifice, Ritual*, 19.

a menacing affirmation of Hitlerism. The feeling of togetherness at the German Theater conduced not to social egalitarianism, but to political submission.

Reviewers also manipulated the classics to substantiate the Nazi myth of an eternal, unified, and exclusive German race. Major von Tellheim and Minna von Barnhelm represented timeless, eternal ideals, "veritable symbols of race and nation."[169] Lessing's greatest accomplishment was his inclusion of low-ranking military men and civilians, such as Werner and Just, respectively, in his portrayal of ethnic virtue.[170] Johannes Franze arrogated Goethe to campaign for National Socialist values of kinship, self-sacrifice, and social equality. During the siege of the Jagsthausen castle, Götz acted as a mouthpiece for the "growing intuition of our people's Germanic strength." Götz, who eats from the same plate as his serfs, advocates the construction of a nation pervaded by deep horizontal comradeship when he exhorts Georg to devote his life to improving the welfare of the common people.[171] Lessing and Goethe foreshadowed a National Socialist community, which was racially exclusive but admitted all German followers of Hitler into its fold.

The nationalist German community in Argentina could only be fully imagined through the exclusion of "Others."[172] Some authors were celebrated as much for not being French as for being German. Herder was lauded for steering Goethe away from French rationalism, and Lessing, too, was credited for liberating the comic genre from French influences.[173] Peter Stallybass and Allon White have asserted that such tactics of exclusion are the effect of a mobile, conflictual fusion of power, fear, and desire in the construction of subjectivity. Exclusion results in a psychological dependency upon precisely those Others who are being rigorously opposed and excluded from the community being built.[174] In Buenos Aires this

---

169. "Lessings 'Minna von Barnhelm,'" *DLPZ*, April 1, 1943.

170. "Lessings 'Minna von Barnhelm,'" *DLPZ*, April 7, 1943.

171. Goethe, *Götz von Berlichingen*, in *Johann Wolfgang von Goethe: Werke, Kommentare und Register*, 4:143.

172. Stallybass and White, *Politics and Poetics of Transgression*, 5.

173. "Goethes 'Götz von Berlichingen,'" *DLPZ*, June 16, 1940.

174. Stallybass and White, *Politics and Poetics*, 5.

opposition found expression in racial anti-Semitism and xenophobia. Celebrating Götz as an exemplary German, the *La Plata Zeitung* vilified Metzler and Link as sadistic, materialistic, democratic Jewish agitators.[175] Johannes Franze excoriated enemies of Nazism in Goethe's drama, including the pompous, perfidious, mercenary army of Great Britain, the salon aesthetics and literary prattle of the 1920s Jewish intelligentsia, and the corrupt judges presiding over scandalous trials in the Weimar Republic.[176] The reader must rely on the calumny against the greed, cowardice, deceit, arrogance, and corruption of Others to glean German traits, such as generosity, bravery, honesty, humility, and integrity. Both reviews are remarkable for their stress on institutions, individuals, and traits antithetical to Nazi visions of Germanness.

In the creative process of imagining nationhood through tactics of exclusion, periphery and center can trade places. In Lessing's *Minna of Barnhelm,* the Frenchman Riccaut is socially peripheral, but symbolically central. Although he figures in only a few scenes, Riccaut was played by the German Theater's first actor, Ludwig Ney. Critics praised Ney for giving the most effective performance of the production even as they condemned Riccaut's Gallic aristocratic conceit and passion for gambling and chicanery.[177] Rejected as un-German, Riccaut is as central to definitions of ethnic virtue as Minna, Tellheim, Werner, and Just—all model Germans. The *La Plata Zeitung* corroborated the primacy of the Others by remarking that Ney's depiction of the outcast Frenchman represented an "accomplishment that will go down in the history of Germans on the River Plate."[178] His portrayal of a figure excluded from this population paradoxically garnered Ney's legacy within it. To enact the strength and the stability of the community's center, dramatic presentations had to depict its boundaries and inveigh against its enemies as well. By means of encountering difference through theatrical excursions beyond their colony's fringes, the German Theater imagined a community of illusory fullness by performing what nationalists believed they were not.

---

175. "Goethes 'Götz von Berlichingen,' " *DLPZ*, May 26, 1940.
176. "Goethes 'Götz von Berlichingen,' " *DiA*, June 1940.
177. " 'Minna von Barnhelm,' " *DLPZ*, April 5, 1943.
178. " 'Minna von Barnhelm,' " *DLPZ*, April 5, 1943.

The German classics illustrate a dual transatlantic alignment on- and offstage between the German Theater and the Nazified press in Argentina, on the one hand, and fascist dramatic theory and propaganda in Germany, on the other. Without fail, thespians and reviewers in Buenos Aires endorsed and enacted the precepts of conservative scholars, authors, and actors in Germany. These included meticulous rehearsals and rigidly programmed speech, movements, and gestures onstage; fanatical reverence for the spoken word and literary text as immutable ethnic exaltation; disdain for erudite analysis in favor of populist posturing; and abhorrence for anything associated with theater in Weimar Republic, such as improvisational acting and extravagant stage designs. Additionally, Lessing, Schiller, and Goethe were uniformly subsumed under the mandate to foment fealty to Hitler's regime. The ensemble and media manipulated every production to indoctrinate theatergoers with tenets of Nazism, such as the cult of the leader and the principle of the authoritarian state, the glorification of war, the ignominy and nemesis of treason, as well as racial anti-Semitism and ethnically exclusive community building. In contrast to the refugee population, which lacked a central orientation beyond opposition to Hitler, nationalist Germans followed clear models from across the Atlantic to pilot their project of transatlantic theatrical nationhood. Moreover, whereas refugees often rejected overtly political theater, German nationalists embraced the fusion of drama and dogma. At least in public, they unvaryingly submitted to Nazi ideology on- and offstage. Unlike the Free German Stage, the German Theater existed as a remarkably homogenous cultural institution, braced by the stability of government funding and a cohesive constituency. Its productions of the German classics effectively harnessed the energy of live theater to construct and sustain a close-knit community in support of Adolf Hitler.

Nationalist Hybrids: Local German Dramatists in Argentina

In addition to the German classics, Ney's group also put on plays written by emigrants, such as Werner Hoffmann's *Utz Schmidl* (1941) and Otto Czierski's *The Farmer General* (1940). *Utz Schmidl* was such a success in Argentina that it reportedly was later reprinted and staged in Germany, and Ludwig Ney honored Czierski by choosing his *Farmer General* to celebrate Hitler's birthday on April 20, 1941.[179] By presenting canonical authors alongside local community members, the German Theater aimed to instill a sense of common cultural heritage among the nationalist population. In the only dramas set outside of Germany, Czierski and Hoffmann upheld Nazism, but they also underscored the vast distance separating emigrants from their native Europe and revealed a complex sense of identity that belied the uniform veneer of German nationalism in Argentina.

Czierski's *Farmer General* is a historical play about the 1788 Turkish siege of Werschetz, a settlement with many German inhabitants on the current eastern border of Serbia. In the drama, Werschetz is surrounded by 40,000 Turks and has been abandoned by both Hapsburg troops and most of its residents. Just seventy Germans, led by the courageous farmer general, Johann Jakob Hennemann, remain. Through an elaborate scheme of deception, Hennemann's troops dupe the Turks into believing that Hapsburg forces still occupy Werschetz. After the Turkish military withdraws, the municipal council ennobles Hennemann for rescuing the town.[180] The birthday performance was well timed, because the Yugoslav Union had fallen to the Nazis in the war just four days earlier, on April 17, 1941. German officials later renamed the town Hennemannstadt in honor of the legendary farmer general.

In its content and aesthetics, Czierski's drama was a conformist, propagandistic drama. It affirmed the central tenet of national aestheticism—namely, the supremacy and power of the word.[181] In *The Farmer General* a choir recited verses to inspire the German residents of Werschetz to take up arms against the Turks:

God gave us a plow,
sharp, heavy, and good,
Now we till with our lives,

---

179. Johannes Franze, "Das künstlerische Leben in Buenos Aires 1941," *JdVA* (1941).
180. Tafferner, *Quellenbuch zur donauschwäbischen Geschichte*, 88.
181. Biccari, *"Zuflucht des Geistes"?*, 101.

with our German blood.
The farmer lives, and can die
for his precious land.
He who wastes his field,
may he lose his hand![182]

Czierski's stanzas evoked dramas in Nazi Germany, such as Richard Euringer's *German Passion* (1933) and Wolfgang Eberhard Möller's *Frankenburg Dice Game* (1936), which also featured choral verses. For the *La Plata Zeitung* the choral deployment of the spoken word activated a militant patriotism that had long lain dormant in the soul of the German people.[183] In the 1941 presentation, German emigrants from Transylvania, near Werschetz, recited these verses onstage. Augmented by transatlantic links to current German dramatists as well as the living, physical memory of the immigrant performers, Czierski's verses reinforced the perception of a besieged homeland that urged loyalty and defense from all Germans.

The Farmer General fortified the nationalist community in Argentina by emphasizing that Werschetzer Germans' greatest strength was their unity. Underscoring previous interpretations of the German classics and comedies, Czierski's work demonstrated that wherever they might live, Germans' intrinsic solidarity stemmed from a timeless national identity. The *La Plata Zeitung* called the work a people's play because it depicted an ethnically inspired kinship and courage that "bound the fate of the individual to that of his people, and defined nationhood as eternal."[184] Furthermore, the Werschetzers' innate German traits foretold Germany's National Socialist destiny.[185] As Nazi troops invaded Yugoslavia, nationalists found justification for the aggression in Czierski's allegory of the timeless mantra of German striving.[186]

---

182. Czierski, *Der Bauerngeneral*, 22.
183. " 'Der Bauerngeneral': Festspiel anlässlich des 52. Geburtstages Adolf Hitler," *DLPZ*, April 21, 1941.
184. " 'Der Bauerngeneral,' " *DiA*, September 1940.
185. " 'Der Bauerngeneral,' " *DLPZ*, December 5, 1940.
186. " 'Der Bauerngeneral,' " *DLPZ*, April 21, 1941.

Invoking an immortal spirit of "ethnic order," the *La Plata Zeitung* asserted that Werschetzers' obedience to Hennemann revealed an inborn German characteristic—the ability to recognize a leading personality—that anticipated Adolf Hitler and proved that Nazism manifested Germans' ethnic destiny.[187] This historical framework inspired the *Deutsche in Argentinien* to declare its blind faith in the Nazi state: "We survey the past, present, and future, and we know that under Adolf Hitler the German people are invincible."[188] Acclaiming emigrants' European heritage with a bold prophecy of victory in World War II, the Ney Stage's performance of Czierski's *The Farmer General* on April 20, 1941, was a birthday gift from the nationalist colony to its reverential leader.

Yet, not all local nationalist playwrights projected such seamless transatlantic unity with Nazi Germany. A teacher at the Goethe School and frequent contributor to the *Deutsche La Plata Zeitung* and the *Jahrbuch des deutschen Volksbundes in Argentinien*, Werner Hoffmann wrote his drama as a retrospective on the life of German adventurer Utz Schmidl. After fighting with Spanish soldiers on numerous exploratory expeditions in Paraguay and Argentina, Schmidl returns to his hometown, Straubing, Bavaria, and converses about South America with old acquaintances in a local tavern. Their reunion functions as a framing device that fades into the main body of the work: Schmidl's experiences with the Spanish colonial army in Paraguay. Caught in a web of intrigue between rival officers, Schmidl obeys the military hierarchy because he is certain that this is the only way to maintain order, but the Spanish troops do not share his values. Instead, they scoff at his convictions and ridicule him for being a mercenary. The soldiers' insults deeply offend Schmidl, who, for all his exploits and devotion to the Spanish mission, remains a lowly sergeant due to his German nationality. Ultimately, he is unable to stay clear of their power struggles. Bitter and impoverished, but with ambitions for strong armed forces under German command, Schmidl returns to Straubing only to find that his visions of national military might literally lull his tavern companions to sleep.

---

187. " 'Der Bauerngeneral,' " *DLPZ*, April 18, 1941.
188. "Zur Aufführung des Festspiels 'Der Bauerngeneral,' " *DiA*, April 1941.

Like Czierski's Hennemann, Hoffmann's Utz Schmidl represents National Socialist archetypes of Germanness. A disciplined and selfless soldier, he is brave in battle and committed to the racially motivated Spanish mission, the conquest of the so-called New World for the white race.[189] Hoffmann emphasizes Schmidl's loyalty, contrasting him with the capricious Spaniards. Schmidl refuses a promotion when he learns it would require him to spy on a Spanish general, and the sanctity of military order moves him to assure his commander that authority trumps morality: "I will be loyal to you, my führer, whether you do right or not."[190] Disillusioned by the Spaniards' refusal to reward his service, Schmidl returns to his hometown of Straubing. However, he is not content in Straubing either. As Hoffmann himself explained, his protagonist longs to sail again, but for Germany. The times, however, are "not yet ripe, so he will remain in Straubing and dream of a united German Reich."[191] Explicitly encouraging theatergoers to draw parallels between *Utz Schmidl* and Nazi Germany, Hoffmann inculcated his contemporaries with an awareness of their patriotic duty as German emigrants in 1940.

Schmidl's German traits distinguish him from the Spanish and indigenous characters in the play. Where they are fickle, unreliable, dishonest, and lazy, Schmidl is loyal, dependable, forthright, and industrious. These differences, which Hoffmann always traces to ethnicity, are so definitive that the Spaniards address Schmidl as "German" instead of calling him by name or rank. Surrounded by foreigners, who scorn his German idealism and integrity, Schmidl is ostracized and returns to Bavaria bitter and impoverished. The *Jahrbuch des deutschen Volksbundes* lamented that many Germans abroad shared Schmidl's plight. They, too, were burdened with obligations but denied civic rights, economic opportunities, and political influence.[192] Equating the undervalued, maltreated

---

189. "Das künstlerische Leben in Buenos Aires," *JdVA* (1941).

190. Hoffmann, *Das Spiel vom deutschen Landsknecht Utz Schmidl*, 82.

191. "Das Spiel vom deutschen Landsknecht Utz Schmidl," *DLPZ*, June 26, 1940.

192. "Das künstlerische Leben," *JdVA* (1941).

Schmidl with other German emigrants, the yearbook admonished its readers always to be mindful that Germany was their true home. Or, as the *Deutsche in Argentinien* put it, "German people, remember that you are Germans!!"[193] Funded by the German embassy, both media organs opposed integration with Argentine society and advocated instead for the primacy and perseverance of emigrants' German heritage.

Yet there exists crucial slippage between *Utz Schmidl* and the official Nazi platform in Argentina. Although Hoffmann is at pains to distinguish Schmidl from Spanish soldiers and native Americans, his protagonist lived in South America for decades. As the author perhaps unwittingly reveals, Schmidl is no longer only a German. His identity is now hyphenated and, like so many German-Argentines in Buenos Aires, Schmidl has become a hybrid. This is clear in the drama's frame when, upon his return to Straubing, the adventurer is distinctly not at home in Germany. Although he sits and converses with them for some time, his former friends do not recognize him and insist on calling him "foreigner."[194] The residents of Straubing have a fundamentally different worldview from Schmidl and betray utter ignorance when they speak of South America. Oblivious that a fire devastated Buenos Aires years earlier, they also believe Paraguay is inhabited by cannibalistic women and giants roam Patagonia. Schmidl is incensed as he listens to them, muttering, "Lies, lies upon lies!" Although they are overjoyed to see him when he identifies himself, Schmidl's compatriots fall asleep when he recounts his travels. They do not understand why he left Bavaria nor, really, why he has returned. His experiences abroad distinguish him from local citizens. When asked whether he has gained wealth abroad, Schmidl states: "Little and lots, when I think of what I've accumulated up here (*points to his forehead*)."[195] His cohorts do not have this knowledge, and neither party can overcome the gulf it opens between them. The barman sums the resultant alienation up neatly when, after they

---

193. "Verpflichtung," *DiA*, June 1940.
194. Hoffmann, *Utz Schmidl*, 8.
195. Hoffmann, *Utz Schmidl*, 9.

have chatted for hours, he tells Schmidl: "You've become rather foreign."[196]

The only German nationalist drama set in South America, *Utz Schmidl* was not officially presented by the German Theater, although some ensemble members participated in its performance. Thus, its locale and cast were removed somewhat from the official Nazi propaganda machine, allowing for more nuanced treatment of nationalists' feelings toward their German past and Argentine present. *Schmidl* challenged the notion of a seamless unity between Germans in Buenos Aires and their compatriots across the Atlantic. Even propagandists like Johannes Franze agreed with Hoffmann— German-Argentines were hyphenated Hitlerites. Franze recognized that in 1940, too, many Germans had a false idea of life in Argentina. He lamented that his countrymen failed to comprehend emigrants' drive to search for opportunities and spread German virtues throughout the world. Indeed, this "essential aspiration of Germans abroad" struck other Germans as lunacy. Despite their mutual patriotism, there existed fundamental, widespread, and enduring differences that separated emigrants from Germans in Europe. Neither would ever truly comprehend the other—a dilemma that Franze viewed as the tragedy of Germans abroad.[197]

Emigrants' self-identification with Schmidl consisted partly in his alienation from Germany, but also in the affection he developed for South America. Initially, Schmidl had traveled to South America to seek adventures; however, in time his feelings toward his new environs evolved: "I began to love this land, its forests and rivers."[198] Franze also remarked that Schmidl's inextinguishable affinity for South America motivated him to leave Germany again at the drama's conclusion. Both Germany and Argentina exerted a strong pull on many nationalist emigrants. Max Tepp, who like Hoffmann taught at the Nazified Goethe School, wrote a book, *The Environment of Ethnic Germans in South America* (1930), which instructed German pupils to love Argentina. Hoffmann

---

196. Hoffmann, *Utz Schmidl*, 93.
197. "Das künstlerische Leben in Buenos Aires," *JdVA* (1941).
198. Hoffmann, *Utz Schmidl*, 64.

himself wrote poetry about South American flora and fauna,[199] and the German League even referred to Argentina as a new "fatherland."[200] Even "Hitler's banner" on the River Plate,[201] the *La Plata Zeitung*, indicated the broad appeal of Hoffmann's drama when it asked: "Who among the millions of Germans abroad is not another Ulrich Schmidl?"[202]

A year after the inaugural performance Hoffmann published a verse epilogue, entitled "Homeland."[203] Reflecting on emigrants' varying degrees of integration in Argentina and their consequent alienation from Germany, Hoffmann conveyed the conflicted identity of Argentina's nationalist German population. Whereas some emigrants are scarcely aware of their heritage and are discomforted by their peers' patriotism, others feel an inexorable sense of diremption. These emigrants long for a homeland to which they will never return. Their nostalgia will never translate into action, and steady estrangement is the inevitable result. The poem concludes with individuals who act on these bonds and sustain a vital connection to Germany through deeds. In his epilogue, Hoffmann goaded Germans to participate actively in the preservation and cultivation of their culture in Argentina. A stand-in for contemporary ethnic Germans, that is, German-Argentines, the hybrid, Schmidl had been alienated from his native country by his experiences abroad, precluding his reintegration into German society. Many Germans in Argentina supported Nazism; however, Hoffmann's drama and epilogic poem exposed their allegiance to being distinct from Germans in Germany. As emigrants, they lived abroad, and many were genuinely fond of their new home.

The relationships between the nationalist German population and non-Germans, the Argentine host country, and their German fatherland represented an emotional entanglement that Nazi

---

199. "Das Spiel vom deutschen Landknecht Utz Schmidl," *DLPZ*, July 7, 1940.
200. "Aufgaben des Deutschen Volksbundes," *Evangelisches Gemeindeblatt für die La Plata Staaten* 23 (1916): 317.
201. Ismar, *Der Pressekrieg*, 80.
202. "Das Spiel vom deutschen Landknecht Utz Schmidl," *DLPZ*, July 7, 1940.
203. "Epilog zu *Utz Schmidl*," *JdVA* (1941).

officialdom and its media were loath to admit. Indeed, coordinated press organs had hitherto squelched all dialogue about any sort of cultural ambivalence. As illustrated in numerous instances at the antifascist Free German Stage, it took the shared spectacle of live theater to push this polemical conversation into the public sphere, although one imagines that many emigrants in both colonies had debated such questions of national affection and alienation in private. Hoffmann's dramatized historical analogy thus represented a powerful rhetorical strategy, which raised contested ideological issues onstage and thereby attenuated the offstage discursive practices used in more controllable political contexts such as government-funded publications. Despite strict oversight by the German embassy, the dramatic presentation and ensuing repercussions of *Utz Schmidl* revealed an onerous truth to Nazi authorities: German speakers in Argentina comprised a distinct community characterized by a plurality of cultural and national identities. Their conflicting affinities undercut and destabilized the National Socialist project to construct a single, transatlantic German community under the swastika.

5

Enduring Competition

German Theater in Argentina, 1946–1965

After rising to power in the military and then as minister of labor and vice president, Juan Domingo Perón was elected president of Argentina in 1946 and held power until late 1955 primarily by advocating for the nation's lower classes. Catalyzed by Eva Perón, the government granted women's suffrage and funded an array of social welfare programs, subsidizing workers' access to housing, health care, education, and leisure activities. At the same time, the regime purged dissidents from the government, media, and education sectors. Controversially, Perón encouraged European immigration to Argentina, particularly from Germany. From 1945 to 1955 approximately 400,000 Europeans emigrated to Latin America, and Argentina quickly became a first choice for many German and Austrian citizens.[1] According to Gerald Steinacher, Argentina received just over 100,000 German- and Austrian-born emigrants

---

1. Pace, *La via del demoni*, 4.

in the decade following World War II; however, many of them later remigrated, leaving Argentina with a net gain of approximately 20,000.[2] While the majority were anonymous and politically dis-interested, the new arrivals also included an estimated 40,000 war criminals. Numerous high-ranking Nazi functionaries and collabo-rators were among the new arrivals, including Adolf Eichmann and his adjutant Fritz Stangl; physician and SS captain Josef Mengele; Wilfred von Oven, Joseph Goebbels's press secretary; Belgian Rex-ist Pierre Daye; industrialist and banker Ludwig Freude; and deco-rated pilot Hans-Ulrich Rudel.[3] Bilingual articles in the nationalist German press in Buenos Aires encouraged postwar immigration,[4] which scholars and members of the pre-1945 nationalist commu-nity claim increased sympathy and nostalgia for Nazism among Germans in Argentina.[5] Statistically, the total number of emi-grants during the postwar period roughly equals figures between 1933 and 1945.[6] Antifascists and nationalists alike referred to mi-grations of both periods as diasporas.[7]

In the media landscape this last large wave of German emigrants to Argentina supported several new nationalist publications. The *Freie Presse* first appeared at newsstands in Buenos Aires in De-cember 1945. Although the *Deutsche La Plata Zeitung* had been banned following Argentina's declaration of war on Germany that March, the *Freie Presse* was its direct successor. The *Freie Presse* featured many of the same staff as the *La Plata Zeitung*, includ-ing its founder, Frederico Müller, and likely was under the same ownership.[8] Like the *Argentinisches Tageblatt* during the 1930s,

---

2. Steinacher, "Argentinien als NS-Fluchtziel," 243–244.

3. Holger Meding, "La emigración a la República Argentina de los Nacional-socialistas buscados: Una aproximación cuantativa," *Estudios migratorios latino-americanos* 43 (1999): 241–259.

4. "Gobernar es poblar/Regieren heißt bevölkern," *FP*, May 15, 1947.

5. Michael Frank, *Die letzte Bastion*; Lamm, interview by author, Decem-ber 10, 2010; Ney, interview by author, February 3, 2009.

6. Holger Meding, "Der Nationalsozialismus und die deutsche Einwanderung an den Rio de la Plata," in Eick, *Nach Buenos Aires!*, 36.

7. "Geistige Lage des Nazismus heute," *AT*, May 31, 1949; "Die Lüge der sechs Millionen," *Der Weg*, March 1955.

8. Ismar, *Pressekrieg*, 197.

the *Freie Presse* gained readers and writers by targeting German emigrants to Argentina. Its circulation rose steadily throughout the 1950s, reaching 30,000 by the end of the decade. For much of the 1950s and 1960s, it had the highest circulation of any German-language newspaper printed outside of Europe.[9] Politically, the *Freie Presse* was equivocal. Despite links to the *La Plata Zeitung*, the *Freie Presse*'s vehemently anti-Communist tone garnered it support among West German diplomats in Buenos Aires.[10] It also eventually distanced itself from blatantly neo-Nazi publications like *Der Weg*. Nonetheless, in 1952 Wilfred von Oven, formerly Joseph Goebbels's press secretary, became editor in chief of the *Freie Presse*. Although West German diplomats defended the paper,[11] von Oven himself described the *Freie Presse* as a National Socialist publication.[12] The war of words between the *Argentinsches Tageblatt* and the *Deutsche La Plata Zeitung* from 1914 to 1945 continued largely unabated between the *Tageblatt* and the *Freie Presse* in the postwar period.

Another prominent voice among Argentina's postwar German-language media was the monthly magazine *Der Weg*. Founded in 1947 by the Hitler Youth leader and Nazi pedagogue Eberhard Fritsch, *Der Weg* was published by the Dürer Press in Buenos Aires. Authors published by Dürer read like a who's who of unapologetic Nazis, including Johann Leers, Mathilde Ludendorff, Wilfred von Oven, Hans-Ulrich Rudel, Rudolf Heß, and Reinhard Kopps (alias Juan Maler). Although *Der Weg* and the *Freie Presse* had partially coinciding readerships, the former was a stridently neo-Nazi publication that was banned in occupied Germany and Austria in 1949.[13] After Perón's downfall in 1955, various overlapping antifascist, Jewish, and governmental groups campaigned against *Der Weg*. It lost many advertisers, including the *Freie Presse*, and

9. Ismar, *Pressekrieg*, 198–199.
10. West German Embassy (WGE) to Federal Foreign Office (FFO), November 16, 1962, Bestand B33, Band 248, PAAA.
11. WGE to FFO, September 30, 1965, Bestand B33, Band 386, PAAA.
12. Meding, *Flucht vor Nürnberg?*, 268.
13. Meding, *Der Weg*, 116–117.

folded in 1957.[14] Known for its political content, initially *Der Weg* was chiefly an arch-conservative cultural magazine, which reported regularly on Ludwig Ney's ensemble.

The Free German Stage: Stymied Reconciliation, 1945–1953

Admired internationally for its accomplishments as the world's only regularly performing exilic theater during World War II, after the conflict the Free German Stage featured guest performances by some of the most famous names in German theater, including Ernst Deutsch (1946), Ellen Schwanneke (1946), Hans Moser (1948), Viktor de Kowa (1949, 1952), Theo Lingen (1954), and the entire ensembles of the Viennese Theater in the Josefstadt (1956) and the Berlin Comedy (1957). In the 1950s the FGS grew increasingly dependent on subventions from Bonn, which sponsored performances throughout the Southern Cone and financed the troupe until 1965. Thus, from 1940 to 1965 the theater reversed roles from debunking to projecting German soft power.

Paul Walter Jacob saw the war's end as an opportunity to fulfill both political convictions and professional ambitions. Jacob hoped that the FGS could help to heal ill will between Argentina's German populations, and he also realized that the company needed to expand beyond the refugee population. Aging, remigration, and integration into Argentine society would cause audiences from this group to shrink in the ensuing years. New emigrant theatergoers and thespians were arriving in the postwar emigration from Europe, but the FGS would alienate itself from them unless it mended relations with German nationalists. On the other hand, its public would more than double if the group could establish itself as a less political, more inclusive German-language theater abroad for both colonies. As early as 1943 Jacob had begun planning for this maneuver, which he believed was the only path to long-term financial

---

14. Meding, *Der Weg*, 138.

solvency for the stage.[15] Yet the director's ambitions threatened to sow deeper discord within the already contentious antifascist population, because many of its members had no wish for reconciliation and opposed his strategy.

The media landscape quickly reflected the changing tactics of the FGS. In one of its very first issues, the *Freie Presse* began reporting on Jacob's troupe. With effusive praise, the paper even undertook to endorse the stage retroactively by weaving applause for past performances into reviews of current productions.[16] Jacob advertised regularly in the *Freie Presse*, which he perceived as a conduit to the nationalist population. The relationship developed into a close partnership. The awkward coupling of the antifascist, predominantly Jewish Free German Stage and the nationalist *Freie Presse* was underscored visually when the paper published a review of the theater's 1947 almanac alongside an advertisement for a local screening of the Nazi propaganda film *Der Herrscher* (1937).[17] In another instance, Jewish Jacques Arndt's reports from Vienna in 1950 were printed next to advertisements for books such as Hans-Ulrich Rudel's *Nevertheless* and Wilfred von Oven's *With Goebbels until the End*.[18] Still, both parties advanced their cooperation. On December 30, 1947, Jacob sent the founder of the *Freie Presse*, Frederico Müller, his best wishes for the coming year and thanked him for being a true friend and supporter of the FGS.[19]

Their cooperation elicited divisive reactions throughout German Buenos Aires. The Free German Stage offended its extant public by advertising in the *Freie Presse*, which was taboo among Jews.[20] Most Jews, antifascists, and nationalists were against reconciliation, and refused even to read the other colony's newspaper. Members of the nationalist colony, too, were baffled by this

---

15. Jacob to Berger, November 22, 1943, PWJAK.
16. "FDB: *Marilou*," *FP*, December 3, 1945.
17. "Deutsches Kino," *FP*, April 15, 1947.
18. "Wiener Theaterbrief," *FP*, January 8, 1950.
19. Jacob to Müller, December 30, 1947, PWJAK.
20. Ernesto Curt Damerau to Jacob, March 22, 1950, PWJAK.

development. One reader, who explained that she had lived in Argentina for decades and was writing on behalf of many prewar emigrants, asked Jacob directly: "Is the FGS a German-language theater for the Jewish colony, or not?"[21] The overwhelming number of Jews in its public, cast, and repertoire indicated that it was, and the group's name also displeased many of her acquaintances. In Germany and especially in Argentina, there were no "unfree" German theaters. But then again, she went on, Jacob continually advertised in the *Freie Presse*, the paper of the "other" German-speaking population in Buenos Aires. The writer of the letter concluded that Jacob would have to be more consequential. If he wanted to expand his public, he had to change the cast. Representatives from both colonies needed to be onstage; otherwise readers of the *Freie Presse* would feel alienated from Jacob's troupe.

The director appears to have taken her advice to heart. In addition to organizing celebrity guest performances, he engaged Werner Zamelka, Egon Straube, and Ina Maria Müller, all of whom had been members of Ludwig Ney's company during the war. He also attempted to contract Roman Riesch, who had starred in a 1935 guest performance sponsored by the German consulate and Strength through Joy.[22] Indicating ongoing political divisions, Riesch declined the offer.[23] Jacob's strategy also encountered stiff resistance among the refugee population. Despite their turbulent relationship, the Zionist *Jüdische Wochenschau* had publicized the FGS since 1940; however, in 1948 the *Jüdische Wochenschau* desisted from further reporting on the ensemble. The antifascist organization and journal *Das Andere Deutschland* had already reduced its coverage toward the end of the war and, although Jacob protested personally to its editor, August Siemsen, *DAD* continued this trend during the postwar period.[24] There was also fallout with the leftist Forward Club, where Jacob previously had lectured and directed the choir. By 1946, however, Jacob complained that his

---

21. Frau Rosenlöcher to Jacob, July 28, 1947, PWJAK.
22. Breslauer to Riesch, February 4, 1946, PWJAK.
23. Roman Riesch to Breslauer, February 12, 1946, PWJAK.
24. Jacob to Siemsen, July 29, 1946, PWJAK

efforts had not been reciprocated. He discontinued his membership and broke off all contact in August of that year.[25]

The Free German Stage's relationship with the *Argentinisches Tageblatt* suffered the worst repercussions. Long his greatest champion, the *Tageblatt* was infuriated by Jacob's decision to advertise in the *Freie Presse*. The deterioration in the paper's relationship with the FGS was evident in its coverage of the 1946 season, which, despite celebrity guest performances by Ernst Deutsch and Ellen Schwanneke, was markedly shorter and less prominently positioned than in the past. The *Freie Presse*, by comparison, consistently published much longer reviews on the front page of its arts section.[26] The 1946 theater almanac, in which shorter excerpts from the *Tageblatt* were printed beneath lengthier quotes from the *Freie Presse*, also evinced the ramifications of the alienation between the former and the FGS. Announcing his intent to break off all contact with Jacob, the *Tageblatt*'s theater critic, Werner Katzenstein, cited the director's friendship with the *Freie Presse* as his primary motive. Katzenstein felt personally slighted that after all the *Tageblatt* had done to aid his enterprise during its tenuous first years, Jacob had established close relations with its primary commercial and political competitor.[27] Jacob did not answer Katzenstein, but days later he complained to Sigmund Breslauer that the *Tageblatt* had slashed coverage of the FGS but printed page-long reports on amateur stages in Rio de Janeiro and Montevideo. Despite Katzenstein's explanations, Jacob described this treatment as bewildering and then complained that the paper "intentionally harms us with every theater article."[28] The quarrel worsened when a leading journalist for the *Tageblatt*, Peter Bussemeyer,

25. Jacob to Forward Club, August 21, 1946; Vice President Sternberg to Jacob, September 2, 1946, PWJAK.

26. This began at the outset of the 1946. Compare "*Ball im Savoy*," *FP*, April 14, 1946 and "*Ball im Savoy*," *AT*, April 10, 1946; "George Bernard Shaw *Frau Warrens Gewerbe*," *FP*, April 28, 1946 and "Shaws *Frau Warrens Gewerbe*," *AT*, April 28, 1946; "*Frühlingswind*, Lustspiel von Johann von Bokay," *FP*, May 5, 1946 and "*Frühlingswind* in der FDB," *AT*, May 5, 1946.

27. Katzenstein to Jacob, March 13, 1947, PWJAK.

28. Jacob to Heinrich Fränkel, April 16, 1947, PWJAK.

published an article in the New York magazine *Aufbau* attacking the "readiness to reconcile" of Jacob and others who seemed to have already forgotten about the catastrophe of Nazism. The Free German Stage had abandoned the "Free" in its name and now spurned antifascist thespians in favor of actors from the former "Nazi theater" in Buenos Aires as well as artists associated with the Miklós Horthy government in Hungary. Furthermore, Busse-meyer lauded Alexander Berger for leaving the troupe and forming a rival, moral theater company.[29]

The imbroglio did not abate. Compared to previous years, Ale-mann's paper had cut the average length of its reviews by half.[30] After the Latin American premiere of Carl Zuckmayer's *The Devil's General* (1946) in 1948, Liselott Reger complained from Uruguay that the *Tageblatt*'s reporting was so colorless that she could not tell whether the sold-out, widely acclaimed production had been a success.[31] For this information Reger could have turned to the *Freie Presse*, which ran a 1,225-word review of the performance as opposed to the 425-word report in the *Tageblatt*. The tension impacted Jacob's journalistic activities, too. In 1945 he published forty-one articles in the paper; just a year later the number had dwindled to six and did not recover. Jacob's lukewarm farewell let-ter to Ernesto Alemann before his departure for Europe, in which he thanked the *Tageblatt* owner for having supported the FGS "a good while," indicated the unhealed rift.[32]

Jacob's strategy of reconciliation and expansion created contro-versy behind the curtain, too. Several actors were irate when Jacob began cooperating with the *Freie Presse* and contracted thespians formerly in Ney's cast. To conclude the 1945 season, the stage

---

29. "Jannings ist nur ein Symptom," *Aufbau* 13 (1947): 11.

30. Compare 1948 and 1943: "*Vergelt's Gott*," AT, April 28, 1948; "*Schnei-der im Schloss*," AT, May 12, 1948; "*Gaslicht*," AT, May 25, 1948; "*Fuhrman Henschel*," AT, June 9, 1948; "*Saison im Kurhotel*," AT, May 23, 1943; "*Zweiter Stock, Tür 19*," AT, May 30, 1943; "*Das Schwedische Zündholz*," AT, June 6, 1943; "*Dorine und der Zufall*," AT, June 13, 1943; "*Dr. Juci Szabo*," AT, June 26, 1943.

31. Reger to Jacob, June 24, 1948, PWJAK.

32. Jacob to Alemann, March 3, 1950, PWJAK.

commemorated the twenty-fifth anniversary of FGS member Annie Ernst's acting debut with the world premiere of *Marilou* (1945), an operetta by composer Lyle Frey and librettist Karl Völlmer, both emigrants to Argentina. Between acts Alexander Berger gave a speech to honor Ernst. The gesture struck the *Jüdische Wochenschau* as heartwarming and passed without comment by the *Tageblatt* and *Freie Presse*.[33] Jacob, on the other hand, was incensed because a fellow actor felt the speech was deliberately offensive to "Aryans." Berger retorted that only antifascist Aryans had visited the FGS during the war. All others attended Ludwig Ney's German Theater. They had boycotted, besmeared, and threatened Jews at every opportunity. Berger concluded that antifascists could only have applauded his speech, and if the second group "was offended by my 'slap in the face' (your words), then I am delighted."[34] Just days later Max Wächter, a founding member of the ensemble, reinforced Berger's actions when he accused Jacob of flirting with the Nazis.[35] The rancor within his own cast imperiled Jacob's project of reconciliation through theater, and it even put the FGS itself at risk.

The mounting tension culminated when, for the first time since its inauguration, the Free German Stage broke apart. Eight longtime members formed their own competing ensemble, the Musical Players, which performed six operettas during the 1946 season. In response Jacob partnered with the exilic Independent Hungarian Theater and Otto Werberg's ballet group to perform a competing program of prewar German, Austrian, and Hungarian operettas. Noting that Ernö Szilágy's orchestra and the Hungarian actors' accents created an exotic atmosphere, the *Jüdische Wochenschau* reported that the operettas filled thousands of seats as well as the coffers of both stages.[36] Various Spanish-language newspapers also lauded the presentations.[37] The upstart Musical Players were

---

33. "FDB: Uraufführung von *Marilou*," *JW*, December 7, 1945.

34. Berger to Jacob, January 3, 1946.

35. Wächter to Arndt, January 15, 1946, JAC.

36. "FDB und Ungarische Bühne *Gräfin Mariza* von Kalman," *JW*, May, 17, 1946.

37. "Tiene Éxito la Opereta de P. Abraham," *La Hora*, July 25, 1946; "Bilingüe," *Hoy*, September 7, 1946.

overmatched, and in 1948 they dissolved and most re-signed with the FGS. Paul Walter Jacob's collaboration with the Independent Hungarian Theater again ratified his strategy of drawing from the strength of intercultural partnerships to overcome external threats and internal dissension. Nevertheless, the widespread aversion to his rapprochement with German nationalists portended that the divisive theatrical energies unleashed during the war had woven a web of hostilities that would not easily be undone.

From 1946 on, wagering that the broad appeal of international theater and film stars could surmount tenacious animosities in German Buenos Aires, Jacob organized numerous celebrity guest performances. Another goal was to reestablish ties to Germany, specifically West Germany. Ernst Deutsch (1946), Ellen Schwanneke (1946), Hans Moser (1948), Fritz Gehlen (1948), Viktor de Kowa (1949, 1952), and Theo Lingen (1954) visited the FGS. These events were acclaimed throughout the Argentine capital. Leading personalities of the Argentine entertainment industry gave speeches at Ernst Deutsch's welcome reception, including the president of the Argentine Actors Association, Florindo Ferrario, and Faustino Tezanos, general intendant of the Buenos Aires theater system. The director of the Smart Theater, Nestor Ibarra, requested permission to attend all Deutsch's rehearsals, and the Emelka television program announced plans to film the dress rehearsal for Ibsen's *Ghosts* (1882). Afterward, with Deutsch in attendance for the FGS's 150th premiere and 500th production, Hans José Rehfisch's *Water for Canitoga* (1936), Jacob declared to the audience that the exiled Jewish actor's presence initiated a new epoch in the stage's existence.[38]

Deutsch's agenda in Buenos Aires included an evening of poetry recitations as well as performances of *Ghosts*, John Galsworthy's *Loyalties* (1922), and the world premiere of Alfred Neumann's *Abel* (1946). Although Deutsch was famous for playing the title role in Lessing's *Nathan the Wise* (1779), the repertoire during his stay prioritized caution and inclusion. Jacob and his donors had

---

38. "Ernst Deutsch in Südamerika," *Sonntagsblatt Staatszeitung und Herold*, June 7, 1946.

engineered the guest performances to establish the FGS as *the* German theater in Buenos Aires, and they refused to jeopardize this endeavor.[39] The approach proved effective. *La Nación*'s drama critic, Samuel Eichelbaum, devoted a full-page article to Deutsch's depiction of Oswald in Ibsen's *Ghosts*, which he compared to the renowned Yiddish actor Ben Ami's portrayal in 1941 and hailed as a landmark in Argentine theater history.[40] Theater reviewers for dozens of local newspapers, including German, Spanish, Hungarian, Polish, and Italian media, gushed over Deutsch's sold-out performances at the National Theater.[41] The Free German Stage had appeared in some of these publications before, but never had so many of them covered the company in such depth at once.

A month later Ellen Schwanneke arrived in Buenos Aires. Her performances in Dario Nicodemi's *Scampolo* (1932), George Bernard Shaw's *Saint Joan* (1923), and Christa Winsloe's *Yesterday and Today* (1930) brought the FGS another round of publicity in Buenos Aires and beyond.[42] But unlike Deutsch's visit, which

39. Deutsch to Lifezis, December 12, 1945; Fränkel to Jacob, January 10, 1946; Lifezis to Jacob, January 18, 1946, PWJAK.

40. "Ernst Deutsch en *Espectros*," *LN*, June 3, 1946.

41. The following is a sampling; many newspapers printed multiple articles on Deutsch's visit: "Gastspiel von Ernst Deutsch," *JW*, May 13, 1946; "*Gespenster* und *Oswald* . . . Ernst Deutsch," *FP*, June 1, 1946; "Actuó Ernesto Deutsch," *El Pueblo*, June 1, 1946; "La temporada de Ernst Deutsch," *La Hora*, June 1, 1946; "Presentóse anoche con *Espectros*," *La Prensa*, June 1, 1946; "E. Deutsch se presentó en El Nacional," *La Razón*, June 1, 1946; "Aplaudióse al actor Ernst Deutsch," *El Mundo*, June 2, 1946; "Ernst Deutsch," *Kurjer Polski*, June 2, 1946; "El actor Alemán Ernesto Deutsch," *El Diario*, June 2, 1946; "E. Deutsch *Gesellschaft* von Galsworthy," *AT*, June 18, 1946; "Entrevistamos al intérprete Alemán Ernst Deutsch," *Noticias Gráficas*, July 5, 1946.

42. "Ellen Schwanneke en Buenos Aires," *La Tarde*, August 8, 1946; "Muchachas de uniforme," *Antena*, August 20, 1946; "Veremos hoy a Schwanneke," *La Hora*, August 13, 1946; "Ellen Schwannecke Makes Her Debut," *BAH*, August 14, 1946; "Mädchen in Uniform," *The Standard*, August 14, 1946; "Se presentó anoche Ellen Schwanneke," *La Prensa*, August 14, 1946; "Ellen Schwanneke en Internado de Señoritas," *Argentina Libro*, August 15, 1946; "Gastspiel Ellen Schwanneke," *AT*, August 15, 1946; "Presentóse Ellen Schwanneke," *El Lider*, August 15, 1946; "Debutó Ellen Schwanneke," *La Argentina*, August 15, 1946; "Pierwszy Wystep Ellen Schwanneke," *Kurjer Polski*, August 15, 1946; "Ellen Schwanneke interpretó una pieza de Nicodemi," *LN*, August 21, 1946; "FDB:

was universally praised and caused no discernible controversy, Schwanneke's sojourn revealed simmering tensions in Buenos Aires. Her signature performance was Winsloe's *Yesterday and Today*, which also had been produced as a film, *Girls in Uniform* (1931), by Carl Froehlich, with Leontine Sagan as director. Both Schwanneke as Ilse von Westhagen and the FGS's Hedwig Schlichter-Crilla as Fräulein von Kesten had played major roles in the film, which denounced the militaristic atmosphere at a Prussian boarding school for girls. The film was an international success, and the *New York Times* singled out Schlichter-Crilla's performance as "deserving of the highest praise."[43]

Although it had potential to stir polemics, the presence of two stars from the movie compelled the FGS to stage the play. Conflict rapidly ensued. The *Freie Presse*'s report on Schwanneke's arrival mentioned the Nazi period just twice and emphasized that the actress had left Germany voluntarily in 1933.[44] Then, its review of *Girls in Uniform* denounced the Allied occupation, noting that Winsloe had been shot mistakenly in France in 1944. It also dismissed the play's condemnation of militarized education in interwar Germany as a world of backward nobility that had disappeared decades earlier. By contrast, the *Argentinisches Tageblatt* contended that *Girls in Uniform* proved the obvious—that, for example, young people require compassionate teachers, and the traditional Prussian method of education forever damaged children's souls by forcibly turning children into mindless robots compliant with the authoritarian state.[45] The *Jüdische Wochenschau* was

---

Gastspiel Ellen Schwanneke *Scampolo*," *JW*, August 23, 1946; "Ellen Schwanneke en El Nacional," *Hoy*, August 28, 1946; "Pequeña comedia fue estrenada anoche," *El Pueblo*, August 28, 1946; "Animó E. Schwanneke una graciosa comedia," *El Mundo*, August 29, 1946; "Ellen Schwanneke, estrella de *Internado de Señoritas*," *La Película*, August 30, 1946; "Ellen Schwanneke in Buenos Aires," *New Yorker Staatszeitung*, September 8, 1946; "Ellen Schwannecke in Buenos Aires," *Hamburger Volkszeitung*, September 8, 1946; "En la voz reside el mágico secreto," *Qué*, September 12, 1946. "*Die heilige Johanna* in der Freien Deutschen Bühne," *DAD*, September 15, 1946;

43. "*Girls in Uniform*," *New York Times*, September 12, 1932.
44. "Grüß Gott, Ellen Schwannecke!," *FP*, August 7, 1946.
45. "Gastspiel Ellen Schwanneke," *AT*, August 15, 1946.

more explicit, asserting that Winsloe unmasked a national German pedagogy responsible for sowing the evil ideology that had brought Nazism into the world.[46] Spanish-language media uniformly corroborated the *Tageblatt*'s interpretation, and many newspapers, from the proletariat *El Pueblo* to the bourgeois *La Nación*, directly accused Prussian educators of systematically inculcating their pupils with totalitarian, militaristic values to avenge Germany's defeat in the First World War.[47] Of fifteen reviews in Argentina and abroad, only the *Freie Presse* did not directly link *Girls in Uniform* to the militarization of German society during the interwar period.

Further controversies followed. In 1948 Jacob contracted the Viennese comic Hans Moser. Although his wife was Jewish, Moser had acted in over thirty films between the Nazi annexation of Austria and 1945. Since the *Argentinisches Tageblatt* mentioned only the actor's postwar work,[48] one reader solicited clarification of Moser's position toward Nazism, noting rumors that he had starred in an early anti-Semitic film.[49] The *Revista Familiar Israelita del Uruguay* argued that Moser only could have continued acting after 1938 if his political views had coincided with the Nazi regime.[50] One theatergoer pressured Jacob for an explanation, claiming the widespread rumors about Moser warranted a response in the *Revista Familiar Israelita* and the *Tageblatt*. This would convince skeptics to attend the presentations.[51] Three days later, Jacob blamed lackluster sales on "anti-Moser propaganda."[52]

---

46. "FDB: Gastspiel Ellen Schwanneke *Mädchen in Uniform*," *JW*, August 16, 1946.

47. "En torno a la presentación de Ellen Schwanneke," *El Pueblo*, August 15, 1946; "Ellen Schwanneke ha sido aplaudida en El Nacional," *LN*, August 15, 1946; "Ellen Schwanneke en *Internado de Señoritas*," *Argentina Libre*, August 15, 1946; "E. Schwanneke rebutó en el teatro alemán," *La Hora*, August 17, 1946.

48. "Hans Moser eingetroffen," *AT*, May 15, 1948.

49. "Ein mit Grund Neugieriger," *AT*, June 13, 1948. The film goes unnamed, but the letter likely references erroneously an interpretation of Moser's portrayal of the anti-Semitic lawmaker, Rat Bernhard, in Hans Breslauer's *Die Stadt ohne Juden* (1924).

50. "Carta a la redacción," *Revista Familiar Israelita del Uruguay*, August 27, 1948.

51. Kraemer to Jacob, August 28, 1948.

52. Jacob to Reger, September 1, 1948, PWJAK.

Figure 8. Hans Moser and Paul Walter Jacob on the *Voice of the Day* radio program in Montevideo, Uruguay, 1948.

Source: Paul Walter Jacob, ed., *Almanach der Freien Deutsche Bühne in Buenos Aires* (Buenos Aires: Editorial Jupiter, 1948), 49.

The dissension continued during Moser's visit, and Jacob felt compelled to address the situation after his closing performance in Herrmann Mostar's *When the Snow Melts* (1948). Attended by Austrian consul Otto Günther, the production benefited the newly formed Austrian Charity, which led the *Freie Presse* to describe the FGS as the epitome of Schiller's concept of the theater as a moral institution. After the final curtain Jacob gave a farewell speech, expressing the hope that the FGS could thaw the snow in Buenos Aires, which still kept many people away from its performances.[53] Yet Moser's visit, including the charity performance, had the opposite effect. Jacob's publicist in Montevideo even advised against publishing a theater almanac for the 1948 season. He could not find any advertisers, because the FGS had become too divisive. The benefit had angered many Jews, who protested that the Austrians

53. "*Wenn der Schnee schmilzt*," *FP*, September 15, 1948.

had behaved no better than the Germans during the Nazi period. Jacob's support for reconciliation between Jews and Austrians riled Zionists and antifascists, costing him longtime supporters, who felt betrayed.[54] An almanac did appear for the 1948 season, and it was warmly received in the local and international press;[55] however, when Jacob engaged Viktor de Kowa in 1949, he took preemptive measures against resurgent polemics.

The guest performances brought Paul Walter Jacob notoriety in Europe. In 1949 he and the well-known actor and director Viktor de Kowa elaborated a plan for individual appearances in Buenos Aires and Berlin during alternate years, to which they would add more ensemble members over time.[56] The arrangement appealed to both parties, but De Kowa's biography was problematic. De Kowa had continued acting during Hitler's regime, featuring in thirty-five films from 1933 to 1945, and was named to the Important Artist Exempt List to shield him from military service. Unlike Moser, De Kowa had been a member of the NSDAP and directed overtly pro-pagandistic productions, such as the 1941 film *Chin Up, Johannes!* The film commended the transformational education and character development that young Johannes, an ethnic German from Argentina, receives in the Nazi National Political Institutes of Education. The visit of an actor and director with such a background augured a casus belli in German Buenos Aires.

To finalize the contract, Jacob visited De Kowa in Berlin in April 1949 and, while he was there, wrote a piece about his impressions for the *Argentinisches Tageblatt*. In addition to the city's political climate, sights, and citizens, Jacob reported on a concert by Rudolf Nelson at De Kowa's Berlin Tribune theater. A pianist, composer, and founder of the illustrious Nelson Review cabaret, the Jewish artist was performing in Berlin for the first time after fifteen years in exile. Jacob quoted from De Kowa's introduction, in

54. Widetzky to Jacob, October 1, 1949, PWJAK.

55. "Theater-Almanach auf das Goethe-Jahr 1949," *FP*, March 12, 1949; "10 Jahre FDB," *Frankfurter Rundschau*, January 12, 1949; "FDB Almanach," *Basler Nationalzeitung*, January 29, 1949; "Freie Deutsche Bühne," *Detroiter Abend-Post*, June 19, 1949.

56. De Kowa to Jacob, April 16, 1949, PWJAK.

which the actor professed his own culpability and begged Nelson's forgiveness. Then, as if to be sure that nobody missed the message, Jacob reiterated that in private conversation it was impossible not be moved by De Kowa's sincerity and his uncompromising commitment to reconciliation and pacifism.[57] Operating in the guise of travel journalism, Jacob's main objective was to forestall attacks against De Kowa during his visit to Buenos Aires.

Upon his arrival in Argentina, the *Freie Presse* and *Argentinisches Tageblatt* ran reports characterizing De Kowa as a pacifist whose credo, peace is the precondition for mankind's happiness, would resonate in Buenos Aires.[58] When the curtain rose, De Kowa performed J. B. Priestley's *Ever since Paradise* (1946), Marcel Achard's *I Know My Love* (1946), a variety show entitled "The Unknown Goethe," and Charlotte Rißmann's *Promise Me Nothing* (1936). He received rave reviews from the *Tageblatt*, which exclaimed that Achard owed the guest a medal of honor and fawned over De Kowa's direction of the intercultural Goethe variety evening. A week later, however, the German-language radio program from Montevideo, *The Voice of Day*, told of a different reaction. In a segment entitled "Viktor de Kowa and the Malice," the program's producer, Hermann Gebhardt, reported that the visitor had received several anonymous letters upbraiding him for acting with a Jewish theater. Then, when he arrived in Montevideo, emigrants vilified him for being a Nazi. Himself an antifascist refugee, but one whom Zionists assailed for advocating rapprochement, Gebhardt concluded that these threats represented larger blocs of agitators in both German-speaking populations.[59] Instead of striving for peace, both factions stoked rancor in an enduring pattern of systemic group hatred. Jacob and Gebhardt were willing to draw a distinction between Germans who had remained active in Hitler's Germany and those who had not. In the case of De Kowa, they also accepted apologies from a person whom they saw as a truly

---

57. "Mit Viktor de Kowa im blockierten Berlin," *AT*, July 18, 1949.

58. "Empfang bei Viktor De Kowa," *FP*, July 9, 1949; "Hoppla, es ist ja Frieden!" *AT*, July 15, 1949; "Viktor De Kowa und der Weltfrieden," *FP*, July 19, 1949.

59. "Viktor de Kowa und die Bosheit," *La Voz del Día*, August 30, 1949.

repentant collaborator. Many other emigrants, however, were not open to reconciliation—let alone forgiveness—in either instance.

Jacob faced staunch, multifold resistance to his efforts to render the FGS the theater of all Germans in Buenos Aires. His strategy did not win over enough people from the nationalist colony to increase attendance significantly and, furthermore, alienated many former supporters and ensemble members. The upshot of theatergoers' intransigence was insolvency. As the stage ran ever deeper deficits, its sponsors grew impatient. Heinrich Fränkel, the primary donor to the stage, complained with increasing vehemence about having to fund the enterprise month after month.[60] Eventually, as he fretted to conductor and frequent spectator at the FGS, Fritz Busch, Jacob worried not about funding the stage from season to season, but from weekly premiere to weekly premiere.[61] Busch himself had to intervene, meeting with several leading members of the antifascist colony to convince them to save the theater. He argued that its closure would irrevocably damage the cultural prestige of the antifascist movement, "our cause."[62] As a motivation to save the stage, Busch invoked the enmity that Jacob was trying to overcome. The group created a theater commission to shore up the FGS's finances, but this precarious endeavor was founded on the very polarization that precluded the enterprise's solvency.

The intractable animosity in German Buenos Aires, the distressing state of the theater's finances, and his own professional ambition all convinced Jacob that his future was in Europe. Through the Free German Stage, he had made a name for himself in Germany,[63] Switzerland,[64] the United States,[65] and England.[66] Jacob parlayed

---

60. Fränkel to Jacob, July 3, 1947, PWJAK.

61. Jacob to Fritz Busch, August 1, 1947, PWJAK.

62. Busch to Fränkel, Alemann, Koch, Zacharias, (date illegible) 1947, PWJAK.

63. "Ellen Schwannecke," *Der Spiegel* 16, April 19, 1947; "Spielzeitbeginn in Buenos Aires," *Der Morgen*, April 16, 1948; "Theater in Buenos Aires," *Telegraf*, April 29, 1948; "Deutsches Theater in Argentinien," *Main Post*, June 1, 1948.

64. "Grüße," *Luzerner Neuste Nachrichten*, May 5, 1948; "Deutsche Bühne in Buenos Aires," *Neue Zürcher Zeitung*, May 26, 1948; "Theaterrundschau," *Basler Nationalzeitung*, June 16, 1948.

65. "185 Premieren in 8 Jahren," *Aufbau* 14, April 16, 1948; "Deutsches Theater in Argentinien," *Sonntagsblatt Staatszeitung und Herold*, May 16, 1948.

66. "Old Acquaintances," *Association of Jewish Refugees Information*, July 1948.

this fame into guest performances in Germany with the goal of gaining a high-level position in Europe. In 1948 and 1949 he appeared as an actor and director in Baden-Baden, Nuremberg, Mainz, and Essen,[67] and lectured on Argentine music and theater in Cologne, Frankfurt, Vienna, Munich, and Berlin.[68] He also applied for the position of general intendant at numerous state theaters, ultimately with success in Dortmund.[69] Jacob initially planned to continue managing the FGS from Dortmund together with Sigmund Breslauer, its administrative manager since 1946; however, this proved untenable.[70] Neither was satisfied with sharing influence, and, furthermore, the evolving political and economic situation in Argentina alienated Jacob from the reality Breslauer had to navigate. In 1952 they agreed that Jacob would cease his involvement with the enterprise, which would be renamed the German Stage of Buenos Aires. The 1953 season was a watershed year for the troupe. Not only did its founder, first actor, artistic director, and business manager leave Buenos Aires for good, but shortly thereafter Hermann Terdenge arrived as the first West German ambassador in Argentina. The German Stage's divorce with Jacob swiftly transitioned to a cozy coupling with the new leading man from Bonn.

The failure of Paul Walter Jacob's strategy to make peace with the nationalist colony and grow the FGS's audience beyond the small and factious refugee colony is attributable in part to several theatrical energies that have surfaced throughout this book. For years both the FGS and the German Theater had deployed dramatic performances to construct bitterly competitive communities on the River Plate. The constitution of these communities relied on tactics of exclusion and stigmatization. The Free German Stage was anathema to nationalist Germans, who would not commit cultural treason and abandon Ludwig Ney to visit a theater made up of Germany's enemies and castaways. Meanwhile, the dissentious

---

67. "Rückkehr von P. Walter Jacob," *AT*, June 26, 1949.

68. Jacob to Antonio Castro (President, Argentine National Culture Commission), December 17, 1948, PWJAK.

69. Jacob to Mannheim Secretariat of Culture, March 21, 1949; Jacob to Heidelberg Secretariat of Culture, March 1949; Erich Otto to Jacob, May 24, 1949; Jacob to Kassel Secretariat of Culture, February 2, 1950.

70. "P. Walter Jacob in Dortmund," *AT*, March 17, 1950.

refugee colony had at times been united by nothing other than their bitter opposition to Nazism. At least in the immediate post-war years, many refugees hardly differentiated between Nazis in Germany and their supporters in Argentina. In this polarized atmosphere, Herbert Blau's concept of theater as a memory machine had potent, divisive force. If, as Blau postulates, the audience is not so much a gathering of human beings, but "a body of thought and desire," the nucleus of this entity at both theaters was competition against their crosstown rivals.[71]

Ludwig Ney: Further Fascism and the Nazi Diaspora, 1945–1951

Ludwig Ney was dealt a heavy blow when the Argentine government issued a ban on his group after declaring war on Nazi Germany in late 1944. Even after he returned to the stage, the actor must have lamented the remarkable reversal of fortunes he and his antifascist adversaries experienced. In contrast to the Free German Stage, which had reached new levels of fame and prestige, if not solvency, in the postwar period, Ney found himself with no theater, very little institutional support, a precarious legal situation, and a downtrodden public in political, financial, and psychological crisis. As Ney reeled from the ban of his group and the loss of funding from the German Labor Front and embassy, the FGS had intensified competition against him by taking over the lease of the National Theater, vying with him in nationalist media, and prying away members of his ensemble.

Amid this array of challenges, when Ney's group resumed performing in 1948 the embattled director renewed his coalition with German nationalists in Argentina. Renamed the New Stage, the troupe instituted a program that was consistent with its wartime repertoire, ranging from the German classics to lighter comedies and excluding all authors who had been prohibited in Nazi Germany. Both the *Freie Presse* and *Der Weg*, to which Ney contributed

---

71. Blau, *Audience*, 25.

several articles, covered the theater. Initially the fascist Dürer publishing house, which printed numerous neo-Nazi publications including *Der Weg*, functioned as a box office for the ensemble's productions.

The New Stage renewed and contemporized nationalist German unity by presenting dramas written by recent and prewar emigrants, such as Julius Demuth's *Didi* (1952) and Otto Czierski's *Ulrich of Hutten* (1949), respectively. Although plans for a guest performance by Emil Jannings did not materialize, numerous European emigrant thespians acted with the New Stage.[72] Angelika Hauff, who later earned the honorary title of Chamber Actress for her work at Vienna's Court Theater, visited in 1948 and 1950,[73] and Zita Szeleczky, Hungarian actress and prizewinner at the 1941 Venice Film Festival, performed with Ney from 1948 to 1953.[74] Arpad Bubik, theater director in Budapest and Berlin, directed several productions in 1949,[75] Rexist journalist Pierre Daye was a frequent reviewer,[76] and in 1948 the theater put on the world premiere of *Hundreds of Millions* by Heinz Coubier, whose brother lived in Argentina.[77] Echoing antifascist media from a decade earlier, *Der Weg* editor Eberhard Fritsch emphasized the New Stage's edifying role in times of spiritual hardship, positing it as a guardian of German cultural heritage for future generations in exile.[78] Ney's troupe played a key part in reconstituting a cohesive community of German nationalists, as well as incorporating postwar emigrants into its fold.[79]

Reviews of dramatic performances from this period, such as *Mary Stuart* in 1948, are strikingly analogous to coverage during

---

72. "Emil Jannings Gastspiel," *FP*, February 1, 1948.

73. "Angelika Hauff, Star in Argentinien," *FP*, August 31, 1950.

74. "Interview mit Fräulein Ypsilon," *FP*, October 4, 1948.

75. "Der bedeutende Berliner Spielleiter Arpad Bubik als Gastregisseur in Buenos Aires," *FP*, May 4, 1949.

76. "Das deutsche Theater in Buenos Aires," *Der Weg*, March 1950.

77. "Neue Bühne Ludwig Ney," *FP*, June 3, 1948.

78. "Die Spielzeit 1949 der Neuen Bühne Ludwig Ney," *Der Weg*, December 1949.

79. "Zufällige Zuschauermenge oder Theatergemeinschaft?," *Der Weg*, April 1949.

World War II. Although numerous critics warned against drawing such concrete parallels, the postwar publications *Der Weg* and the *Freie Presse* correlated Schiller's drama to current events in Germany, just as the *La Plata Zeitung* and *Der Deutsche in Argentinien* had done years earlier.[80] Verging on apologism for National Socialism, *Der Weg* construed Schiller's "contemporary" drama as well-warranted opprobrium against the concurrent Nuremberg trials, which were dominated by the suffocating rationalism and boundless vengeance of intellectual statesmen similar to the figure of Lord Burleigh in *Mary Stuart*, who strove to purge Germany of its fervent humanity.[81] Recalling the Nazi press's harangues on the legal system in the Weimar Republic, *Der Weg* praised Ney for setting an ambitious and noble goal for the evening: to defend human rights and human dignity against the "devious distortion and diabolical perversion of the law, which characterizes the most urgent of today's world crises."[82] The *Freie Presse* depicted Mary Stuart and Burleigh as a falsely accused defendant and a vengeful Allied politician, respectively: "Mary was already hopelessly lost before the beginning of the trial. The court issued the death sentence based not on evidence, but solely in compliance with Burleigh's agenda. Power, not justice, drags her to the gallows."[83] Particularly in such godless times of material and moral destruction, the *Freie Presse* declared, audiences longed for the catharsis, spiritual purification, and moral guidance of the classics: "Schiller is *the* author of our times. His poetic fire invigorates those who, tired and broken, contemplate the ruins of their homes and of their ideals."[84] The defeated, devastated, and plundered German people could not allow themselves to be further denigrated, the paper continued; they required Schiller to revitalize their moral fortitude. Finally,

---

80. Gert Vonhoff, "*Maria Stuart*," in Luserke-Jaqui, *Schiller-Handbuch: Leben—Werk—Wirkung*, 164.

81. "*Maria Stuart*," *Der Weg*, August 1948.

82. "Goethes 'Götz von Berlichingen,'" *DiA*, June 1940; "Gedanken zur 'Faust'-Aufführung durch das Deutsche Theater, Buenos Aires," *DLPZ*, March 8, 1943; "*Maria Stuart*," *Der Weg*, July 1948.

83. "*Maria Stuart*," *FP*, June 26, 1948.

84. "*Maria Stuart*," *FP*, June 26, 1948 (emphasis in original).

both the *Freie Presse* and *Der Weg* emphasized the exemplary, proud, well-trained delivery of the drama's blank verse; language represented a vital cultural bulwark for Germans abroad during this crisis.[85] Peppered with a litany of Nazi cultural tropes as well as tenets of conservative drama, the reviews agreed with earlier coverage in the now banned *Deutsche La Plata Zeitung* and *Der Deutsche in Argentinien*.

As a result of strong demand, *Mary Stuart* ran through August in the Smart Theater, a midsize venue with a capacity of 700 spectators. The final production sold out in advance despite conflicting directly with Hans Moser's appearances at the FGS.[86] While Paul Walter Jacob lamented lackluster ticket sales, blocks away Ludwig Ney was drawing full houses. Sites of bitter disputes about postwar identity and Allied politics, theatrical performances hardened hostilities in German Buenos Aires. Antifascist concerns about deficient denazification were countered by conservative theater critics who defended Nazi officials, upheld German nationalism, furthered fascism, and accused the Allies of war crimes against their desecrated, fettered fatherland.[87]

Aside from the German classics, comedies formed the backbone of the New Stage's repertoire during the crisis-ridden postwar years, including for the 1948 season Rudolf Presber's *Queen of Hearts* (1932), Hans Müller-Nürnberg's *Cool Wind* (1936), Ludwig Bender's *Sparrows in God's Hand* (1934), and Maximilian Böttcher's *Trouble Backstairs* (1934). Apart from *Queen of Hearts*, all these plays premiered in Hitler's Germany, and Presber, Bender, and Böttcher each had featured at the German Theater during the war. Writing for *Der Weg*, critic Charlotte Thomas posited the theater as a refuge from a troubled reality: "Life has performed many tragedies during the past years. We all are looking for hours of relaxation, and where would we find them more than in witty

---

85. "*Maria Stuart* und die geschichtliche Wirklichkeit," *FP*, July 2, 1948; "*Maria Stuart*," *Der Weg*, August 1948.

86. "*Maria Stuart* Wiederholung," *FP*, August 15, 1948.

87. "Entnazifizierung von Auslandsdeutschen," *AT*, March 7, 1946; "Renazifizierung," *AT*, January 13, 1948.

renditions of the spoken word?"[88] Thomas's conclusion evoked the therapeutic function of the FGS for Jewish theatergoers, but within the theoretical framework espoused by Nazi poet laureate Hanns Johst and Professor Julius Petersen, who emphasized the primacy of the spoken word.[89] Reviews of *Trouble Backstairs* and *Cool Wind* extended the continuity with expressions such as "people's poet," "pure and uncorrupted Berliner north," "true-to-life German figures," "people of flesh and blood," and "fountain of ethnic humor."[90] All repeated earlier coverage in the Nazified press nearly verbatim.[91]

Unlike the FGS, in the aftermath of World War II Ludwig Ney perpetuated a politically and ethnically insular approach to sustaining his theater. Eschewing intercultural collaboration with Argentine artists as well as anything remotely resembling reconciliation with the antifascist colony, the New Stage held fast to National Socialist repertory and fascist drama theory to retain the allegiance of conservative media and theatergoers, as well as attract postwar emigrants. Meanwhile, the *Freie Presse* and *Der Weg* seized on performances to abet enduring sentiments of nationalism and fan resentment against the Allied occupation of Germany. Although the strategy was initially effective, both Ney and the *Freie Presse* would soon question the long-term viability of exclusionary ethnocentric survival tactics. Eventually both came to recognize that sectarian politics and fascist drama theory were malleable within the dynamics of live theater. Onstage, both could coalesce with the intercultural imperative inherent in preserving German cultural heritage amid immigratory dispersion.

---

88. "Kleine Plauderei," *Der Weg*, May 1948.

89. Biccari, *"Zuflucht des Geistes"?*, 85–87.

90. *"Krach im Hinterhaus,"* FP, April 14, 1948; "Neue Bühne Ludwig Neys," *FP*, April 25, 1948.

91. See "Zum Spielplan der Ney-Bühne," *DiA*, September 1940; "Geschichte einer jungen Schauspielschule," *DiA*, June 1941; " 'Krach im Hinterhaus,' " *DLPZ*, July 30, 1942; " 'Krach im Hinterhaus,' " *DLPZ*, August 13, 1942; " 'Frischer Wind,' " *DLPZ*, May 13, 1942.

Bowing to Bonn: The German Classics in the Cold War, 1955–1965

In the immediate aftermath of the Second World War, before the West German embassy opened in Argentina, the two colonies relentlessly expressed deeply discordant views of modern German history. Thus, although both populations esteemed Carl Zuckmayer's *The Captain of Köpenick* (1931) as a contemporary "classic," and donors saw nothing polemical about the play, it should have been no surprise that the drama's presentation at the Free German Stage triggered derisive disputes about the Wilhelmine monarchy.[92] For the *Jüdische Wochenschau* the play augured Nazism, laying bare the pernicious defects of an authoritarian Prussian state machinery that recently had threatened to become the world order.[93] The *Argentinisches Tageblatt* saw the piece as a dire, sadly unheard warning; the world would have been spared an ocean of blood and tears had it heeded Zuckmayer's message.[94] The *Freie Presse* demurred. Blithely dubbing the drama a "cheerful idyll from the Serenissimus period," it declared categorically that Zuckmayer's *Captain* was not relevant to later events.[95] Whereas nationalists regarded Wilhelmine Germany with fond nostalgia and posited Nazism as anomalous (at worst), antifascists insisted that National Socialism had its origins in the monarchy, and vigorously denounced the militaristic authoritarianism of both eras.

The Allied occupation of Germany was another thorny subject. The *Freie Presse* exploited Zuckmayer's *The Devil's General* (1946) to denounce the occupation as a slap in the face to justice, equating the ruthlessness of Allied authorities with the Gestapo.[96] The *Tageblatt* also linked distinct epochs, praising Zuckmayer for exhibiting the same political acumen and creative talent in

---

92. Fränkel to Jacob, July 17, 1946, PWJAK.
93. "*Der Hauptmann von Köpenick*," *JW*, May 4, 1947.
94. "*Der Hauptmann von Köpenick*," *AT*, May 4, 1947.
95. "*Der Hauptmann von Köpenick*," *FP*, May 4, 1947.
96. "*Des Teufels General*," *FP*, June 23, 1948.

his depiction of Hitler's Germany as he had in portraying the Wilhelmine monarchy. Both the *Tageblatt* and the *Buenos Aires Herald* highlighted Wolfgang Vacano's portrayal of the "quietly dignified" resistance fighter, Oderbruch, a figure the *Tageblatt* already had lauded when discussing the piece's reception in Germany.[97] The *Freie Presse* commended Zuckmayer for his nuanced portrayal of German society and affirmed his differentiation between the eternal Germany of Goethe and the ephemeral Hitler regime. On the other hand, although Zuckmayer had written earlier in the *Hannoversche Presse* that surely everyone could agree that artists must eulogize German resistance fighters so they would serve as role models for future generations, the *Freie Presse* repudiated Oderbruch. His arguments were highly controvertible, and Oderbruch himself was a murderer for conspiring in deadly acts of sabotage against German soldiers. The *Argentinisches Tageblatt* and the *Freie Presse* agreed that Zuckmayer's dramas were modern German classics—the papers called him a "living legend" and the "greatest living German dramatist," respectively—however they vehemently disagreed about the moral obligations of ordinary Germans to resist Hitler's regime.[98] While their conflicting positions on Nazism and modern German history always were evident, this divergence rarely found direct, concurrent expression in both papers. Theatrical performances potentiated their quarrel. Zuckmayer's plays represented clear instances of hyper-historian actors working in tandem with dramatic texts, directors, and designers to create an aesthetic experience that presented something genuine from the past.[99] Audiences ratified the historicity of the depictions, yet their interpretations of the relevance of both the historical and the theatrical event were passionately oppositional. These emotive instances of performing history catalyzed immediate, simultaneous, reverberant clashes between the antifascist and nationalist populations.

---

97. "*Des Teufels General*," *AT*, June 23, 1948; "*The Devil's General*," *BAH*, June 25, 1948; "*Des Teufels General* in München," *AT*, March 28, 1948.

98. "Carl Zuckmayer, der lebende Klassiker," *AT*, September 9, 1951; "Carl Zuckmayer, der größte deutsche Dramatiker," *FP*, August 9, 1950.

99. Rokem, *Performing History*, 35.

In 1952, against this backdrop of antagonism, the West German embassy opened in the Argentine capital. Aiming to assemble a robust bulwark against Communist expansion in South America, West German diplomats viewed the New Stage and the Free German Stage as mechanisms to push Buenos Aires's German populations to reconciliation.[100] Wary of divisive dramatists, such as Zuckmayer, the embassy avoided tendentious plays and touted the German classics, which it saw as having timeless cultural validity for all Germans in Argentina.[101] This approach was burdened by problematic precedents. Schiller's *Mary Stuart* had failed when the FGS put on the play in 1940, and the German embassy had conscripted both Schiller and Lessing into its propaganda machine. More recently, the New Stage's performance of *Mary Stuart* had redoubled belligerent nationalist sentiments. Even so, shortly after the war voices in both factions hoped that canonical dramas by the likes of Lessing, Goethe, and Schiller could initiate a dialogue.[102]

Despite obvious direct links between the *Freie Presse* and the *La Plata Zeitung*, the West German embassy reported to Bonn that upon its founding the *Freie Presse* had assumed responsibility to counteract the mistaken views of its readers and reeducate them.[103] The paper's interpretations of the classics were ambivalent, ranging from traces of Nazi sympathy to cooperation with the Western powers against the new foe of communism. In 1943 the *La Plata Zeitung* had twisted Schiller's *Robbers* into a prescient apotheosis of Adolf Hitler; however, thirty months later its successor boasted that the drama had catalyzed the French Revolution and earned its author honorary French citizenship. In another heretofore unthinkable passage the *Freie Presse* compared Schiller to Ben Franklin, claiming that both men had ripped the scepter from the grasp

---

100. Moltmann (FFO) to WGE, October 18, 1956, Bestand B33, Band 010; Guild of the German Stage to FFO, July 8, 1958, Bestand B95, Band 765; WGE to FFO, April 2, 1959, Bestand B95, Band 558; WGE to FFO, September 10, 1959, Bestand B95, Band 765; WGE to FFO, January 17, 1963, Bestand B95, Band 907, PAAA.

101. WGE to FFO, March 25, 1958.

102. Rudolf Baer to Jacob, January 11, 1944, PWJAK.

103. WGE to FFO, May 10, 1962, Bestand B33, Band 248, PAAA.

of tyrants.[104] A few years later, framed by the incipient Cold War, the newspaper declared that Schiller, too, would have fled from East Germany to West Berlin.[105] No longer a proto-Nazi visionary, the playwright now was posited as a trailblazer for European democracy.

Other articles, however, were equivocal. Beyond the polemical reviews of Ney's *Mary Stuart*, a 1947 historical overview of Schiller reception referred to the poet as a "führer," leading Germany to glory and overpowering the world's resistance with his indomitable "heroic will." Literati and intellectuals of the Weimar Republic often misconstrued Schiller, but soon thereafter the German people, who had always understood him intuitively, liberated their national poet from the shackles of academic formulas and raised him to the pedestal of his own rightful "Reich"—the stage.[106] Another piece trashed Hannes Razum's 1948 production of *The Robbers* in Hamburg. In the rapid, two-hour performance, Karl Moor's robbers spoke soldiers' jargon and wore military uniforms and prison jumpsuits. The *Freie Presse* sneered that the protests of theatergoers must signify German citizens' lamentations over recent military strength and current pride for demilitarization. Certainly, the reviewer acerbically concluded, the "storm of whistles" had nothing to do with the Allied occupation nor Razum's treatment of the national poet.[107] The *Freie Presse* conscripted Schiller into a nascent anti-Communist political front while simultaneously invoking him to perpetuate nostalgia for Nazism and rebel against Allied influence in postwar Germany. Its commentary on Schiller in the late 1940s is the ambivalent voice of a publication in transition.

By the time of the 150th anniversary of Schiller's death in 1955, however, both German colonies had sided decisively with the West against the USSR and obligingly converted Schiller into a Cold Warrior. Both in 1955 and four years later, on the 200th anniversary of his birth, dozens of articles in the *Freie Presse* and

---

104. "Gedanken über Schiller," *FP*, March 21, 1946.
105. "Auch Schiller floh nach West Berlin," *FP*, May 21, 1950.
106. "Schiller im Wandel der Zeiten," *FP*, February 2, 1947.
107. "Schiller contra Razum," *FP*, December 23, 1948.

the *Argentinisches Tageblatt* shared a litany of references to freedom. Quoting from "On the Sublime," the *Tageblatt* declared that Schiller's most significant contribution to the German people and, indeed, all of humanity was his ceaseless toil as an apostle of freedom under the mantra "Culture will set man free."[108] For once, the *Tageblatt* concurred with the *Freie Presse*, which interpreted Schiller's *Love and Intrigue* as a clarion call for freedom in choosing one's spouse, while *The Robbers* and *Don Carlos* warned against despotism.[109] More broadly, the *Freie Presse* proclaimed that Schiller's dramas upheld Western values, especially political, moral, and creative freedom.[110] On May 1, 1955, there was a ceremony honoring Schiller at the Argentine-German Cultural Institute, which had closely collaborated with Nazi officials and, to the consternation of antifascists, reopened in 1952.[111] The homage included lectures by Professor Friedrich Wilhelm Wentlzlaff-Eggebert and Werner Bock, and the Colón Theater's Angel Mattiello sang Schiller's ballads, accompanied by Werner Hoffmann on piano.[112] The event was noteworthy because surrogates of both German theaters participated. While Werner Bock was a poet and a cultural critic for the *Argentinisches Tageblatt*, Hoffmann and Mattiello had worked with Ludwig Ney. Schiller assembled previously inconceivable constellations of personalities and politics. Their stance against communism, alliance with the West German embassy, and mutual cultivation of the German classics demonstrated that a measure of common ground existed between Argentina's German populations.

In June 1955, six weeks after West Germany had joined NATO, and East Germany the Warsaw Pact, the German Stage performed *Don Carlos* (1787) under the auspices of the West Germany embassy and the watchful eye of Ambassador Hermann Terdenge. The *Freie Presse* and the *Argentinisches Tageblatt* seized this moment

---

108. "Schiller über Freiheit und Menschenwürde," *AT*, May 8, 1955.

109. "Schiller als Dramatiker der Gegenwart," *FP*, May 9, 1955.

110. "Zu Schillers geistiger Gestalt," *FP*, May 9, 1955.

111. Thermann to FO, October 4, 1940, Band R55, Akte 20553, BB; "20 Jahre Institución Cultural Argentino-Germano," *DLPZ*, September 13, 1942; "Was wir vom Instituto Argentino-Germano erwarten," *AT*, November 11, 1951.

112. "Institución Cultural Argentino-Germana," *FP*, May 1, 1955.

to designate Schiller, the preeminent poet of the German people, a clairvoyant proto–Cold Warrior.[113] Both papers emphasized the eternal preponderance of Schiller's manifesto for freedom, asserting that Marquis Posa's fight for freedom was against both current Soviet oppressors and the sixteenth-century Spanish court.[114] The *Tageblatt* announced Schiller's "guiding principle of a single ideal: freedom!" which the *Freie Presse* corroborated by asserting that *Don Carlos* was not a historical play, but depicted "man's unending struggle for his moral freedom."[115] In 1959, celebrations of the 200th anniversary of Schiller's birth were again synonymous with panegyrics to freedom. Nonetheless, the *Freie Presse* reflected with brazen hypocrisy that Bonn assiduously avoided politicizing the dramatist while in East Germany the Soviets arrogated his oeuvre to consolidate Communist terror.[116] Meanwhile, the German Stage read aloud congratulations from Foreign Minister Heinrich Brentano and Chancellor Konrad Adenauer before inaugurating its twentieth season with Schiller's *Mary Stuart*, and Ambassador Georg Rosen and his entire staff presided over a guest performance of the play in Montevideo.[117] The reception evinced a convergence of the two German colonies, since the New Stage had put on *Mary Stuart* in 1948. This time the *Tageblatt* and the *Freie Presse* showed malice against neither the Western powers nor each other. Instead both newspapers marched to the poet's politicized protocol: "The idea of freedom is Schiller's original ideal, the innermost demand of his being."[118] Or, as the *Tageblatt* put it, "Schiller's political significance culminates in his ideas of personal freedom."[119]

Though to a lesser extent than Schiller, Lessing was also drafted into the crusade against communism. While scholars have noted that Lessing was depoliticized in postwar West Germany, this was

---

113. "Schiller und sein *Don Carlos*," *FP*, May 26, 1955.

114. "*Don Carlos*," *AT*, June 27, 1955.

115. "*Don Carlos*," *AT*, June 29, 1955; "*Don Carlos*," *FP*, June 29, 1955.

116. "Schiller —eine politische Bekenntniskraft," *FP*, January 31, 1959.

117. "*Maria Stuart*," *FP*, May 14, 1959; "Nachrichten aus Montevideo: *Maria Stuart*," *AT*, July 26, 1959.

118. "Der Freiheitsgedanke bei Friedrich Schiller," *FP*, September 15, 1959.

119. "Der Weg zu Schiller," *AT*, November 8, 1959.

not the case in Buenos Aires.[120] By the mid-1950s both the *Freie Presse* and the German Stage had grown increasingly dependent on subventions from Bonn, which conditioned the paper's reporting and the theater's performances.[121] As I have stated above, the West German embassy deployed the theater to project soft power in the Cold War, and it also was wary of dissent against its agenda on stages in Argentina.[122] When the popular actress Hedwig Schlichter-Crilla left the German Stage and founded the influential leftist theater group The Mask, the embassy criticized her project as an effective tool for spreading Communist propaganda.[123] It also is noteworthy that neither the German Stage nor Ludwig Ney ever staged an East German playwright, including Bertolt Brecht, his immense popularity in Argentina notwithstanding.[124] Despite the paper's reluctance to confront the past, repudiate Hitlerism, or even acknowledge Nazi war crimes and genocide, West German diplomats supported the *Freie Presse* for its anti-Communist tone. This political posturing found expression in the paper's criticism of Brechtian drama in its review of the German Stage's performance of Lessing's *Nathan the Wise* (1779) in 1956, which was presided over by Bonn's chargé d'affaires in Argentina, Dr. Luitpold Werz: "Arndt guarded himself against the epic theater, and its alienation technique."[125] The *Freie Presse*'s rapid transition from its predecessor's function as "Hitler's banner in Buenos Aires" to a dutiful ally of West German diplomats indicates that its politics likely were conditioned by conformism or opportunism as much as by

---

120. Eckardt, "Das Lessingbild im Dritten Reich," 75–76; Barner et al., *Lessing—Epoche—Werk—Wirkung*.

121. FFO to WGE, March 12, 1959; FFO to WGE, March 15, 1960, Bestand B33, Band 98, PAAA.

122. Moltmann (FFO) to WGE, January 26, 1956, Bestand B33, Band 010, PAAA; WGE to FFO, January 27, 1965, Bestand B33, Band 386, PAAA.

123. WGE to FFO, January 6, 1956, Bestand B33, Band 010, PAAA.

124. Jorge Dubatti, "El teatro de Bertolt Brecht en Buenos Aires: Observaciones de Teatro Comparado," *La Escalera* 22 (2013): 13–24; Osvaldo Pellettieri, "Brecht y el teatro porteño 1950–1990," in *De Bertolt Brecht a Ricardo Monti: Teatro en lengua alemana y teatro argentino 1900–1994*, cd. Pellettieri (Buenos Aires: Editorial Galerna, 1995), 37–53.

125. "Nathan der Weise," *FP*, June 27, 1956.

ideological conviction. Onstage and off, West German efforts to realign emigrants against the perceived Communist menace in the Cold War were evident. Coined in the common cultural currency of Lessing and Schiller, by 1956 dramatic productions occasioned utterances of unity from factious German Buenos Aires. Yet, this theatrical solidarity against a common foe was largely performative. Under the gaze and financial pressure of Bonn, metonymically represented by Ambassadors Terdenge and Rosen as well as Chargé d'affaires Werz, Germans on the River Plate affected a cohesion that was far more tenuous than outward appearances suggested.

From Emigration to Immigration, 1945–1965

Unlike the government-funded Ney Stage, during the Nazi period the Free German Stage was a private enterprise playing for small audiences composed mostly of impoverished refugees. Out of political conviction and economic necessity, it had formed intercultural alliances with Argentine artists from the start. By maximizing these partnerships and the publicity from celebrity guest performances, already in the late 1940s members of the FGS cast had gained a foothold in the South American entertainment industry. In 1943 Herman Geiger-Torel became conductor of the national SODRE (Official Service of Broadcasting, Television, and Entertainment) orchestra in neighboring Uruguay. Paul Walter Jacob directed a Spanish-language production of Bert Rosé and Harald V. Hanstein's musical comedy ¡*Vamps!* in 1946, and both Jacob and Hedwig Schlichter-Crilla received laudatory reviews for their roles in Mario Soffici's feature film *Land of Fire* (1948).[126] Schlichter-Crilla also starred in the film *Paradise* (1951), directed by Carlos Ritter.[127] Jacques Arndt, too, played a leading role in the Chilean-Argentine production of *Hope* (1949), codirected by Francisco

---

126. "Se presentan con un espectáculo musical," *El Mundo*, March 15, 1946; "*Tierra del Fuego*," *Teatros y Cines*, October 1, 1948; "Lo que vi anoche," *El Laborista*, December 1, 1948; "*Tierra del Fuego*," *El Mundo*, December 1, 1948.

127. "*El Paraiso*," *FP*, March 18, 1951.

Mugica and Eduardo Boneo. Shortly thereafter, Renato Salvati of the Municipal Theater in Santiago, Chile, contracted Arndt to form an operetta ensemble for the stage.[128] Arndt went on to enjoy a prolific career in Argentine film and radio, acting in thirty-nine locally and internationally produced films, perhaps most notably as the Chilean dictator Augusto Pinochet in *Of Love and Shadows* (1994), based on the novel of the same title by Isabel Allende. From 1993 until shortly before his death in 2009 he also had his own radio program, *Jacques's Agenda*, which aired twice weekly on the Radio Culture station. In 2006 the Argentine Film Critics Association awarded him a Silver Condor, Argentina's equivalent of an Oscar, for lifetime achievement.

Several members of the Free German Stage had success in the local entertainment industry, but Hedwig Schlichter-Crilla left the deepest imprint. Before founding her own drama school in 1947, the School of Performance Arts of the Argentine Hebrew Society, she worked with pupils at the Pestalozzi School, most of whom were refugees from Nazism. In October 1945, Schlichter-Crilla directed a group of pupils, together with actors from the FGS, the Yiddish People's Theater, and the French Comedy, in a performance of Hans Christian Andersen's *The Princess and the Swineherd*. Schlichter-Crilla adapted the tale to fit the lives of local refugee children, setting the action in contemporary Buenos Aires instead of medieval Europe.[129] Geographically, the play followed a course of emigration parallel to the that of theatergoers and actors themselves. The Spanish-language plot featured a framing device in which the main characters were two emigrant children: a newspaper boy, Juancito, and his friend, a chocolate vendor named Cachito. Onstage and in real life, the boys had humble lives like the youthful spectators, who also grappled with poverty, a new language, and adaptation to Argentine society.

One afternoon Juancito notices an old, tattered book in a pile of rubbish. Intrigued, he leafs through it, eventually realizing it is a collection of marvelous stories from a place and time far away

---

128. "Jacques Arndt wieder in Buenos Aires," *FP*, March 11, 1949.
129. "Kindertheater," *AT*, October 23, 1945.

from twentieth-century Buenos Aires. Later that afternoon, Juancito and Cachito come across a title that sparks their imaginations,
The Princess and the Swineherd. They cannot satisfy their interest
because the rest of the tale is badly damaged and illegible, and so,
perplexed by this unlikely relationship, they concoct plots, characters, and settings to contrive encounters between the princess and
the swineherd. Their self-invented worlds of fiction are an escape
from the struggles of emigration, and their tale eventually follows
the boys into their dreams, where they take part in the action personally. At the end of the prologue Juancito drew a spoon from
under his shirt and opened a gate to "the land of dreams," initiating the three-act drama. After each act, the protagonists met
in front of the curtain and conversed with the spectators, leading
them into their colorful fantasy world. Through friendship and
imagination, Juancito and Cachito affirmed each individual's in-
corruptible spiritual and creative freedom, even those as vulnerable
as child refugees.

The *Argentinisches Tageblatt* described *The Princess and the
Swineherd* as the most inspiring fairy-tale performance in years.[130]
The work behind the curtain was also inspirational. Under Schlichter-
Crilla's direction, young emigrants collaborated with professional
actors from Argentine, French, Yiddish, and German theaters.
They learned diverse acting styles and interacted with artists from
a variety of cultural backgrounds, which helped them to heal the
wounds of racial persecution that many had suffered in Germany.
Furthermore, Schlichter-Crilla encouraged the youthful actors to
individualize the characters assigned to them. Nourished by the
close working relationships they developed with professional adult
actors, this creative freedom enabled them to reach higher levels of
self-respect and artistic accomplishment.[131]

Hedwig Schlichter-Crilla exerted an enormous influence on
Argentine theater. When her school put on another performance
of *The Princess and the Swineherd* in 1954, the participants included some of the most brightest young talents in Argentine

---

130. "*Die Prinzessin und der Schweinehirt*," *AT*, October 25, 1945.
131. Roca, *Días de Teatro*, 189.

theater, including Osvaldo Riofrancos, who later became dean of the School of Drama at the North Carolina School of the Arts, and director of the New York Shakespeare Festival in Central Park.[132] Schlichter-Crilla introduced Stanislavsky's system to local thespians, which critic and professor Osvaldo Berenguer credits with transforming acting in Argentina in the same way that Astor Piazzolla transformed the tango.[133] Now famous as Hedy Crilla, an Argentine version of her name, she taught many celebrities in the nation's cinema and theater, including Norma Aleandro, Zulema Katz, Agustín Alezzo, Cecilio Madanes, Augusto Fernandes, and more.[134] One of her students, Frank Nelson, recalled that Schlichter-Crilla encouraged students to lose their inhibitions and experiment with their own abilities to metamorphose. For Schlichter-Crilla and her students as well, acting enhanced expressive and receptive faculties on- and offstage, honed a range of versatile communicative skills, and cultivated the capacity to empathize.[135] As a theater pedagogue, Schlichter-Crilla trained her students and herself in the critical skills that empower emigrants to transition into immigrants.

As a performance artist, Schlichter-Crilla briefly led the German Stage in 1963, but she is better known for her work in Argentine theaters. In 1953, she founded the influential ensemble The Mask, which the West German embassy criticized for its leftist political tilt.[136] The Mask's production of Shaw's *Candida* (1898), which Schlichter-Crilla codirected with Carlos Gandolfo, won the Argentine Theater Critics' Prize for best performance in 1959. Other notable productions included Frank Wedekind's *Spring Awakening* in 1976 and David Edgar's *Mary Barnes* in 1982. Her performance in the leading role of Colin Higgins's *Only 80*, which was written especially for her and ran for three years, represented a final ovation for her career.

---

132. "*La Princesa y el Pastor* im Teatro Nacional," *AT*, May 23, 1954.
133. Roca, *Días de Teatro*, 195.
134. "Todo comenzó con Hedy Crilla," *LN*, September 2, 1998.
135. Roca, *Días de Teatro*, 189.
136. WGE to FFO, January 6, 1956, Bestand B33, Band 010, PAAA.

Himself a victim of Nazi persecution who found refuge in South America, Egon Schwarz has described the slow changes that convert an emigrant into an immigrant, including the search for a stable economic position; the struggle, frequently, with a new language; the process of adjusting to a new, often exotic and unwelcoming environment; and ultimately the need to integrate into a new population, with new customs and moral norms. In brief, it is a matter of acclimating to a new culture.[137] As an actress and a pedagogue Schlichter-Crilla facilitated this transition for scores of refugees, including herself. However, Schwarz noted that this process is essential to any emigrant who wants to become an immigrant—that is, to become a productive member of a new nation and participate in its society at all levels. In this sense, Schwarz's vision of integration applied to both German populations in Argentina.

Throughout the Ney Stage's first decade of existence its director and reviewers paid scant attention to the Argentine host society. During World War II, assisted by the German government, the German Theater had been solvent on its own. After the war, with no government funding and the nationalist colony financially strained, Ludwig Ney found himself in a situation similar to the early years of the FGS, which depended on intercultural relationships to subsist. In the postwar period, Ney's troupe struggled to remain financially viable by playing only for the German public in Buenos Aires. Shifting away from wartime ethnocentric survival tactics, the *Freie Presse* touted new nationwide tours and collaborative projects with Argentine artists as the path to sustainability for German theater in Argentina.[138] The Talmudic scholars Daniel and Jonathan Boyarin have postulated that immigrant groups should recognize the strength derived from a diversity of communal arrangements and concentrations, both among themselves and with other cultural groups. To assure their own survival, these communities should understand that the copresence of others is not a threat, but rather the condition of their existence as residents in

137. Egon Schwarz, "La emigración de la Alemania nazi," in Rohland de Langbehn, *Paul Zech y las condiciones del exilio en la Argentina*, 18.

138. "Spanische Fassung Molieres *Der Geizige*," *FP*, February 4, 1953.

foreign countries. Furthermore, diasporic cultural identity teaches that cultures are not preserved by being protected from mixing but probably can continue to exist only as a product of such mixing.[139] From the early 1950s, Ludwig Ney was emblematic of this position.

Initially, Ney extended his activities beyond the capital by organizing guest performances in rural German communities. His group's first trip was to Eldorado, a German settlement in the Argentine rain forest wedged between Paraguay and Brazil, where they performed Molière's *The Miser* (1668) and Franz and Paul von Schönthan's *The Robbery of the Sabines* (1883). By circulating European theater to this isolated area, over 700 miles from Buenos Aires, Ludwig Ney both brought Germans in Argentina together and broadened his professional profile. He earned the esteem of Germans throughout the country, beginning with the mayor of Eldorado, who published a letter of gratitude in the *Freie Presse* thanking the cast for its visit.[140] Partnering with director Steven Wiel, a postwar emigrant, during the next years Ney and his company toured throughout Argentina. He became a cultural ambassador who, together with the conservative *Freie Presse*, coordinated journalism and drama in the spirit of integration. In 1951, as the troupe visited the cities of Rosario, Córdoba, and Mendoza,[141] the *Freie Presse* paired its coverage with reports on each region's geography, industry, and local customs.[142]

Unlike during the Nazi period, these productions were not confined to the German population. The tours caught the attention of Córdoba province's minister of education, Dr. Enrico Bonetto, who contracted Ney to put on Spanish-language performances of Shakespeare, Molière, and Schiller in Córdoba, Argentina's second most

---

139. Boyarin and Boyarin, "Diaspora," 721.

140. "Abschluss des Misiones-Gastspiels des Deutschen Theaters Ludwig Ney," *FP*, December 13, 1950.

141. "Ney in Rosario," *FP*, November 2, 1951; "Ney-Bühne in Córdoba," *FP*, November 3, 1951.

142. "Llanura Chaqueña," *FP*, October 10, 1951; "Sierra Córdoba," *FP*, October 20, 1951; "Süd Anden/Tierra del Fuego," *FP*, November 1, 1951.

populous city, from 1952 to 1954.[143] Ney and Wiel's intercultural ensemble, the Renewal Theater Corporation, produced Moliere's *The Miser* at the amphitheater Leopoldo Lugones in Sarmiento Park, with a capacity of 3,780 spectators. The *Diario Córdoba* promoted the performance as a transatlantic spectacle, integrating European dramatic theory with local visual artists and actors.[144] Ney and Wiel created a new script for the play, based on the French original, as well as Spanish, German, and English translations. Emphasizing that these cross-cultural influences would tailor the play to the current context of Argentina, Ney explained that each language corresponded to a specific national environment. Convinced that performance art resists abstract universalism, Ney and Wiel strove for differentiation, believing that every production must adopt a specific jargon to suit the national spirit of its audience.[145]

Ney was staking out a new hybrid position here, at once confirming and resisting the nationalist theories of language that previously had guided his ensemble. By tying the individual characteristics of the Argentine, French, English, and German people to language, Ney echoed Nazi sociolinguist Hans Naumann, who argued that the mother tongue is foundational to ethnic identity. Other linguists, including Heinz Kloss and Georg Schmidt-Rohr, theorized that race determines potential members of a nation, but language establishes who is an "ethnic comrade."[146] These theories cut two ways across Ney's new program. On the one hand, they underscored his view that language and cultural identity were inextricably linked. On the other hand, by translating and performing in Spanish, Ney approximated the calamitous vision that Nazi linguists had articulated around the power of language. The vitality of language could unify Germans abroad, while simultaneously functioning as a protective shield against assimilation.[147] Nationalist

---

143. Director General of Secondary Education to Ney, March 11, 1953, CNC.

144. "Spanische Fassung von Moliere," *FP*, February 26, 1953.

145. "En la representación de *El Avaro* actuarán elementos de Córdoba," *Diario Córdoba*, February 5, 1953.

146. Schmidt-Rohr, *Die Sprache als Bildnerin der Völker*, 130.

147. Hutton, *Linguistics and the Third Reich*, 292.

German linguists tended to see German history as a stateless confusion in which only language had held the German people together and marked boundaries between themselves and others. Both historically in Europe and currently in the Americas, the cultivation of their mother tongue was elemental to Germans' racial or ethnic cohesion.[148] Transcending religious, regional, political, and class divisions, language could unite an otherwise divided national consciousness. However, the infiltration of a foreign language threatened to annihilate emigrants' Germanness first by eroding the preservation of their native tongue and then by corrupting their racial identity.[149] Under the rubric of mother-tongue fascism, dramatic productions in Spanish transgressed against the linguistic buffer of the German idiom. They were an initial alienation that ultimately risked assimilation and the loss of ethnic identity. The Argentine press, by contrast, praised this adaptation as a great success, lauding the localized vernacular and noting that the revisions augmented suspense and humor in *The Miser*. The presentation marked a turning point in Ney's career, in which he rejected ethnocentric theater and recognized instead that intercultural partnerships were fundamental to his livelihood and creativity.

Ney's commitment to intercultural theater did not, however, signify his disavowal of all fascist cultural politics or the Nazi theatrical repertoire. Reich dramatist Rainer Schlösser, an influential voice in decisions to ban or approve foreign playwrights, had pointed to Molière as worthy of stages under the swastika in 1934. According to Schlösser, Molière (1622–73) belonged to a France that had not yet lost its most commendable cultural and political virtues to the Revolution and the Napoleonic wars. Analyzing *The Miser* specifically, Schlösser concluded that "even if it is not our blood," such creativity is welcomed for the sake of its morality and linguistic skill.[150] The case for Shakespeare's *Merchant of Venice* (1600) is even stronger. Before discussing the Nazi politics surrounding this

---

148. Hutton, *Linguistics and the Third Reich*, 5.

149. Schmidt-Rohr, "Die zweite Ebene der Volkserhaltung."

150. John London, *Theatre under the Nazis* (Manchester: Manchester University Press, 2000), 235.

drama, let me offer a brief analysis of perhaps the most legendary villain of Shakespeare's oeuvre, the Jewish Shylock.

Although *The Merchant of Venice* has received innumerable contrasting representations over the centuries, there can be no doubt that Shakespeare intended Shylock to be the antagonist of the drama. Shylock's motives are debatable, but the text precludes any real dispute about his actions. Given the opportunity, which is of his own creation, he tries to commit legalized murder. Additionally, his religion seems to reflect a deliberate choice of the playwright. There were Christian moneylenders in Venice, and the plot would function with a Gentile villain. The antagonist himself emphasizes his religion, and all other characters claim that his faith is the core of his identity. His character matches anti-Semitic stereotypes. Shylock is a usurer, he is devious and cruel, and he pursues revenge against Antonio, whose altruism establishes him as a noble Gentile foil to his Jewish nemesis. The central conflicts of the drama position Christian virtue against Jewish depravity, and Shylock's murderous fantasies insinuate Jews' role in the crucifixion. Possibly the most famous Jewish character in all of world literature, Shylock is integral to the history of anti-Semitism.[151]

The Merchant of Venice was not among the most frequently performed plays in Nazi Germany, but it was a repertory staple, and performances upheld racial policy in the so-called Third Reich. Beyond the Jewish Cultural League, of course, under Nazism it was impossible to present an interpretation of Shylock that protested the persecution of Jews through history. Instead, *The Merchant of Venice* was produced in a comic style, exploiting anti-Semitic stereotypes. A production in 1936 in Erfurt presented a ruthless usurer, defined by his blind hatred toward all the Gentiles. This Shylock did not even exhibit remorse for the loss of his daughter, who turned out to be adopted, allowing the union of Jessica and Lorenzo to comply with the racial laws of Nuremberg. Even worse was a less documented production of the German Theater in Minsk in 1943 for the benefit of the German army, which coincided with

---

151. John Gross, "Shylock and Nazi Propaganda," *New York Times*, April 4, 1993.

the liquidation of the last Jewish ghettos in Belarus.[152] Of course, such anti-Semitic interpretations of *The Merchant of Venice* were not confined to Hitler's Germany. Years later in Argentina the neo-Nazi magazine *Der Weg* would praise Shakespeare for presaging National Socialist models of eugenics, noting the contrasting figures of Shylock and Portia as evidence.[153]

On July 9, 1953, Ludwig Ney's Renewal Theater Corporation presented Shakespeare's *The Merchant of Venice* in Córdoba. Reviews, especially with reference to thematic purport and anti-Semitism, largely tallied with Nazi interpretations of the drama. First, critics agreed that the drama was a cheerful, uplifting comedy.[154] *Los Principios* emphasized the "atmosphere of youth and optimism; everything turns out well."[155] Furthermore, the paper condemned Shylock for "loving his religion; being a miserly usurer; having an astonishing capacity for speculative investments; hating and despising Christians; and especially detesting the merchant Antonio because he lends without charging interest."[156] Even the so-called virtues of Shylock confirmed anti-Semitic stereotypes: the villain was "endowed with penetrating insight, calculating, incomparable cunning, and a manner of speech characterized by irony and sarcasm."[157] The newspaper praised the heroine Portia in terms antithetical to Shylock, underlining her "joyful spirit, pure, tender, noble, generous and charming eloquence."[158] The Christian Portia

---

152. Andrew Bonnell, "Shylock and Othello and the Nazis," *German Life and Letters* 63 (2010): 166–178, 173.

153. "Menschenwürde und Gattenwahl," *Der Weg*, January 1957.

154. "Otro ponderable esfuerzo: *El Mercader de Venecia*," *Los Principios*, July 11, 1953; "*El Mercader de Venecia*: La más bella de las comedias de William Shakespeare," *Los Principios*, July 4, 1953; "*El Mercader de Venecia* se ofrece hoy en el San Martin," *Los Principios*, July 9, 1953; "*El Mercader de Venecia* obtiene éxito sostenible," *Diario Córdoba*, February 24, 1954.

155. "*El Mercader de Venecia* se ofrece hoy en el San Martin," *Los Principios*, July 9, 1953.

156. "*El Mercader de Venecia* se ofrece hoy en el San Martin," *Los Principios*, July 9, 1953.

157. "*El Mercader de Venecia*: La más bella de las comedias de Shakespeare," *Los Principios*, July 4, 1953.

158. "*El Mercader de Venecia*: La más bella de las comedias de Shakespeare," *Los Principios*, July 4, 1953.

earned praise for exhibiting the opposite qualities of her nemesis, the Jewish Shylock.

Like his collaboration during World War II with the Nazi organization Strength through Joy, the Renewal Theater Corporation's productions of *The Merchant of Venice* were heavily subsidized by the Córdoban government.[159] The purpose, according to the press, was to edify and unify members of the working class by bringing them together to witness live theater. The newspaper *Meridiano* emphasized the formative influence that Shakespearean drama could exert on the moral sensibilities of an uneducated audience.[160] Christian figures such as Portia, Bassanio, and Antonio were models for Argentine spectators, but Ney's depiction also relied on Nazi German tactics of community building, particularly the exclusion of "Others." Like nationalist representations of the Frenchman Riccaut in Lessing's *Minna of Barnhelm* in 1934 and 1943, the Jewish Shylock was a pariah, but he too remained symbolically central. Newspapers confirmed the primacy of Shakespeare's Jewish villain by devoting far more text to him than other more "noble and generous" characters.[161] To promulgate, protect, and promote the morality of their community, the Córdoban government, press, and artists pointed out transgressors and attacked their depraved and potentially corrosive behavior. Evoking propagandistic performances at the Nazified German Theater, the Renewal Theater Corporation's presentation of *The Merchant of Venice* imagined a population of moral virtue through the dramatic depiction of what its members should never do.

Despite Ney's lingering fascist tendencies, however, it is indisputable that the intercultural, Spanish-language presentations of his Renewal Theater Corporation contradicted German nationalists' ethnocentric approach to community building. Capitalizing

159. "Será ofrecido un espectáculo original: En el lago paseo sobremonte se representará *El Mercader de Venecia*," *Meridiano*, February 13, 1954.

160. "Extraordinaria expectativa ha despertado la representación de *El Mercader de Venecia*," *Meridiano*, February 2, 1954.

161. "*El Mercader de Venecia*: La más bella de las comedias de Shakespeare," *Los Principios*, July 4, 1953.

on its success the previous year, in 1954 the Córdoban government contracted the Renewal Theater Corporation to put on a series of grand open-air productions of *The Merchant of Venice* in a municipal park. Engineers from the Argentine military helped build a series of stages in the park's lake to recreate the atmosphere of Venice,[162] and the general manager of Córdoba's Saint Martin Theater, Manuel Martín Frederico, the theater professor Pascual Salvatore, and local ballet and choral groups also collaborated in the presentation.[163] With ticket prices subsidized by the Perónist government, the performances attracted over 10,000 spectators. Finally, during the next holiday season the Renewal Theater Corporation twice staged Ney's self-authored drama, *Glory to God and Peace to Men* (1953), in the main city square in front of Córdoba's sixteenth-century cathedral. *Los Principios* praised Ney for bringing high art to the working class, a pillar of Perónism, and educating them in religion, morality, and aesthetic sensibilities.[164] The *Diario Córdoba* lauded his incorporation of the natural environment as a landmark event in Argentine theater history, likening Ney to Copeau in France or, ironically, Reinhardt in Germany.[165] Performances of the play were the centerpiece of celebrations for Christmas and the New Year in Córdoba, with police reports estimating total attendance for the two performances at 50,000, including the city mayor and archbishop, as well as the provincial governor.[166] The Córdoban government also filmed the production to promote tourism in the city. Through his new intercultural agenda, Ludwig Ney had morphed from Nazi propagandist to a marketing man for Argentina.

Over time Ney strengthened his commitment to interculturalism and integration. Inspired by student-centered theater projects

---

162. "*El Mercader de Venecia*," *Los Principios*, February 28, 1954.

163. "En el lago paseo sobremonte se representará *El Mercader de Venecia*," *Meridiano*, February 13, 1954.

164. "Pueblo e iglesia en la navidad," *Córdoba*, January 11, 1954.

165. "Será representada hoy en el lago del paseo sobremonte la obra 'El Mercader de Venecia,'" *Córdoba*, February 22, 1954.

166. "La escenificación de navidad," *Los Principios*, December 27, 1953; "Pueblo e iglesia en la navidad," *Córdoba*, January 11, 1954.

in Germany, in 1957 he began a new ensemble composed of professional thespians and students from the North School, successor to the former, Nazified Goethe School. The group, called the Chamber Theater, followed the model of small, postwar stages in Germany and existed until 1972. Such intimate, often improvised venues were popular in Germany because many theaters had been destroyed in the war; however, the format also suited Ney's new focus on touring and pedagogy. The intimate setting fused onstage fantasy with offstage reality while also opening more direct avenues of emotion and creativity between audience and actors.[167] Another consideration was the changing composition of the cast. Many in Ney's cast now belonged to a new generation born in Argentina, and the preservation of the German language among the youth was acutely important to older immigrants. Lacking dramatic aids, such as an elaborate stage setting, footlights, and prompters, the small auditorium demanded the sovereignty of the spoken word.[168] The actors replaced other props with the art of language, thus buoying the maintenance and cultivation of the German idiom.

In 1959, as part of an embassy-sponsored project to celebrate the 200th anniversary of Friedrich Schiller's birth, Ney's ensemble put on German and Spanish performances of *Love and Intrigue* (1784) throughout Argentina. Such linguistic hybridity directly contradicted the tenets of mother-tongue fascism, because the act of translation often represents a pivotal step in emigrants' integration with the host society.[169] Furthermore, by facilitating contact among Germans and their Argentine hosts, as well as circulating German culture throughout Argentina, Ludwig Ney put the literary scholar Ottmar Ette's concept of literature as knowledge for living together into action.[170] Both Regine Enzweiler and Ursula Siegerist, young student-actresses with Ney, stressed that the tours brought them to

---

167. Thiess, *Theater ohne Rampe*, 8.

168. Thiess, *Theater ohne Rampe*, 14.

169. Alfrun Kliems, "Transkulturalitat des Exils und Translation im Exil: Versuch einer Zusammenbindung," in Krohn et al., *Übersetzung als transkultureller Prozess. Exilforschung*, 31.

170. Ette, "Literature as Knowledge for Living, Literary Studies as Science for Living," 989.

areas they otherwise never would have visited, catalyzing connections that increased their fondness for Argentina and boosted their cultural fluency. Siegerist noted that before these journeys she had tended to subordinate Argentina to Germany. During her journeys with Ludwig Ney, and especially when performing in Spanish, she learned "to also love my Argentine homeland."[171] In the words of the French-Lebanese author Amin Maalouf, the tours exploited literature's capability to create passageways between vastly different cultures.[172]

The presentations of Schiller's *Love and Intrigue* introduced the canonical dramatist to many Argentine audiences. In Rosario, La

Figure 9. Ludwig Ney and his ensemble on tour in rural
Argentina.

Source: Author's collection, with thanks to Ursula Siegerist.

---

171. Siegerist, interview by author, November 15, 2012.
172. Maalouf, "Je parle du voyage comme d'autres parlent du leur maison," 101.

Falda, and Córdoba, university professors held lectures present-ing the play and author in Spanish before the curtain rose. The West German consul attended the play in Rosario, and National Radio Córdoba broadcasted the performance there live.[173] *La Voz del Interior*, Argentina's most widely circulating newspaper outside of Buenos Aires, emphasized the intellectual interchange between Germans and Argentines. Ney himself added that he was excited to see how his cast of "Argentine-Germans" would contribute to theater in Argentina, a country whose vibrant spirit and art they fervently admired.[174] With these words Ludwig Ney revealed him-self to be a hybrid. Argentina had become his adopted homeland, a sentiment demonstrated by his description of his cast's binational identity. Having thrived on stages in Nazi Germany and in Ar-gentina during World War II as well as the Perónist and Frondizi regimes, Ney proved himself an opportunist adaptable to volatile political climates in Europe and South America.

The performance in Alta Gracia, a town near Córdoba, en-capsulated this inexorable hybridity and adroit flexibility. The Spanish-language presentation stood out because all proceeds went to support the local Anglo-American School. This caught the at-tention of the *Buenos Aires Herald*, which had been vehemently antifascist during the war and still regarded nationalist German institutions with suspicion. Yet the *Herald* had warm words for Ney's group, highlighting the fruitful cultural approximation be-tween local inhabitants and the traveling thespians.[175] As Ney put it himself, through the shared event of live theater representatives of disparate cultures could "counter the atrophy of artistic sensibil-ity" among young people. In canonical dramas such as *Love and Intrigue*, spectators observed the embodiment of timeless dilemmas by actors onstage, and then after the presentation the two groups exchanged perspectives and discussed alternative actions that

---

173. Program, *Intriga y Amor*, Rosario, July 1, 1959; program, *Intriga y Amor*, Córdoba, July 4, 1959.

174. "Expresión de gran jerarquía artística del conjunto alemán," *La Voz del Interior*, July 21, 1959.

175. "Culture on Tour," *BAH*, July 20, 1959.

might have prevented the tragedy.[176] The *Herald* was so taken with the endeavor that its headline declared the tours as "something to be emulated."[177] In 1959 alone, the troupe covered over 5,000 kilometers and played for over 4,000 people.[178] The translingual productions undercut Ney's earlier project of ethnocentric drama, and they fomented closer relations with the Argentine host society and other, previously adversarial emigrant populations.

Ney's program appears to have resonated with Argentine artists and academics. There were commemorations of Schiller's poetry in Rosario and La Plata that October, and the Argentine-German Cultural Institute partnered with the Argentine Association of Literature and Art and the University of Buenos Aires to put on an intercultural homage to the author in November.[179] Hedwig Schlichter-Crilla led a group in a Spanish-language dramatic recitation of Schiller's unfinished drama, *Demetrius* (1857), before another canonical author, Jorge Luis Borges, lectured on the Goethe-Schiller monument in Weimar.[180] The Argentine National Radio station broadcasted a three-part series on the author, including live performances of scenes from *Mary Stuart* and *The Maid of Orleans*. Finally, in January 1960, directors Fernando Llabat and Ernesto Bianco put on an open-air presentation of *The Robbers*.[181] Schiller created connections within German Buenos Aires and externally to Argentine performers and audiences.

Meanwhile, Ludwig Ney embarked on new intercultural endeavors with Argentine artists in the nation's capital. Grand open-air presentations of canonical European playwrights became annual events for the German colonies. From 1956 to 1966 Ney put on

---

176. Program, *Intriga y Amor*, Alta Gracia, July 11, 1959.

177. "Culture on Tour," *BAH*, July 20, 1959.

178. Carl Hillekamps, "Kulturelle Jugendpflege durch Laienspiel und Diskussion," *Institut für Auslandsbeziehungen* 11 (1961): 2–3.

179. "Schiller Ehrung in Rosario," *FP*, October 27, 1959; "Schiller Ehrung in La Plata," *FP*, October 28, 1959; "Schillerfeier in der UBA," *AT*, November 11, 1959.

180. "Schiller Vortrag von Borges," *FP*, November 12, 1959.

181. "Schillerjahr," *AT*, December 9, 1959; "Freilichtaufführung von den *Räubern*," *AT*, January 13, 1960.

Figure 10. Scene from performance of William Shakespeare's
A Midsummer Night's Dream at the Summer Festival
in December 1962.

Source: Regine Lamm Collection.

Shakespeare's *Midsummer Night's Dream* in 1956 and 1962, *Merry Wives of Windsor* in 1957, and *Othello* in 1966, Hofmannsthal's *Everyman* in 1963, Molière's *Miser* in 1964, Schiller's *Robbers* in 1965, and his own *Glory to God and Peace to Men* in 1961. Held outdoors at the New German Gymnastics Club, the productions included ensembles of over ninety people, plus technical staff and stage crew.[182] The facilities featured seating for 2,000 spectators, who watched the action unfold on a series of three stages each 240 square meters in size.[183] Reports on the event, which was called the Summer Festival and attracted 4,000–6,000 spectators for two to three presentations, repeatedly emphasized its importance for the cohesion of the German population.[184] With the explicit purpose

---

182. "Freilichtvorstellung von *Jedermann*," *FP*, December 8, 1962.

183. "Freilichtvorstellung von *Jedermann*," *FP*, December 8, 1962.

184. "Mitwirkende im weihnachtlichen Festspiel," *FP*, December 10, 1961; program, *Othello*, December 17, 1966.

of cultivating immigrants' ties to their European heritage, the West German, Swiss, and Austrian ambassadors attended the festival: "Think of the forests in our homeland, which the legends of our people also have inhabited with magical beings. The beauty of our language will also find a happy echo in your heart."[185] The festival reinforced immigrants' linguistic and cultural affinity to Germany, which newspapers and promotional materials continued to call their homeland.

During World War II the German Theater's open-air performances at the Strength through Joy park were exclusionary events that reinforced Germans' ties to Europe, purposefully estranged them from the host society, and subordinated Argentina to Germany. The Summer Festival, by contrast, was an intercultural production. The cast for the 1961 production of *Glory to God* featured the Italian immigrant Angel Mattiello, one of the most-renowned opera singers of his generation and first baritone at the Colón Theater for over thirty years. *Glory to God* also included the entire ballet group of the Colón Theater under the choreography of José María Antelo and featured the percussion soloist Desiderio Barilli of the Buenos Aires Philharmonic Orchestra.[186] The festival cultivated immigrants' nostalgic bonds to Germany while evincing their steady integration into Argentine society.

Eventually, Ludwig Ney dissociated himself from the ethnocentric survival tactics that characterized his troupe during the World War II period. Ney and many of his colleagues, such as Steven Wiel, continued to espouse fascist dramatic theory, took a hypernationalistic view of German history, and never publicly disavowed Nazism. Nonetheless, through a blend of opportunism and gradual hybridity, Ney came to recognize the stability, endurance, and vitality created by cross-cultural partnerships and collaborative ventures with Argentine and other immigrant artists. Furthermore, Ney grasped that the viability of German theater in Argentina was contingent upon the participation and enthusiasm of first-generation Argentine-Germans. By mentoring younger thespians, Ney bridged

---

185. WGE to FFO, December 19, 1962, Bestand B95, Band 733, PAAA; program, *Ein Sommernachtstraum*, December 15, 1962.

186. Program, *Weih—Nacht: Ein Mysterienspiel*, December 23, 1961.

German and Argentine cultures. In 1961 *La Nación*, an august journalistic institution and the Argentina's second most–widely circulating newspaper, highlighted Ney's group as an example of successful integration.[187] The tellingly entitled article, "When They Begin to Be Argentines," declared that through theater he and his cast had put down deep roots in a new world: "What do the Neys think of Argentina? We don't need them to answer. We can see it in their eyes and smiling faces. They are no longer itinerant artists. They have found a new home, full of happiness."[188] The "border skills" of flexibility, adaptation, and reinvention that Sandra McGee Deutsch stresses in her book *Crossing Borders, Claiming a Nation: A History of Argentine Jewish Women* apply without political distinction to immigrants.[189] Thanks to his cultivation of these skills, *La Nación* was provoked to acclaim the Nazi collaborator Ludwig Ney as a model immigrant.

A Scripted Silence: Confronting the Past on the River Plate

Ney's evolving strategy showed confidence in the efficacy of integration and interculturalism to achieve professional success in postwar Argentina, but did not reflect a rejection of his earlier propagandistic activities. By continuing to advertise and write in *Der Weg*, Ney courted the neofascist right. In 1949, he compared audiences at the two German stages in Buenos Aires. Each public's choice of theater revealed its essence. In the jargon of Nazi anti-Semitism, Ney inveighed against theatergoers enticed by star guest performances at the predominantly Jewish Free German Stage as "rootless, coincidental, and superficial," because they lacked lasting cultural values. These spectators differed from a theater community, such as the spiritual kinship that existed between audience and ensemble at the New Stage. Quoting the playwright Hermann

---

187. A few illustrious contributors to *La Nación* include José Martí, Miguel de Unamuno, José Ortega y Gasset, Jorge Luis Borges, and Mario Vargas Llosa.
188. "Cuando Empiezan a Ser Argentinos," *LN*, April 2, 1961.
189. McGee Deutsch, *Crossing Borders, Claiming a Nation*, 3.

Bahr's assertion that true dramatic art exists as a buoyant, mutually edifying expression of togetherness between thespians and nation, Ney clarified that the "nation" was not determined by national borders, but by a shared ethnic identity founded on cultural values. The older immigrants and recent arrivals in Ney's public thus formed a genuine German theater community; however, Jews, thinly disguised in Ney's insidious euphemism "rootless," would never have a fixed, grounded identity. Jews opted for the emotional poverty of sensationalist spectacle, unlike culturally and ethnically anchored theatergoers, who preferred the richness of a permanent theater community.[190]

Ney's partner, Steven Wiel, also contributed to *Der Weg*. In one essay, Wiel excoriated Allied forces for their actions in the aftermath of World War II. He declared that Roosevelt, Churchill, and Truman had expelled 14 million Germans from their homes, and 40,000 German parents were still searching for their children. Meanwhile, Wiel's teenage nephew had been hanged for war crimes committed at a place he had never been. Furthermore, thousands of German girls served their "liberators" as prostitutes. Accusing Czech, Russian, and US-American troops of war crimes, murder, torture, gang rape, and sex-trafficking, Wiel implored all Germans to never forget these crimes because forgetting is treason. Laden with lingering loyalty to Nazism, Wiel's piece concluded that remembrance was the first step toward vengeance.[191]

Anti-Semitism was a marketing tool as well. Founded in 1952, the German Chamber Players featured actors associated with Ludwig Ney's New Stage, including Egon Straube, Zita Szeleczky, and Eduard Radlegger. Although it was never his focus, Ney himself collaborated with the company, and in 1953 it fused with his own group. A brief phenomenon in a cluttered theater landscape, the Players launched a polemical advertising campaign emphasizing their "Jew-free" ensemble. Outraged, the *Argentinisches Tageblatt* suggested that the group rename itself the Julius Streicher Stage or

---

190. "Zufällige Zuschauermenge oder Theatergemeinschaft?" *Der Weg*, April 1949.
191. "Flucht ins Vergessen," *Der Weg*, March 1951.

the S.S. Players. It exhorted all Germans to protest this so-called German theater, whose members clearly had nothing to do with Germany.[192] The rebellion never occurred. Instead, the Players garnered positive reviews in the *Freie Presse*, their performances often sold out, and FGS manager Sigmund Breslauer worried about new competition from a new "Nazi Stage."[193] Far from blacklisted, Straube, Szeleczky, and Radlegger continued performing in Buenos Aires, including with Ludwig Ney.[194]

Weeks after Ney's cast had presented *A Midsummer Night's Dream* at the inaugural Summer Festival, the neo-Nazi magazine *Der Weg* celebrated Shakespeare's clairvoyant vision of fascist ideology. Drawing heavily from Hitler's *My Struggle*, Hans F. K. Günther theorized that the improvement of a race is only possible by promoting procreation between genetically worthy persons. For this reason marriages must never occur among people of higher and lower races—for example, between Germans and Jews. One's choice of spouse decides whether the quality of a nation will be improved or worsened, and young Germans would do well to seek guidance in the works of Shakespeare. After listing various examples, Günther stated that beyond their Germanic virtues, Shakespeare's feminine characters should be understood both rationally and emotionally, especially with youthful emotions. The "Nordic poet" depicted the essence of love in the Teutonic Middle Ages, in which there was still no separation of body, heart, and mind. As with all forms of great "Germanic art," Shakespeare represented an eternal model for spiritual health and the improvement of German youth.[195]

Der Weg saw Shakespeare as a vehicle for recovering the spirit of World War II in Germany.[196] Foreign powers tried to confine the

---

192. "Verwirrung der Begriffe," *AT*, March 16, 1952.

193. "Deutsche Kammerspiele," *FP*, March 23, 1952; "Deutsche Kammerspiele: *Der Strom*," *FP*, June 10, 1952; "Deutsche Kammerspiele: *Didi*," *FP*, August 26, 1952; Breslauer to Jacob, April 14, 1952, PWJAK.

194. Despite antifascist protests, in 2015 Hungary issued a stamp celebrating Szeleczky as a cultural treasure.

195. "Menschenwürde und Gattenwahl," *Der Weg*, January 1957.

196. "William Shakespeare," *Der Weg*, January 1957.

triumphs, convictions, and sufferings of German soldiers to history books with the intention of nullifying their influence in postwar Germany, but Shakespeare's eternal art was the antidote to this oppression. The Bard's forests, seas, and battlefields eclipsed all boundaries of time and space, and in his immortal example veterans could find inspiration to uphold Nazi ideals and define the future of European culture. In William Shakespeare, *Der Weg* envisioned a Germanic prophet who would legitimize and resurrect the Teutonic visions of national "greatness."[197] With dozens of Nazi war criminals currently residing in Argentina, this appeal did not have to travel far to reach its target readership.

There is no demonstrable link between *Der Weg* and the Summer Festival, but the timing of the magazine's unabashed arrogation of Shakespeare to the neo-Nazi cause does not seem coincidental. Indeed, Günther's piece about love and "youthful emotions" appeared to target Ney's youthful ensemble of student-actors directly. Its message can be construed as a warning against integration, lest Argentine spouses and parents diminish the German race. While Ney had little influence over *Der Weg*, he publicly repudiated the messages in none of its articles, nor did he criticize the publication in general. Ney now pursued a program of intercultural outreach to Argentine artists and theatergoers, and his projects could well lead to the full integration that the magazine so vehemently opposed. Nevertheless, he continued to support Nazi ideology and fascist drama theory, as well as ally himself with like-minded emigrants. Furthermore, neither Ney nor his colleagues publicly renounced their words and deeds. In the postwar period both antifascist and nationalist thespians made significant progress toward integration with the Argentine host society, and the West German embassy rallied all actors and audiences against the common foe of communism. Yet dramatic presentations revealed that internally German Buenos Aires continued to be suffused with a scripted silence that propelled ongoing malice.

Just as the *La Plata Zeitung* shunned the Free German Stage, for eighteen years the *Argentinisches Tageblatt* never once reported

197. "William Shakespeare," *Der Weg*, January 1957.

on Ludwig Ney. He did not appear in its pages until 1956, and even then the paper was loath to acknowledge him, mentioning his name only once at the end of its review, even though he had led the ensemble and directed the production.[198] Slowly, however, its disdain gave way to recognition of Ney's evolving posture and pedagogical work, which also received approbation from the West German embassy.[199] Not only did West German ambassadors attend the Summer Festival and Ney's Chamber Theater, but the embassy supported his tours in 1959 and repeatedly solicited funding for his troupe from the Foreign Office in Bonn.[200] The embassy regarded his work as urgent and irreplaceable for the preservation of German identity among immigrants and especially their children. Diplomats also agreed that the theater's traveling presentations were an effective tool for projecting West German soft power in the nation's interior, and they regarded Ney as a crucial, unifying figure in their endeavor to forge a united front against communism among Germans throughout the country.[201]

Citing budgetary restrictions, the Foreign Office denied the theater funding. Ney's work during the Nazi period did not figure prominently in diplomatic correspondence, which referred only briefly to his collaboration with Strength through Joy and tensions between Ney and the FGS.[202] By contrast, the correspondence of Paul Walter Jacob, who in 1962 was considering a return to Argentina, overflowed with bitterness. Sigmund Breslauer was concerned that Ambassador Werner Junker, a former NSDAP member with extensive experience in the Nazi German foreign service,[203] was

---

198. "Axel an der Himmelstür," *AT*, July 8, 1956.

199. WGE to FFO, March 5, 1958, Bestand B33, Band 248, PAAA.

200. Werner Brückmann to Literary Artistic Society, October 24, 1960, CNC.

201. WGE, Yearly Report 1961, Bestand B33, Band 248, PAAA; WGE to FFO, January 11, 1962, Bestand B95, Band 765, PAAA; WGE, Yearly Report 1963; WGE to FFO, December 19, 1962, Bestand B95, Band 733, PAAA; Frank to Ney, November 13, 1963, CNC.

202. FFO to WGE, January 22, 1962, Bestand B95, Band 765, PAAA; WGE to FFO, October 11, 1962, Bestand B95, Band 733, PAAA.

203. Ambassador from 1956 to 1963, Werner Junker appears in studies on Nazi criminals escaping to Argentina, especially Adolf Eichmann: Stangneth, *Eichmann before Jerusalem*; Gaby Weber, *Los expedientes Eichmann* (Buenos Aires: Penguin, 2013).

courting Ludwig Ney.[204] In a vitriolic exchange, the FGS ensemble, the *Jüdische Wochenschau*, the *Argentinisches Tageblatt*, the Guild of the German Stage, and the German Stage Association referred to Ney as "a star of the Third Reich,"[205] "Nazi criminal in Buenos Aires,"[206] "clearly hired and maintained as theater director by Nazi authorities,"[207] "leader of the Strength Through Joy Stage,"[208] "baleful,"[209] and "highly questionable."[210] Others speculated that cooperation with Ney would cause a boycott of the FGS by actors and spectators alike, because the hostilities were the same as decades ago.[211] Underscoring the multilayered discord pervading the German-speaking populations, Bernhardi Swarsensky of the *Jüdische Wochenschau* also warned Jacob that he would not intervene in the matter, because he refused to support German culture in any way.[212] The German-born diplomats at the embassy were not attuned to immigrants, for whom past conflicts continued to weld current relationships and goad ongoing rancor.

Two years later Carl Hillekamps, a correspondent for the *Neue Zürcher Zeitung* whose daughter performed with the Chamber Theater, intervened with the Foreign Office on Ney's behalf. Having lived in Buenos Aires during the Nazi period, Hillekamps claimed he had witnessed firsthand how Ney resisted pressure from the German embassy, never promoted National Socialism, and refused to put on propagandistic dramas. This of course was utterly false. An outspoken and unapologetic Nazi propagandist, Ney had written for the *La Plata Zeitung*, *Der Deutsche in Argentinien*, and, later, *Der Weg*. He had presented blatantly propagandistic

---

204. Breslauer to Jacob, January 12, 1962, PWJAK.

205. Erich Raeder (German Stage Association) to Jacob and Breslauer, January 22, 1962, PWJAK.

206. Breslauer to Jacob, January 12, 1962, PWJAK.

207. Jacob to Heinrich Wüllner (Guild of the German Stage), January 22, 1962, PWJAK.

208. Breslauer to Raeder, February 20, 1962, PWJAK.

209. Lilly Wichert (FGS ensemble) to Jacob, March 17, 1962, PWJAK.

210. Bernhardi Swarsensky (*JW*) to Jacob, January 8, 1962, PWJAK.

211. Jacob to Heriberto Dresel, January 22, 1962, PWJAK; Alemann to Jacob, April 30, 1962, PWJAK; Wichert to Jacob, March 17, 1962, PWJAK.

212. Swarsensky to Jacob, January 8, 1962, PWJAK.

works, including Hanns Johst's *Schlageter*, Eberhard Wolfgang Möller's *Frankenburg Dice Game*, and numerous plays by NSDAP members, such as August Hinrichs, Rudolf Presber, and Maximilian Böttcher. Despite his program of intercultural outreach and his rapprochement with the *Argentinisches Tageblatt*, Ney's past stirred unresolved tensions in German Buenos Aires. The actor's efforts at vindication were steeped in duplicity. All discourse remained in the private sphere of self-interested personal correspondence, often conducted via surrogates such as Hillekamps who were willing to collaborate in a ruse of anti-Nazi resistance that precluded admitting the truth, let alone repenting for it. In a public environment still polarized by bitterness and denial, Ney never confronted or acknowledged his misdeeds.

In 1947, the *Freie Presse* printed an article entitled "Lessing, the Truth Seeker." Although just four years had passed since the *La Plata Zeitung*'s polemical reviews of *Minna of Barnhelm,* the *Freie Presse* mentioned neither Lessing's crusade against French corruption of German drama nor his glorification of Prussian military values, lauding instead his unwavering commitment to uncovering and promoting the truth throughout a life marred by setbacks and personal tragedy. Lessing's most enduring achievement in pursuit of the ideal of truth was *Nathan the Wise*. Its moral, which the paper declared to have universal validity, was that one's actions must be guided by tolerance and love because "truth ultimately means nothing less than striving for true humanity."[213] The *Freie Presse* was politically ambivalent, and its motivations were inscrutable, even dubious, yet the article intimated that Lessing could inspire Argentina's German populations to improve relations after decades of strife.

In the ensuing years both colonies repeatedly invoked Lessing as a catalyst for rapprochement, and the compatibility of their views on the author reflected recognition that a measure of common ground existed between them. In 1951, the *Argentinisches Tageblatt* published an article written in the form of a letter from Lessing himself to the newspaper. Lessing states that he has heard of a

---

213. "Lessing, der Wahrheitssucher," *FP*, December 21, 1947.

theater in Argentina, the Free German Stage, for which he feels his *Nathan* is eminently well suited. Arguing that the play's wisdom is eternal, and asserting, "I believe that Nathan is as relevant today as he was back then," the dramatist concludes that the FGS has an unfulfilled obligation to present this work.[214]

It was not until 1956, by which time the renamed German Stage relied heavily on subventions from Bonn, that *Nathan the Wise* finally had its German-language premiere in South America. The commemorative presentation on the 175th anniversary of Lessing's death received positive reviews in the *Freie Presse* and the *Argentinisches Tageblatt*. Both reviews lauded the performance as a highlight in the sixteen-year existence of the stage, and they praised *Nathan* in nearly the same language, calling the work "canticles of humanity" and the "canticles of true humanity," respectively.[215] Both papers admitted that the play's impact would be limited to those who were already receptive to its purport, but the *Freie Presse* hoped that the rousing applause and numerous curtain calls reflected genuine enthusiasm among theatergoers for Lessing's compassion.

Language was another intersection. Though it lacked the bellicose overtones of the *La Plata Zeitung*'s 1943 review of *Minna*, in its discussion of *Nathan* the *Freie Presse* continued to focus on the spoken word. It praised Wolfgang Schwarz's Templar as "masterful in its modern diction," and Joseph Halpern's Patriarch was a "linguistic masterclass" and a model for younger actors.[216] The *Tageblatt* also devoted considerable space to language, although it was more critical and complained that the script was at times "disimproved" by excessive editing, cutting off syllables from Lessing's iambic verse.[217] Their mutual emphasis on language in the *Tageblatt* and the *Freie Presse* demonstrated a bond between both German colonies.

---

214. "Leserbrief bittet um Aufführung von Nathan," *AT*, October 14, 1951.

215. *"Nathan der Weise," FP*, June 27, 1956; "Lessings *Nathan*," *AT*, June 24, 1956.

216. *"Nathan der Weise," FP*, June 27, 1956.

217. *"Nathan der Weise," AT*, June 27, 1956.

The *Tageblatt*'s review of *Nathan* exposed the limits of dialogue by addressing the politically charged issue of struggling to overcome the past or, in German, *Vergangenheitsbewältigung*. The *Tageblatt* made explicit references to the biographical parallels between Lessing's protagonist and the leading actor in the presentation, Jacques Arndt. It noted that a scene in which the Jewish Nathan told the Friar the story of his own suffering and persecution was excruciatingly personal on- and offstage.[218] The *Freie Presse*, perhaps remembering its own role during Nazism, did not comment on this striking aspect of the performance. Even worse was a scene in which the Patriarch of Jerusalem repeated: "Do nothing. The Jew will burn." At this moment, a section of the audience began to laugh. A shudder, the *Tageblatt* opined, would have been more appropriate. The *Freie Presse*, again, was silent. Although it commended the production, the *Tageblatt* criticized the closing that Arndt had grafted onto Lessing's work, in which the cast joined hands and formed a circle as the sultan exclaimed: "Let's be friends!"[219] Arndt later explained that he had believed theater could bring the antagonistic populations together, and felt that *Nathan* was singularly suited to this aim. Thus, he had added the rather heavy-handed ending to be sure not to miss the unique opportunity that the performance presented.[220] Indeed, both the *Tageblatt* and the *Freie Presse* urged their readers to attend the presentation and learn from its message of tolerance and empathy. Reviews of Lessing's *Nathan the Wise* revealed common ground and acute discord between the German blocs. The newspapers voiced a will to heal, and they found bonds of language and cultural heritage in Lessing's drama that helped them make a start. On the other hand, their reviews also made clear that fallout from the recent past continued to preclude truly open dialogue and full reconciliation.

On July 1, 1962, Ney and his ensemble chose Lessing's *Minna of Barnhelm* to open a permanent facility for his Chamber Theater

---

218. "*Nathan der Weise*," *AT*, June 27, 1956.
219. "*Nathan der Weise*," *AT*, June 27, 1956.
220. Arndt, interview by author, December 25, 2008.

at the Goethe School in Buenos Aires. Lessing's comedy drew thousands of spectators during a nine-week run, proving to be an apt choice to inaugurate the theater, which hosted the stage until Ney's retirement in 1974. The *Tageblatt* warmly welcomed the venue, noting that Ney's Chamber Theater provided public and ensemble alike a wholesome connection to German cultural and intellectual values.[221] The *Freie Presse* remarked that a German-Argentine who has acted under Ney "embraces his cultural heritage in the most beautiful sense" and contributes to the joy of the local community.[222] Attended by Ambassador Werner Junker and Rudolf Junges, counselor to the West German diplomatic mission in Uruguay, the presentation of *Minna* became a celebration of German cultural identity shared by both German colonies. However, these optimistic festivities were contingent on a selective view of German history and current politics. Two years after Adolf Eichmann's capture in Buenos Aires and just a month after his execution in Israel, the presentation and reviews conspicuously avoided any mention of Nazism, World War II, or the Shoah.

This scripted silence had reverberated with undeniable and perhaps insurmountable enmity a few years earlier. No play unmasked the intransigent discord between Argentina's German populations as forcefully as *The Diary of Anne Frank* (1955). When it premiered in multiple German cities in 1956, the *Tageblatt* applauded the drama and noted the reflective, solemn atmosphere at the performances, but the *Freie Presse* made no mention of the event.[223] Instead it published an account by Wilfred von Oven, formerly Goebbels's press secretary, of his trip to Germany.[224] When the *Tageblatt* reviewed the play at the Yiddish People's Theater it speculated that although Yiddish-, Italian-, and Spanish-language theaters had already put on *Anne Frank* in Argentina, a German-language presentation was unlikely. The next week a reader

221. "Eröffnung des neuen Zimmertheaters," *AT*, July 1, 1962.

222. "Deutsches Zimmertheater," *FP*, July 1, 1962.

223. "*Das Tagebuch der Anne Frank* erschüttert das deutsche Publikum," *AT*, October 9, 1956.

224. "Ausklang im Schwabenland," *FP*, October 6, 1956.

rebuked the German Stage for eschewing the play because it was afraid to reopen old wounds. She reminded the theater's management that it had its "old," Jewish public to thank for its success and not the "other" audience whose sensibilities it was shielding.[225] When the stage finally scheduled *Anne Frank* for the 1958 season it encountered resistance from the West German embassy, which protested to Bonn that this unfortunate selection would be a "terrible burden" for the German-speaking public, including Jews who all surely wished "to forget the past."[226] Since renewed polarization of German-speaking theatergoers into "Jewish and Gentile" camps was not in the interests of West German diplomacy, the embassy urged the Foreign Office to intervene against the production.[227] The embassy failed to differentiate between Gentile antifascists and supporters of Nazism and, worse, preferred to repress confrontation with the past in the interest of political expediency.

Against the embassy's objections, the German Stage performed *Anne Frank* on June 2, 1958. Already the prelude to the presentation portended conflict. While several previews accompanied regular advertisements in the *Tageblatt*, the *Freie Presse* printed nothing on the upcoming performance. The reviews then laid bare the colonies' starkly divergent perspectives. The *Tageblatt*'s review began with innuendo, noting that Anne Frank would be twenty-nine years old, had it not been for people who now say, " 'I only followed orders' and 'I only did my duty' and 'I didn't know.' " Exuding aspersion, the paper explicitly denounced the many German emigrants who avoided the presentation, because they had already excused the six million dead Jews for being naive enough to allow themselves to be tortured, raped, and murdered. The drama's greatest deed was to tell Anne Frank's story for "our children—so they know." In its review, the *Tageblatt* launched a withering diatribe against the nationalist colony, including Ambassador Junker, and then castigated the lot of them for failing to uphold the memory of the Shoah for the sake of future generations. That same day the *Freie Presse* printed a review that read as if its theater

225. "Leserbrief: *Das Tagebuch der Anne Frank*," *AT*, September 1, 1957.
226. WGE to FFO, March 25, 1958, Bestand B95, Band 558, PAAA.
227. WGE to FFO, March 25, 1958, Bestand B95, Band 558, PAAA.

critic had deliberately coordinated with the *Tageblatt* to validate its admonishments and incriminations. It noted only once that the Franks were Jews, also mentioned the word "Jewish" only once, and devoted not a single word to Nazis, the Holocaust, concentration camps, deportation, or the SS. The critic saw neither relevance to contemporary West Germany nor warnings for future generations. Anne Frank's diary was not a historical artifact documenting Nazi genocide, but functioned dramatically as the protagonist's companion and friend. Moreover, viewers should interpret the play simply as the story of a young girl entering adulthood and "certainly not as an attack on the prevailing conditions at that time." For the *Freie Presse*, this was the last word.

Despite a subsequent performance in Montevideo and the widely publicized release of the film *The Diary of Anne Frank* (1959), the *Freie Presse* had no further comment. The *Tageblatt*, by contrast, ran a lengthy piece on the presentation at the Uruguayan national theater. Many theatergoers, Uruguayan ambassador Rosen stressed in an emotional letter to Bonn, had suffered in concentration camps or lost loved ones to the Shoah. Rosen lamented the absence of others, who remained reluctant to confront the recent past.[228] When the film premiered in Buenos Aires on April 20, 1959, the *Tageblatt* reiterated that its salient contribution was to promote awareness of the Shoah among future generations.[229] While the *Tageblatt* emphasized remembrance, the *Freie Presse* celebrated the birthday of Johannes Franze, who had been a Nazi propagandist in Argentina during the 1940s.[230] The date of the premiere, Hitler's birthday, discreetly underscored the unrelenting schism.

Curtain Call: Death in Buenos Aires

By the late 1950s, as deficits mounted and its cast aged, the German Stage was encountering adversity on multiple fronts.[231] For

---

228. WGE (Uruguay) to FFO, July 8, 1958, Bestand B95, Band 558, PAAA.
229. "*Das Tagebuch der Anne Frank*," *AT*, April 20, 1959.
230. "Johannes Franze wird 70," *FP*, June 15, 1959.
231. See also Lemmer, *Die "Freie Deutsche Bühne*," 95–104.

political reasons both Bonn and the embassy had been reluctant to stop funding the only regularly performing antifascist theater since 1940; however, they were unsatisfied with its presentations, and solutions were elusive. Under pressure from the German Stage's cast, the *Tageblatt*, the German Theater Guild, and prominent German-speaking Jews, the Foreign Office had rebuffed Ney's suggestions to fuse his Chamber Theater with the exilic ensemble. Ney's more accomplished students such as Regine Enzweiler, who later went on to a successful acting career in Argentina, might have provided the youthful energy that the ensemble lacked.[232] Yet, despite improved relations in some areas, the unyielding malice between Jews and antifascists, on the one hand, and nationalist Gentile Germans, on the other, precluded a partnership. This exacerbated the problems of aging thespians and financial struggles at the German Stage. Hiring actors from Germany was expensive and risked shutting out the refugees who had been members of the stage for decades.[233] As its artistic level declined, continual economic crises in Argentina caused the troupe to run ever increasing deficits, reaching 60,000 German marks for the 1962 season.[234] This was untenable, and as early as 1960 Bonn had already begun considering whether to deny the German Stage further funding and look instead for a fresh start with an alternative enterprise.[235]

Founded in 1949, Reinhold Olszewski's German Chamber Theater in Santiago, Chile, had staged guest performances in Buenos Aires since 1961, consistently receiving positive media coverage.[236] The Foreign Office invested heavily in the company—170,000

---

232. Known today as Regine Lamm, the actress had a leading role in Leonel Giacometto's prize-winning play, *¡All Jews out of Europe!* (2009), the first in a trilogy about the Shoah.

233. WGE to FFO, March 2, 1961; WGE to FFO, July 20, 1961; WGE to FFO, November 22, 1961, Bestand B95, Band 765, PAAA.

234. FFO to WGE, November 8, 1961, Bestand B95, Band 765, PAAA.

235. Internal memorandum, FFO, March 24, 1960; WGE to FFO, December 15, 1962, Bestand B95, Band 765; WGE to FFO, January 1, 1964, Bestand B95, Band 1066, PAAA.

236. "*Die Kinder Eduards*," *AT*, September 15, 1961; "Saison der Deutschen Kammerspiele," *FP*, April 29, 1962; "Deutsche Kammerspiele: *Prätorius*," *AT*, September 10, 1962; "Deutsche Kammerspiele: *Scherz, Satire, tiefere Bedeutung*," *FP*, September 1, 1963.

German marks for the 1962 season—which gave Olszewski artistic capabilities that the German Stage could not match.[237] Furthermore, the Foreign Office reasoned, it could fund even higher-quality performances and cut costs by supporting Olszewski alone.[238] Since Buenos Aires had a much larger German population than Santiago, in 1965 Bonn decided to relocate Olszewski's entire group to Argentina. From 1965 to 1971 his outfit was centered in Buenos Aires and traveled throughout South America. Although Olszewski promised to employ members of the German Stage, only Jacques Arndt and Lilly Wichert found work with him.[239] The Foreign Office never did fund Ludwig Ney; however, Olszewski supported the Chamber Theater with props, costumes, and technical assistance.[240]

The Germany-based magazine *Vorwärts* reacted with a darkly titled article, "Death in Buenos Aires," which lambasted Bonn for belligerence against German culture.[241] The Foreign Office defended itself by citing the unsustainable costs of maintaining two theaters in South America, as well as the older cast's deficient artistic vitality.[242] Perhaps the most insightful indictment came from Paul Walter Jacob. In an op-ed for the *Israel Forum*, Jacob bitterly lamented the demise of a theater that offered the world a better image of Germany during its most shameful and tragic hour.[243] In defining the German Stage by its role during the Nazi period, Jacob pinpointed the need to install a new troupe with an unburdened past. The final theater program of the German Stage itself had highlighted the obdurate divisions in the Argentine capital: "It is wholly indifferent to us who you are, what school you attended, what newspaper you read, or to which 'group' you belong."[244] In the act of declaring reconciliation, or at least indifference, the program corroborated

---

237. FFO to WGE, November 8, 1961, Bestand B95, Band 765, PAAA.

238. Stuhlmann, *Vater Courage*, 144.

239. Stuhlmann, *Vater Courage*, 155.

240. WGE to FFO, November 24, 1964, Bestand B95, Band 1066, PAAA.

241. "Sterben in Buenos Aires: Deutsches Theater zum Tode verurteilt," *Vorwärts*, August 1965.

242. Internal memorandum, FFO, August 23, 1965, Bestand B95, Band 1495, PAAA.

243. "Tragisches Ende einer Emigrantenbühne," *Israel Forum*, June 1965.

244. Program, Deutsches Schauspielhaus Buenos Aires, Heft 2, Spielzeit 1964.

partisanship, including sectarian schools, such as the North School vs. Pestalozzi School; newspapers, the *Argentinisches Tageblatt* vs. the *Freie Presse*; and factions, the so-called new and old colonies, names that persisted even though the "new" colony was now over twenty-five years old. Two decades after the Second World War, even an institution whose survival depended on overcoming these blocs was compelled to acknowledge their existence.

In 1951 West Germany's first ambassador to Argentina, Hermann Terdenge, asserted that Argentina's conflicting German populations should work together for the future and not lose themselves in the past. Mutual love for the fatherland, Terdenge concluded, was the bridge to understanding.[245] During the postwar period theatrical performances were a crucial vehicle for initiating a dialogue and rediscovering the common cultural heritage that Terdenge hoped could bring the antagonists closer together. Not long beforehand, however, the same media, thespians, and theatergoers had deployed theater to drive German Buenos Aires asunder. Postwar rapprochement required a willful and ultimately impossible avoidance of this recent history. It was a history that would splinter Argentina's German communities for years to come.

---

245. "Terdenge tritt ins Amt," *FP*, December 2, 1951.

Epilogue

There can be no question that from the 1930s through the 1960s Buenos Aires was a volatile, conflict-ridden place. To an extent, the city's German populations mirrored their hosts, who also were in nearly constant political and social turmoil. The polarization of Argentine society allowed both antifascist and nationalist German blocs to cultivate intercultural alliances without modifying many aspects of their own political platform. The competition among emigrants to define German culture also was shaped by events in Europe, including German dramatic theory, Bonn's domestic and foreign policies, and new waves of emigration to Argentina. Neither off- nor onstage were the disputes stable; instead they evolved over time as the emigrants became immigrants, and their relationships to their respective countries of origin and residence shifted. By the 1960s, there was an expanding stretch of common ground among the German immigrants, although their historical animosity remained unresolved.

The West German government intervened at both the German Stage and Ludwig Ney's Chamber Theater, and its actions are one measure of how closely dramatic performances were intertwined with the social and political agendas of German Buenos Aires. Furthermore, Bonn's level of investment in theater—up to 180,000 German marks per annum in Buenos Aires alone—is testimony to the power of this cultural medium.[1] On the occasion of the 1965 Summer Festival, against the backdrop of Ney's presentation of Friedrich Schiller's *Robbers*, the immigrant population revealed both how much they now approximated each other and to what extent historical hostilities remained entrenched. Recognized as Germany's preeminent national poet by all parties, Schiller elicited a shared and largely congruous emphasis on language and Cold War politics. The *Argentinisches Tageblatt* devoted an entire preview to Irene Ney's individualized language instruction with each actor to practice enunciation and delivery, often reciting, recording, and listening to a single passage dozens of times. Although this technique was reactionary for rehearsals in the 1960s and even recalled fascist dramatic theory, Irene Ney's meticulous focus on language resonated throughout German Buenos Aires.[2] By this time many actors in Ney's group were Argentine-born, and most spoke imperfect German. Crucial to this new generation's propensity to sustain transnational attachments over time, the preservation of the German language among younger members was vital to immigrants in Argentina.[3] The press reinforced this priority and fretted over tenuous linguistic links to the fatherland.[4] Writing to Bonn

---

1. Internal memorandum, FFO, March 24, 1960; WGE to FFO; FFO to WGE, November 8, 1961, Bestand B95, Band 765; WGE to FFO, December 15, 1962, Bestand B95, Band 765; WGE to FFO, January 1, 1964, Bestand B95, Band 1066, PAAA.

2. Spolin, *Improvisation for the Theater*, 112.

3. Rubén Rumbaut, "Severed or Sustained Attachments? Language, Identity, and Imagined Communities in the Post-Immigrant Generation," Levitt and Walters, *Changing Face of Home*, 43–95, 47–48.

4. "Du mete dich nicht in was dich nicht importart," *FP*, March 13, 1956; "Deutsche Eltern haben argentinische Kinder," *AT*, August 22, 1957; "Deutsche lernen Deutsch," *FP*, March 11, 1959; "Die Musik der deutschen Sprache," *AT*, January 22, 1961; "Deutsche Kulturpolitik im Ausland," *FP*, March 1, 1964.

on Ney's behalf, both the journalist Carl Hillekamps and West German ambassador Werner Junker had stressed the improvement of younger actors' spoken German under the director's tutelage.[5] The German populations of Buenos Aires coalesced around an emotional sense of cultural identity based on their native tongue and concern for its perseverance among future generations.

With obsequious lines such as "For his entire life Friedrich Schiller fought for the freedom and dignity of man," the *Freie Presse* and the *Tageblatt* coordinated their previews of the 1965 production of *The Robbers* with West German ambassador Ernst-Günther Mohr's panegyric to Schiller's crusade for freedom and justice in his introductory speech at the event.[6] The show of unity against the perceived Communist menace provoked the *Tageblatt* to assert that a single German colony filled the seats at Ney's Summer Festival.[7]

While media coverage of *The Robbers* found common values in linguistic preservation and Western democratic principles, the aftermath of the festival revealed the projection of unity to have been showy indeed. A week after the final presentation, the *Argentinisches Tageblatt* published an anecdote by a young Jewish actress in Berlin in 1936.[8] Dismayed by Hitler's order to remove the Schiller monument at the Gendarmenmarkt in Berlin to create a military parade ground, she remembered discovering a new tribute in a nearby phone booth. It was a poem prophesying the inexorable dawn of the Marquis Posa's vision of freedom, because no nation had ever chosen subjugation to leaders such as Spielberg or Franz Moor. The actress had memorized the poem, because it was too dangerous to write it down. There was of course no corresponding piece in the *Freie Presse*. Written by a Jewish actress just a week after the all-Gentile performances of *The Robbers*,

---

5. Hillekamps to FFO, January 1, 1964; WGE to FFO, March 5, 1958, Bestand B33, Band 248, PAAA.

6. "*Die Räuber*," *AT*, October 24, 1965; "*Die Räuber*," *FP*, October 31, 1965; "Schillers *Räuber* als Freilichtaufführung," *AT*, December 6, 1965.

7. "Letzte Vorstellung der *Räuber*," *AT*, December 12, 1965.

8. "Lesebrief über Schiller von Elfi Zweig," *AT*, December 19, 1965.

the article prodded at the underlying disunity in German Buenos Aires. Harmony among Argentina's German-speakers was contingent upon a willful amnesia of the past, especially Nazism, World War II, and the Shoah. When either colony refused to engage in this exercise of selective memory, the thin veneer of rapprochement was exposed to be a contrivance.

Both the oldest and newest directors in town, Ludwig Ney and Reinhold Olszewski, respectively, seem to have recognized that playing theater in Buenos Aires was still a precarious balancing act. The potential of theatrical energies to stir polemics, unearth memories, and vitalize lingering rancor by violating the uneasy scripted silence among immigrants remained even in the mid-1960s. Furthermore, by this time, the German-speaking public was shrinking. The last wave of postwar immigration had ended with Germany's economic recovery in the 1950s. Aging, integration, and remigration to Germany also caused the number of potential theatergoers to drop. It was imperative for Olszewski's large, supraregional, government-funded operation as well as Ney's smaller community ensemble to draw from as wide a swath of German Buenos Aires as possible. The two men confronted this challenge with pragmatism. In key productions Ney and Olszewski opted for universalism as a means of reducing the risk of alienating theatergoers and reigniting the explosive antagonism still pervading the populations.

For Ludwig Ney the highlight of the theater season was the Summer Festival. His cast began preparations months ahead of time, because instead of the approximately 200-seat capacity of his regular facility, audiences at the Summer Festival numbered in the thousands. This event attracted extensive media coverage in both populations, and Ney hoped that the large attendances would eventually garner him funding from the Foreign Office in Bonn. Taking care to avoid controversies, at least as much as possible, Ney chose dramas that were politically unobjectionable and universally accepted as worthy of performance. Of the Summer Festivals from 1956 to 1966, nearly half featured Shakespearean dramas, including *A Midsummer Night's Dream* (1956 and 1962), *The Merry Wives of Windsor* (1957), and *Othello* (1966). No other dramatist received more than a single performance. Nobody questioned Shakespeare's literary merit, and through the ages he had been staged by German speakers of all faiths and political convictions. Through the universality of William Shakespeare, Ney's company could appeal to spectators from across German Buenos Aires, irrespective of their ongoing differences.

For the 1966 festival, Ney's group presented *Othello* (1604). At first glance, this selection seems finally to represent Ney's definitive departure from Nazi dramatic politics. The noble African protagonist, Othello, is a tragic hero, and the plot focuses on interracial sex and marriage. Although in Nazi Germany Othello would have been deported to a concentration camp and sterilized for racial defilement, the drama did not disappear from the nation's stages. In fact, during the Nazi era *Othello* generally was presented more frequently and in more theaters than the *Merchant of Venice*, although the latter's plot dovetailed with Nazi anti-Semitism.[9] Critics underscored Othello's passions, describing him as a paragon of masculine virtues and military bearing in an aristocratic and morally decadent society. The protagonist's race could not be ignored, of course, so Othello was depicted as a light-skinned Moor, very different from the black Africans in numerous productions during the Weimar Republic. Othello's behavior was conditioned not by race but by the agony of a proud and dignified soldier who finds himself isolated and betrayed in a foreign and decadent world.[10]

Authored by Ludwig Ney himself, the introductory essay in the Summer Festival program coincided with National Socialist interpretations. Evoking articles on Shakespeare in *Der Weg*, Ney praised the spirituality of Othello's love for Desdemona and rejected his subsumption into contemporary "sex sensations."[11] Ney criticized Venetian society, which he saw represented by the "selfish, amoral and cold" behavior of the "degenerate" Jago.[12]

---

9. Thomas Eicher, "Spielplanstrukturen 1929–1944," in *"Theater im Dritten Reich": Theaterpolitik, Spielplanstruktur, NS-Dramatik*, ed. Thomas Eicher, Barbara Panse, and Henning Rischbieter (Seelze-Velber: Kallmeyer, 2000): 298–301.

10. Bonnell, 173–174.

11. "Menschenwürde und Gattenwahl," *Der Weg*, January 1957; program, *Othello*, December 1966.

12. Program, *Othello*, December 1966.

Othello's soldierly idealism contrasted thus with the "materialistic values" of the Republic of Venice.[13] Ney never mentioned Othello's race, which, represented by a blond actor, was "Aryanized" in the presentation. Instead, the director lamented the "broken soul" of the solitary military officer upon losing his most sacred treasure: his love for Desdemona. Instead of opening a new chapter, Ney's essay stands out for its consistency with National Socialist interpretations of the Shakespearean tragedy. Even in 1966, the director advanced his fusion of conservative dramatic theory with an intercultural cast, setting, and audience. Contrary to the program, the *Tageblatt* lamented the tragic destruction of an inspirational love that transcended artificial and unjust racial barriers.[14] In another reference to the racial background of the play, the paper observed that the diabolical intriguer, Jago, had white skin but a black soul. The discrepancy between the program and the review demonstrated the evolution of relations between the German-speaking populations of Buenos Aires. Conflicts between the groups persisted, especially concerning any discourse related to Nazism, but Shakespeare's universalism drew members of both blocs to the same theatrical presentation, something that would have been unthinkable years earlier.[15]

The year before the German Chamber Theater moved from Santiago to Buenos Aires to replace the German Stage, Olszewski's cast played Shakespeare's *Hamlet* as part of a five-day run in the Argentine capital. The company presented five different dramas; however, *Hamlet* was the only sold-out performance, indicating that both German populations attended the production. The *Freie Presse* emphasized that *Hamlet* represented an artistic challenge for any theater, and was concerned that an inadequate interpretation would transgress against Shakespeare's genius.[16] However, subsequent reviews praised the scenic design, dramatic diction, and expressive unity of performance. The *Argentinisches Tageblatt*

13. Program, *Othello*, December 1966.
14. "Shakespeares *Othello* in Los Polvorines," *AT*, December 12, 1966.
15. "Deutsche Kammerspiele: *Hamlet*," *AT*, September 2, 1964.
16. "Spielplan der Deutschen Kammerspiele", *FP*, August 18, 1964.

referred to the event as a delight for all spectators, and the *Freie Presse* also affirmed the group's impressive artistic achievement.[17] Faced with the challenge of attracting various demanding and divided populations, and almost certainly aware that a potential move to Buenos Aires and an accompanying windfall of embassy funding hung in the balance, the troupe chose Shakespeare's *Hamlet* as its final argument. The following year, with lavish support from Bonn, Olszewski's group moved permanently to Buenos Aires. Although their European "homeland" boasted literary giants like Goethe, Schiller, Lessing, Brecht, and many others, during the postwar period from 1945 to 1966 no playwright was performed on German-language stages in Argentina as often as Shakespeare. This unexpected statistic is as much a testament to the universality of the Bard of Avon, who transcended all political, social, and artistic agendas, as it is to the unending competition between Argentina's immigrant factions. Even in the 1960s, depictions of German dramatists remained fraught with divisive interpretations of the nation's culture, history, and identity.

* * *

In the introduction to this book I posed a series of questions to guide its readers (and its writer) along the winding paths it follows from Europe in the 1930s to South America in the 1960s. Many pages have passed in the interim, so it is helpful to restate those queries here: How did the German Theater and the Free German Stage contribute to transatlantic and transnational projects, such as delineating and consolidating German identity in South America, staking political allegiances, and integrating with the Argentine host society? Why, more than any other form of art or cultural representation, did theater have such wide, enduring appeal in German Buenos Aires and beyond? Finally, how does putting theater at the center revise perceptions of German-speaking nationalist, antifascist, and Zionist populations in Argentina? I revisit these questions here by linking them to a more poignantly profiled reflection

---

17. "Deutsche Kammerspiele: *Hamlet*," *FP*, September 2, 1964.

on the salient themes of this study, including inclusion and exclusion, integration, transnationalism, drama theory, theatrical energies, and, of course, competition. The central role of theater in this book enables a reexamination of German-speaking immigrants in Argentina, emphasizing previously underexplored events and individuals while offering new perspectives on more frequently studied topics. The conclusion depicts the impact of theater on existing narratives about Germans in Argentina, as well as the power of a focus on culture and the arts to inform and shape studies of migrant groups.

Inclusion and Exclusion

Putting theater at the center profoundly changes our perceptions of German speakers in Buenos Aires, including how the groups constituted themselves and delineated their limits. As noted in chapter 1, many scholars have ratified the emigrant Balder Olden's observation that the city's German-speaking population consisted of two absolutely separated groups—a mostly Jewish antifascist bloc, which also included earlier republicans during the Weimar Republic, and a Gentile nationalist faction, which transitioned from monarchists to Nazi sympathizers during the 1930s.[18] The lens of theater reveals this definition to be problematic not only with respect to social, religious, and generational groupings that predate the period under consideration, but also on multiple levels also during the 1930s and beyond. Germán Friedmann rightly differentiates between antifascist activists and politically disengaged emigrants, and he also questions whether the separation was as absolute as

---

18. Kießling, *Exil in Lateinamerika*, 73–74; Meding, *Flucht vor Nürnberg*, 230; Ismar, *Der Pressekrieg*, 29; Ana María Cartolano, "Editoriales en el exilio: Los libros en lengua alemana editados en la Argentina durante el período de 1930–1950," in Rohland de Langbehn, *Paul Zech y las condiciones del exilio en la Argentina*, 81–92, 82; Rojer, *Exile in Argentina*, 97; Anne Saint Sauveur-Henn, "Das Exil der 'kleinen Leute' (1933–1945): Ein Spezifikum?," in *Alltag im Exil*, ed. Daniel Azuélos (Wurzburg: Königshausen & Neumann, 2011), 41.

Olden suggests.[19] In this study another group emerges—Zionists. Theatrical performances demonstrate that German-speaking Zionists are not subsumable into the antifascist colony. While the antifascists welcomed a plurality of faiths and nationalities into their fold, Zionists founded their own independent social, religious, philanthropic, and journalistic institutions. They excluded Gentiles from the ranks of anti-Nazis despite the existence of obvious examples to the contrary, including the founder of *Das Andere Deutschland*, August Siemsen; the owner of the *Argentinisches Tageblatt*, Ernesto Alemann; and members of the Free German Stage's ensemble. For their part, antifascists and moderate Jews rejected the Zionist platform by boycotting Zionist dramas, such as Nathan Bistritzky's *That Night* and J. Aialti's *Father and Son*. The Free German Stage's public attended plays with religious and political themes, including Lillian Hellman's *Watch on the Rhine* and Carl Rössler's *The Five Frankfurters*, but it consistently rebelled against stridently Zionist dramas. Finally, the FGS concluded that an inclusive community of theatergoers was possible only by excluding Zionists. For their part, Zionist groups broke irrevocably with the FGS after controversial celebrity guest performances and the addition of nationalist Germans to its personnel. As Bernhardi Swarsensky, editor of the *Jüdische Wochenschau*, made clear in 1962, the foundation of this rift was Zionists' rejection of German culture in general.[20] German-speaking Zionists refused to define themselves as Germans, and they did not belong to the antifascist colony. Thus, although the Free German Stage touted itself as an open, intercultural anti-Nazi community-building institution, opposition to Hitler alone did not signify unity or even inclusion.

Despite individual interactions, in their competition to define Germanness victims and supporters of Nazism excluded each other. During World War II, these groups shunned the opposing faction in the spheres of education, media, and entertainment. Both

---

19. Friedmann, "Los alemanes antinazis de la Argentina," 205–226.
20. Swarsensky to Jacob, January 8, 1962, PWJAK.

German stages had their origins in this polarized and antagonistic environment. Supported by the antitotalitarian *Tageblatt*, the Free German Stage defined itself as an anti-Nazi theater; Ludwig Ney's German Theater was sponsored from the outset by National Socialist organizations, including the German embassy, the German Labor Front, Strength through Joy, and the Ministry of Propaganda. Each troupe actively contributed to the entrenchment of these positions through divergent repertoire, personnel, advertising, and media coverage. Both directors, Ludwig Ney and Paul Walter Jacob, published essays further demarcating the opposing factions and intensifying their own rivalry.

In this light, each theater can be viewed as a collective representative of its public, reflecting and hardening extant hostilities. This exclusionary community-building created divisions that could not be undone. During the postwar period, Paul Walter Jacob attempted to redirect policy at the Free German Stage by pushing an agenda of inclusion and reconciliation with nationalist Germans. By advertising in the *Freie Presse*, successor to the *La Plata Zeitung*, and contracting actors from Ludwig Ney's ensemble, Jacob demonstrated that in the realm of theater the split between Argentina's German populations was not absolute. To his chagrin, however, for many emigrants the tactics of exclusion had not ended with the war. After years of inculcating their constituencies with antithetical visions of Germanness, there was no possibility of postwar reconciliation. As he opened relations with nationalist Germans, Jacob estranged many of the theatergoers, artists, and journalists who had supported him. His efforts at inclusion resulted in his own exclusion.

Nationalist Germans, by contrast, were a more coherent population. At least publicly, there was no infighting about political objectives or cultural values. Dramas such as Werner Hoffmann's *Utz Schmidl* demonstrated that there was variation among nationalist emigrants' level of identification with Germany and affinity for Argentina; however, audiences, artists, and the press all consistently upheld a National Socialist view of Germanness. In public forums, all nationalist Germans were accepted as members of the colony, and this continued after World War II when nationalists included postwar emigrant actors, journalists, and spectators in their ranks. Explicitly neo-Nazi organizations that did not find sufficient support to survive on their own, such as *Der Weg* and the German Chamber Players, integrated with older, nationalist counterparts like the *Freie Presse* and Ludwig Ney's ensemble. Although some eventually opened paths to contact, communication, and limited cooperation with antifascist groups, such as the Free German Stage, even in the 1960s many leading nationalist institutions and individuals never renounced Nazism. They thereby implicitly affirmed ongoing tactics of exclusionary community-building.

A final aspect of inclusion is this book itself. By analyzing both German theaters, it tracks the evolving relationships not only within, but also between antagonistic German populations. Viewed over the full period covered in this study, Ludwig Ney's troupe and the Free German Stage reveal that they had much in common. They adopted parallel tactics in publicity by cultivating close relationships with media, educational, and social organizations; in repertoire by favoring the comic genre in times of crisis and performing historical plays to mold current cultural identity and foster political cohesion; in intercultural outreach by embarking on multiple collaborative projects with Argentine artists, audiences, and media; and in constructing community by promulgating a sense of togetherness based on a shared history and common foes. Ironically, the similarities in their approaches to constituting a loyal audience precluded rapprochement even when both directors wanted to expand audiences. Neither Paul Walter Jacob nor Ludwig Ney was able to surmount the barriers they themselves had helped to construct. Whereas Zionists denied Germanness altogether, neither antifascists nor nationalists could imagine allowing the opposing faction into their community. The groups could inhabit common areas, such as certain dramatic performances, and by the mid-1950s both theaters found their way into the pages of the *Freie Presse* and the *Argentinisches Tageblatt*. Nonetheless, the contrast in reporting on performances such as Zuckmayer's *The Captain of Köpenick*, Winsloe's *Girls in Uniform*, Lessing's *Nathan the Wise*, Hackett and Goodrich's *The Diary of Anne Frank*, and Schiller's *The Robbers* disclosed intransigently antipathetic positions on German history, World War II, and the Shoah that did not waver from the late 1940s through the mid-1960s. There may have existed overlapping political alliances against communism, and a measure of common cultural heritage, but neither group ever truly regarded the other as among its own ranks. This is why Bonn ultimately opted to relocate a new, postwar theater from Santiago, Chile, to the Argentine capital. Strong campaigns of antagonistic exclusion had been mounted for years, so there was no path to a single, inclusive German-speaking community in Buenos Aires.

Integration

Perhaps unexpectedly, given their divergent views on politics and cultural identity, this study shows that German nationalists, antifascists, and Zionists all cultivated relationships with the Argentine host society. Their motivations varied. Zionists had decisively rejected Germany. As Bernhardi Swarsensky wrote in the *Jüdische Wochenschau*, there was no possibility of Zionists returning to Germany or forgiving Germans after what Jews had suffered.[21] Twenty-five years after the fallout from Hellman's *Unvanquished*, he reiterated the Zionist position: "Smoke billowed from the gas chambers. Fires were visible for miles. Ignorance is an unconvincing excuse. Everyone knew it and they kept silent."[22] Zionists did not seek integration with Argentine Gentiles; however, they supported dramas, such as Pico and Eichelbaum's *The Nutshell*, that steered refugees away from Europe by familiarizing them with Argentine culture and customs. Zionists also sought to utilize theater to build relationships with Argentine Jews, exemplified by the production of Bistritzky's *That Night*. While the performance failed, many Zionists persisted in their efforts and participated in intercultural professional and religious organizations. Swarsensky, for example, eventually became president of Centra, an umbrella organization for central European Jews throughout South America.

---

21. "Einig wie nie zuvor," *JW*, April 26, 1940.
22. "Das deutsche Volk," *JW*, February 3, 1967.

To disseminate their religious message to a larger public, Zionist publications increasingly appeared in Spanish.[23] Zionists' goal was to convince Jews to make aliyah, not integrate into Argentine society, but they realized that they could not achieve this goal without cross-cultural cooperation and outreach to other Jews in Argentina.

The Free German Stage was a different case. Unlike Zionists, many members of its cast self-identified as Germans and considered returning to Germany after the war. Still, they also had to persevere in exile. As a politically vulnerable, privately funded theater company, the enterprise could survive only if it forged partnerships with Argentine artists and institutions. A model for internationalism and interculturalism, from its foundation the Free German Stage established a presence in Argentine media, initiated dramatic projects with local artists and venues, joined and participated in administrative organizations, staged benefits for international charities, and attracted a diverse public to its productions. The troupe drew from these connections to secure venues, process visas and work permits for actors, and gain recognition beyond German Buenos Aires, as well as withstand pressure from Argentine fascist sympathizers and nationalist Germans. Its intercultural relationships helped save the stage from bankruptcy in 1944 and 1946, and were fundamental to its ability to woo celebrities for guest performances after the war. Politically, especially through its diverse repertoire and charity productions, the Free German Stage played a key role in the formation of an international community of antifascists. Through intercultural dramatic performances, the FGS also pushed sometimes reluctant refugees to transition from emigrants to immigrants in Argentina. Members of its own ensemble, including Jacques Arndt and Hedwig Schlichter-Crilla, integrated so successfully that they became celebrities in the Argentine

---

23. The magazine *Porvenir* appeared from 1942 to 1945. The *Jüdische Wochenschau* was also called *La Semana Israelita* and featured articles in Spanish, and Bernhardi Swarsensky published in Spanish, including his book *Historia de la Noche de cristal* (Buenos Aires: Ejecutivo Sudamericano del Congreso Judío Mundial, 1968).

entertainment industry. In accord with the Argentine constitution, which promotes European immigration to improve and teach the sciences and the arts, Schlichter-Crilla's innovative Mask ensemble and her pioneering projects in children's theater left lasting imprints on drama theory and pedagogy in Argentina.[24] It is not possible to evaluate every individual in these pages; however, the successful integration of several refugee actors confirms Ottmar Ette's concept of literature as a science for living together.[25] The Free German Stage demonstrates, at least in this instance, the efficacy of interculturalism and internationalism to persevere, construct community, and even achieve prosperity amid the multifold challenges of diaspora.

At a more gradual pace, Ludwig Ney's ensembles, too, initiated a process of intercultural outreach and integration. Already in 1941 dramas such as Hoffmann's *Utz Schmidl* demonstrated that many nationalist emigrants considered themselves to be immigrants, or at least hybrids, and harbored a sense of national affection for both Germany and Argentina. Nevertheless, during World War II the German Theater essentially was a monocultural enterprise. Thanks to its sizable and affluent public as well as ample funding from state-sponsored German organizations, the troupe had no need to collaborate with Argentine organizations. All this changed after the war, when the nationalist colony suffered losses of wealth, prestige, and influence as a result of the Argentine government's declaration of war on Germany and the Allied victory in the conflict. Finding himself with greatly reduced institutional support and no public funding, in the early 1950s Ludwig Ney's posture toward Argentine artists and public organizations underwent a remarkable shift. He initiated intercultural relationships with the Cordoban government, local artists, and media, and even began performing in Spanish. Although his collaboration with the Argentine government ended after Perón's downfall, Ney advanced his intercultural agenda by launching translingual tours

---

24. www.argentina.gov.ar/argentina/portal/documentos/constitucion_nacional. pdf, 4.

25. Ette, "Literature as Knowledge for Living," 989.

with the Chamber Theater as well as incorporating Argentine performers into the annual Summer Festival. Ludwig Ney never repented for his work as a Nazi collaborator, and there is ample evidence that he remained sympathetic to fascist ideology through his retirement in 1972; however, he too came to recognize interculturalism as the most viable and effective route to professional success in Argentina.

Zionists, antifascists, and Nazi collaborators comprised a diverse cast of characters. They advocated oppositional political platforms, professed distinct religious beliefs, and cultivated contrasting relationships to Germany and German culture. Yet all emigrated from German-speaking Europe, and most morphed into immigrants in Argentina. As noted in chapter 5, Daniel Boyarin and Jonathan Boyarin have argued that interculturalism is not a menace to the preservation of ethnic identity, but rather is probably necessary for the protection and survival of emigrant communities. The Germanist Egon Schwarz also theorized that integration is essential for emigrants to thrive in their new countries of residence.[26] While Schwarz speaks as a Jewish refugee and the Boyarins refer to Jewish diasporic identity, this study suggests that their theses hold true for emigrants of diverse political, ethnic, and religious affiliations.[27] Groups as various and conflictive as Zionists, Nazi sympathizers, antifascists, and politically disinterested refugees came to consider integration as an imperative to achieve their objectives and pursue their divergent political agendas in Argentina. For all German-speaking blocs in Buenos Aires, integration signified expanding one's horizons, honing skills, forging intercultural alliances, and participating in cultural and artistic life beyond the fringes of their ethnic population. Within the purview of this book, the process of integration was essential to any emigrant who wanted to become an immigrant—that is, to become a productive and prosperous member of a new nation and to participate in its society at all levels.

---

26. Egon Schwarz, "La emigración de la Alemania nazi," in Rohland de Langbehn, *Paul Zech y las condiciones del exilio en la Argentina*,13–28, 19.

27. Boyarin and Boyarin, "Diaspora," 721.

Transnationalism

From the start, both German theaters in Argentina were fundamentally transnational projects. In the first years of its existence, Ludwig Ney's troupe relied on funding from the German Labor Front, Strength through Joy, the German embassy, and, eventually, the Ministry of Propaganda in Berlin. In numerous reports to Berlin, Ambassador Edmund von Thermann emphasized the propagandistic value of the stage, which other emigrants also noted was crucial to the cohesion of the nationalist population. Nazi officialdom saw the German Theater as a vehicle to promote loyalty to Hitler in Argentina, and they appear to have been successful in this endeavor. Many nationalist German emigrants had an abiding relationship with National Socialism; they never dissented publicly against Nazi influence in Buenos Aires, even long after 1945. Nonetheless, Werner Hoffman's *Utz Schmidl* demonstrated that some of them had a sense of transatlantic identity that did not match National Socialist visions of Germanness. These emigrants viewed themselves as patriotic Germans, but also felt genuine sentiments of national affection toward Argentina. They regarded themselves as hybrids, and understood that their transnational sense of identity contrasted profoundly with the identity of their European countrymen.

The foundation of the antifascist Free German Stage stemmed in large part from a will to compete against the nationalist German Theater.[28] Nazi officialdom thus had a germinal influence on both theaters in Argentina. Furthermore, the German government pursued a transatlantic agenda of oppression against the FGS, including denaturalizing its director, blacklisting the theater in Germany, blocking publishers from sending it materials, and leveraging German influence to impede the troupe from continuing to perform in Argentina. The theater fought back, however, and pursued transcontinental alliances by presenting an international dramatic repertoire and coordinating with antifascists in Europe and the Americas, as well as with various nationalities in Buenos

---

28. Jacob to Weil, January 29, 1941, PWJAK.

Aires, to combat Nazism in South America. These partnerships enabled the stage to survive amid mounting adversity during the war, and then contributed to a new area of transnational celebrity guest performances in Argentina and Germany in the postwar period.

Zionists added other international elements at the Free German Stage. Leading figures in the local Zionist movement, such as Bernhardi Swarsensky and Günter Friedländer, worked to disrupt connections to Germany by inveighing against nostalgic depictions of Germany and Austria at the theater, and well as indicting Germans collectively for the Shoah. Zionists saw the FGS as a Jewish theater that performed in German, while antifascists, including founder, Paul Walter Jacob, regarded the German in the theater's name as a reference to the Europe of yesteryear and, they hoped, of tomorrow.[29] Finally, Zionists rejected the concept of diaspora as an indication that Jewish life in exile could become tolerable.[30] Zionists regarded any existence outside Eretz Israel as galuth, which connotes suffering, dislocation, and alienation from a true home.[31] Thus, they also seized on the Free German Stage to promote aliyah, including by inviting Nathan Bistritzky, who resided in Palestine, to attend a performance of his drama, *That Night*, and then donating the proceeds to Keren Kayemet Leisrael y Keren Hayesod.[32] Although only a small percentage of the refugee population made aliyah, the Free German Stage did contribute to the transnational project of Zionism during World War II. After the war, Zionists abandoned the theater out of vehement opposition to Paul Walter Jacob's dual program of outreach to the nationalist German

29. "Deutsches Theater in Argentinien," *AT*, September 7, 1941.

30. "Galuth und Diaspora," *JW*, September 18, 1951.

31. Krüger, *La diáspora*, 56–57.

32. Established as the Jewish National Funds at the Fifth Zionist Congress in Basel, Switzerland, in 1901, Keren Kayemet Leisrael purchased land in Eretz Israel for the Jewish people. The central fund-raising organization for Israel, Keren Hayesod was founded at the World Zionist Conference in Britain in 1920 and moved to Jerusalem in 1926. The chief tasks of Keren Hayesod included financing immigration and absorption, settlement, defense, development of water resources, and public works.

population and Germany itself. Rather than engaging in rapprochement, Zionists renounced German culture altogether.

Postwar celebrity guest performances at both stages indicated a
shift in the transnational projects being undertaken by Argentina's
German theater companies. Ludwig Ney courted the Nazi diaspora
to Argentina by allying himself with the fascist monthly *Der Weg*,
and contracting actors who had formerly featured in Nazi Germany
and other countries under fascism. Initially then, Ludwig Ney espoused the transnational agenda of some nationalist Germans and
recent postwar emigrants to advance fascist ideology in Argentina.
The extent to which the Peronist government welcomed Nazis, facilitated their emigration to Argentina, and permitted or even abetted the perpetuation of their ideology will remain a thorny subject
of debate, yet it is striking that Ludwig Ney collaborated on several large-scale productions with the Peronist government at a time
when he was openly advocating fascist ideology in neo-Nazi publications, adhering to Nazi drama theory onstage, and collaborating
with ensembles that touted their refusal to work with Jewish actors.

During the same period, Paul Walter Jacob launched numerous transatlantic endeavors. At first Jacob mostly contacted fellow exiles; however, by 1948 the director's focus had shifted to
individuals and organizations based in Germany. Guest performances endowed with international star power boosted the stage's
domestic and international profile, which facilitated Jacob's project
to reinvent the Free German Stage as a formally transnational institution. At the exclusion of East Germany, Jacob extended and
deepened networks with West German artists and institutions, par-
laying his fame across the Atlantic into professional opportunities
in Europe. When he accepted the position of general intendant in
Dortmund, Jacob became the first actor at either stage to remigrate
to Germany. Although many others still were struggling to adapt
to Argentina, nobody followed Jacob's route across the Atlantic.
The entire refugee ensemble at the Free German Stage remained
in the Americas, the vast majority in Argentina. Few in the troupe
espoused a Zionist point of view; however, they concurred on the
point that their break with Germany was permanent.

Nonetheless, transnational programs continued at the institutional level. There was significant concern in West Germany about

the spread of communism in the Southern Cone, and the West German embassy in Buenos Aires wasted little time in recruiting both German theaters to form an alliance against this perceived threat. The interventions of the embassy, particularly its financial lure, pulled both theaters into its cultural and political orbit. Although Bonn was reluctant to grant funding to Ludwig Ney because of his past as a Nazi collaborator, diplomats agreed that his traveling presentations were an effective tool for projecting West German soft power in the nation's interior. They regarded Ney as a crucial, unifying figure in their endeavor to forge a united front against communism among Germans throughout the country and exerted a heavy influence on his performances in service of this aim. Whereas Ney misrepresented his role during the Nazi period in numerous attempts to garner funding from Bonn, actors at the Free German Stage also felt compelled to moderate their tone if they sought financial support from West Germany. As individuals, leftist actors embarked on cross-cultural projects with Argentine artists, most notably Hedwig Schlichter-Crilla's ensemble, The Mask. Yet, their dependence on funding from the West German embassy incentivized thespians, including Schlichter-Crilla herself, who directed the FGS in 1963, to strictly avoid a progressive political agenda when working with this theater. Once a singular expression of resistance to German officialdom in Argentina, the exilic enterprise became a mouthpiece for projecting West German cultural politics in the Southern Cone. Under instructions from the Federal Foreign Office, the embassy molded emigrants' national affections and incorporated them into a transnational crusade against communism. It is possible that actors of both competing theaters would have adopted alternative modes of cultural and political expression had it not been for Bonn's financial clout.

Theatrical Energies

More than any other art form or mode of cultural expression, during the tumultuous years from 1934 to 1965 theater garnered the lasting attention and sponsorship of German political institutions, media organs, and antagonistic German-speaking populations. The collective sacrifices of time, work, and financial resources required to sustain the Free German Stage and Ludwig Ney's ensembles ratify them as vital community-building institutions. The prominence and endurance of both stages raise the question of why theater was such a singular focus of effort, resources, and debate among emigrant populations in Argentina.

Freddie Rokem's concept of theatrical energies—that is, the emotional, cultural, and political forces generated and unleashed by live theatrical performances—helps resolve this conundrum.[33] The environment of mass migration, cultural conflict, and political antagonism that characterized Buenos Aires in the mid-twentieth century was germane to theatrical communication, especially among immigrant populations. Drawing from a blend of literary text and dramatic performance, theatrical communication releases aesthetic, social, and political energies that interpret contemporary and historical events onstage and, often, intend to bring people together and shape their actions offstage in the present or future. Deployed to effect catharsis—the emotional, intellectual, moral, or even physical reactions that may be experienced by spectators during or following a performance—theatrical energies reverberated among and within Argentina's German-speaking blocs. By creating the illusion of reality, theater joins often distinct aspects of human experiences and social practices and elevates them for spectators to witness and decipher onstage. This shared event can trigger explosive, often unforeseeable offstage energies, which theater critics and journalists refract and often attempt to steer through the media. Even before Paul Walter Jacob and Ludwig Ney had arrived in the Argentine capital, Ferdinand Bruckner's antifascist play, *Race*, and the German Drama's propagandistic portrayals of Lessing's *Minna of Barnhelm* and Schiller's *Mary Stuart* had witnessed such an impact locally. The theatrical event generates a reaction that often resonates beyond the theater, spilling into the public sphere, frequently with the intention of catalyzing transgressive behaviors against existing groups, social norms, or ideologies.[34] The

---

33. Rokem, *Performing History*, 188–204.
34. Goldmann, *Actor's Freedom*, 23–24.

reverberations of theatrical communication are thus characterized by aggression, a salient feature of interactions in German Buenos Aires throughout the period under consideration.

Therefore, as exemplified by the Free German Stage and Ludwig Ney's ensembles, theater can act potently as both a unifying and a polarizing force. For decades, the aggressions that sprang from dramatic presentations cleaved and coalesced German-speaking blocs on the River Plate. When the dispersed tensions residing on- and offstage became attuned, these theatrical energies detonated the controversies and discord pervading German Buenos Aires. During the war, performances of Lillian Hellman's *The Unvanquished*, Carl Rössler's *The Five Frankfurters*, the German classics, and Werner Hoffmann's *Utz Schmidl*, for example, roused public responses to questions of religion, national affection, and political loyalty that united and strengthened certain German-speaking groups while attacking other blocs and the religious beliefs, cultural identities, and political programs they were seen to represent. At the same time, the failure of other productions to discharge theatrical energies, such as the Free German Stage's productions of *Mary Stuart*, Bistritzky's *That Night*, and Aialti's *Father and Son*, also delineated the boundaries of the refugee community, which embraced neither the German canon nor the Zionist agenda.

Theatrical energies remained a vigorous and unstable force after the war. Sentiments and alliances stemming from the Nazi period and the aftermath of World War II found expression in incendiary reactions to Carl Zuckmayer's *The Captain of Köpenick* and *The Devil's General* at the Free German Stage, as well as Ludwig Ney's presentation of *Mary Stuart*. The hardened hostilities stymied Paul Walter Jacob's program of celebrity-infused outreach to all German speakers in Buenos Aires, in which exilic actors and fascist thespian collaborators were ghosted by their roles on- and offstage during the recent past. Despite this setback, the West German embassy recognized and exploited theatrical communication to project Western soft power during the Cold War; however, despite the care taken to contrive harmony, theater proved divisive. The depictions of historical events onstage transformed actors into hyperhistorians, whose representations in *Anne Frank* and *Nathan the*

Wise rendered these figures from the Nazi occupation of Holland and the Third Crusade in Jerusalem poignantly "present" at the theatrical performances. Imbued with the Stanislavskian "magic if," the presentations carried the mimetic force of dramatized historical events. The thespians interpreted and stirred past and present onstage, inciting theatergoers.[35] The blend of identification and involvement inherent to witnessing performances of history was intensified because the audiences had personally endured the suffering depicted in *Anne Frank* and the racial trauma emphasized in *Nathan*. The spectators-cum-witnesses-cum-participants then reported their catharsis to a wider public, which experienced the theatrical energies vicariously beyond the venue of the production. Members of both populations contested the history performed, accusing those who advocated contrary perspectives of immoral, politicized revisionism. In the case of *Anne Frank*, the West German embassy foresaw the ensuing strife and unsuccessfully intervened against the presentation. *Nathan the Wise* represents a contrasting instance, in which the embassy, media, and thespians all hoped that catharsis would conduce to reconciliation. Instead Lessing's drama vitalized conflicts, catalyzed aggression, and restored behaviors that transgressed against the embassy's campaign for unity against communism. Though performed long after the death of the author and the culture for which they originally were intended, canonical German dramas, including *Nathan* and Schiller's *Robbers*, transmitted a social and historical energy that arose from their long life as performed literary works.[36] The polemical aftermath of *The Robbers* resembled the trajectory of Schiller's drama, and the dramatist's conscription into the National Socialist propaganda machine continued to be the subject of emotive debates through the 1960s. The volatility of the German classics reflected the volatility of German culture and history itself.

---

35. Colin Counsell, *Signs of Performance: An Introduction to Twentieth-Century Theatre* (London: Routledge, 1996), 28.

36. Stephen Greenblatt, *Shakespearean Negotiations: The Circulation of Social Energy in Renaissance England* (Oakland: University of California Press, 1988), 2.

Their confidence, albeit often mistaken, that they could harness these theatrical energies to promote their own interests motivated diverse local and transnational institutions to support the Free German Stage and Ludwig Ney's ensembles over the span of four decades. At the same time, the sense of community and catharsis experienced by spectators inspired durable loyalty to their theaters, sustaining them for a full generation.

Dramatic Theory and Repertoire

Beyond theatrical energies, other approaches to dramatic theory also open new approaches to historical and cultural examination. For example, it is tempting to view Ludwig Ney's career as a course of integration into Argentine society accompanied by his steady alienation from fascist ideology. Productions in Spanish, collaborative efforts with Argentine and other immigrant artists, and the inclusion of non-German dramatists in his repertoire all support such an interpretation. Furthermore, given Ney's steady popularity among emigrant-cum-immigrant audiences, this perspective also would indicate that nationalist Germans themselves had followed a similar course.

Drama theory problematizes this analysis. Especially concerning integration and interculturalism, Ney and other nationalist Germans eventually moved beyond their ethnocentric survival tactics and cultural practices of the Nazi period, yet the director's work evinces much aesthetic, cultural, and political continuity. During World War II, the German Theater's repertoire mirrored theater programs in Nazi Germany, including extending all Nazi bans on dramatists to Argentina. Ney and his troupe also upheld fascist drama theory. Onstage and behind the curtain, this included reverence for the dramatic text and the spoken word as the highest form of ethnic artistic expression, an understated mis-en-scène to repudiate the elaborate stage designs of the Weimar Republic, meticulous rehearsals to eliminate improvisation, and the exaltation of the director as the dramatic embodiment of the cult of the leader.

Offstage, nationalist theater critics in Argentina followed transatlantic models that wielded theater as part of their propagandistic arsenal to consolidate and legitimize the National Socialist state. Reviews posited German dramatists as harbingers of Hitler's rise to power and exploited historical dramas to justify Nazi government policies, including the glorification of military power and war, racial anti-Semitism, and exclusionary community-building.

Ney's postwar productions, too, revealed unflinching adherence to National Socialist aesthetics, drama theory, and repertoire policy. Even as he internationalized his repertoire, collaborated with Argentine artists, and began performing in Spanish, Ney never staged dramatists who had been proscribed in Nazi Germany. Furthermore, whether in German or Spanish, from 1948 to 1966 his presentations of the German classics, Molière, and Shakespeare abided by axioms of fascist drama theory. Although the productions in Córdoba and the Summer Festival showcased grand stage designs, Ney held fast to the primacy of the word and assiduous preparation to squelch improvisatory acting. Reviewers, too, manipulated Schiller according to the same pattern of politicized contemporization, brandishing him as proto-Nazi visionary, anti-occupation crusader and, finally, strident Cold Warrior. Molière and especially Shakespeare were among the foreign dramatists favored by the Reich Theater Chamber, and Ney's productions of *The Miser*, *The Merchant of Venice*, and *Othello* dovetailed with interpretations of these works in Nazi Germany, including anti-Semitism, exclusionary community-building, the glorification of the soldier as a paragon of masculinity, and, in the case of *Othello*, the Aryanization of Shakespeare's protagonist. From his South American debut in 1938 until his retirement in 1972, Ludwig Ney neither staged a Jewish dramatist nor engaged a Jewish thespian. It is striking to what degree Argentine artists, media, and Peronist functionaries embraced his archconservative approach to theater. Ney collaborated with dozens of local actors and musicians, and was featured in numerous national press organs, as well as the antitotalitarian *Argentinisches Tageblatt*, without ever renouncing Nazism, implementing a more inclusive repertoire, nor altering the fascist drama theory that undergirded his theatrical performances.

The case of Ludwig Ney demonstrates that even nationalist emigrants are compelled to integrate, and, furthermore, that they can
do so successfully without a pervasive ideological shift.

When the Free German Stage debuted in 1940, it already was
navigating deep fissures in its public. Its repertoire was exceedingly
cautious and betrayed refugees' estrangement from German culture. Although he personally believed in a reformed postwar Germany and eventually remigrated to Dortmund, in 1941 Paul Walter
Jacob explicated the adjective "German" in the ensemble's name
by foregrounding the formal aspect of its work with the German
language to present international dramas. Cognizant of his public,
Jacob associated "German" less with a specific country than with
European cultural diversity and cosmopolitanism.[37] Many theatergoers broke with Germany, including much of its literary canon.
The most performed dramatist at the German Theater, Friedrich
Schiller, flopped at the Free German Stage. Its public wanted to
see dramas from the recent past, especially light, early twentieth-
century comedies by European Jews. The troupe willfully deployed
the comic genre as a therapeutic memory machine to foster a buoyant sense of community and provide refugees with a temporary
escape from their troubles outside the theater. This fed emigrants'
often chimerical nostalgia for their previous lives in Europe, which
met with reprobation from Zionists and antifascist activists. During the postwar period, the stage attempted to attract all German-
speaking theatergoers; however, celebrity guest performances
revealed the predicament of playing to audiences who had contradictory definitions of German theater. Whereas the refugee population preferred actors who had starred in the Weimar Republic
and then emigrated when Hitler seized power, nationalist Germans
expected thespians and dramas that did not break with Nazism.
Actors and plays that implied criticism of this period were anathema to them. The Free German Stage failed to bridge this gap; in
fact many members of its own cast rebelled against conciliatory
gestures in personnel and repertoire.

---

37. "Deutsches Theater in Argentinien," *AT*, September 7, 1941.

Dramatic theory also discloses the weighty influence of the West German embassy, which prohibited leftist agitprop theater at the stage. Hedwig Schlichter-Crilla could only fully develop her pedagogical theater and propagate Konstantin Stanislavsky's acting system in Argentina outside of the bounds of the Free German Stage, despite the Russian actor's tense relationship with Soviet authorities. At Bonn's behest, the FGS shunned Brechtian mechanisms such as the alienation technique and the principle of historicization, although the dramatist was popular among Argentines and exilic actors alike.[38] Neither Brecht nor any playwright living in East Germany or the Eastern bloc countries was selected for performance. Instead, the repertoire comprised only canonical European and contemporary Western authors. The lens of dramatic theory belies a convergence between Argentina's competing German theaters. On the contrary, theatrical performances depict Ludwig Ney's adherence to fascist dramatic theory and the Free German Stage's remarkable transformation from political dissidence to conformism, underscored by the pervasiveness of West German soft power.

Competition

From 1933 to 1966, Argentina's German nationalist and anti-fascist populations—Zionists eventually withdrew themselves by renouncing Europe altogether—existed in a state of implacable competition. Multiple communities of German speakers had existed since the beginning of large-scale immigration to Argentina in the 1880s. Lutherans and Catholics, for example, formed separate, sometimes competing populations of German speakers. Christian denominational conflicts are absent from all discourse on German theaters in Argentina, however, likely because of the waning role of denominational difference in immigrant identity formation among Gentiles as well as the predominance of Lutherans

---

38. Arndt, interview by author, 2006.

in most nationalist German institutions in Buenos Aires. Competition between Lutherans and Catholics also would have had little relevance for the Free German Stage, because its cast and public were overwhelmingly Jewish. In the aftermath of the First World War, new, political discord between monarchists and republicans emerged, and the advent of National Socialism profoundly exacerbated these tensions. From the outset, the groups waged their rivalry across multiple fronts, including education, media, and cultural forums. Although the rivalry was defined by the participants' positions vis-à-vis Nazism, it was also messy—along with animosity came linkage, crisscrossing, disunity, and ambiguity. The conflict represents a singular instance of immediate, local, and fully open competition to dispute German politics, history, and culture throughout the Nazi period and for decades beyond. More than a contact zone, Buenos Aires was a battleground for oppositional definitions of German identity.

Surpassing any other venue, theater became the proving ground for contesting what it meant to be German. After nationalists contracted Ludwig Ney to launch the German Theater, German-speaking antifascists and Jewish refugees retaliated by establishing the Free German Stage. Thus, the two stages were conceived under the rubric of competition. The troupes and their constituents portrayed themselves as soldiers on cultural front-lines, and sought financial backing on this basis.[39] Neither side was willing to acknowledge the other's legitimacy throughout the Nazi period. The *Deutsche La Plata Zeitung* never mentioned the Free German Stage by name, and implied it was illegitimate by labeling its reports on Ludwig Ney's ensemble, "German Theater in Argentina." Meanwhile, the *Argentinisches Tageblatt* snidely remarked that even a few "Nazis" may have enjoyed the performances at the antifascist stage, because it was the only "truly German theater" in Buenos Aires.[40] Although they adopted similar tactics in community building, integration, publicity, and transnational alliances,

39. "Gespräch mit Ludwig Ney," *Teutonia*, September 1938; "Ein Sieg auf der Kulturfront," *DAD*, August 15, 1940.

40. "Die erste Spielzeit der Freien Deutschen Bühne," *AT*, November 17, 1940.

and even drew some of the same spectators to their performances, the two stages remained in fierce competition during the postwar period. Striving to become director of the Free German Stage, Ney denied and concealed his past as a Nazi collaborator. Under Paul Walter Jacob, the Free German Stage curried favor with nationalist Germans in an attempt to force Ludwig Ney off Argentine stages. Even gestures of rapprochement were steeped in competition against the rival ensemble.

Irreconcilable understandings of German identity were at the core of their competition. Each troupe designated itself as German; however, they held starkly antithetical views on what this signified. Adhering to fascist dramatic theory from across the Atlantic, Ludwig Ney relentlessly deployed theater to justify nationalists' claims that they represented an eternal, racially exclusive German nation. Numerous actors at the Free German Stage argued that Nazism was neither essence nor continuity, but aberration. For them, to perform in German was to fight for the restoration of the fundamentally German values of tolerance and cosmopolitanism that Nazism had trampled. The competition continued unabated after the war, when many nationalists never revised their conception of Germanness and adamantly rejected accusations of war crimes and guilt for atrocities during the Nazi period. Antifascists and Jews would not forgive them for these transgressions, and clashing performances of German history onstage vitalized, prolonged, and sharpened these conflicts over decades. Despite the efforts of numerous parties to achieve rapprochement, Argentina's competing German theaters had helped inculcate hostilities that could not be extinguished for many years to come.

REFERENCES

Public Archives

Bundesarchiv Berlin. Berlin.
Exilbibliothek im Literaturhaus Wien. Vienna.
Fundación IWO. Buenos Aires.
Goethe-Schule Archiv. Boulogne, Argentina.
Max Wächter Collection, Institut für Theaterwissenschaft, Universität Hamburg. Hamburg.
Paul Walter Jacob-Archiv. Hamburg.
Pestalozzi-Schule Archiv. Buenos Aires.
Politisches Archiv des Auswärtigen Amts. Berlin.

Private Collections

Cornelia Ney Collection. La Cumbre, Argentina.
Jacques Arndt Collection. Vicente López, Argentina.

Interviews

Arndt, Jacques. Interview by author. August 2, 2006.
———. Interview by author. December 25, 2008.
———. Telephone conversation with author. April 2007.
Bauer, Alfredo. Interview by author. August 9, 2007.
Lamm, Regine. Interview by author. December 5, 2010
Ney, Cornelia. Interview by author. February 3, 2009.
Siegerist, Ursula. Interview by author. November 15, 2012.

Newspapers, Magazines, Yearbooks, and Other Media, 1916–1971

Argentina

Das Andere Deutschland, Buenos Aires, 1937–1943.
Antena, Buenos Aires, 1944.
La Argentina, Buenos Aires, 1945–1950.
Argentina Libre, Buenos Aires, 1945–1950.
Argentinisches Tageblatt, Buenos Aires, 1934–1971.
Die Brücke, Buenos Aires, 1942–1944.
Buenos Aires Herald, Buenos Aires, 1940–1942.
Cine, Buenos Aires, 1944.
Córdoba, Córdoba, 1952–1954.
Czechoslovakia Libre, Buenos Aires, 1940.
Délamerikai Magyarság, Buenos Aires, 1940.
Der Deutsche in Argentinien, Buenos Aires, 1935–1943.
Deutsche La Plata Zeitung, Buenos Aires, 1937–1944.
El Diario, Buenos Aires, 1946–1950.
Diario Córdoba, Córdoba, 1952–1953.
El Diario Israelita, Buenos Aires, 1941–1943.
Evangelisches Gemeindeblatt für die La Plata Staaten, Buenos Aires, 1916.
Freie Presse, Buenos Aires, 1945–1965.
Freies Wort, Buenos Aires, 1945.
La Hora, Buenos Aires, 1945–1949.
Hoy, Buenos Aires, 1945–1949.
Jahrbuch des deutschen Volksbundes in Argentinien, Buenos Aires, 1938–1944.
Jüdische Wochenschau, Buenos Aires, 1940–1947.
El Lider, Buenos Aires, 1946.
Meridiano, Córdoba, 1952–1954.
MMM, Buenos Aires, 1947.
El Mundo, Buenos Aires, 1945–1950.

La Nación, Buenos Aires, 1940–1961, 2006
Noticias Graficas, Buenos Aires, 1940–1950.
La Película, Buenos Aires, 1946.
El Plata, Buenos Aires, 1944.
La Prensa, Buenos Aires, 1938–1957
Di Presse, Buenos Aires, 1943.
Los Principios, Córdoba, 1952–1954.
El Pueblo, Buenos Aires, 1945–1950.
La Razón, Buenos Aires, 1945–1950.
Schulnachrichten, Buenos Aires, 1943.
La Tarde, Buenos Aires, 1945–1950.
Teatros y Cines, Buenos Aires, 1948.
Teutonia, Buenos Aires, 1938.
Volksblatt, Buenos Aires, 1942–1943.
La Voz del Interior, Córdoba, 1952–1960.
Der Weg, Buenos Aires, 1947–1955.

Austria

Die Furche, Vienna, 2005.
Neues Wiener Tagblatt, Vienna, 1938.

Czechoslovakia

Der Abend, Teplitz-Schönau, Czechoslovakia, 1937.
Wegweiser, Teplitz-Schönau, Czechoslovakia, 1937.

Germany

Bergische Heimat, Wuppertal, 1932.
Berliner Zeitung, Berlin, 1934.
Deutscher Reichsanzeiger und Preußischer Staatsanzeiger, Berlin, 1938.
Essener National Zeitung, Essen, 1933.
Frankfurter Rundschau, Frankfurt am Main, 1949.
Fränkischer Kurier, Nuremberg, 1935.
Landeszeitung für Rhein-Main, Wiesbaden, 1935.
Main Post, Würzburg, 1948.
Rhein-Neckar-Zeitung, Heidelberg, 1948.
Der Spiegel, Hamburg, 1948–1950.
Der Telegraf, Berlin, 1948–1950.
Wiesbadener Tageblatt, Wiesbaden, 1936.
Würzburg General Anzeiger, Würzburg, 1935.

Luxemburg

Luxemburger Volksblatt, Luxemburg City, 1935.
Luxemburger Zeitung, Luxemburg City, 1935.

Paraguay

Deutsche Zeitung für Paraguay, Asunción, 1937.

Switzerland

Basler Nationalzeitung, Basel, 1948–1949.
Luzerner Neuste Nachrichten, Luzern, 1948.
Neue Zürcher Zeitung, Zurich, 1948–1950.
Tages-Anzeiger für Stadt und Kanton Zürich, Zurich, 1949.

United States

Aufbau, New York, 1942–1947.
Detroiter Abend-Post, Detroit, 1949.
New York Times, New York, 1932.
Staatszeitung New York, New York, 1946–1950.

Uruguay

Das Andere Deutschland, Montevideo, 1944.
Mundo Uruguayo, Montevideo, 1940.
Revista Familiar Israelita del Uruguay, Montevideo, 1944–1948.
La Voz del Día, Montevideo, 1939–1965.

Unpublished Promptbooks (Paul Walter Jacob-Archiv)

Aialti, J. *Vater und Sohn*. PWJA VI, j) 305.
Ardrey, Robert. *Leuchtfeuer*. PWJA VI, j) 305.
Bistritzky, Nathan. *In jener Nacht*. PWJA VI, j) 309.
Eichelbaum, Samuel, and Pedro E. Pico. *Die Nussschale*. PWJA VI, j) 346.
Hellman, Lillian. *Die Unbesiegten*. PWJA VI, j) 329.
Rössler, Carl. *Die fünf Frankfurter*. PWJA VI, j) 350.
Thomas, Brandon. *Charleys Tante*. PWJA VI, j) 357.
Werfel, Franz. *Jacobowsky und der Oberst*. PWJA VI, j) 358.

Published Fictional Works

Böttcher, Maximilian. *Krach im Hinterhaus*. Munich: Blanvalet, 1976.
Czierski, Otto. *Der Bauerngeneral*. Buenos Aires: Verlag Junges Volk, 1941.
Erasmus, Desiderius. *The Praise of Folly*. New Haven, CT: Yale University Press, 2003.
Hellman, Lillian. *Four Plays*. New York: Random House, 1942.
———. *Scoundrel Time*. Boston: Little, Brown, 1976.
Hinrichs, August. *Für die Katz!* Berlin: Drei Masken Verlag, 1938.
Hoffmann, Werner. *Das Spiel vom deutschen Landsknecht Utz Schmidl*. Buenos Aires: Verlag Junges Volk, 1940.
Goethe, Johann Wolfgang von. *Dramen 2*. Edited by Herbert von Einem, Hans Joachim Schrimpf, and Erich Trunz. Vol. 4 of *Johann Wolfgang von Goethe: Werke, Kommentare und Register*. Hamburger Ausgabe. Munich: C.H. Beck, 1999.
Lessing, Gotthold Ephraim. *Gotthold Ephraim Lessing: Werke*. Vol. 1, *Gedichte, Fabeln, Lustspiele*, edited by Herbert G. Göpfert. Darmstadt: Wissenschaftliche Buschgesellschaft, 1996.
Presber, Rudolf, and Leo Stein. *Liselott von der Pfalz*. Leipzig: Reclam, 1921.
Roessler, Carl. *The Five Frankforters*. Translated by James Fuchs. New York: H.K. Fly Company, 1913.
Rosenow, Emil. *Kater Lampe*. Leipzig: Gustav Richter, 1927.
Schiller, Friedrich. *Friedrich Schiller: Sämtliche Werke*. Vols. 1–2, *Dramen*. Munich: Artemis and Winkler, 1994.
Schmidt, Otto Ernst. *Flachsmann als Erzieher*. Leipzig: L. Staackmann, 1901.
Thomas, Brandon. *Charley's Aunt*. London: Samuel French Inc., 1935.
Winsloe, Christa. *Mädchen in Uniform*. Göttingen: Daphne Verlag, 1999.
Zuckmayer, Carl. *Die deutschen Dramen*. Frankfurt am Main: S. Fischer, 1951.

Secondary Sources

Alberdi, Juan Bautista. *Bases y puntos de partida para la organización política de la República Argentina*. Buenos Aires: Ediciones Jackson, 1938.
Albert, Claudia. "Ende der Exilforschung? Eine Überlegung anlässlich neuerer Veröffentlichungen zum Thema Exilliteratur." *Internationales Archiv für Sozialgeschichte der deutschen Literatur* 24:2 (1999): 180–187.
Alemann, Roberto. "75 Jahre *Argentinisches Wochenblatt*.'" *Argentinisches Wochenblatt*. Jubiläumsausgabe zum 75.jährigen Bestehen, March 1953.
Anderson, Benedict. *Imagined Communities*. London: Verso, 1991.
Arendt, Hannah. *Eichmann in Jerusalem: A Report on the Banality of Evil*. New York: Penguin, 1994.

────. *The Origins of Totalitarianism*. New York: Harcourt, 1973.

Argachá, Celomar José, and Orlando César Busiello. *Nazismo y otros extremismos en Entre Ríos: A través de la prensa y otros documentos, 1930–1945*. Concepción del Uruguay, Argentina: Artes Gráficas Yusty S.R.L., 2013.

Aristotle. *Aristotle's Poetics*. Ed. John Baxter and Patrick Atherton. Montreal: McGill-Queen's University Press, 1997.

Arndt, Karl, and May Olson. *Die deutschsprachige Presse der Amerikas/The German Language Press of the Americas, 1732–1968*. Pullach, Germany: Verlag Dokumentation, 1973.

Arntz, Helmut. *Germanen und Indogermanen: Volkstum, Sprache, Heimat, Kultur; Festschrift für Herman Hirt*. Heidelberg: C. Winter, 1936.

Austenfeld, Thomas. *American Women Writers and the Nazis*. Charlottesville: University of Virginia Press, 2001.

Avni, Haim. *Argentina y la historia de la inmigración judía (1810–1950)*. Buenos Aires: Universidad Hebrea de Jerusalén/AMIA, 1983.

Bannasch, Bettina, and Gerhild Rochus. *Handbuch der deutschsprachigen Exilliteratur*. Berlin: De Gruyter, 2013.

Bannasch, Bettina, Helga Schreckenberger, and Alan E. Steinweis, eds. *Exil und Shoah*. Exilforschung: Ein internationales Jahrbuch 34. Munich: Text und Kritik, 2016.

Baranowski, Shelley. *Strength through Joy*. Cambridge: Cambridge University Press, 2004.

Barner, Wilfred, Gunter Grimm, Helmuth Kiesel, and Martin Kramer. *Lessing—Epoche—Werk—Wirkung*. Munich: C.H. Beck, 1975.

Barrault, Jean-Louis. *Ich bin Theatermensch*. Frankfurt am Main: Sammlung Luchterhand, 1989.

Bauer, Alfredo. *La Asociación Vorwärts y la lucha democrática en la Argentina*. Buenos Aires: Biblioteca Nacional, 2008.

Baumgartner, Karin. "Illness and Health as Strategies of Resistance and Identity Formation in the Letters of Liselotte von der Pfalz." *Women in German Yearbook* 17 (2001): 57–76.

Ben-Dror, Graciela. *The Catholic Church and the Jews: Argentina, 1933–1945*. Lincoln: University of Nebraska Press, 2008.

Berendsohn, Walter. *Die humanistische Front: Einführung in die deutsche Emigranten-Literatur*. Worms: G. Heintz, 1976.

Biccari, Gaetano. *"Zuflucht des Geistes"? Konservativ-revolutionäre, faschistische und nationalsozialistische Theaterdiskurse in Deutschland und Italien 1900–1944*. Tübingen: G. Narr, 2001.

Bischoff, Doerte. *Dinge des Exils*. Exilforschung 31. Munich: Text und Kritik, 2013.

Blau, Herbert. *The Audience*. Baltimore: Johns Hopkins University Press, 1990.

Borge, Jason. *Latin American Writers and the Rise of Hollywood Cinema*. New York: Routledge, 2008.

Botana, Natalio. *El orden conservador: La política argentina entre 1880 y 1916*. Buenos Aires: Sudamerica, 1994.

Boyarin, Daniel. *A Radical Jew*. Berkeley: University of California Press, 1997.

Boyarin, Daniel, and Jonathan Boyarin. "Diaspora: Generational Ground of Jewish Identity." *Critical Inquiry* 19 (1993): 693–725.

Brah, Avtar. *Cartographies of Diaspora: Contesting Identities*. London: Routledge, 1996.

Brinkmeyer, Robert. *The Fourth Ghost*. Baton Rouge: Louisiana State University Press, 2009.

Brodsky, Adriana, and Raanan Rein. *The New Jewish Argentina: Facets of Jewish Experiences in the Southern Cone*. Leiden: Brill, 2013.

Brüstle, Andrea, *Das Deutsche Ausland-Institut und die Deutschen in Argentinien, 1933–1945*. Berlin: Wissenschaftlicher Verlag Berlin, 2007.

Bryce, Benjamin. *To Belong in Buenos Aires: Germans, Argentines, and the Rise of a Pluralist Society*. Stanford: Stanford University Press, 2018.

Bussemeyer, Peter. *50 Jahre "Argentinisches Tageblatt": Werden und Aufstieg einer auslandsdeutschen Zeitung*. Buenos Aires: N.p., 1939.

Buxbaum, Elisabeth. *Transit Shanghai: Ein Leben im Exil*. Vienna: Steinbauer, 2008.

Cane, James. *The Fourth Enemy: Journalism and Power in the Making of Peronist Argentina, 1930–1955*. University Park: Penn State University Press, 2012.

Carlson, Marvin. *The Haunted Stage*. Ann Arbor: University of Michigan Press, 2001.

Clifford, James. *Routes: Travel and Translation in the Late Twentieth Century*. Cambridge, MA: Harvard University Press, 1997.

Cordes, Gerhard, and Dieter Möhn, eds. *Handbuch zur niederdeutschen Sprach- und Literaturwissenschaft*. Berlin: Erich Schmidt Verlag, 1983.

Cruz, Jorge. *Samuel Eichelbaum*. Buenos Aires: Ediciones Culturales Argentinas, 1962.

"Del Archivo: El Censo de 1936; Cuarto Censo General de la Ciudad de Buenos Aires," *Población de Buenos Aires: Revista semestral de datos y estudios demogräaficos* 6 (2009): 103–123.

della Paolera, Gerardo, and Alan M. Taylor, eds. *A New Economic History of Argentina*. Cambridge: Cambridge University Press, 2003.

Demetz, Peter. *Prague in Danger*. New York: Farrar, Straus and Giroux, 2008.

Dewey, John. "The Theory of Emotion." *Psychological Review* 1 (1894): n.p.

Dickmann, Enrique. *La infiltración nazi-fascista en la Argentina*. Buenos Aires: Ediciones Sociales Argentinas, 1939.

Di Núbila, Domingo. *La época de oro: Historia del cine argentino*. Buenos Aires: Ediciones del Jilguero, 1998.

Douer, Alisa, and Ursula Seeber. *Wie weit ist Wien: Lateinamerika als Exil für österreichische Schriftsteller und Künstler*. Vienna: Picus Verlag, 1995.

Drewniak, Boguslav. *Das Theater im NS-Staat: Szenarium deutscher Zeitgeschichte 1933–1945*. Düsseldorf: Droste, 1983.

Dujovne, Alejandro. "Cartografía de las publicaciones periódicas judías de izquerda en Argentina, 1900–1953." *Revista del Museo de Antropología de la Universidad Nacional de Córdoba* 1 (2008): 121–138.

Dumont-Lindemann, Louise. *Vermächtnisse*. Düsseldorf: Bagel, 1932.

Durzak, Manfred. *Die deutsche Exilliteratur 1933–1945*. Stuttgart: Reclam, 1974.

Ebel, Arnold. *Das Dritte Reich und Argentinien: Die diplomatischen Beziehungen unter besonderer Berücksichtigung der Handelspolitik (1933–1939)*. Cologne: Böhlau, 1971.

Eckardt, Jo-Jacqueline. "Das Lessingbild im Dritten Reich." *Lessing Yearbook* 23 (1991): 69–78.

Eick, Simone, ed. *Nach Buenos Aires!* Bremerhaven: Deutsches Auswandererhaus Bremerhaven, 2008.

Emmerich, Wolfgang, ed. *Lyrik des Exils*. Stuttgart: Reclam, 1985.

Ette, Ottmar. "Literature as Knowledge for Living, Literary Studies as Science for Living." Edited with an introduction by Vera M. Kutzinski. Translated by Vera M. Kutzinski. *PMLA* 125 (2010): 977–993.

———. "Literaturwissenschaft als Lebenswissenschaft: Eine Programmschrift im Jahr der Geisteswissenschaften." *Lendemains* 125:32 (2007): 7–32.

———. *ZwischenWeltenSchreiben: Literatur ohne festen Wohnsitz*. Berlin: Kadmos, 2005.

Falcoff, Mark, and Ronald H. Dolkart. *Prologue to Perón: Argentina in Depression and War, 1930–1943*. Berkeley: University of California Press, 1975.

Farnsworth-Alvear, Ann. *Dulcinea in the Factory: Myths, Morals, Men, and Women in Colombia's Industrial Experiment, 1905–1960*. Durham, NC: Duke University Press, 2000.

Fischer, Barbara, and Thomas Fox, eds. *A Companion to the Works of Gotthold Ephraim Lessing*. Rochester: Camden House, 2005.

Fischer-Lichte, Erika. *Theatre, Sacrifice, Ritual: Exploring Forms of Political Theatre*. London: Routledge, 2005.

Foote, Nicola, and Michael Goebel, eds. *Immigration and Naitonal Identities in Latin America*. Gainesville: University Press of Florida, 2014.

Forster, Elborg. *A Woman's Life in the Court of the Sun King*. Baltimore: Johns Hopkins University Press, 1984.

Frank, Michael. *Die letzte Bastion: Nazis in Argentinien*. Hamburg: Rutten und Loening Verlag, 1962.

Frankl, Viktor. *The Doctor and the Soul*. New York: Alfred Knopf, 1960.

———. *Viktor Frankl Recollections: An Autobiography*. New York: Insight Books, 1997.

Franz, Margit. *Gateway India: Deutschsprachiges Exil in Indien zwischen britischer Kolonialherrschaft, Maharadschas und Gandhi*. Graz: CLIO-Verlag, 2015.

Friedmann, Germán. "Los alemanes antinazis de la Argentina y el mito de las dos aldeas." *Ayer: Revista de historia contemporánea* 77 (2010): 205–226.

———. *Alemanes antinazis en la Argentina*. Buenos Aires: Siglo Veintiuno Editores Argentina, 2010.

Fröschle, Hartmut, ed. *Die Deutschen in Lateinamerika: Schicksal und Leistung*. Tübingen: Horst Erdmann, 1979.

Fry, William, and Waleed Salameh. *Humor and Wellness in Clinical Intervention*. Westport, CT: Praeger, 2001.

Fuchs, James. "Concerning the Jews of Frankfort." Introduction to *The Five Frankforters*, by Carl Roessler, 9–26. New York: H.K. Fly, 1913.

Gaudig, Olaf, and Peter Veit. *Der Widerschein des Nazismus: Das Bild des Nationalsozialismus in der deutschsprachigen Presse Argentiniens, Brasiliens und Chiles 1932–1945*. Berlin: Wissenschaftlicher Verlag, 1997.

Gebhardt, Hermann. *7 Jahre voz del día*. Montevideo: N.p. 1945.

Giffler, Ferdinand. "Hundert Jahre deutsches Schulwesen in Argentinien." *Das Jahrbuch deutscher Volksbund für Argentinien*, 1944, 157.

Goethe, Johann Wolfgang von. *Kunst und Literatur*. Edited by Herbert von Einem, Hans Joachim Schrimpf, and Erich Trunz. Vol. 12 of *Johann Wolfgang von Goethe: Werke, Kommentare und Register*. Hamburger Ausgabe. Munich: C.H. Beck, 1999.

Goldmann, Michael. *The Actor's Freedom: Toward a Theory of Drama*. New York: Viking Press, 1975.

Goltz, Joshua. "Memories of Heimat: National Socialist Propaganda and the Homelands of German Emigrés in Argentina." Master's thesis, University of Oxford, 1998.

Goñi, Uki. *La auténtica Odessa*. Barcelona: Paidós, 2002.

González Lutier, Mariana. "La Comisión de Investigación de las Actividades Anti-argentinas: El caso de la Goethe Schule, 1938–1942." *Cuadernos DIHA* 5–6 (2019).

González-Rivera, Victoria, and Karen Kampwirth. *Radical Women in Latin America, Left and Right*. University Park: Penn State University Press, 2001.

Grimm, Reinhold, ed. *Bertolt Brecht: Poetry and Prose*. London: A&C Black, 2003.

Heller, Fred. *Das Leben beginnt noch einmal: Schicksale der Emigration*. Buenos Aires: Editorial Cosmopolita, 1945.

Hermand, Jost. *Culture in Dark Times*. New York: Berghahn Books, 2012.

Hilberg, Raul. *The Destruction of the European Jews*. New Haven, CT: Yale University Press, 2003.

Hilfsverein deutschsprechender Juden/Asociación Filantrópica Israelita. *Zehn Jahre Aufbauarbeit in Südamerika*. Buenos Aires: Asociación Filantrópica Israelita, 1943.

Holdsworth, Nadine. *Theatre and National Identity: Re-imagining Conceptions of a Nation*. New York: Routledge, 2014.

Horkheimer, Max, and Theodor Adorno. *Dialektik der Aufklärung*. Frankfurt am Main: Fischer, 1986.

Hutton, Christopher. *Linguistics and the Third Reich: Mother-Tongue Fascism, Race, and the Science of Language*. London: Routledge, 1999.

Ismar, Georg. *Der Pressekrieg: Argentinisches Tageblatt und Deutsche La Plata Zeitung, 1933–1945*. Berlin: Wissenschaftlicher Verlag Berlin, 2006.

Jackisch, Carlota. *El nazismo y los refugiados alemanes en la Argentina*. Buenos Aires: Editorial de Belgrano, 1997.

Jackman, Jarrell C., and Carla M. Borden, eds. *The Muses Flee Hitler: Cultural Transfer and Adaptation, 1930–1945.* Washington, DC: Smithsonian Institution Press, 1983.

Jacob, Paul Walter. *Theater: Drei Jahre Freie Deutsche Bühne in Buenos Aires.* Buenos Aires: Editorial Cosmopolita, 1943.

———. *Theater: Sieben Jahre Freie Deutsche Bühne in Buenos Aires.* Buenos Aires: Editorial Jupiter, 1946.

Johst, Hanns. *Standpunkt und Fortschritt.* Oldenburg: Gerhard Stalling, 1933.

Kalinna, Lea. "Exil und Identität: Die deutsche Emigration in Argentinien während des Nationalsozialismus am Beispiel der Freien Deutschen Bühne." Bachelor of arts thesis, Europa-Universität Viadrina Frankfurt (Oder), 2009.

Keiper, Wilhelm. *Der Deutsche in Argentinien.* Berlin: Julius Beltz Verlag, 1938.

Kelz, Robert. "Desde la emigración a la inmigración: Actuaciones interculturales en el Teatro Alemán Independiente, Buenos Aires Argentina, 1940–45." *Anuario argentino de germanística* 2 (2010): 193–211.

———. "Los escritos de Hardi Swarsensky: Culpabilidad, seguridad, desagravio." *Estudios migratorios latinoamericanos* 74 (2013): 119–136.

———. "German Buenos Aires Asunder: Lessing Onstage in the Argentine Capital, 1934–1962." *Lessing Yearbook/Jahrbuch* 40 (2012/2013): 167–186.

———. "El teatro y la concepción de lo nacional: El Deutsches Theater, Buenos Aires, Argentina." *Estudios migratorios latinoamericanos* 70 (2011): 177–194.

Kießling, Wolfgang. *Exil in Lateinamerika.* Leipzig: Philip Reclam, 1980.

Kindheit und Jugend im Exil—Ein Generationsthema. Exilforschung: Ein internationales Jahrbuch 24. Munich: Text und Kritik, 2006.

Klee, Ernst. *Das Kulturlexikon zum Dritten Reich: Wer war was vor und nach 1945.* Frankfurt a.M.: S. Fischer, 2007.

Koch, Edita, ed. *Exiltheater und Exildramatik, 1933–1945: Tagung der Hamburger Arbeitsstelle für deutsche Exilliteratur.* Maintal: Koch, 1990.

Koebner, Thomas, Wulf Köpke, Claus-Dieter Krohn, and Sigrid Schneider, eds. *Fluchtpunkte des Exils und andere Themen.* Exilforschung 5. Munich: Text und Kritik, 1987.

Koebner, Thomas, Wulf Köpke, and Joachim Radkau, eds. *Stalin und die Intellektuellen und andere Themen.* Exilforschung 1. Munich: Text und Kritik, 1983.

Koebner, Thomas, et al., eds. *Vertreibung der Wissenschaften und andere Themen.* Exilforschung 6. Munich: Text und Kritik, 1988.

Köpke, Wulf, and Michael Winkler. *Exilliteratur 1933–1945.* Darmstadt: Wissenschaftliche Buchgesellschaft, 1989.

Krohn, Claus-Dieter, ed. *Handbuch der deutschsprachigen Emigration 1933–1945.* Darmstadt: Wissenschaftliche Buchgesellschaft, 2008.

Krohn, Claus-Dieter, Erwin Rotermund, Lutz Winckler, and Wulf Köpke, eds. *Aspekte der künstlerischen Inneren Emigration 1933–1945.* Exilforschung 12. Munich: Text und Kritik, 1994.

————. *Exil, Entwurzelung, Hybridität.* Exilforschung 27. Munich: Text und Kritik, 2009.

————. *Exil und Remigration.* Exilforschung 9. Munich: Text und Kritik, 1991.

————. *Exil und Widerstand.* Exilforschung 15. Munich: Text und Kritik, 1997.

————. *Frauen und Exil: Zwischen Anpassung und Selbstbehauptung.* Exilforschung 11. Munich: Text und Kritik, 1993.

————. *Kulturelle Räume und ästhetische Universalität: Musik und Musiker im Exil.* Exilforschung 26. Munich: Text und Kritik, 2008.

————. *Metropolen des Exils.* Exilforschung 20. Munich: Text und Kritik, 2002.

————. *Politische Aspekte des Exils.* Exilforschung 8. Munich: Text und Kritik, 1990.

————. *Publizistik im Exil und andere Themen.* Exilforschung 7. Munich: Text und Kritik, 1989.

————. *Übersetzung als transkultureller Prozess.* Exilforschung 25. Munich: Text und Kritik, 2007.

Krohn, Claus-Dieter, Erwin Rotermund, Lutz Winckler, Wulf Köpke, and Irmtrud Wojak, eds. *Jüdische Emigration: Zwischen Assimilation und Verfolgung, Akkulturation und jüdischer Identität.* Exilforschung 19. Munich: Text und Kritik, 2001.

Kroll, Maria, ed. *Letters from Liselotte: Princess Palatine and Duchess of Orleans, "Madame," 1652–1722.* New York: McCall, 1971.

Kruger, Loren. *The National Stage: Theatre and Cultural Legitimation in England, France, and America.* Chicago: University of Chicago Press, 1992.

Krüger, René. *La diáspora: De experiencia traumática a paradigma eclesiológico.* Buenos Aires: Instituto Universitario ISEDET, 2008.

Laberenz, Lennart. "Vom Kaiser zum Führer- deutschsprachige Nationalismusdiskurse in Buenos Aires, 1918–1933." Master's thesis, Humboldt University of Berlin, 2006.

Laming, Dieter. *Über Grenzen.* Göttingen: Vandenhoeck and Ruprecht, 2001.

Le Goff, Jacques. *History and Memory.* New York: Columbia University Press, 1992.

Leiva, María Luján. "La inmigración en la Argentina de posguerra." *Todo es historia: Registra la memoria nacional inmigración; Integración y prejuicio,* 1992, 8–22.

Lemmer, Anne. *Die "Freie Deutsche Bühne" in Buenos Aires 1940–1965.* Hamburg: Hamburger Arbeitsstelle für deutsche Exilliteratur, 1999.

Levitt, Peggy, and Mary C. Walters, eds. *The Changing Face of Home: The Transnational Lives of the Second Generation.* New York: Russell Sage Foundation, 2002.

Luserke-Jaqui, Matthias. *Schiller-Handbuch: Leben—Werk—Wirkung.* Stuttgart: Metzler, 2005.

Lützeler, Paul Michael. *Hermann Broch.* Frankfurt: Suhrkamp, 1985.

Maalouf, Amin. "Je parle du voyage comme d'autres parlent du leur maison." *Magazine littéraire* 394 (2001): 98–103.

Maaß, Ingrid. *Repertoire der deutschsprachigen Exilbühnen, 1933–1945.* Hamburg: Wagner, 2000.

Maaß, Ingrid, and Michael Philipp. *Handbuch der deutschsprachigen Exiltheaters*. Berlin: De Gruyter, 2013.

Mandelkov, Karl Robert. *Goethe in Deutschland*. 2 vols. Munich: C.H. Beck, 1989.

Marshall, Alan. "Naturalism and Nationalism." *German Life and Letters* 37 (1984): 91–104.

McGee Deutsch, Sandra. *Crossing Borders, Claiming a Nation: A History of Argentine Jewish Women, 1880–1955*. Durham, NC: Duke University Press, 2010.

———. *Las Derechas: The Extreme Right in Argentina, Brazil, and Chile, 1890–1939*. Palo Alto, CA: Stanford University Press, 1999.

Meding, Holger. *Flucht vor Nürnberg? Deutsch und österreichische Einwanderung in Argentinien 1945–1955*. Cologne: Böhlau, 1992.

———, ed. *Nationalsozialismus und Argentinien: Beziehungen, Einflüsse und Nachwirkungen*. Frankfurt: Peter Lang, 1995.

———. *"Der Weg": Eine deutsche Emigrantenzeitschrift in Buenos Aires 1947–1957*. Berlin: Wissenschaftlicher Verlag Berlin, 1997.

Meding, Holger, and Georg Ismar, eds. *Argentinien und das Dritte Reich Mediale und reale Präsenz, Ideologie Transfer, Folgewirkungen*. Berlin: Wissenschaftlicher Verlag, 2008.

Mejcher, Sonja. *Geschichten über Geschichten: Erinnerung im Romanwerk von Ilyas Huri*. Wiesbaden: Reichert, 2001.

Mirau, Leo. *Argentinien von heute: Schilderungen von Land und Leute*. Buenos Aires: Librería Mirau, 1920.

Möbus, Frank, Friederike Schmidt-Möbus, and Gerd Unverfehrt, eds. *Faust: Annäherung an einen Mythos*. Göttingen: Wallstein Verlag, 1996.

Morreall, John. *Taking Laughter Seriously*. Albany: State University of New York Press, 1983.

Morrison, Toni. *Playing in the Dark: Whiteness and the Literary Imagination*. New York: Vintage, 1992.

Müller, Walter. "Der Erziehungswert der landschaftsgebundenen und handwerksgerechten Gestaltung des Schullandheimes." *Das Schullandheim* 11:2 (1939).

Naumann, Uwe. *Ein Theatermann im Exil, P. Walter Jacob*. Hamburg: Kabel, 1985.

Neumeyer, Alfred, Roberto Schopflocher, and Rainer Traub. *"Wir wollen den Fluch in Segen verwandeln": Drei Generationen der jüdischen Familie Neumeier; Eine autobiografische Trilogie*. Berlin: Metropol, 2007.

Newton, Ronald. *German Buenos Aires, 1900–1933: Social Change and Cultural Crisis*. Austin: University of Texas Press, 1977.

———. *The "Nazi Menace" in Argentina, 1931–1947*. Stanford: Stanford University Press, 1992.

Nouwen, Mollie Lewis. *Oy, My Buenos Aires: Jewish Immigrants and the Creation of Argentine National Identity*. Albuquerque: University of New Mexico Press, 2013.

O'Donnell, Krista, Renate Bridenthal, and Nancy Reagin, eds. *The Heimat Abroad: The Boundaries of Germanness*. Ann Arbor: University of Michigan Press, 2005.

Ortiz, Scalabrini. *Política británica en el Río de la Plata*. Buenos Aires: Reconquista, 1940.

Pace, Giovanni Maria. *La via del demoni: La fuga en Sudamerica dei criminali nazisti; Secreti, complicità, silenzi*. Milan: Sperling & Kupfer, 2000.

Pantförder, Manfred. *"Das andere Deutschland," Buenos Aires 1938–1949: Ein Beitrag zur deutschsprachigen Publizistik im Exil*. Berlin: Freie Üniveristät Berlin, 1986.

Penny, H. Glenn. "Latin American Connections: Recent Work on German Interactions with Latin America." *Central European History* 46 (2013): 362–394.

Perón, Juan. *Yo Perón*. Edited by Enrique Pavón Pereya. Buenos Aires: MILSA, 1993.

Petersen, Julius. *Die Sehnsucht nach dem Dritten Reich in deutscher Sage und Dichtung*. Stuttgart: Metzler, 1934.

Pfanner, Helmut. *Exile in New York: German and Austrian Writers after 1933*. Detroit: Wayne State University Press, 1983.

———. *Hanns Johst: Vom Expressionismus zum Nationalsozialismus*. The Hague: Mouton, 1970.

Pigna, Felipe. *Los mitos de la historia argentina*. Vol. 3, *De la Ley Sáenz Peña a los albores del peronismo*. Buenos Aires: Planeta, 2006.

Pohle, Fritz. *Emigrationstheater in Südamerika abseits der "Freien Deutschen Bühne," Buenos Aires*. Hamburg: Hamburger Arbeitsstelle für deutsche Exilliteratur, 1989.

———. "Paul Walter Jacob am Rio de la Plata: Exilprominenz und Zwang zur Politik." *Exil* 8 (1988): 79–96.

———. "Paul Walter Jacob am Rio de la Plata: Der Kurs der FDB—eine exilpolitische Gratwanderung." *Exil* 7:2 (1987): 34–58.

———. "Paul Walter Jacob am Rio de la Plata: Rahmenbedingungen und Bestimmungsfaktoren eines exilpolitischen Engagements." *Exil* 7:1 (1987): 34–52.

Poutrus, Patrick. "Zuflucht Nachkriegsdeutschland: Flüchtlingsaufnahme in der Bundesrepublik und DDR von den späten 1940er bis zu den 1970er Jahren." *Exilforschung* 27 (2009): 182–205.

Pratt, Marie Louise. *Imperial Eyes: Travel Writing and Transculturation*. London: Routledge, 1992.

Roach, Joseph. *Cities of the Dead: Circum-Atlantic Performance*. New York: Columbia University Press, 1996.

Roca, Cora. *Días de Teatro: Hedy Crilla*. Buenos Aires: CELCIT, 2001.

———. *Días de Teatro: Hedy Crilla*. Buenos Aires: CELCIT, 2001.

Rodriguez, Julia. *Civilizing Argentina: Science, Medicine, and the Modern State*. Chapel Hill: University of North Carolina Press, 2006.

Rohland de Langbehn, Regula, ed. *Paul Zech y las condiciones del exilio en la Argentina*. Buenos Aires: Universidad de Buenos Aires, 1999.

Rohland de Langbehn, Regula, and Miguel Vedda, eds. *Teatro y teoría teatral*. Buenos Aires: Universidad de Buenos Aires, 2001.

Rohrbacher, Stefan, and Michael Schmidt. *Judenbilder*. Reinbek: Rowohlt TB, 1990.

Rojer, Olga Elaine. *Exile in Argentina, 1933–1945: A Historical and Literary Introduction*. New York: Peter Lang, 1989.

Rokem, Freddie. *Performing History: Theatrical Representations of the Past in Contemporary Theatre*. Iowa City: University of Iowa Press, 2000.

Ruppelt, Georg. *Schiller im nationalsozialistischen Deutschland*. Stuttgart: Metzler, 1979.

Saint Sauveur-Henn, Anne. *Un siècle d'emigration allemande vers l'Argentine 1853–1945*. Vienna: Böhlau, 1995.

Schirp, Kerstin. *Die Wochenzeitung "Semanario Israelita": Sprachrohr der deutsch-jüdischen Emigranten in Argentinien, 1969–1999*. Münster: LIT Verlag, 2001.

Schlösser, Rainer. *Das Volk und seine Bühne: Bemerkungen zum Aufbau des deutschen Theaters*. Berlin: Langen und Müller, 1935.

Schmidt-Rohr, Georg. *Die Sprache als Bildnerin der Völker: Eine Wesens- und Lebenskunde der Volkstümer*. Jena: Diedrichs, 1932.

———. "Die zweite Ebene der Volkserhaltung." *Rasse* 6 (1939): 81–89.

Schmitz, Helmut. *Von der nationalen zur internationalen Literatur: Transkulturelle deutschsprachige Literatur und Kultur im Zeitalter globaler Migration*. Amsterdam: Rodopi, 2009.

Schnorbach, Hermann. *Por "la otra Alemania": El Colegio Pestalozzi en Buenos Aires, 1934–2004*. Buenos Aires: Asociación Cultural Pestalozzi, 2004.

Schoepp, Sebastian. *Das Argentinische Tageblatt, 1933–45: Eine "bürgerliche Kampfzeitung" als Forum der antinationalsozialistischen Emigration*. Berlin: Wissenschaftlicher Verlag Berlin, 1996.

———. "Das Argentinische Tageblatt als Forum der Emigration 1933–1945." *Vierteljahresheft für Zeitgeschichte* 43 (1995): 75–113.

Schopenhauer, Arthur. *The World as Will and Idea*. 3 vols. London: Routledge, 1964.

Schopflocher, Robert, and Dirk Niefanger. *Buenos Aires: Eine deutsche Kulturinsel 1933–1945; Erinnerungen: Erweiterte Fassung eines Vortrags an der Friedrich-Alexander-Universität Erlangen-Nürnberg am 30. Oktober 2012*. Erlangen: Friedrich-Alexander-Universität, 2013.

Schott, Georg. *Goethes Faust in heutiger Schau*. Stuttgart: Tazzelwurm, 1940.

Schulze, Mathias, James Skidmore, David John, Grit Liebscher, and Sebastian Siebel Achenbach, eds. *German Diasporic Experiences: Identity, Migration, and Loss*. Waterloo, Canada: Wilfrid Laurier University Press, 2008.

Schvarzer, Jorge. "The Argentine Riddle in Historical Perspective." *Latin American Research Review* 27 (1992): 169–181.

Schwarcz, José Alfredo. *Trotz allem . . . : Die deutschsprachigen Juden in Argentinien*. Cologne: Böhlau, 1995.

Schwarz, Egon. "Franz Werfel und das Judentum." Lecture, Wiener Werfel-Symposium, Vienna, 1990.

———. *Keine Zeit für Eichendorff: Chronik unfreiwilliger Wanderjahre*. Königstein im Taunus: Athenäum, 1979.

Smith, Helmut. *Modern German History*. Oxford: Oxford University Press, 2011.

Spalek, John, and Joseph Strelka, eds. *Deutsche Exilliteratur seit 1933*. Studien zur deutschen Exilliteratur 1.1: Kalifornien. Tübingen: Francke, 1976.

Spitta, Arnold. *Paul Zech im südamerikanischen Exil, 1933–1946*. Berlin: Colloquium, 1978.

Spolin, Viola. *Improvisation for the Theater: A Handbook of Teaching and Directing Techniques*. Evanston, IL: Northwestern University Press, 1963.

Stallybass, Peter, and Allon White. *The Politics and Poetics of Transgression*. Ithaca, NY: Cornell University Press, 1989.

Stangneth, Bettina. *Eichmann before Jerusalem: The Unexamined Life of a Mass Murderer*. New York: Knopf, 2014.

Steiman, Lionel. *Franz Werfel: The Faith of an Exile*. Waterloo, Canada: Wilfrid Laurier University Press, 1985.

Steinacher, Gerald. *Nazis on the Run: How Hitler's Henchmen Fled Justice*. Oxford: Oxford University Press, 2011.

Strelka, Joseph. *Exilliteratur: Grundprobleme der Theorie, Aspekte der Geschichte und Kritik*. Bern: Peter Lang, 1983.

Strobl, Gerwin. *The Swastika and the Stage*. Cambridge: Cambridge University Press, 2007.

Strohmeyer, Heidrun, Reinhold Bidner, Georg Hobmeier, and Fritz Hausjell. "Spiel, Spaß, Ernst: Computerspiele zum Thema Flucht." Roundtable at the University of Vienna, January 11, 2016.

Stuhlmann, Andreas. *Vater Courage: Reinhold K. Olzewski und die Deutschen Kammerspiele in Lateinamerika 1949–1974*. Munich: Belleville Verlag, 2016.

Tafferner, Anton. *Quellenbuch zur donauschwäbischen Geschichte*. Stuttgart: Kepplerhaus, 1995.

Tanzi, Vito. *Argentina: An Economic Chronicle*. New York: Jorge Pinto, 2007.

Tepp, Max. *Die Umwelt des Auslandsdeutschen in Südamerika*. Buenos Aires: Umwelt Verlag, 1938.

Thiess, Frank. *Theater ohne Rampe: Stücke für Zimmertheater und Studiobühnen*. Darmstadt: Luchterhand, 1960.

Van der Cruysse, Dirk. *"Madame seyn ist ein ellendes Handwerk": Liselotte von der Pfalz—eine Deutsche am Hof des Sonnenkönigs*. Munich: Piper, 1990.

Volberg, Heinrich. *Auslandsdeutschtum und drittes Reich: Der Fall Argentinien*. Cologne: Böhlau, 1981.

Wächter, Hans-Christoph. *Theater im Exil: Sozialgeschichte des deutschen Exiltheaters 1933–1945*. Munich: Carl Hanser Verlag, 1973.

Wagener, Hans. *Understanding Franz Werfel*. Columbia: University of South Carolina Press, 1993.

Waisman, Carlos. *The Reversal of Development in Argentina: Postwar Counterrevolutionary Policies and Their Structural Consequences*. Princeton, NJ: Princeton University Press, 1987.

Walter, Hans-Albert. *Deutsche Exilliteratur 1933–1950*. Darmstadt: Luchterhand, 1974.

Walter, Horacio. "Los Alemanes de Rusia en la Argentina: Una comunidad visible." Paper presented at "La inserción de la minoría de habla alemana en la Argentina: Asociaciones e instituciones de las colectividades de habla alemana en la Argentina," Buenos Aires, Argentina, June 8, 2018.

Willet, Ralph. *The Americanization of Germany*. London: Routledge, 1989.

Williams, Raymond. *New Keywords: A Revised Vocabulary of Culture and Society*. Malden, MA: Blackwell, 2005.

Wolfgang, Vivian. "Paul Walter Jacob und die Freie Deutsche in Argentinien." PhD diss., Vienna University, 1980.

Zimmermann, Eduardo. *Los liberales reformistas: La cuestión social en la Argentina, 1890–1916*. Buenos Aires: Sudamérica, 1994.

INDEX

Page numbers followed by letters *f* and *n* refer to figures and notes, respectively.

CPSIA information can be obtained
at www.ICGtesting.com
Printed in the USA
LVHW011758160120
643876LV00004B/279